In loving memory of Dr. James Howard Cremin, who, along with his family, gave me a place in which to find a sense of self during my early days of tumult and who managed to keep his cool when I blew out half the electricity in his house one Christmas morning. And to the loving memory of his son, and my friend, John Cremin, who was kind, completely selfless, and a truly good heart. I miss you both.

—Rickford

To Nan,
You were right, we're not!

—Phil

PRAISE FOR *UBUNTU FOR NON-GEEKS*

"A fast, crystal-clear topical tour of the amazing collective accomplishment embodied in Ubuntu. I learned something new in every chapter, and ended up with a computer that did more of what I wanted it to do, faster. This book should come with every Ubuntu Live CD—it's just the documentation I needed to take some of the mystery out of my machine."
—BOING BOING

"Highly recommended to all Ubuntu newcomers."
—PC WORLD

"If you're a Linux novice, or an experienced user who wants a good book to recommend, I give this book a big thumbs up."
—LINUX TODAY

"This very nice book on Ubuntu Linux is clearly targeted at the neophytes who wish to take their first steps in installing and using Ubuntu. The author explains in a step-by-step manner the solutions to the problems that one might face in installing, configuring and using Ubuntu Linux."
—SLASHDOT

"Grant makes it seem easy with his step-by-step instructions and plenty of screen shots."
—LINUX.COM

"This is a good, practical book that reads well and doesn't involve the victim in lots of superfluous stuff."
—UNIX REVIEW

"With books like this in the hands of non-geeks, the lines of distinction between geeks and non-geeks might just begin to blur!"
—IT WORLD

"The best thing in Rickford Grant's *Ubuntu Linux for Non-Geeks* is plenty of practical examples."
—LINUX MAGAZINE

"Highly recommended for both new Linux users and new computer users in general."
—BLOGCRITICS

UBUNTU FOR NON-GEEKS

4TH EDITION

A Pain-Free, Get-Things-Done Guide

by Rickford Grant with Phil Bull

no starch
press

San Francisco

UBUNTU FOR NON-GEEKS, 4TH EDITION. Copyright © 2010 by Rickford Grant and Phil Bull.

14 13 12 11 10   1 2 3 4 5 6 7 8 9

ISBN-10: 1-59327-257-X
ISBN-13: 978-1-59327-257-9

Publisher: William Pollock
Production Editors: Ansel Staton and Megan Dunchak
Cover and Interior Design: Octopod Studios
Developmental Editor: Keith Fancher
Technical Reviewer: Milo Casagrande
Copyeditor: Kim Wimpsett
Compositor: Susan Glinert Stevens
Proofreader: Linda Seifert

For information on book distributors or translations, please contact No Starch Press, Inc. directly:

No Starch Press, Inc.
38 Ringold Street, San Francisco, CA 94103
phone: 415.863.9900; fax: 415.863.9950; info@nostarch.com; www.nostarch.com

The Library of Congress has cataloged the first edition as follows:

Grant, Rickford.
 Ubuntu Linux for non-geeks : a pain-free, project-based, get-things-done guidebook / Rickford Grant.
      p. cm.
 Includes index.
 ISBN 1-59327-118-2
1. Linux. 2. Operating systems (Computers) I. Title. QA76.76.063.G7246 2006
 005.4'32--dc22
                                    2006015576

Printed in Canada.

BRIEF CONTENTS

CONTENTS IN DETAIL

3
A NEW PLACE TO CALL HOME
Getting to Know the Desktop   25

4
MORE THAN WEBBED FEET
Connecting to the Internet   45

5
SLIPPING AND SLIDING
Exploring the Internet, Linux Style 59

6
ROUNDING OUT THE BIRD
Downloading, Installing, and
Updating Programs the Easy Way 79

7
A TIDY NEST
File and Disc Handling in Ubuntu 93

8
DRESSING UP THE BIRD
Customizing the Look and Feel of Your System 123

9
SIMPLE KITTEN WAYS
Getting to Know the Linux Terminal and Command Line . . . and the Cool Things It Can Do   155

10
GUTENBIRD
Setting Up and Using Your Printer and Scanner   193

11
POLYGLOT PENGUINS
Linux Speaks Your Language   211

12
PENGUINS AT WORK
Getting Down to Business in Linux 227

13
BRUSH-WIELDING PENGUINS
Linux Does Art 243

14
TUX ROCKS
Music à la Linux 261

15
PLUGGIN' IN THE PENGUIN
Working with Your iPod, iPhone, and Other Digital Media Devices

277

16
COUCH PENGUINS
Video and DVD Playback in Ubuntu

291

17
FEATHERED FLIPPERS
Linux Gaming
305

18
PENGUINS AT THE GATES
Working with Ubuntu in a Windows World
323

19
DEFENDING THE NEST
Security   339

20
A COLONY OF PENGUINS
The Ubuntu Community   355

21
WOUNDED WINGS
Fixing Common Problems   **375**

A
INSTALLING UBUNTU FROM A USB FLASH DRIVE   **405**

ABOUT THE AUTHORS

Rickford Grant

My computing life began long ago, in the Commodore/Atari days. No doubt inspired by Alan Alda's television commercials at the time, I purchased my first machine, an Atari 600XL with a cassette drive for storage and 16KB of RAM—more than I thought I would ever need. Most of my time on that machine, I must admit, was spent playing cartridge-based games and transcribing pages and pages of machine code from the now-defunct magazine *Antic* to create even more games. Eventually, my interest in computers increased, especially after seeing my first (and actually the first) Macintosh at the UCLA bookstore. The very in-your-face nature of the Mac's operating system caused me to become an operating system maniac. To date, I have worked with a lot of different operating systems, including Mac OS up to and including OS X, every Windows version from 3.1 to 7, and even IBM's much forgotten OS/2.

Though tempted to join the Linux fray, I continued to steer away from it for a long time because I could not help but see it, as so many others do, as a system for never-seen-the-light-of-day-faced, late-night Dr Pepper–drinking, Domino's-pizza-eating compu-geeks. However, when I moved to Japan and was suddenly surrounded by machines loaded with Japanese versions of Windows, I encountered numerous problems, especially language constraints. Since everything, including Help files, was written in Japanese, I ended up using only a fraction of the full potential of most software. Then there were those annoying Windows-type problems, such as the constant freezes and restarts and the gradual system slowdowns, which were eventually remedied only by reinstalling the system. Getting the software I needed to do the things I wanted to do also took its toll on my wallet, and I began to rethink my initial resistance to Linux. With Linux's multilingual support, system stability, and extensive and free software packages, there were plenty of incentives for me to get over my preconceived notions about the typical Linux user.

After a few failed attempts at getting Linux to work on the oddball, Frankenstein-like collection of junk that was my computer, I finally succeeded with a CD-based Knoppix distribution, which worked well enough to reel me in a little further. I moved on to Mandrake (now known as Mandriva), since that was claimed to be the most newbie-friendly version, and then I tried SUSE as well, which I found to be rather quirky. Eventually, I tried Red Hat Linux and stuck to that because it just didn't give me any grief; and I, like most others, do not want any more grief than necessary.

I started off with my three desktop machines at work and home set up as dual-boot systems running both Linux and Windows, but I gradually found myself using only Linux. Although I had expected to encounter numerous limitations in Linux that would force me to return to Windows often, I instead found that I had actually increased my productivity. Other than lack of native support for Windows streaming media, I was actually able to do more because of the extensive software base that was now installed on my machine. Without having to fork out money that I could ill afford to spend, I was able to manipulate my digital images, rip songs from CDs, create vector drawings, create PDF files, and do a variety of other things that I wasn't able to do under Windows. It was only a matter of time before my dual-boot setups became full Linux-only setups. I ceased to be a Windows user.

Since those early Linux days, I have gone on to try a number of other distributions, including JAMD, Xandros, Damn Small Linux, and more recently, Ubuntu. I am happy to report that things have continued to get easier and better, and those early frustrations I suffered trying to get things to work with this machine or that piece of hardware have become more and more a thing of the past. Best of all, with even more distributions being available as live CDs, which allow you to try Linux before you actually install it, you usually don't even have to take a leap of faith to get started.

Of course, getting started in the world of Linux can be a bit intimidating, especially when you don't have anyone around to help you out. In fact, I actually started writing this book as a primer on Red Hat 9 for my mother, whom I had just given one of my extra computers with Red Hat installed. At that time, I was not planning on writing a book at all; it was just that there really weren't any books out there written with average users in mind. The books available then were all more or less geek-oriented, and as such, they would just not do for the mater. I thus created a somewhat elaborate instruction set that would tell her everything she might want to do on the machine in a way that she could understand.

My auntie caught hold of the "manuscript" and decided that I must try to publish it. I responded with the obligatory, "Yeah, right," before putting it out of my mind for a while. My auntie, being a rather persistent character, however, did not relent, and so I moved to quiet her by submitting the book for publication. Surely a rejection slip would do the trick; however, I did not get a rejection slip, and instead my first book, *Linux for Non-Geeks*, based on Fedora Core I, was born. I later switched to Ubuntu, and the *Non-Geeks* line followed along with *Ubuntu for Non-Geeks*.

I continued with two subsequent editions of the Ubuntu books, but my new day job was making it harder and harder to devote the time necessary to keep the whole book up-to-date and up-to-snuff and get it all written in a rather limited timeframe. It seemed time to bring in a coauthor to keep things moving. Enter Phil Bull. Phil was the technical editor on the third edition of *Ubuntu for Non-Geeks*, and because of his familiarity with the book, in addition to his work on Ubuntu documentation, he seemed a perfect candidate for the job. The fact that he lives closer than I to Stanage Edge, where I imagine myself one day standing, pulling the Keira Knightley *Pride and Prejudice* pose, didn't hurt matters either.

Such *rêves de vacances* aside, having Phil in on the project has allowed us to not only update the book so as to reflect changes in the system and bundled applications, but also to expand it to cover changes in available technology and hardware and to address suggestions from readers of past editions. These changes, I believe, have made for an even more well-rounded volume than before—a book that even better serves the original purpose of the series: helping you get into the world of Linux easily and comfortably.

Phil Bull

I worked as the technical reviewer on the previous edition of *Ubuntu for Non-Geeks*. This time around, Rickford and Bill felt that the book could use some fresh input and asked me to coauthor. I was happy to oblige!

So, what's my background? Well, computers have taken up most of my free time since I was eight years old. I started off playing games on my uncle's old DOS machine, and I soon found myself ripping apart our home PC and putting it back together again just to see how it worked. The geekiness doesn't stop there; I taught myself to program using Microsoft Word and Visual Basic for Applications (ugh) when I was 14, and I even worked in technical support for a while in my teens. However, physics became my calling in life at the end of school, and now I study cosmology full time. I haven't completely forsaken computers, though; it turns out that numerical simulations are pretty important in my line of work, and I currently spend a lot of time simulating particle collisions on an eight-core Mac inexplicably named "WiganPier."

My Linux journey started off with an old copy of *PC Pro* magazine from 1999. There was an article on this weird, alien-looking operating system in there, and I just knew I had to try it out. Unfortunately, my dial-up modem balked at the prospect of downloading a 650MB file, so I had to wait until some time around 2004, when a friend sent me a Xandros Linux CD. The rest, as they say, is history: I rapidly migrated to Fedora, and then settled down with Ubuntu in 2006. Not long after, I started writing documentation for Ubuntu, a pastime that I've kept up ever since. I just love to figure out problems, and writing clear, understandable instructions for people felt more productive (and often, more challenging!) than doing the crossword.

Writing this book with Rickford is, in many ways, the culmination of the last decade or so of my computing life, and I hope you'll find my contributions to this volume fun, easy to read, and above all, useful. In the rest of this section, I'll explain the changes I made and some of the logic behind them.

All manner of online activities, formerly the preserve of hard-core nerds, are now part of the non-geek's daily routine, so I've given our Internet coverage a significant overhaul to reflect this. New in this edition are an introduction to social networking with Twitter and Gwibber, setup instructions for "3G" mobile broadband connections, and extra tips on using the Firefox web browser.

Ubuntu isn't just a collection of software; there's a large, friendly community behind the project, and everyone is invited to participate. This can be a little unexpected for those used to the rigid, corporate world of computer stores and support hotlines that most other operating systems inhabit, but the "community vibe" really is one of Ubuntu's killer features. I've tried to get that message across in the new Chapter 20. You'll learn about how the community works, what the community can do for you, and how you can join in and help out if you like. In particular, there's lots on getting help and support via IRC and the forums.

Computers go wrong from time to time, so chances are you've learned a few tricks to deal with Windows hiccups or Mac disasters over the years. However, experiencing a problem as a new Ubuntu user can be daunting, since you may not yet have the experience to know how to handle it. To help you out, I've included a whole new chapter of troubleshooting tips and tricks. Although some specific, common problems are covered, I've kept most of the discussion quite general. The idea is to equip you with a problem-solving toolkit comparable to the one you painstakingly built up over the years for your previous operating system, and I hope that by the end of Chapter 21 you'll feel much more confident if faced with an unexpected error or misbehaving hardware.

One of the most common stumbling blocks for Linux newcomers is the first one, installation—so we've really beefed up our coverage of it this time around. A big chunk of Chapter 21 is dedicated to solving installation problems, so you can feel more confident than ever to try out Ubuntu. There's one new appendix (A) dedicated to installing from a USB memory stick, which is the method of choice for owners of netbooks and other computers lacking a CD drive. Hard disk partitioning is another oft-cited source of bewilderment, so I've added another new appendix (C) packed with advice on how to manually partition your hard disk during installation, too.

Once Ubuntu is installed, you may find that you miss certain aspects of your former operating system. For most people, that former operating system is Windows, so I've added a new chapter (18) on getting Ubuntu and

Windows to play together nicely. There's some enhanced coverage of Wine too, so running Windows programs in Linux need no longer be a chore.

This Ubuntu release comes with some big changes in the way you install applications. Things are much simpler now, so to reflect this we've consolidated pretty much everything you need to know about software installation into Chapter 6. Gone are the ugly workarounds and complicated programs that were sometimes necessary to get a program installed; they've been replaced by safer, more elegant ways of doing things, like the Ubuntu Software Center, PPAs, and APT-URL.

Finally, in response to the common, but erroneous, gripe that there are "no games for Linux," Rickford and I have dedicated the whole of Chapter 17 to the state-of-the-art in Linux gaming. (Rumors that it was inserted purely so that we could goof off and play a bunch of games have been greatly exaggerated.) Don't forget to check it out; we tried to include something for everyone.

New material aside, we've been over the book with a fine-toothed comb to check that everything is accurate, up-to-date, and easy to understand. I hope you enjoy reading it. Oh, and one last thing . . . welcome to Ubuntu!

ACKNOWLEDGMENTS

There are a good number of people who deserve thanks for the help and support they provided either while or before this book was written, and there are still others whose help will come after the book is released. I (Rickford) would like to acknowledge all of them now.

Starting with my family and friends, I'd like to thank my mother, Dixie Angelina Burckel-Testa; my auntie and uncle, Danica Lucia and David Zollars; and Sumire, who continues to inspire me with her art and creativity. And, somewhere in the dimension between family and *geistfreund,* a special shout-out to Mini—"*Pakalaka!*" I also send thanks to my long-time friends Donald Hammang, Tracy Nakajima, and Kimberly Jo Burk, who help to give me a needed sense of continuity and balance; and to my very dear friends back in Japan, Keith Hagan, Enryo Nagata, and Setsu Uesaka, who keep me connected with the sensibilities and joys I acquired there. Very special thanks also go out to my godfather, Theophan Dort, who is an always kind and patient ear for my incoherent ramblings and who does his best to keep me relatively sane in the context of my otherwise whacko world.

In the production of any book, editors are so very important, and so I would like to thank the editor of this edition of *Ubuntu for Non-Geeks,* Keith Fancher, who had the unenviable task of dealing with files flying in from two different authors, one of whom (me) is particularly good at mucking things up in the numbering and attachments department. Good job, Keith! Thanks also go out to Milo Casagrande, the technical editor on this edition, who did his best to ensure that all of the details in the book were straight duck, and Kim Wimpsett, the copyeditor, who made sure that every *t* was crossed and bit of orphaned text was found and dealt with. Thanks also to those folks whose job it is to turn the jumble of text and images we submit into a book—Megan Dunchak, Ansel Staton, and Riley Hoffman, who also taught us a thing or two about indexing. Sweet! And finally, a very special set of thanks go out to William Pollock for not only taking a chance on the completely unknown writer that I was but also for turning me on to a great *pupuseria* in San Mateo, California.

Having worked on my own for the previous editions of this book, working with a coauthor this time around was a new and pleasant experience, and for that reason I would also like to add a couple lines of thanks to that coauthor, Phil Bull. Working with Phil not only provided me with some new inspiration and ideas for the book, but it also made working on this edition a lot more fun and less lonely than working on the previous editions had been. It's always nice to have someone to bounce ideas around with.

Finally, a special thanks to my sweet little black cat and dear feline friend, Muju, who, despite vociferously protesting as I spent *her* time writing this book, continues to listen to whatever I have to say and keeps me sane when I'm feeling down—though I admit to losing it a bit when she demands that I spin her around on my swivel chair at 4 AM. Such is life in service to one's cat. Meow.

With two authors you get two sets of acknowledgments, so I'd like to take this opportunity to thank all of the people who've helped me (Phil) through the writing of this book, too.

First and foremost, I want to thank my parents, Julie and Jeff, for all of the love, support and home cooking they've provided over the years. Someday, as an expression of my gratitude, I might even remove all of my old computer junk from their house! I'd also like to acknowledge my sister, Ellen, for keeping things interesting; Nan, Gramps, and Nana for their affection; and my auntie and uncle, Pam and Roy Beeson, for being (mostly) willing Ubuntu guinea pigs.

Emily Johnstone has been superb in putting up with my nonsense and helping me through some of life's little obstacles. I hope she knows how much I appreciate her friendship. My good friends (and fellow nerds) Kiran "K-Dizzle" Joshi and Leo "Tenacity" Huckvale waded through my initial scribblings and gave me the confidence to keep writing, and Will "Willybobs" Whyles was the inspiration for the troubleshooting chapter; thanks, guys! I'm also grateful to Adam Blundred who, despite his misguided attempts to convince me that Windows is better than Linux, has been a wonderful friend, and to Matt Glover, Jamie Poole, and the other folks back in Stoke for all the fun times.

While I've been in Manchester, Christina Smith, Amanda Jackson, Michel Schammel, Sarah Johnson, Sara Rehman, and Jack Mason have made every day interesting, and their friendship has been so important to me. Sally and the Millican family have also been a big part of my life these past few years, and I'm grateful to them for all the adventures we've shared. Thanks must go out to the guys in the physics department at the University of Manchester, too; Bob, Richard, Fred, Lucio, Giampaolo, and all the rest have turned me into the cosmologist I am today (whether they intended to or not), and I'm sincerely grateful for their support.

Being part of the open source documentation community maintains my faith in humanity. It's a privilege to be involved in the Ubuntu and GNOME projects, and people like Matthew East, Shaun McCance, Paul Cutler, Daniel Holbach, and Emma-Jane Hogbin are the reason why. In particular, I'd like to single out Jim Campbell for his endless generosity and Rich Johnson for trying to get me use my accent for no good.

This is my first book, and the guys at No Starch Press have turned the process from a daunting leap into the unknown into a rewarding and pleasurable experience. Keith Fancher, our editor, has been a rock; his comments and advice always cut straight to the point, and without his guidance it's fair to say I would have been lost. As our copyeditor, Kim Wimpsett has dealt admirably with the task of turning the output of two different authors into a readable, coherent whole, and Milo Casagrande deserves thanks not only for the sterling job he made of the technical reviewing but also for giving me a place to stay one windy night after a post-conference visit to a blues bar. Riley Hoffman, Ansel Staton, and all the other folks behind the scenes should also be praised for their hard work in getting this book out on the shelves. Lastly, I want to say thanks to William Pollock for a series of out-of-the-blue job offers that have kept me pleasantly occupied over the last couple of years. It's always fun working with you!

Finally, I'd like to express my gratitude to my coauthor. This edition of *Ubuntu For Non-Geeks* wouldn't have been possible without the extremely solid base he's put in place over the course of the previous revisions, and working with him has been nothing less than enjoyable. Thanks, Rickford!

INTRODUCTION

If you're standing in the aisle of your local bookstore reading this right now, you may well be wondering who this book is for. *Ubuntu for Non-Geeks*, as you might imagine, is for readers who are interested in Linux but who feel the need for a jumping-off point of sorts.

If you're familiar with computers but unfamiliar with Linux, or if you are somewhat familiar with Linux but not with Ubuntu, this book is for you. This is not primarily a book for those seasoned geeks or power users; it's an introductory guide that will provide you with some hands-on experience that will get you up, running, and comfortable with the Ubuntu Linux distribution without pain. Think of this book as a map, a compass, and a comfy pair of hiking boots, rather than a harness, a rope, and a set of crampons.

Version Compatibility

This fourth edition of *Ubuntu for Non-Geeks* is based on Ubuntu 10.04 (Lucid Lynx) Desktop edition. The CD bundled with this book is the Ubuntu Desktop CD, which lets you both try Ubuntu without installing it and install

Ubuntu to your hard drive once you're ready. It's called a *live CD*. You can boot your computer from the CD and run Ubuntu directly off the CD without touching your hard disk so that you can see if you like Ubuntu and make sure that Ubuntu will work with your hardware. If, after running the live CD, you like what you see and everything seems to work, you can install Ubuntu on your computer using the same disc. (There are instructions for doing so in Chapter 2.)

NOTE   *The world of computers is dynamic, and there may be changes in the software or the links to the files for projects in this book after publication. Please see* http://www .edgy-penguins.org/UFNG/ *for updates.*

Concept and Approach

This book is intended as both a handy reference and a dynamic learning experience: You'll get some hands-on experience as you work through it. The text is organized by increasing skills, so that as much as possible you won't be asked to do something that you haven't already learned. In addition, you can put the various morsels of knowledge you acquire into practice through several exercises, or *projects*.

The projects in this book serve a secondary purpose as well: By working through them, you will learn to configure and customize your Ubuntu system. By the time you finish this book, you should have pretty good mastery over Ubuntu.

These chapter descriptions should give you a better idea of what is in store:

Chapter 1: Becoming a Penguinista—Welcome to the World of Linux
What's Linux? What's Ubuntu? What's a distribution? Can I . . .? Will my . . .? Chapter 1 holds the answers to these and many other questions you might have as it introduces you to the world of Linux and what it takes to get it up and running on your machine.

Chapter 2: Wading and Diving—Running and (If You Like) Installing Ubuntu
The CD that comes with this book works as both a live CD and an install CD. Chapter 2 tells you how to run a live Ubuntu session from the CD and, assuming you catch the Linux bug after doing so, how to install Ubuntu on your hard disk either as your sole operating system or together with Windows.

Chapter 3: A New Place to Call Home—Getting to Know the Desktop
Regardless of whether you are an émigré from the Windows or Mac worlds, you're probably already familiar with the concept of a desktop. Chapter 3 points out the differences between Ubuntu's GNOME desktop and the one on your previous operating system, and it teaches you a number of cool tricks you can use to customize the look and feel of things. It also includes a couple of nifty GNOME Easter eggs (hidden surprises).

Chapter 4: More Than Webbed Feet—Connecting to the Internet

"Have computer, will cybertravel" could well be the mantra of the Internet age, and that being the case, Chapter 4 is an indispensable part of your Ubuntu experience. In this chapter, you will learn how to connect to the Internet and set up wireless and mobile broadband connections. You'll also find tips for using a modem and some handy troubleshooting advice just in case you struggle to get connected.

Chapter 5: Slipping and Sliding—Exploring the Internet, Linux Style

With Chapter 4 behind you, it's time to get serious about all this Internet business and start putting it to good use. Chapter 5 takes you on a tour of Ubuntu's suite of Internet applications, in particular the Firefox web browser. You're introduced to Ubuntu's email and instant messaging tools before embarking on a crash course in social networking with Twitter and Gwibber.

Chapter 6: Rounding Out the Bird—Downloading, Installing, and Updating Programs the Easy Way

The default Ubuntu installation includes most of the software you need, but there is still much more available out there, free and waiting on the Internet. Chapter 6 teaches you how to easily download and install applications using the Ubuntu Software Center. You'll learn about system and application updating and how to broaden your software horizons using third-party repositories.

Chapter 7: A Tidy Nest—File and Disc Handling in Ubuntu

From creating folders to copying files to browsing your system and network, Chapter 7 covers all things file management. You'll learn how to work with USB storage devices, transfer files via Bluetooth, burn data CDs and DVDs, deal with CD-RW disks and multisession CDs, and create space-saving compressed archives of files and folders.

Chapter 8: Dressing Up the Bird—Customizing the Look and Feel of Your System

Tired of looking at the same old desktop? Feeling nostalgic for the desktop in your previous operating system? Chapter 8 tells you how to beat the déjà vu blues by changing the look and feel of just about every visual element of your system and how to take control of Ubuntu's visual effects engine, Compiz.

Chapter 9: Simple Kitten Ways—Getting to Know the Linux Terminal and Command Line . . . and the Cool Things It Can Do

Many people shy away from Linux because they perceive it as a system in which everything still needs to be done by entering commands. That perception is, as the saying goes, a load of squashed avocados. Still, there is a lot of cool stuff that can be done via the command-line based Terminal, and Chapter 9 will tell you all about it as it tames your fears and piques your interest in commands. Really.

Chapter 10: Gutenbird—Setting Up and Using Your Printer and Scanner

Just about everyone with a computer has or needs a printer. Chapter 10 tells you exactly how to get your printer (or scanner) working with Ubuntu.

Chapter 11: Polyglot Penguins—Linux Speaks Your Language

Need to jot off a note in Urdu? Write a book in Korean? Send a letter in Chinese to your friend in Chengdu? Chapter 11 gives you what you need to read and write in just about any language in the world.

Chapter 12: Penguins at Work—Getting Down to Business in Linux

Work can be a drag, especially when there are so many other things you could be doing. Still, wearing the ole' fingers to the bone is part of life for just about everyone outside of a Jane Austen novel, and you'll be glad to know that Linux has lots to offer in this regard. Chapter 12 introduces you to the various productivity applications available.

Chapter 13: Brush-Wielding Penguins—Linux Does Art

Those with an artistic bent will find Chapter 13 especially useful. Working with your digital camera, modifying images, and building web albums are just some of the topics covered.

Chapter 14: Tux Rocks—Music à la Linux

Chapter 14 is the music lover's treasure trove. You'll learn how to rip CDs, encode MP3 or Ogg Vorbis audio files, and even create your own mix-and-match audio CDs. Several audio ripping and playback applications are also covered.

Chapter 15: Pluggin' In the Penguin—Working with Your iPhone, iPod, and Other Digital Media Devices

Do you have an iPod? An iPhone? A Droid? A $19 MP3 player from the flea market? Want to use it in Ubuntu? Chapter 15 tells you how.

Chapter 16: Couch Penguins—Video and DVD Playback in Ubuntu

Sitting in your dorm room trying to figure out how to play your DVD copy of *The Baxter* on your Ubuntu-ized computer? Just finished filming a video of your sibling talking while asleep and want to do some creative editing of the evidence? Chapter 16 covers these and other video-related topics.

Chapter 17: Feathered Flippers—Linux Gaming

If music and art don't keep your mind off things enough, Chapter 17 presents you with more diversions: games. In addition to learning what games your system comes with, you will also learn how to add more and even how to run Java-based games.

Chapter 18: Penguins at the Gates—Working with Ubuntu in a Windows World

Like it or not, Microsoft Windows is probably here to stay (for the foreseeable future, at least). Chapter 18 shows you how to share files between Windows and Ubuntu over a network, install Windows fonts, and even install Windows programs to run under Ubuntu. Dual-booters take note: You'll learn how to access your Windows files from Ubuntu and change the boot menu.

Chapter 19: Defending the Nest—Security

Although Linux is about as safe and secure an operating system as you are likely to use, Chapter 19 tells you how to add a few additional lines of defense to your system.

Chapter 20: A Colony of Penguins—The Ubuntu Community

If there's one thing that sets Ubuntu apart from most Linux distributions, it's the friendly, ever-growing Ubuntu community that surrounds it. In Chapter 20 you'll learn how to participate in the Ubuntu community by reporting bugs, sharing ideas, and talking to other users.

Chapter 21: Wounded Wings—Fixing Common Problems

Don't panic! If a computer problem crops up and is spoiling your fun, flip to Chapter 21 and take heed of the many (and varied) troubleshooting tips within. You'll find fixes for the most common issues, and some general advice on diagnosing and treating your poor PC.

Appendix A: Installing Ubuntu from a USB Flash Drive

What with the proliferation of netbooks in recent years, installing Ubuntu from CD is beginning to seem a little *passé*. Appendix A shows you how to install Ubuntu from a USB memory stick, which will be particularly useful if your computer lacks a CD drive or if you found the disc included with this book far too attractive to *not* be used as a coaster.

Appendix B: Ubuntu Desktop CDs for AMD64, Opteron, or Intel Core 2 Users

The CD bundled with this book is designed to work with i386 processors. It will also work with most 64-bit processors, although not in 64-bit mode. If you've got what it takes to run Ubuntu in 64-bit mode, Appendix B will show you how to get what you need to do it.

Appendix C: Manually Partitioning Your Hard Disk

If the basic partitioning advice in Chapter 2 wasn't enough for you, Appendix C shows you how to carve up your hard disk as you desire, free from the constraints of the Ubuntu installer's sensible, but ultimately simple, suggestions. If you're a dual-booter and want an easy way to share files between Windows and Ubuntu, this appendix is for you.

Appendix D: Resources

Are you crazy for Ubuntu and want to say so? Check out a forum. Do you have a hardware compatibility question? Some websites seem to have all the answers. Are you looking for free downloads, or do you want to read up on the other Linux distributions? Appendix D is a great place to start.

How to Use This Book

You can use this book simply as a reference, but that's not the main idea behind its design. Ideally, you should go through the book chapter by chapter, doing the projects along the way. This will give you a much broader understanding of how things are done (and of how you can get things done), and it will reduce the chance for anxiety, confusion, and, worse yet, mistakes.

It is best to read this book and complete its projects when you are relaxed and have time to spare. Nothing makes things go wrong more than working in a rush. And keep in mind that Linux and the projects in this book are fun, not just work exercises. Linux is fun so enjoy it!

About the Conventions Used in This Book

There are a few points worth noting about the conventions used in this book. Items in **bold** type are ones that you need to click or manipulate in any way, such as buttons, tabs, and menus. Where words or phrases are defined, they have been set in *italics*. Text to input into a Terminal window is in a bold `monospace` font.

About the Projects in This Book

The projects and other information in this book are primarily geared toward readers who have installed Ubuntu using the CD that comes with this book. Most of the information also applies to Ubuntu live sessions run from the live CD. Note, however, that some projects and actions cannot be performed in live sessions because they require write access to your hard disk, which is not possible during live sessions.

1

BECOMING A PENGUINISTA

Welcome to the World of Linux

In this first chapter, we begin our project to get you up and running in the world of Linux. If you have already made the commitment and have Ubuntu installed on your machine, you are essentially ready to go. Others of you might have made the commitment psychologically but have yet to act on that commitment. And some of you are probably reading these words in the aisle of a bookstore, wondering about Linux and about whether you should spend your money on this book or on a latté every morning for the next couple of weeks. For those in this last group, I can only say, "Get this book." Save the wear and tear on your stomach and nerves.

In any case, the first thing we need to do is get you up to snuff on what this Ubuntu thing is all about, why you might want to install and use it, and what you will need in order to do so. I expect you will have lots of questions along the way and, if you are like most people, a few doubts. I hope that by the time you finish this book and have your Linux system up and running, your doubts will be gone and your questions, for the most part, will be answered. Anyway, until you are ready to make the commitment, you can still follow along, because the CD that comes with this book contains, in addition to the

Ubuntu installer, a live Ubuntu environment—meaning that you can get a taste of the Ubuntu Linux experience without having to even touch what you have on your hard drive. You can kick back, put your worries in check, and go with the flow.

What Is Linux?

Your computer, despite being a collection of highly sophisticated parts, is really just . . . well, a collection of highly sophisticated parts. On its own, it can do nothing other than switch on and off and spin a disk or two. For it to do anything truly useful, it needs an operating system (OS) to guide it. The OS takes a well-endowed but completely uneducated hunk of a machine and educates it, at least enough so that it will understand what you want it to do.

You already know of and have probably used at least one of the many operating systems that exist today, or did in the past. Windows, DOS, OS/2, and Mac OS are all such operating systems, and Linux is yet another. Linux is, however, different from these other operating systems, in terms of both its capabilities and its heritage. Linux was not created by a corporation or by some corporate wanna-be out to make money. The Linux core, referred to as the *kernel*, was created by computer enthusiast Linus Torvalds, a member of Finland's Swedish ethnic minority, who wanted to create a Unix-like system that would work on home computers—particularly his.

Rather than keeping his creation to himself, Torvalds opened it up to the world, so to speak, and compu-geeks around the globe worked to make it better and more powerful. It is this combination of applications built around the core of the Linux kernel that is the essence of all Linux distributions today.

Linux has acquired many fans and followers since its creation in 1991. Such devotees praise Linux for its many features, as well as for being robust, reliable, free, and open. Despite these positive characteristics, however, Linux is, on its own, just a text-based system. There is no pretty desktop, and there are no windows or charming little icons to make you feel safe and comfy once you are behind the keyboard. Powerful though it may be, Linux is still strictly a black-screen, command line–driven operating system. I guess you could think of it as DOS on steroids, though a Linux purist will surely cringe at the thought. Sorry.

Although you can use Linux by itself, accomplishing all your tasks by typing commands on a black screen (the most common way of doing things when Linux is used as a server), you don't have to do that. It is fair to say that with the advent in 1984 of the Macintosh and its easy-to-use graphical user interface (GUI, pronounced "goo-ee"), DOS users began suffering something akin to GUI envy. They began clamoring for a GUI to call their own. The final result was Windows, which gave DOS a GUI and eased many command-wary users into the Microsoft world.

Similarly, many members of the Linux world felt the need and desire to go graphical. The community at large developed various GUIs (called *window managers* and *desktop environments*) and a subsystem with which to handle them (somewhat confusingly referred to as the *X Window System*) to bring about the change. The graphical desktop environment that is included in your Ubuntu distribution—GNOME—is one example of the fruit of that development.

About the Penguin

You may have been wondering about the penguin in the chapter title, so I might as well explain that now. The penguin was chosen by Linus Torvalds as the Linux mascot, and what has come to be thought of as *the* Linux penguin was designed by Larry Ewing and is named Tux (see Figure 1-1). This explains not only the ornithological references and graphics throughout the book but also why there are so many penguin icons in Linux distributions and so many programs that include *penguin* or *Tux*, such as TuxRacer, XPenguins, and Pingus. This, combined with the fact that Linux is a revolutionary OS, helps explain why Linux users are sometimes referred to as *Penguinistas*. True, Ubuntu doesn't play up the penguin as much as other distributions, but Linux is Linux, and so the penguin lives in Ubuntu too . . . just a bit less conspicuously.

Figure 1-1: Tux, the Linux mascot

Why Should You Use Linux?

People use Linux for different reasons. For many, it is a matter of power, stability, multilingual capabilities, or even personal philosophy. However, for others, crass as it may sound, it is a matter of money. Just think for a moment about what it usually costs to get started with an operating system. Go to wherever it is you go to buy software, and take a walk down the aisles. Make a list in your head of all the things you want to buy and how much each costs: an office suite; a game or two; maybe a graphics program with which to make yourself look better in your digital photos; and a collection of all those firewall, antispam, antivirus, and anti-adware programs that you really need to protect yourself in the Windows world. Now do the math.

After you pick yourself up off the floor, you will understand that we are talking big bucks here. On the other hand, for the price of this book, you will have all of the things you wanted and more in the Linux world. Despite the worries that many people have, making the move to Linux means not only savings for you but also more computing versatility. You will not be hamstrung at some point along the way because you don't have this or that program when you need it most—you'll have it all from the get-go or else be able to download it easily . . . and at no cost!

You might counter with the fact that there are a lot of freeware applications out there for other operating systems, but c'mon, let's face it—these are often rather limited in terms of their capabilities. The programs with a little more oomph are mostly shareware, and most shareware programs these days are limited in some way, or they let you use them only for a short time unless you are willing to pay for them. Sure, their costs are relatively low, but $25 here and $35 there eventually adds up to a considerable chunk of change. There is also the problem that some of these programs, unbeknownst to you, install backdoors or keyloggers or make your system a sudden garden of adware. Finally, at least in my experience, the majority of such programs are hardly worth the money asked.

Is It All Just About Money?

Although money is important to the average user, it is certainly not the only reason for taking the Linux plunge; there are a variety of other reasons as well. As I mentioned, Linux is noted for its stability. Try running your current system for a month without restarting and see what happens. Linux has been known to run without a reboot for more than a year without a hitch or decrease in performance. With its multilingual capabilities, Linux is also a perfect choice for language students or users in a multilingual environment.

In addition, Linux is infinitely customizable: You can get your system to look and act the way you want it to without being "wizarded" to death. And then there are the applications that come with most Linux distributions. In addition to their wide variety, most are well up to industry snuff, with some, such as Evolution, the GIMP, and Inkscape, being sources of envy for those outside the Linux world.

Finally, with the advent of Microsoft's Windows 7 system and its more demanding hardware requirements (especially if you want to take advantage of its most touted new features), you may find your current machine on the fast track to obsolescence. Turning it into a Linux machine will ensure it several more years of working life. After all, it's a shame to put good hardware out to pasture so early.

But Is Linux Really Ready for the Desktop?

Despite the advances Linux has made in recent years, this question still pops up quite often, and that's fair enough. But consider this: When you install a program on your current Windows system and get an error message saying that the program can't run because some DLL file is missing, or when you connect a piece of hardware and can't get it to run, no one asks if that operating system is ready for the desktop.

In my own experience, I have found no reason to doubt that Linux is ready. Sure, Linux has its occasional quirks, but so does every other operating system. Linux is ready and able. If my mother, hardly a computer wiz, can do the work she needs to do and can keep herself amused until the middle of the night using her Linux system (without blowing the whole thing up), then I think it's pretty safe to say that you'll do all right too.

What Is a Distribution?

An operating system consists of a lot of files that perform a lot of different functions. And because there is no Linux corporation to package and distribute the files that make up Linux, the task of getting Linux onto your computer in working order, along with the applications that you are likely to want, has fallen to a varied group of entities—companies, universities, user groups, and even private individuals. These entities create Linux system and application collections called *distributions*, or *distros*. You could bypass such distros and try to collect everything you'd need to set up a system all on your own, but you would undoubtedly lose your mind in the process. Most people, even the geekiest, opt for the distros.

Most of these distros, whatever their ultimate target audience, basically consist of the same main elements: the core operating system (that's the Linux kernel I mentioned earlier); some sort of installer program to get all the system parts and applications properly installed on your machine; the X Window System to provide graphical interface support; one or more graphical desktop environments; and a series of applications, such as word processors, audio players, and games; as well as all the files needed to make these things work.

There are, of course, a large number of distros. Some are geared toward specific audiences, such as businesses, educators, gamers, students, programmers, system administrators, and specific language users. What makes each distro different is the software that is bundled with the Linux kernel, as well as other convenience features such as the package (or application) installation mechanism and the installer for the system itself. Some distros are especially appropriate for home users because of their ease of installation. Ubuntu, a relative newcomer to the Linux world, is one of these, joining other distros that have long been popular in the ease-of-use arena, such as Mandriva, SUSE, and Fedora Core. Although some of these entities charge for their distros, most also provide them free for download.

What Is Ubuntu?

Ubuntu is a completely free, easy-to-use, and extremely popular Linux distribution that is geared toward the desktop user. It is one of the hottest Linux distros in the marketplace today. It is also one of the few Linux distros with what could be described as a social agenda behind it.

Ubuntu was the brainchild of South African millionaire entrepreneur Mark Shuttleworth, who is probably better known for being one of the first space tourists—the first African in space, to be exact. Shuttleworth invested more than $10 million in starting the Ubuntu Foundation based on his belief in free software and in order to fix what he describes as "bug #1"—Microsoft's dominance of the desktop PC marketplace (*https://bugs.launchpad.net/ubuntu/ +bug/1*).

As Shuttleworth states the following in his blog (available at *https:// wiki.ubuntu.com/MarkShuttleworth*):

> I believe that free software brings us into a new era of technology, and holds the promise of universal access to the tools of the digital era. I drive Ubuntu because I would like to see that promise delivered as reality.

As you can see, it's a vision thing.

Befitting the nationality and goals of the man who brought it into being, the word *ubuntu* comes from the Zulu and Xhosa languages. Ubuntu, according to Wikipedia, is a concept meaning something along the lines of "humanity toward others" or "I am because we are." If you're interested, the 2005 film *In My Country*, although not one of the greatest films ever produced, is on many levels a 100-minute examination of the concept of ubuntu.

Why Ubuntu Then?

With so many distros out there, you may wonder why you should opt for Ubuntu. Well, as they say, numbers don't lie, and Ubuntu's popularity is not without good cause. These traits are especially crowd pleasing:

Easy to install
It's fair to say that most Linux distributions these days are pretty easy to install (and definitely easier and faster to install than Windows). Ubuntu is right in line with these improvements, and the fact that you can install it with only a few mouse clicks while running the live CD means it is pretty much ready to go whenever you are.

Easy to use
Ubuntu is easy to use in that it is very Windows-like in operation, and yet it's more Linux-like than other Windows user–oriented distributions. It is designed with the needs of real people in mind, not just compu-nerds and geeks.

DEB based
Ubuntu is based on the *Debian* distribution, which means that it utilizes Debian's very convenient DEB package system for application handling and installation. The two preconfigured, graphical package installers that come with Ubuntu make installing applications even easier. So many packages are available for Debian systems like Ubuntu that you are likely to find more software out there than you'll ever know what to do with.

Up-to-date

Some distros are updated at a snail's pace, while others strive to be so cutting edge that they are often plagued with bugs. Ubuntu, with its reasonable six-month release cycle, tries to stay as up-to-date as possible, while at the same time making sure that things are not released before they are ready for prime time. In this way, you are ensured of having an up-to-date yet less buggy distro at your disposal.

Dependable and robust

I know these terms come across as mere hype, but after you smack Ubuntu around a bit, you come to understand what they mean. Knock things down and around, and they bounce right back—this is very important for beginners who often have a knack for screwing things up. Nothing turns a new user off more than a twitchy system that has to be velvet-gloved all the time.

Desktop user–oriented

A lot of Linux distributions, although quite capable in the desktop arena, cater more to geeks and developers, taking up valuable disk space with a lot of junk you'll probably never use. Ubuntu's purpose is to grab desktop market share from the Redmond folks, so the needs of the common end user are always in mind. The result is that Ubuntu's GNOME desktop environment is a very comfy place for the average desktop user to be.

Hardware Compatibility

Well, enough of this background babble; it's time to get things rolling. If you haven't installed Linux on your machine yet and are wondering whether you can, rest assured: Ubuntu will run on most machines out there today. Of course, you just never know until you get up and running. There are so many minor parts to your machine that it is difficult to say whether each part will cooperate with your installation. There are video cards, sound chips, LAN cards, monitors, and so on, and they all need to be considered.

Diving In

If you are going to buy a new machine on which to run Ubuntu, then it is reasonable enough to do a bit of worrying and check things out first, but if you are going to install it on the machine you have, I recommend just diving in. After all, you don't really have to install anything the first time out. You have a live CD right here in this book, after all, so you can just pop that CD in your drive, boot up your machine, and, *biff, bam, zowie,* you'll be up and running (or not) in a minute or two. If everything seems to be going as it should . . . well, your worries are over, and you can go ahead and install the system when you're ready and willing. That is one of the Ubuntu advantages—not only do all the essentials fit on a single CD (compared to four or more for other distros), but that CD is both a live operating environment and the installer! You can't get much more convenient than that.

When Research Is Required

If things don't work out for you with the live CD, you can start by taking a look at Chapter 21. If you don't find the answer to your problem there, search the Web to see whether you can identify what part of your hardware puzzle is causing your problems. (Or if you are looking to buy a machine on which to install Ubuntu, you can search for hardware that is supported by Linux.) Of course, before you can do this, you need to know what models of hardware you have. You should know at least what motherboard, central processing unit (CPU), monitor, and video card you have if you want to be able to find out anything of value. Identifying your CPU and monitor should be easy enough, but the motherboard and video card may require a bit more searching.

If you have no documentation that clearly states the make and model of these devices, you can find out most things you need to know from within Windows by going to the Windows Control Panel, double-clicking **System**, and then clicking the **Hardware** tab in that window. Once on the Hardware tab, click the **Device Manager** button, and see what you can find about your system components. Sometimes the information there is rather limited, so you might instead want to try a shareware application such as HWiNFO (*http://www.hwinfo.com/*) or Sandra (*http://www.sisoftware.net/*) to get more useful details, such as the specifications of your motherboard or the supported video modes for your current setup.

Both HWiNFO and Sandra should give you the information you need about your motherboard, but if they don't (or if you don't feel like bothering with them), you can always just open the case of your computer and look at your board, though I wouldn't recommend doing so if you have a laptop. Once inside, you needn't worry about damaging anything because you don't need to touch anything—so don't. You may need a flashlight to find it, but the model name and number should be stamped on there somewhere, either in the middle of the board or around the edges. Mine, for example, says quite clearly in the middle of the board "AOpen MX46-533V." You should be looking for similar information.

Once you have all your information, you can do a variety of things to check out your hardware's compatibility with Ubuntu. You can simply do a Yahoo! or Google search by entering your motherboard's make and model plus the word *Linux*. This works for other hardware devices too.

You can also post a question to the Ubuntu User Forums (at *http://www.ubuntuforums.org/*) or one of the other various Linux forums or mailing lists on the Web. Chapter 20 might provide you with additional sources of information, and Appendix D lists still other sources. When posting a forum question, just write that you are a newbie and want to know whether anyone has had any experience using Ubuntu with the board (or other hardware) in question. You will probably get quite a few responses. Linux users are usually rather evangelical in terms of trying to draw in new Penguinistas.

Hardware Requirements

All worries about compatibility aside, you will need to meet some minimum hardware requirements:

- Any computer with a 1 GHz or higher i386-based processor, or an Intel or AMD 64-bit processor
- About 5 gigabytes (GB) of hard disk space, though having at least 10GB would be a bit more comfy
- Sufficient memory (RAM)

NOTE *The CD that comes with this book is designed to work on machines with i386-based processors (basically, all the Pentium chips, including Celeron, Xeon, and the new Core Duo, as well as processors from AMD). Though this CD will install Ubuntu on a computer with an AMD or Intel 64-bit processor, it will run in 32-bit mode only. To make full use of your 64-bit processor, you need to download the 64-bit version of Ubuntu. Additional information is provided in Appendix B.*

As for random access memory (RAM), the official specs tell you that you need a minimum of 512 megabytes (MB) to run Ubuntu. Although you can no doubt get by with this, you'd get by much better with more. My basic rule of thumb, no matter what OS I am dealing with, is that you need the recommended (not the minimum) memory plus at least 128MB. Regardless of what the official specs say, put in more. You won't regret it.

Saying "the more memory you have, the better" may sound a bit simple, and perhaps even cavalier, but trust me on this one. When you have too little memory, no matter what system you are running, weird things happen: Applications seem to take years to open or don't open at all, menus take forever to render their little icons, and freezes and general system meltdowns just happen much more often. In other words, running your machine on too little RAM is sort of like trying to do jumping jacks in a broom closet. Sure, you could do it, but you would be all contorted, and you'd be smashing your hands into the walls every 1.4 seconds.

Fortunately, it is pretty hard to find a machine with less than 512MB of RAM these days (256MB, perhaps, on the really old beasties), but if you do happen to have such a machine, you can at least take solace in the fact that memory is relatively cheap, so go for it.

Good News for 64-Bit Machine Users

It is again important to mention that the CD that comes with this book is designed to work on machines with i386-based processors, which pretty much covers the vast majority of PCs out there. If your machine is 64-bit compatible, you will be glad to know that it will also work, albeit not in 64-bit mode. Sorry, but no go.

Fortunately, there is good news for those of you who were a bit disappointed by the content of that previous paragraph. Ubuntu is available in a native 64-bit version. Check Appendix B for information on how to get it. The information provided there will also be of use to i386 users who happen to lose or damage the disc that comes with this book.

Mixed News for Mac Users

Those of you with pre–Intel era PowerPC Macs (such as those with G3, G4, and G5 processors) may be aware that previous Ubuntu releases have been available in PowerPC versions. Unfortunately, as of the Ubuntu 7.04 Feisty Fawn release, this is no longer the case. This means that if you are a PowerPC Mac user, you will have to use one of the older Ubuntu releases or use an unofficial, community-supported release of Ubuntu 10.04 Lucid Lynx (more on that name in the following section) for PowerPCs (*http://cdimage.ubuntu.com/ports/*).

Of course, if you are using an Intel-based Mac, you're in luck: The disc that comes with this book will work on your Mac. After all, the *i* in *i386* stands for "Intel."

Speaking Ubuntu

It's worth noting that you are bound to come across a lot of weird phrases when dealing with Ubuntu, especially when searching for information on the Net. In particular, I am referring to seemingly incongruous phrases, such as *Warty Warthog, Hoary Hedgehog, Breezy Badger, Dapper Drake, Edgy Eft, Feisty Fawn, Gutsy Gibbon, Hardy Heron, Intrepid Ibex, Jaunty Jackalope,* and *Karmic Koala.* These are the unlikely code names of each of the releases of Ubuntu since its first appearance in 2004. The important one for you to remember is that of the current release, which is the one on the book's disc: version 10.04, known as *Lucid Lynx.*

You are also likely to come across a few other variations of the Ubuntu theme. These are Kubuntu, a KDE-based version of Ubuntu; Edubuntu, a special version of Ubuntu designed for use in the classroom; Xubuntu, a lightweight version of Ubuntu based on the XFCE desktop; and Ubuntu Studio, a new flavor of Ubuntu, aimed at "creative people," which contains a strong suite of graphics, video, and music applications. There's even a slimmed-down version of Ubuntu, called Ubuntu Netbook Edition, designed specifically for netbooks.

Where Do I Go from Here?

Now that you know more about the world of Linux and Ubuntu and you have your disc in hand, it's time to get down to it. If you have already installed Ubuntu on your machine, just flip ahead to Chapter 3. If your machine is still Linuxless, though, it's time to take it out for a spin and see whether you like it. So for now, strap yourself down in front of that computer, clip on your spurs, and go straight to the next chapter. It's time to become a Penguinista!

2

WADING AND DIVING

Running and (If You Like) Installing Ubuntu

As I have already mentioned, one of the great things about Ubuntu is that it comes on a live CD, which means that you can try it before you install it . . . or never install it at all, if that's what you prefer. Better yet is the fact that, unlike earlier editions of Ubuntu, you don't need an additional installation CD if you do choose to install it—the Ubuntu Desktop CD functions as both a live CD and an install CD. And in the good-better-best swing of things, the best point of all is that installation from the live CD is actually much, much easier than any other installation process you've ever dealt with, and it even gives you more than one way to go about it.

In this chapter, I will cover the basics of starting up and running Ubuntu from the live CD and then, assuming you've caught the Linux bug, the painless steps of installing Ubuntu on your hard disk as your sole operating system, in its own partition on your hard disk in a traditional dual-boot setup (with Windows in its own partition), or, for the slightly less adventurous, from within your Windows system. If your computer doesn't have a CD drive, don't worry, you can still join in—take a look at Appendix A to see how you can run or install Ubuntu from a USB flash drive instead. Whatever way you end up going about things, let's put this book to use and get Ubuntu up and running.

Going for a Dip

To get a taste of what Ubuntu is all about (and to check out your hardware to see whether it's all comfy-cozy with Ubuntu), there is probably no better way to go than to run Ubuntu directly from the live CD. To do this, just place the Ubuntu Desktop CD in your disc drive and restart your machine. When the machine starts up, it should boot up from the CD, and after a second or two, you should see a purple Ubuntu startup screen with a couple of icons at the bottom of it. If the screen does not appear and your machine instead boots up into your usual operating system, then it is very likely that your machine's BIOS settings need to be changed to allow you to boot from a CD.

You can access your machine's BIOS by restarting and then pressing whatever key the onscreen startup instructions assign to accessing the BIOS setup. This is usually DELETE or F1 (F2, F10, and ESC are also common), but not all machines are the same. If the onscreen information passes by so fast that you miss it, you can check your user's manual to see what the correct key is. Once you get into the BIOS setup, change the boot sequence so that your CD drive is first.

Once your machine boots from the live CD and you see the purple Ubuntu startup screen, either you can wait for a few seconds for Ubuntu to start booting into the live CD proper or you can press a key (any key) to display a menu where you can choose your language and other settings. The default settings should suffice for our purposes, so leave the keyboard untouched for a few seconds, and the purple screen will give way to a loading screen (also purple).

After a couple of minutes or so, the loading screen will disappear, and in its place will come an Install window like the one in Figure 2-1. You should now be able to use your mouse as well as the keyboard, so unless you want to change the language using the list on the left of the screen, click the **Try Ubuntu 10.04** button to start a live session. After a few more seconds of loading, you'll be presented with an Ubuntu desktop, all run from the CD. And remember, your hard disk will go untouched, so rest easy—you're not going to change, let alone hurt, anything. When you get to this point, you're ready to roll—but I'll hold off on talking about that until Chapter 3.

NOTE *Special input mechanisms that are required for typing certain languages (that is, Chinese, Japanese, and Korean) are not supported in live CD sessions.*

If you'd like to get out of the live CD and return your computer to normal, click the power button at the top right of the screen, choose **Restart**, and then choose **Restart** again from the window that appears. After a little while, you'll be asked to remove the CD from the drive and press ENTER. The computer will restart and return you to your normal Windows desktop soon after. If you have no luck with the Restart button for some reason, it should be safe to just turn your computer off and then on again using the power button on the front of it.

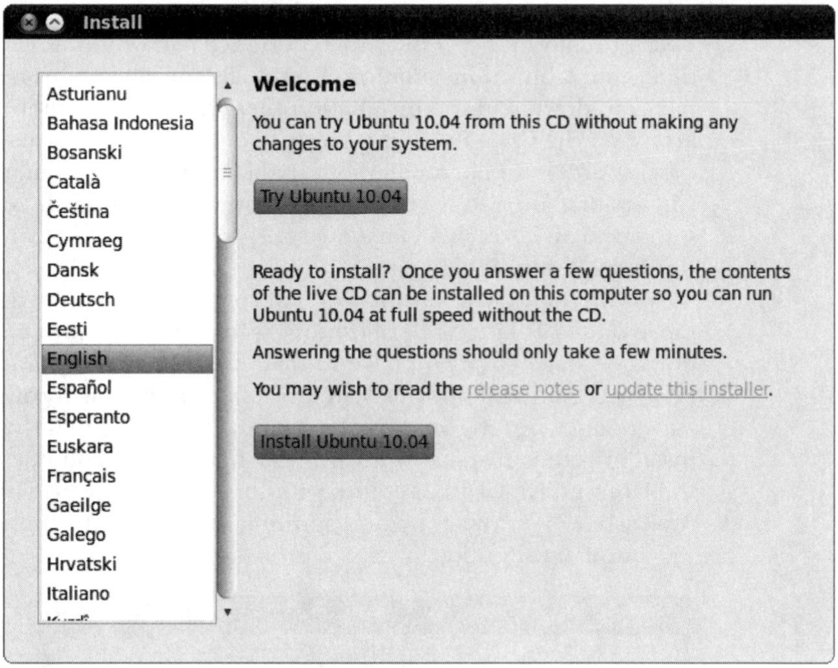

Figure 2-1: The Ubuntu live CD's Install window

Choices, Choices, Choices—Installation Options

If you have already installed Ubuntu on your machine, are satisfied running it from the live CD, or still haven't made up your mind what to do, you can skip the rest of this chapter and continue to the next one to get started working with the Ubuntu desktop. If, however, you haven't installed Ubuntu yet and are ready and rarin' to do so, then you had better stay right where you are and continue reading.

Going for a Swim—Installing Ubuntu Inside Windows (the Wubi Installer)

It used to be that if you enjoyed Ubuntu enough to want to run it off your hard disk but were afraid to do it for fear of damaging the delicate state of your Windows setup, you were . . . well, out of luck. Things have changed, however, because there is now an installation option called *Wubi* that lets you install Ubuntu directly on your Windows C: drive as if it were any other Windows program. Once installed, every time you start up your machine, you will be able to choose between starting up into Windows or into Ubuntu from the Windows bootloader screen. Your Windows system stays as it is; you don't have to partition your hard disk; and if you want to get rid of Ubuntu later for whatever reason, you can do so like you would with any other Windows application. It's a great way to go about things for the faint of heart.

Admittedly, this approach could be described as a half measure, in that it doesn't really give you the full experience you would normally get from a dedicated Ubuntu installation. It also takes longer to install, because Wubi needs to download the installation files from the Internet (the right ones aren't on the CD). But it is a pretty good compromise—it definitely runs quicker and is much, much more usable and enjoyable than an Ubuntu live CD session. You also have the added benefit of being able to save files and settings to disk, which means you can follow along with anything described in this book. Pretty cool.

If this alternative installation approach doesn't seem appealing to you, move on to "Taking the Full Plunge—Installing Ubuntu Outside of Windows" on page 16. If you haven't made up your mind yet and would like to know a bit more about this Wubi installer, point your browser to *http://wubi-installer.org/*. If, on the other hand, you've decided that the Wubi installer is the answer to your prayers, here's what you need to do: Insert the Ubuntu live CD that comes with this book into your computer's disc drive while Windows is up and running. A window like the one in Figure 2-2 will automatically appear.

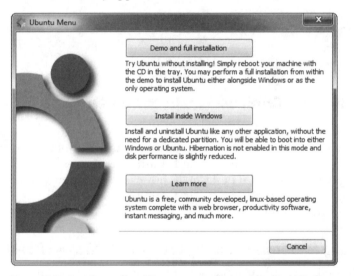

Figure 2-2: An Ubuntu live CD automatically launched in Windows

1. In that window, click the **Install inside Windows** button. The Ubuntu Installer window will appear (Figure 2-3).

2. Use the **Installation drive** option to specify where you want the Ubuntu files to be put. Make sure you have enough space on that drive!

3. Windows and Linux can't share the same disk space, so you need to set some aside for use by Ubuntu only (you can easily reclaim the space by uninstalling Ubuntu, discussed in a moment). Choose how much disk space you'd like to have available in Ubuntu by selecting a size from the Installation size drop-down list. Anything less than 6GB will probably be very restrictive.

4. Leave the Desktop environment set to its default value (Ubuntu), and then choose a username and a password. Click the **Install** button once you're happy with your choices.

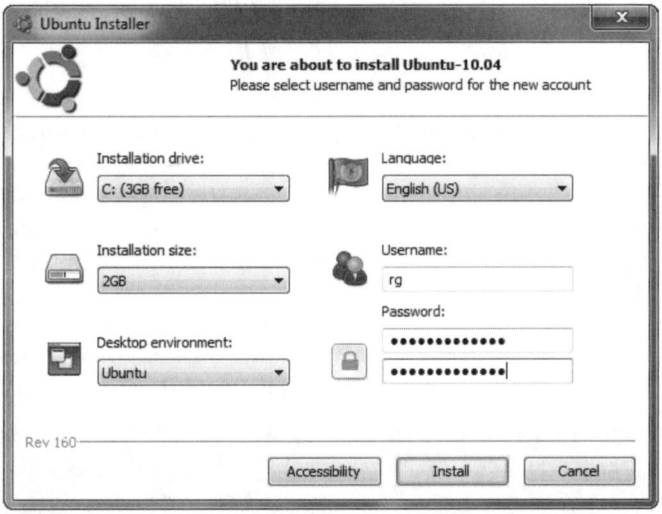

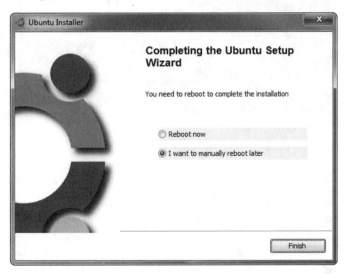

Figure 2-3: Choosing to install Ubuntu inside Windows

5. If your machine is not already connected to the Internet at this point, you will be told to get it connected. Do so if you need to, and click the **Retry** button if the warning window appears.

At this point, Wubi will begin downloading the files it needs in order to create a bootable Ubuntu installation within your Windows environment. Depending on your connection speed, this could take quite some time.

After all is done, you will see a window like the one in Figure 2-4 asking you to reboot.

Figure 2-4: Ubuntu has completed the first phase of its inside-Windows installation.

6. Select *Reboot now* and click the **Finish** button in that window, after which your machine will reboot.

7. When the machine restarts, you will see the Windows bootloader, a black screen with white text, which allows you to decide whether to boot up in Windows or in Ubuntu. Use your down arrow key to select **Ubuntu**, and then press ENTER.

Your machine will then begin the Ubuntu startup process, which should be new territory for you. Once the Ubuntu desktop appears, Ubuntu will get to work setting things up for you, which might take a bit of time, depending on the speed of your machine. When it's done, you will be delivered to the login screen (Figure 2-5); you can now flip to Chapter 3, because you are done here.

If you decide that you do not want to keep Ubuntu on your machine, you can remove it from within Windows by going to the Windows Control Panel, selecting **Add or Remove Programs**, and then selecting **Wubi** for removal.

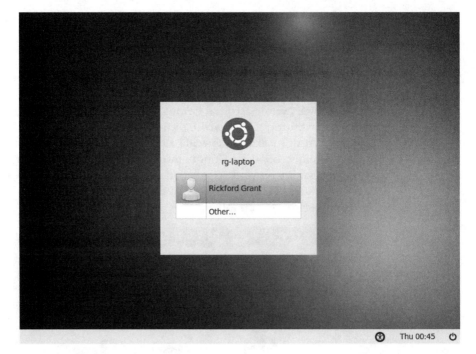

Figure 2-5: The Ubuntu login screen

Taking the Full Plunge—Installing Ubuntu Outside of Windows

If you don't already have Windows installed on your machine, you can skip this section. If you do, then you are going to have to decide whether you want to keep it.

It is possible to have both Windows and Linux installed on the same machine and for them to happily coexist. This is known as a *dual-boot setup*. It has also become incredibly easy to set up such a system. I started out with a dual-boot setup, though I eventually found that I used the Linux side of things exclusively. Having so much disk space being taken up by a Windows system I didn't use seemed a waste of prime real estate, so eventually I just dumped the whole thing and went for a straight Linux-only setup.

My feeling is that you should try the Wubi route of installing Ubuntu inside Windows first and then, when you're ready, go for a Linux-only setup and ditch Windows completely. Most people find that Ubuntu can do everything they need, so there's no need to dual-boot unless you require some specific application that has no equivalent on Linux.

If you do opt for a dual-boot setup, starting up in either system is easy. When you start up your machine, you will be greeted by the GRand Unified Bootloader (better known as GRUB) screen, from which you can choose to continue booting up Linux or choose Windows instead. After that, bootup proceeds as normal for the system you selected. This setup works fine and is easy to use, so you needn't worry.

So as you see, either way you decide to go, you can't really go wrong. Just be sure to back up your important files before starting the installation. Proceed with common sense, patience, and a positive attitude, and you'll be fine. In short, don't worry.

Getting Ready for Action

There is less you need to do to prepare for an Ubuntu installation than for many other Linux distributions. Once you've decided whether you want to go the dual-boot route, all you really need to have on hand is your single Ubuntu Desktop CD and, for guidance and security, this book. The only mental energy you'll probably need to expend is to come up with a username and user password, just as you do for most other operating systems.

Usernames and User Passwords

Your username is something that you will be seeing quite a bit. You will need to click it every time you boot up your system, among other things, so be sure it is something you can live with. It can be just your first name or your initials or whatever you want it to be. It must, however, begin with a lowercase letter, followed by numbers and/or other lowercase letters. Mine, for example, is simply *rg*, but you could use something like *hope4u2pal*, though that would get rather tiring to look at.

You also need to come up with a user password, which you will need to type every time you log in. You will need to use it when you install new software or change certain system settings, as well. It should be a minimum of eight characters in length and consist of numbers and letters (upper- and lowercase) for improved security. You can, of course, get by with fewer characters and only letters if you prefer. The installer will advise you if the password you enter is unacceptable, so don't worry too much. Be sure to write it down and keep the paper you've written it on in a safe place so you don't end up locking yourself out of your system.

NOTE *If you have experience working with other Linux distributions, you may be surprised to learn that the root account is disabled by default in Ubuntu. There is, therefore, no installation step for inputting a root password. You can check the forums* (http:// www.ubuntuforums.org/) *to learn ways of getting around this setup. You can also set up a root password later at any time after the system is installed, so if having a root account is important to you, don't worry.*

Dual-Booters Take Note

If you are going to be creating a dual-boot setup, it is a good idea to first defragment your current Windows disk before moving on to installing Ubuntu. This step isn't strictly necessary, but it can make the repartitioning phase of the installation process a little faster, and it helps guard against unwanted surprises.

If you are using Windows Vista or Windows 7, your system is set up by default to automatically defragment your hard disk on a regular basis, so you should be good to go without any additional effort on your part. On other versions of Windows, however, you'll have to defragment your disk manually. In Windows XP, you can do this by double-clicking **My Computer**, right-clicking the icon for your hard disk, and selecting **Properties**. You can then defragment your hard disk by clicking the **Tools** tab in the Properties window and clicking the **Defragment Now** button. In Windows 2000, you can do this by going to the **Start** menu and selecting **Control Panel ▸ Administrative Tools ▸ Computer Management ▸ Disk Defragmenter**, while in Windows 98 and some other versions, you can do the same by selecting **Programs ▸ Accessories ▸ System Tools ▸ Disk Defragmenter**. Defragmenting can take quite a while, so you might want to leave it running overnight.

Doing the Deed

Well, now that I've covered all that preliminary stuff, let's get down to the actual Linux installation. Set this book on your lap so you can follow along, and then get ready for action. It's time to do the deed!

Fortunately for you, the installation process is extremely easy, because there are very few steps in which you actually have to do anything. Most of what you will be doing is clicking buttons on your screen. Nothing hard about that, eh?

Of course, when you look at the directions and descriptions listed here, it may look like a long and cumbersome process. It is not. It will be over more quickly than you can imagine. As a beginner frequently referring to this text, you might take a bit longer, of course, but all in all, the whole process is faster and easier than that for Windows or Mac OS X. And keep in mind that with Windows and OS X you are installing the operating system with just a few bundled applications. In an Ubuntu installation, on the other hand, you are installing not only the operating system itself but also most of the applications you will ever want or need to use. You will thus be getting a lot done in one fell swoop.

One more thing before we start. Some people approach installing a system with a good deal of trepidation. The process makes them nervous, as if the house is going to go up in smoke if they click the wrong thing somewhere along the line. Needless to say, there is no need for such concern. As long as you have backed up your data, you will be OK. If you screw up the installation the first time out, so what? Just start over again. No harm done, because you have nothing to harm. Just make sure that you give yourself more time than you need for the process. Don't start installing one hour before you have to be at work or before you have to meet your friend downtown. Rushing makes people do weird things. Make things easy on yourself by giving yourself plenty of time and, as I mentioned before, by backing up any data you would mourn the loss of.

If you're ready, here are the steps:

1. **Start 'er up.** If you haven't already done so, boot up your machine from the Ubuntu Desktop CD.

2. **Start the installation.** This time, when you get to the Install window shown in Figure 2-1, click the **Install Ubuntu 10.04** button to start the installation. This will open the first page of the installation wizard, Where are you? (Figure 2-6).

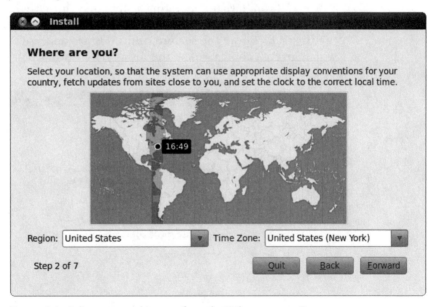

Figure 2-6: Selecting your location from the Where are you? screen

3. **Choose your location.** The Ubuntu installer will select the default location for the installation language you have chosen. If your location is different, select the one appropriate for you by clicking the map directly. Once you've made your selection, click **Forward**.

4. **Select a keyboard layout.** The default keyboard layout for the installation language you have chosen will appear on the next wizard screen. If your keyboard layout is different, select **Choose your own**, make the appropriate choice from the location list in the left pane of the screen, and then choose from among the available layouts for that location in the right pane. If you're not sure you've made the right choice, you can double-check by typing a few words in the text box at the bottom of the window. Once you've done this, click **Forward**. If need be, you can add other keyboard layouts later, after the system is installed.

5. **Prepare disk space.** What you do at this point depends on what you have on your machine. Assuming you have an operating system on the disk already, such as Windows, accept the uppermost option (Install them side by side). This will reduce the size of your Windows (or other OS) installation to allow for installation of Ubuntu in a new partition. By default, the partitioner will use the minimum amount of space necessary to install Ubuntu, but you will no doubt want a bit more so as to give yourself room to grow and store files. To create a bigger partition for Ubuntu, drag the gray button between the two partitions on the colored bar at the bottom of the screen until you come up with a combination that you think will work for you (Figure 2-7). Once done, click the **Forward** button.

    If you have no operating system on your hard disk or if you intend to eliminate what you currently have and replace it with Ubuntu, you should instead choose the second option, **Erase and use the entire disk**; then, if given a choice, select the main drive onto which you want to install the system.

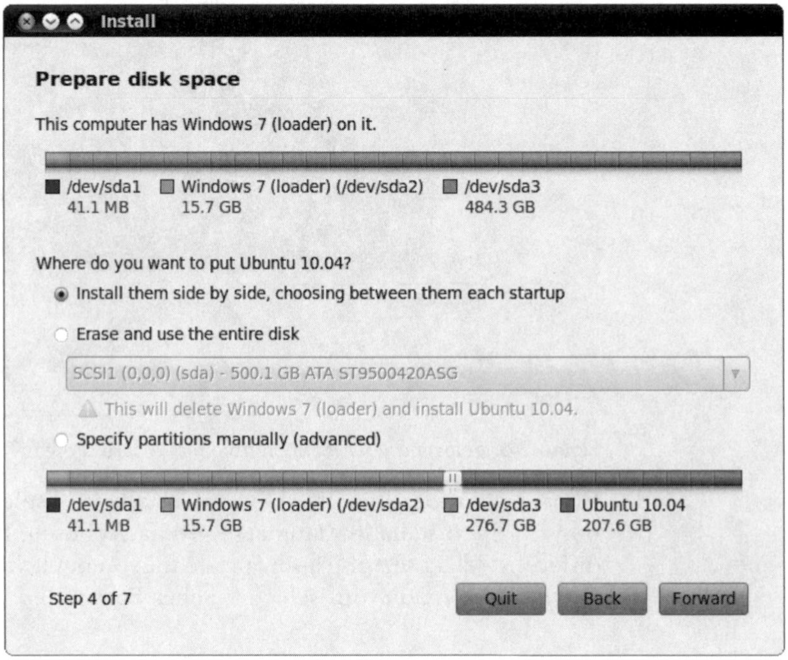

Figure 2-7: Partitioning your hard disk (or not) to make way for Ubuntu

WHAT IS A HARD DRIVE PARTITION?

I've mentioned *partitions* several times so far, but it may not be obvious to you what I meant. A partition is an area of your hard disk that is "cordoned off" from other areas of the disk. It's a useful way of keeping things such as operating systems separate. Because they are isolated from each other, different partitions are treated as if they are different hard disks attached to your computer, even though they're on the same physical hard disk.

Most computers have just one partition that fills up the entire hard disk. This is like having a house with a completely open floor plan—the whole house is just one big room. If you want to completely remove Windows and install Ubuntu instead, Ubuntu can happily take over the entire partition (and thus the entire disk) and kick out its former resident, Windows.

If you want to install two operating systems on the same computer, you have to give each one its own partition (after all, they need their privacy). Back with the house analogy, it's like erecting a partition wall to carve up the house into two rooms. If you choose to dual-boot Windows and Ubuntu, the installer will automatically do this partitioning for you. Of course, you can choose how big each partition is: The bigger you make the Ubuntu partition, the more disk space will be available to you in Ubuntu (and the less in Windows). After all, the house is the same size; it's just the position of the dividing wall that you're changing.

You can find some information on manually partitioning your hard disk in Appendix C, if you fancy taking control of the process yourself. There should be no need to, however, since the Ubuntu installer will be happy to handle the task for you.

If you'd like to do something more elaborate with your disk space, such as having separate partitions for your data and system files (convenient if you ever need to reinstall or want to easily share files between Windows and Ubuntu), you'll need to specify the partitions manually using the last option. This is more advanced—check out Appendix C for some guidance. Once your selection is made, click **Forward**.

Depending on the partitioning scheme you chose, once you've clicked the Forward button, a small window may appear reminding you that any changes you've made thus far will now be written to disk (Figure 2-8).

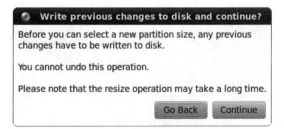

Figure 2-8: A warning that the changes you've requested are about to be made permanent

6. Click the **Continue** button, keeping in mind that, if you saw the warning message, this is the point of no return. After that, wait for the partitioner to do its stuff (depending on the size of your disk and what you have on it, this could take some time).

7. **Specify who you are.** On the next page of the installation wizard, you are asked to provide your real name, your login name, and a password. The wizard will automatically generate a name for your computer based on your username (*rg-laptop* in my case), but you are free to change this to something else if you like (I changed mine to *Ubuntu-Acer*). Once you've filled in all the fields, as I've done in Figure 2-9, click **Forward**. If you're warned that your password is too weak, go back and add a few extra characters to it and try again (or just ignore the message and click **Continue**).

NOTE *The security-conscious among you might consider selecting the Require my password to log in and to decrypt my home folder option at the bottom of the window. This will encrypt your home folder (where all your documents are stored) so that no one can see any of the files in it without your password. This is nice to have if you work with confidential information, since the data will be pretty safe even if your computer is stolen.*

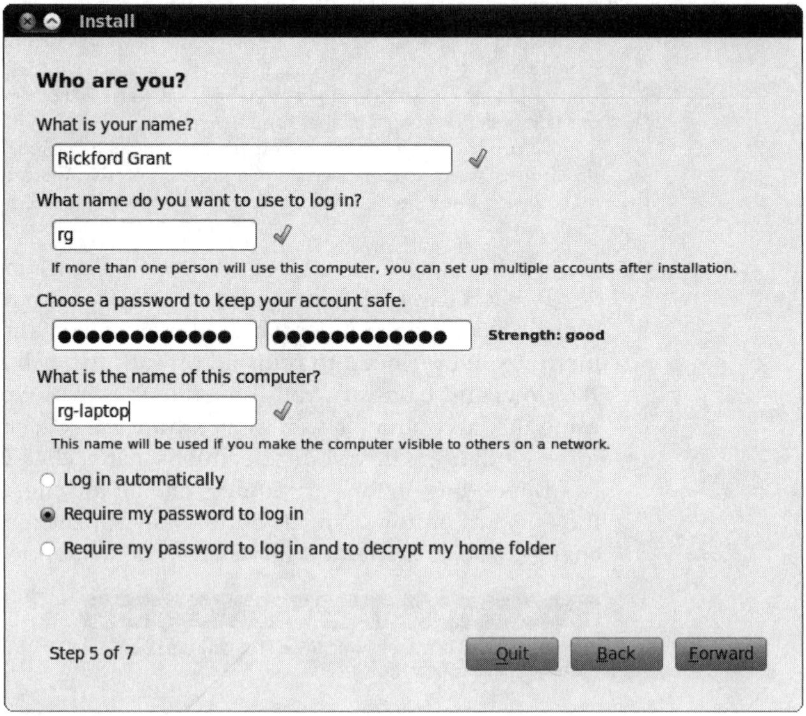

Figure 2-9: Providing your username, password, and computer name in the installation wizard

8. **Migrate documents and settings.** If your machine already has another operating system on it and you are setting up a dual-boot system, the installer will scan your hard disk to try to find certain settings, folders, and documents that it can transfer to your new Ubuntu system environment. If a migration window appears, just check the boxes next to the items you want to transfer, and then click **Forward**.

9. **Get ready to install.** The final page of the wizard (Figure 2-10) lists the details of your soon-to-be installed system and hard disk partition setup, along with a point-of-no-return warning. You've come this far, so you might as well go for it, even though there's no turning back (if you saw the warning message in Figure 2-8, that is). Click **Install**.

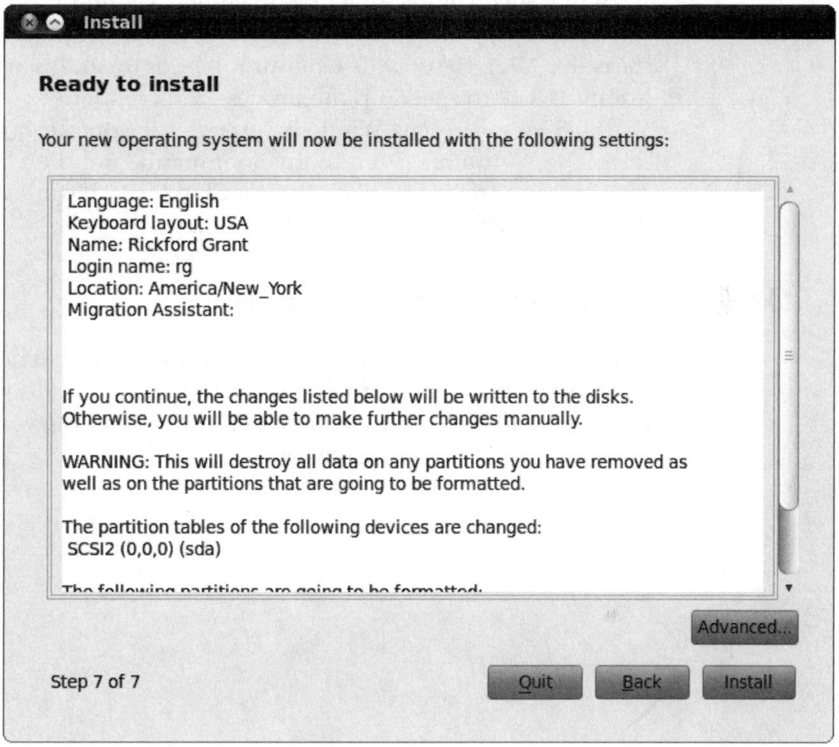

Figure 2-10: Ready to install—the final page of the installation wizard

The partitioner will then do whatever writing to disk it must do in order to finish the partitioning process, after which the installation itself will seamlessly begin, without any additional input necessary from you. The progress of the installation will be indicated in progress windows along with a brief slide show so that you don't have to fret (and so you'll know how much more time you have left to "veg out" in front of the TV).

10. **The installation is complete.** When you've come to the end of the first phase of the installation, you will be notified in a new window. You are given the option of either continuing to use the live CD or restarting the machine and running Ubuntu directly from your hard disk. Well, you didn't go through all of this just to keep using the live CD, so let's go for the second option by clicking the **Restart now** button, removing the live CD from your drive when it is automatically ejected, and pressing ENTER when prompted to do so. Your machine will then restart.

After that . . . well, that's basically it. You now have Ubuntu installed on your machine. Congratulations!

How Can I Get Back into Windows?

If you installed your system in a dual-boot configuration, with Ubuntu along-side Windows, you should see a new boot menu appear when the computer starts up. After 10 seconds Ubuntu will boot up automatically, but you can just hit ENTER to speed up the process.

If you want to start Windows instead, use your keyboard's arrow keys to select the **Windows** option in the boot menu, and then hit ENTER. Windows should start as normal. Take a look at Chapter 18 if you want to make Windows the default or change the boot time delay.

Oh No, My Computer Won't Boot!

If the installation process fails, you may not be able to boot your computer. Thankfully this is very rare, but if it happens to you, don't panic! There's plenty you can do to get up and running again, so flip your way to Chapter 21 for some troubleshooting advice.

3

A NEW PLACE TO CALL HOME

Getting to Know the Desktop

Now Ubuntu is up and running, and you are ready and rarin' to go. If you are running Ubuntu from your hard disk, you will first see the login screen that will appear each and every time you boot up (Figure 3-1). There's no need to keep the login screen waiting, so click your username, type your password, and press ENTER. Within moments, you will be face to face with your desktop in Ubuntu.

Welcome to the GNOME Desktop

Figure 3-2 shows Ubuntu's implementation of the GNOME desktop, and as you can see, it isn't all that different from what you might be used to in a Windows or Mac OS environment, other than that it has taskbars, or *panels*, at both the top and the bottom of the screen. There are also no desktop icons, except when running a live session from the Ubuntu Desktop CD, in which case you'll see a launcher to run the installation wizard (labeled *Install Ubuntu 10.04*) and an *Examples* folder, which contains a number of sample

Figure 3-1: The Ubuntu login screen

files for many of the applications that come bundled with Ubuntu. All in all, it is a very uncluttered place to be, and despite its superficial similarities to other OS desktop environments, things in the GNOME are different enough to be interesting.

The main elements of the GNOME desktop are the panels at the top and bottom of the screen and the icons that appear upon those panels. The desktop itself, although empty at startup, does see its share of action, but I'll come to that later. For now, I'll focus on the two panels.

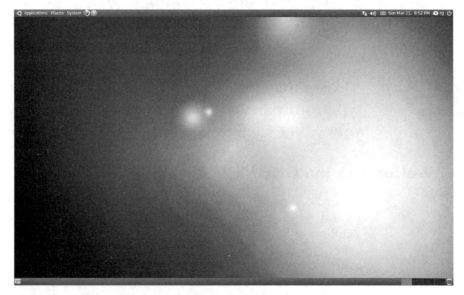

Figure 3-2: The GNOME desktop in Ubuntu

The Top Panel

Of the two GNOME panels on your desktop, the top panel is basically where all the action is. As you can see, there are three menus and a few icons at the left end of the panel and a number of odds and ends at the other end (Figure 3-3). So that you understand what each of the panel items does, I will now briefly describe each of them, moving from left to right, as seems to be the fashion these days.

Figure 3-3: The left and right sides of the top GNOME panel

The Left End

At the far left of the top panel, you will find a set of three menus. These menus provide access to most of what your system has to offer in terms of applications, locations, and utilities:

Applications menu   The access point to the majority of your applications, a software manager, and some system tools

Places menu   Your system navigator, from which you can access your home folder, browse your computer's filesystem and connected networks, and search for files on your hard disk

System menu   The access point for your system preferences and administration tools

Immediately to the right of the three menus is a set of two launchers. When these icons are clicked, they launch the following applications:

Firefox   Your web browser

Help   Access to the Ubuntu Help files installed on your hard disk

The Right End

At the right side of the top panel are a series of icons that can perform a variety of functions. Some of these are indicators, while others are applets that allow you to perform certain functions:

Network Manager Applet   Lets you see your network status and configure your network devices. When used with a wireless network connection, this icon indicates the wireless signal's strength and allows you to switch between wireless networks easily.

Volume Control   A volume controller. Duh.

Mail/Message Indicator   An indicator that lets you know when you receive email or chat messages. It also allows you to easily send email messages, check your address book, and even check and send messages to social networking sites, such as Facebook, Twitter, and Flickr, via an application called Gwibber (Figure 3-4), which you'll learn more about in Chapter 5.

Figure 3-4: Gwibber allows you to see and send messages on social networking sites.

Calendar/Clock   Date and time and weather.

Session Indicator   Shows the name of the current user and allows you to change your IM status and access the options for your social networks, IMs, and Ubuntu One.

Quit/Logout   Allows you to lock your screen, log out, shut down, restart, or switch users.

Other indicators will appear depending on your hardware configuration or system status:

Bluetooth Manager   As the name implies. This appears only on machines with Bluetooth capabilities.

Battery Indicator   On laptops, shows whether you are using battery or line power and, if battery, the amount of power your battery has remaining.

The Bottom Panel

The bottom panel, as you can see in Figure 3-5, is a much simpler affair, containing only the four items I will now briefly describe:

Show Desktop   A button that minimizes all open windows and allows you to see your desktop when it is obscured from view.

Window List   A list of windows or applications you have open. If nothing is open, there will be no windows in the list. This is very similar to what happens in the Windows taskbar.

Workspace Switcher   An application that allows you to switch between virtual desktops. (I'll talk about this more in "Virtual Desktops" on page 40.)

Trash   There is nothing mysterious about the Trash . . . other than its rather Mac OS X–ish location on the panel.

Figure 3-5: The bottom GNOME panel

Project 3A: Customizing the GNOME Panel

The GNOME panel is not a static thing. You can add *launchers* (respectively known as *program shortcuts* or *aliases* to Windows and Mac users), utilities, and even amusements to make it do almost anything you want—within limits, of course. In the various stages of this project, you will customize your panel to get some hands-on experience working with it and to make things more convenient for you as you make your way through the rest of this book. You are, of course, free to change any of the customizations I ask you to make (though you won't have a say in the matter if you're working in a live session from the Ubuntu Desktop CD, because you won't be able to save your settings).

Each of the following subprojects is very simple. Most are only three-step, point-and-click procedures that you should be able to handle without any difficulty.

3A-1: Adding Utility Buttons to the Panel

The GNOME panel allows you to add a number of utility applications, known as *applets*. Each of these has some specific function, such as tracking your stocks, telling you the weather, or performing some particular system-related function. To start, let's add a useful utility to the top panel: the Force Quit button. The Force Quit button lets you quickly and easily deal with non-responding windows.

Yes, it does happen on occasion: A window suddenly refuses to do anything. Regardless of what you want it to do or what it is supposed to be doing, it just sits there as if it is on strike (maybe it is). With just one click of the Force Quit button, your cursor becomes a powerful surgical instrument that will kill the window you click. You definitely don't want to be without this button, so here's how to add it to the panel:

1. Right-click any open space on the top panel.
2. From the pop-up menu, select **Add to Panel**, after which the Add to Panel window will appear.
3. In that window, scroll down, and click **Force Quit** once to highlight it, as I've done in Figure 3-6. Click the **Add** button, and then click **Close** to finish the job.

Figure 3-6: Adding launchers and utility applets to the panel

To reinforce what you've just learned how to do, let's add another utility to the panel: the Run Application applet. Once you start installing applications in Ubuntu, you will find that some of those applications do not automatically install program launchers in your Applications menu. This means that you have to open a Terminal window and type a command every time you want to run such programs, which can get old rather fast. The Run Application applet is one way around this problem.

To add the Run Application applet to the panel, just follow the same steps you used when adding the Force Quit button, but this time in Step 3, highlight **Run Application** in the Add to Panel window instead of Force Quit.

NOTE   *If you later decide not to keep the Run Application applet on the panel or if you just prefer keyboard shortcuts to pointing and clicking, it is worth noting that you can also open the applet by pressing ALT-F2.*

3A-2: Adding Amusing Applets to the Panel

The GNOME panel not only allows you to add very functional utilities, but it allows you to add quite seemingly useless amusements as well. In this part of the project, you will be adding two such amusements: Eyes and a little fish called Wanda.

At first glance, Wanda does little more than bat her tail around and spurt out a bubble or two. However, if you install a little application called Fortune via the Ubuntu Software Center, which you will learn how to use in Chapter 6, and then click Wanda, a window pops up in which she will spew out quotes and offbeat one-liners.

To get a glimpse of Wanda in action, limited though that action may be, the steps are essentially the same as those in Project 3A-1, but I'll run through them one more time:

1. Right-click any open space on the top panel.
2. From the pop-up menu, select **Add to Panel**, after which the Add to Panel window will appear.
3. In that window, click **Fish** once to highlight it, click the **Add** button, and then click **Close**.

With Wanda now in place on your panel, you can add Eyes, which is a pair of eyes that follows your mouse cursor around as it moves around your desktop. Follow the same procedure, but click **Eyes** instead of Fish in Step 3.

3A-3: Adding a Program Launcher to the Panel

Now let's move on to something a bit more practical—adding program launchers to the panel. Although it is very easy to run an application by navigating through the Applications menu, there are no doubt some applications that you will be using frequently enough to want even easier access to them. The OpenOffice.org word processor, Writer, is probably one of those applications.

Method 1

You can add a launcher to the panel in a number of ways, but let's start with the most conventional. To add a panel launcher for OpenOffice.org Writer, follow these steps:

1. Right-click any open space within the top panel.
2. Select **Add to Panel** in the pop-up menu to open the Add to Panel window.
3. In that window, select **Application Launcher**, and click the **Forward** button that then appears.
4. A new screen will then appear, showing the contents of the Applications menu (Figure 3-7). Click the **+** next to **Office** to expand that menu, and then scroll down and click **OpenOffice.org Word Processor** to highlight it.
5. Click the **Add** button, and then click **Close** to complete the process.

Figure 3-7: Adding an application launcher to the panel

Method 2

There's another way to add program launchers to the panel that is actually a tad quicker. As an example, you'll add a launcher for the OpenOffice.org spreadsheet program, Calc. Here are the steps:

1. Go to the Applications menu, and navigate your way to and right-click **Office ▸ OpenOffice.org Spreadsheet**.

2. In the pop-up menu that then appears, select (that's the usual ol' click) **Add this launcher to panel** (Figure 3-8). The spreadsheet launcher will then appear in the panel.

Figure 3-8: Another way to add application launchers to the panel

Method 3

Now that you've learned two ways to add application launchers to the panel, I might as well let you in on a third, even easier method. Just open a menu, select the item you want to add to the panel, and then drag it there. Well, it can't get much easier than that, eh?

3A-4: Changing Panel Launcher Icons

You may think your two new program launchers are somewhat plain, and therefore, it is rather difficult to distinguish one from the other. Fortunately, you can change the icon for any launcher quite easily. To learn how to do it, I'll address any immediate concerns with the two OpenOffice.org launchers. Here's what you need to do:

1. Right-click the first program launcher you added (the word processor), and select **Properties** from the pop-up menu.

2. In the Launcher Properties window that then appears, click the **OpenOffice.org Word Processor** icon, which will open a Choose an icon window.

3. In that window, click the **Browse** button to open the Browse window.

4. At the top of that window, click the **icons** button. In the right pane, double-click the **hicolor** folder, double-click the **48x48** folder within the *hicolor* folder, and then double-click the **apps** folder within the *48x48* folder.

5. Scroll down in that window and click **openofficeorg3-writer.png** once (Figure 3-9).

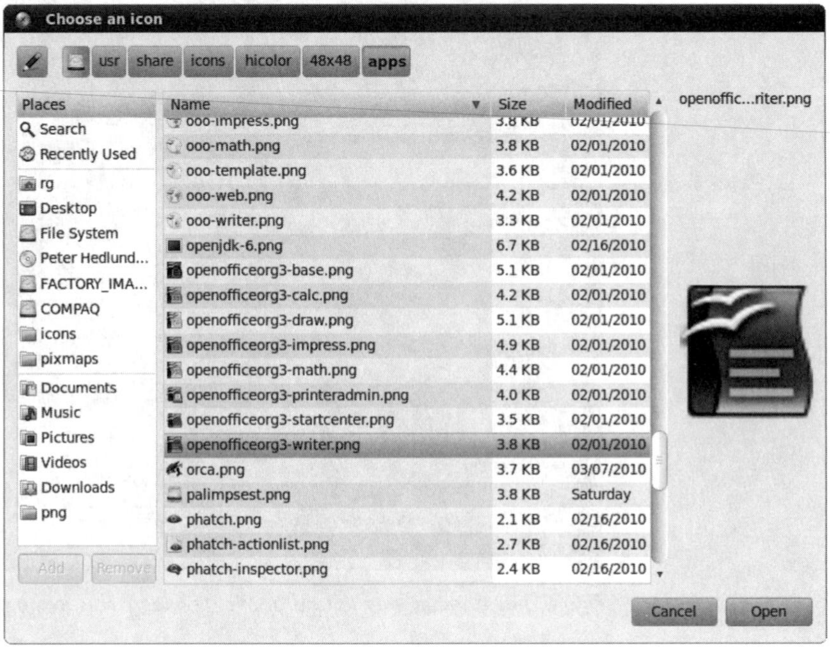

Figure 3-9: Selecting a new panel launcher icon

6. Click the **Open** button in that window, which will close it.

7. You will then be back at the Launcher Properties window, which should now look like Figure 3-10. If so, click **Close**.

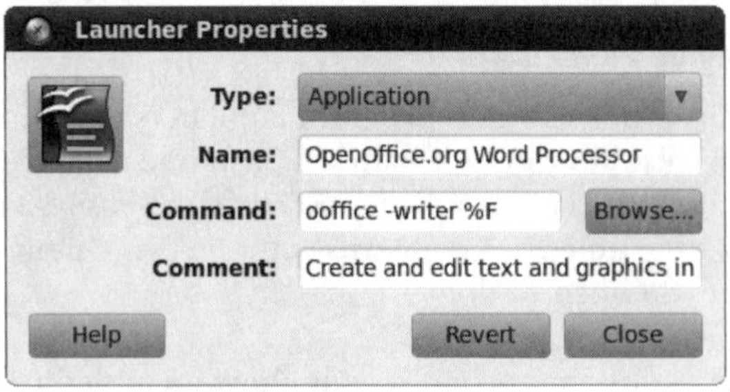

Figure 3-10: A Launcher Properties window

Once you have completed the transformation, follow essentially the same steps for the word processor launcher, but this time around you should select **openofficeorg3-calc.png** as the icon in Step 3.

3A-5: Adding a Drawer to the Panel

One of the features I quite like about the GNOME panel is the drawer. The *drawer* is a little applet that saves on panel space by letting you add drop-down panels, in which you can place launchers that you do not have room to place elsewhere. These drawers are also handy locations to place launchers for applications that you must normally run by typing a command in a Terminal window or via the Launch Application window, such as those you compile yourself from source code or that are run via scripts. You'll learn how to do this in Chapter 9. Of course, you can put anything you want in a drawer, including frequently used files or even whole menus.

Adding a drawer to your panel is very easy and is basically the same procedure that you used to add the Force Quit button to the panel. Here is all you need to do:

1. Right-click any open space on the top panel.
2. From the pop-up menu, select **Add to Panel**, after which the Add to Panel window will appear.
3. In that window, click **Drawer** once to highlight it, and then click the **Add** button. Close the window by, quite logically, clicking **Close**.

3A-6: Adding Program Launchers to the Drawer

The drawer you've just added is empty at this stage, so let's put it to good use by adding launchers for three useful, yet less glamorous, system utilities. These are System Monitor, which allows you to view your computer's running applications and processes, memory and CPU usage, and storage device usage; Terminal, in which you can type and execute commands (slightly geeky, I admit, but very useful); and the Ubuntu Software Center, which you can use to download and install applications.

Here's what you need to do:

1. Right-click the **drawer** applet in the panel, and select **Add to Drawer** in the pop-up menu.
2. In the Add to Drawer window that then appears (and looks and behaves the same as the Add to Panel window), select **Application Launcher**, and then click the **Forward** button that appears.
3. On the next screen, click the small + next to **Accessories**, scroll down and click **Terminal** to select it, and then click the **Add** button. The Terminal launcher will now be loaded into the drawer.
4. Next, scroll way down and click the small arrow next to **Administration**.
5. Scroll down within that category until you find **Ubuntu Software Center**, click it to select, and then click **Add**.
6. Finally, add a launcher for the System Monitor by scrolling down to the System Tools category, clicking the small + next to that category, selecting **System Monitor** from within that group, and then clicking **Add**. You can now close the Add to Drawer window.

The three launchers should now be loaded in the drawer, so click the drawer to sneak a peek. Yours should look the same as mine in Figure 3-11.

Figure 3-11: Launchers in a panel drawer

3A-7: Adding the Entire Contents of a Menu to the Panel

If you find that you use the applications in a particular submenu of your Applications, Places, or System menus a lot, you can opt to add the entire menu to the panel either as a menu or as a drawer in a manner similar to the one you used in Project 3A-3's "Method 2" section on page 32. To learn how to do this, let's add the Games submenu to the panel as a menu and the Sound & Video submenu as a drawer. Here is what you need to do:

1. Add the Games menu to the panel by selecting **Applications ▶ Games** and then right-clicking any of the launchers within that submenu.

2. In the pop-up menu that appears, select **Entire menu ▶ Add this as menu to panel**.

3. Add the Sound & Video submenu to the panel as a drawer by selecting **Applications ▶ Sound & Video** and then right-clicking any of the launchers you find there.

4. In the pop-up menu, select **Entire menu ▶ Add this as drawer to panel**.

Figure 3-12: Adding menus to the panel as menus (left) and as drawers (right)

You should now have two new launchers on your panel with icons matching those found in the Applications menu next to the relevant items. As you can see in Figure 3-12, these two icons act somewhat differently.

3A-8: Moving Things Around on the Panel

Well, now you've added all you are going to be adding to the panel in this chapter. It may seem a little messy up there right now, so let's do a bit of housekeeping by moving things around. You will try to group things together somewhat thematically so as to make them easier to deal with.

Fortunately, you can move panel launchers quite easily by right-clicking the launcher in question, selecting Move from the pop-up menu, and then dragging the launcher to the spot you want to place it. Once the launcher is where you want it to be, click the launcher once, and it will stay there.

To get some practice with this moving business, let's move the launchers, menus, and drawers you added by placing them in the following order, from left to right: Applications, Places, System, Firefox, Help, OpenOffice.org Writer, OpenOffice.org Calc, Sound & Video, Games, Drawer. Place the remaining launchers toward the right end of the panel, to the left of the Network Manager applet or any others that appear their automatically, in the following left-to-right order: Eyes, Wanda (Fish), Force Quit. Finally, place the Run Application applet by itself, midway between the two clusters of launchers. When you've made all your changes, your panel should look pretty much like mine in Figure 3-13.

Figure 3-13: The GNOME panel with the new launchers

More Panel Fun

In addition to the basic customization you did in Project 3A, you can do a lot more to change the look and feel of your panel. Of course, you can remove any of your launchers, drawers, or menus by right-clicking the item in question and then selecting **Remove From Panel** in the pop-up menu, but there are still more options. Most of these are available by right-clicking any open space in the panel and then selecting **Properties**, which will open the Panel Properties window.

From this window you can change the position of the panel, alter its size, change its color, or make it transparent—very cool. You can also set the panel so that it will automatically disappear when you are not using it and have it reappear when you bring your mouse cursor into the area where the panel normally resides. Don't feel afraid to play around—that's half the fun!

Project 3B: Manipulating Menus

Now that you have learned about some of the cool and useful things you can do with your panel, let's now move on to the topic of menus. A very nice feature of GNOME is that it allows you to edit its menus. You can add launchers, remove items, move items, and even change the icons that appear within the menus. All in all, you have a lot of control over things, but for this project, you'll limit the work to two of these areas: changing icons and moving menu items.

3B-1: Changing Icons Within Menus

As you no doubt recall, one of the problems with the OpenOffice.org Writer and Calc launchers you added to the panel was that they shared rather similar icons. If you select **Applications ▸ Office**, you will see that the icons for the various OpenOffice.org modules, although not the same, are also a bit similar. To remedy this state of affairs, you will change these icons to the same set you used for the two panel launchers in Project 3A-4. In this case, just follow these steps:

1. Right-click the **Applications** menu and select **Edit Menus**, or go to the **System** menu and select **Preferences ▸ Main Menu**.

2. In the menu editor window that then appears (Figure 3-14), click **Office** in the left pane. The contents of that menu will then appear in the right pane.

3. In the right pane of the window, click **OpenOffice.org Word Processor** once, and then click the **Properties** button. A Launcher Properties window will then appear.

4. In the Name box of that window, first shorten the name of launcher down to *Writer* or *Word Processor* or whatever naming works for you.

5. Next, click the **Icon** button (it doesn't say *Icon* but rather has the Writer icon on it). Using the method described in "Project 3A-4: Changing Panel Launcher Icons" on page 33, navigate to */usr/share/icons/hicolor/48x48/ apps* in the Choose an icon window that then appears.

6. Scroll down to and click **openofficeorg3-writer.png**, and then click **Open**.

7. The new icon should now appear in the Launcher Properties window. Click **Close**, and you will be able to see the change in the menu editor window.

8. Repeat the process for OpenOffice.org Spreadsheet, and even OpenOffice.org Presentation, if you like. Just be sure to choose an appropriate name and to select the appropriate icon for each (*openofficeorg3-calc.png* for Spreadsheet and *openofficeorg3-impress.png* for Presentation, for example). Once you're done, leave the editor window open to continue work on Project 3B-2.

Figure 3-14: Customizing your menus

3B-2: Changing the Order of Icons Within Menus

While you still have everything open to the Office menu, let's deal with what I consider to be another problem: the order of the items in the menu. It just doesn't make sense to me to have what is arguably the most commonly used office application, your word processor, way down there at the bottom of the menu.

Remedying this situation is easy. Just click the **OpenOffice.org Word Processor** icon in the right pane of the menu editor window. Then click the **Move Up** button on the right side of the window as many times as necessary until the Word Processor icon is right there at the top of the list.

Now that your word processor is up there at the top of the menu, the other OpenOffice.org modules seem a bit out of place down at the bottom, so you might as well move the other OpenOffice.org modules up near the top too by using the same method.

While I'm being logical and all, why not make things even better by getting the Evolution launcher out of the Office menu and moving it over to the Internet menu, which seems a far more natural place for it to be? If you agree and want to hide this instance of Evolution, just uncheck the box next to its name. The name of that entry should then switch to italic typeface, indicating that the item in question will not be visible in the actual drop-down menu. Once you're done, your menu editor window should look something like mine in Figure 3-15. If all seems fine to you, click **Close** and then select **Applications ▸ Office** to check out the results.

Figure 3-15: Managing menus with the menu editor

Now add Evolution to the Internet menu by clicking **Internet** in the left pane of the menu editor window and then clicking the **New Item** button. In the Create Launcher window that appears, type `Evolution Mail and Calendar` in the Name box and `evolution` in the Command box. The Evolution icon should then automatically appear in the icon button. Once done, click **OK**, after which the new Evolution entry will appear in the Internet menu. Close the menu editor window.

Virtual Desktops

It is now time to discuss a rather convenient feature of Linux: *virtual desktops.* Although the virtual desktop feature has only recently made its way into other operating systems, it has been a Linux feature for years (yes, it started here, folks). But rather than babble on about what this virtual desktop business is and what it can do for you, it is probably best to have you learn about it by giving you some hands-on experience.

In your GNOME panel, click the **Wanda (Fish)**, **OpenOffice.org Writer**, and **Firefox** launchers. You will then have three windows open in your present desktop, or *workspace.* Now look at the Workspace Switcher to the right of the bottom panel. There should be four boxes, with the one on the left (your present workspace) in light gray. If you click the box next to that, now in dark gray, all your open windows will suddenly disappear.

Actually, nothing has really disappeared—you are just viewing a new desktop. All your other windows are still open and running in the previous desktop.

In this second desktop, you can open something else: Select **Applications ▶ Games ▶ AisleRiot Solitaire**. The AisleRiot Solitaire card game will soon appear.

You now have windows open in two different desktops, and you can switch back and forth between them. To do so, just go to the Workspace Switcher in your panel, and click the now gray left box, which will take you to your original desktop. Once you've done that, the box for the workspace you were just in will turn dark gray, and you can then click that one to go back to your game desktop.

As you can imagine, this feature has some potential benefits for you, in addition to helping you avoid clutter. Just imagine that you are at work typing some long document in OpenOffice.org Writer. Eventually, you get tired and decide to goof off a bit by playing a game, such as Mines, for a while. To do this, you switch to another desktop where you open and play the game. A bit later, when you notice your boss making the rounds of the office, you simply switch back to the first desktop so that you look busy when he walks by and asks, "Keeping yourself busy, Boaz?"

Phew!

By the way, you can also switch between virtual desktops by simultaneously pressing and holding CTRL-ALT and then pressing your left and right arrow keys to move to your targeted desktop.

So, what happens if, let's say, you are running OpenOffice.org Writer in one workspace and the GIMP in another but suddenly think that it would be handy to have them both running in the same workspace? Do you quit the GIMP and start it up again in the other desktop? Fortunately, things are much simpler than that, and there are actually two ways to get the job done.

The first of these ways is to right-click the title bar of the window you want to move, and then select **Move to Workspace Left** or **Move to Workspace Right**. You can also select Move to Another Workspace and then select the workspace you want to move the window to by number: Workspace 1, Workspace 2, Workspace 3, and so on.

If you prefer keeping your hands more on your keyboard than on your mouse, you can also move a window from workspace to workspace by using hotkeys. With the window you want to move active (on top of the pile, so to speak), press and hold SHIFT-CTRL-ALT, and then use the left and right cursor keys to move the window to the desired desktop

Wanda Revisited—GNOME Easter Eggs

Well, now that you've finished with your work in this chapter, it's time to goof around a bit by revisiting our precocious piscean pal, Wanda. Knowing what you now do about Wanda the fish, you might find it odd for me to start talking about her again, but Wanda has a few more tricks beneath her fins. In fact, she is a good means by which to introduce two of GNOME's most famous Easter eggs. *Easter eggs*, in case you don't know, are hidden snippets of code that programmers seem to love to sneak into their programs. They are usually pretty useless things, but they can be found in all operating systems, numerous applications, and even on DVDs (to find out more about those, go to *http://www.dvdeastereggs.com/*). A good example of an Easter egg is my first encounter with one on my first Mac, an ancient Mac SE with a whopping 2MB of RAM. On that machine, you could bring up an image (or was it a slide show?) of the Mac SE development team by pressing the seldom used debug key on the side of the machine and then typing `G 41D89A`. Pretty cool, I guess, but I would never ever have stumbled upon it had I not read about it in some magazine.

As my example shows, accessing these Easter eggs usually requires some unusual maneuvers, ones that you would never perform in the normal course of things. To see a Wanda-related Easter egg in action, click the **Run Application** button you just added to the panel, type `gegls from outer space` in the Command box, and then click **Run**. You will then see an odd little game of the Space Invaders genre, shown in Figure 3-16, in which Wanda defends our beloved planet from . . . well, gegls, I guess.

Figure 3-16: One of GNOME's Wanda-related Easter eggs

To try the other Wanda Easter egg, open the Run Application panel applet again, but this time type **free the fish**, and then click **Run**. Wanda will now appear swimming around your desktop. If you then click her, she will swim away and out of the picture . . . but she'll be back.

To put an end to Wanda's comings and goings, you will need to restart the GNOME panel. There several rather inelegant ways of going about this, but for now you can do it by opening the Run Application panel applet again, typing `killall gnome-panel`, and then clicking **Run**. Your panels will disappear for a second or two but will shortly reappear. Wanda, however, will be gone.

Shutting Down

Now that you know your desktop environment so well, you may feel like calling it a day and shutting down your machine. To do so, just click the **Quit** button at the far-right corner of the top panel (it looks like a power button). A menu (Figure 3-17) will appear with eight choices to choose from: Lock Screen, Guest Session, Switch from rg (whatever your username happens to be), Log Out, Suspend, Hibernate, Restart, and Shut Down. (Hibernate is not an option when running a live session from the Ubuntu Desktop CD). Select **Shut Down**, and a small window will appear to confirm your decision. Click **Shut Down**, and the shutdown process will begin. If, however, nothing seems to happen within a few seconds, press CTRL-ALT-DELETE in unison, which will open a Shut Down the Computer window (Figure 3-18). In that window, click **Shut Down**, after which shutdown will commence.

Figure 3-17: GNOME's session menu options

The actual shutdown will take a few seconds as the system closes its various services. When it is all done, the system should power down your computer as well, in which case you are done. On a few machines, however, the system might not be able power down your machine. You will know whether this is so in your case because all screen activity will come to an end. If you get to that point and nothing else happens for 15 seconds or so, then just power down the machine manually by pressing the power button. It is completely safe to do so at that point.

Figure 3-18: Pressing CTRL-ALT-DELETE in unison brings up the Shut Down the Computer window

4

MORE THAN WEBBED FEET

Connecting to the Internet

These days, the average home computer user spends more time surfing the Web and writing email messages than doing just about anything else. Even if you're not much of a surfer, there are still numerous other applications that aren't really Internet applications per se but that still use the Internet in some way, such as gathering song and album information when you rip audio CDs to create MP3 files. Having a computer that isn't hooked up to the Internet is like buying a new Maserati and then refusing to take it out of the garage.

Of course, how you connect to the Internet depends on your hardware and provider. There are a number of possibilities in this area, including high-speed local area networks (LANs), cable modems, mobile (3G) broadband, and ADSL connections from phone companies. Some computers still have an internal 56Kbps modem or can be connected to external dial-up modems for slower connections over regular phone lines. Depending on what you have, setting things up on your system should prove a cinch in the case of LAN connections and any others that use your Ethernet port (such as cable modems), possibly a bit more work in the case of wireless and mobile connections, and sometimes a bit of a challenge when it comes to dial-up connections. In this chapter you will learn how to set up these connections, and in the next chapter you will learn a bit about what Linux has to offer in terms of the most commonly used Internet applications.

How Do You Connect?

The way you go about setting up your connection really depends on how you're trying to connect to the Internet. Here's a list to help you decide which method to use:

- If you connect your computer to a wall socket, a router, or a cable modem by using an Ethernet cable, go to "Setting Up a Wired Connection" on page 46.
- If you connect to a wireless network or your own wireless router, head to "Setting Up a Wireless Connection" on page 49.
- If you connect using a dial-up modem connected to your phone line, the section "Setting Up a Dial-up Connection" on page 53 is the one for you.
- If you have an ADSL or DSL modem that is built in to your computer or connects to a USB port, try "Connecting with a DSL or ADSL Modem" on page 52.
- If you connect using a mobile (3G) broadband connection that plugs in to your computer, skip to "Mobile (3G) Broadband Connections" on page 55.

Setting Up a Wired Connection

If you have a high-speed Internet connection from your cable television company or ISP or if you are connected to the Internet by a LAN at your office, you are really in luck, because these setups are probably the easiest to deal with. I'm going to assume that you've already set up your router or modem according to your Internet provider's instructions, so all that remains is to connect an Ethernet cable between the modem/router (or LAN wall socket) and your computer's network socket. After you've done that, you should be ready to go without any further settings to fool with.

Checking Your Connection

If you like, you can see whether you're connected by opening Firefox (click the Firefox launcher in the top panel, right next to the System menu) and then, once it starts up, trying to navigate to a common site, such as *http://www.yahoo.com/*. If the site comes up, you know you're all set.

If you have a problem getting online and you are trying to connect via a LAN or cable modem, you could try to refresh your connection by right-clicking the Network Manager icon in the top panel, unchecking the **Enable**

Networking box in the pop-up menu, waiting a few seconds, and then checking the **Enable Networking** box in the pop-up menu again. If that doesn't work, try restarting your machine while physically connected to your Internet source with the Ethernet cable. If the lack of connectivity persists, it is possible that your network card is not supported by Linux. This is relatively rare but, fortunately, easily remedied (by replacing it).

The problem could also be that your network or service provider does not automatically assign addresses via Dynamic Host Configuration Protocol (DHCP). *DHCP* is a means by which your Internet provider can automatically provide your system with the configuration information it needs in order to connect to the Internet. If your provider does not use DHCP, you will have to get the necessary information about settings from the network administrator or service provider and enter the settings yourself.

Setting Up a Cable or Ethernet Connection for Providers Not Using DHCP

To input your cable or Ethernet settings yourself, first get the settings you need from your network administrator or Internet provider, and then perform the following steps:

1. Select **System ▸ Preferences ▸ Network Connections**.
2. Choose the **Wired** tab (Figure 4-1), and select the network connection from the list by clicking it once (it should have a name like *Auto eth0*). If there are no entries in the list, then your network card hasn't been properly recognized. Take a look at "Installing Drivers for Your Network/Wireless Card" on page 390 to see how to fix this.

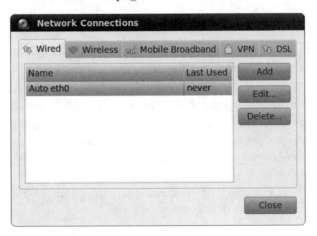

Figure 4-1: The Network Connections window

3. Click **Edit**, and you'll be presented with a settings window. Choose the **IPv4 Settings** tab, and change the Method setting from Automatic (DHCP) to **Manual**.

4. Click the **Add** button to enter the IP address information for your computer. This should have been provided by your ISP or network administrator and will consist of an IP address, default gateway, and netmask (see Figure 4-2 for an example). Enter the DNS server address that you were given too.

Figure 4-2: Manually inputting network IP settings

5. Make sure that the **Available to all users** option is checked if other users of your computer will be using the connection.

6. Click **Apply** to save the settings. You'll be asked to enter the password for your user account, so do that, and click **Authenticate**.

7. Network Manager will try to establish the connection using the details you just provided. If it's successful, a message will pop up saying that the network was connected. If that doesn't happen, click the Network Manager icon on the top panel, and choose *Disconnect*.

8. Then, click the Network Manager icon again, and select your network underneath where it says *Available*.

NOTE *If you are wondering what Internet Protocol (IP) and Domain Name Service (DNS) are all about, you can simply think of them in this way: DNS translates the easy-to-remember URLs that you have come to know, such as* http://www.google.com/, *into numerical, or IP, addresses that the Internet can understand. The address* http://www.google.com/ *thus becomes* http://209.85.229.104. *You can type the numerical version into your browser later to see for yourself.*

Setting Up a Wireless Connection

With the right wireless hardware, you can now surf the Web just about any-where you can catch a (radio) wave, so to speak. Whether you happen to be at your breakfast table, in the library of your university, or at your local Star-bucks, you can now go online without having to physically hook up your com-puter to anything.

Fortunately, the process of setting up wireless networking in Ubuntu is quite easy and not very different from what you just read in the previous section.

Hardware

If you lead a solely wired existence or are just inexperienced in this particular area, there are a few things worth knowing. To get started, you need to have the right hardware. If you just want to go wireless, then all you need is a wire-less network card (sometimes referred to as an *802.11a/b/g/n card* or *WiFi card*). These are built in to almost all modern laptops, while for older models they are usually add-ons in the form of cards that pop into the PCMCIA slot on the side of your computer (as shown on the right of Figure 4-3).

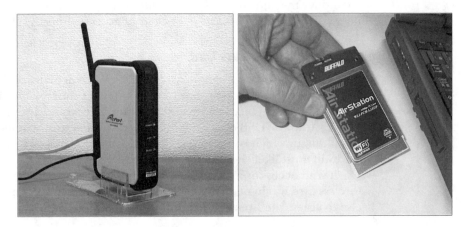

Figure 4-3: All you need for a WiFi setup—an access point and a network interface card

Some wireless cards plug into one of your machine's USB ports or, in the case of desktop models, one of its PCI slots. Although support for cards of this type has improved through the past couple of years, there are still gaps, and some can be rather tricky to deal with. You'll find some tips on how to deal with awkward cards in Chapter 21, but if you're looking for a sure thing, Centrino IPW-2100 and IPW-2200 cards are definitely supported by Ubuntu. As for cards of the built-in or PC card variety, you will find support much better, but even then you have to make sure, or at least hope, that the card you are using is Linux compatible. No matter what wireless card you are wondering about, the easiest way to find out whether it will work is to just try it. The Linux kernel now comes with many wireless drivers built in, and Ubuntu updates often provide new ones, so if you use a card that is compatible with one of those drivers, things will be smooth sailing. If things don't seem to work, check Ubuntu's list of supported cards (*https://help.ubuntu.com/community/WifiDocs/WirelessCardsSupported/*), or check the Ubuntu forums to find a driver that is compatible or to see whether anyone has experience with your particular card.

If you want to set up a wireless system in your home or office, then you will also need to get a *wireless access point* (WAP), shown on the left of Figure 4-3. Fortunately, Linux compatibility is not really much of an issue in this department, because the access point doesn't physically interface with your computer, and the settings are handled via your web browser.

NOTE *Access points come in several different types. The most common type is a wireless router, which many ISPs provide for free.*

You should be aware, however, that a few access points require you to use Internet Explorer to handle their setup chores. Although it is possible to get Internet Explorer up and running in Linux via Wine (as you'll see in Chapter 18), you can't be 100 percent sure that it will work. Unless you have a Windows machine somewhere in your house or office to handle such chores, it is probably a good idea to steer clear of access points of this kind.

Activating Your Wireless Card

Setting up a Linux-compatible wireless PC card is actually relatively simple. First connect your access point to your Internet source, and then turn on the access point. Once it is up and running, plug your wireless card into the PCMCIA slot or USB port on your laptop (unless your wireless connection is built in, in which case you can forgo this step). Any LEDs on the external card will most likely light up at this time.

If your access point was on when you booted up your computer and your wireless card was in place during bootup, you probably don't need to do much else to access the Internet. Just follow these steps:

1. Click the Network Manager icon on the top panel to reveal a drop-down menu showing the wireless signals that are present in your vicinity and the strength of each signal (Figure 4-4).

2. From that menu, select the signal for your access point (or any other wave you are entitled to latch onto) by clicking it.

3. Your system will then try to connect to the Internet. Once a connection is made, the Network Manager icon will morph into a small signal-strength indicator. Pretty handy.

4. If your network has a WEP or WPA password, you'll be prompted to enter it. It can be useful to check **Show password** before you type the password so you can check for any mistakes. Click **Connect** when you're finished.

NOTE *Most access points employ an added level of security in the form of Wired Equivalent Privacy (WEP) or a Wi-Fi Protected Access (WPA) key. If you didn't choose your own password when you set up the access point, try looking for a sticker on the base or side of the access point to see whether a default one is used. If you're trying to connect to a network for which you don't happen to know the key, then chances are you are not supposed to be making the connection in the first place. Naughty, naughty.*

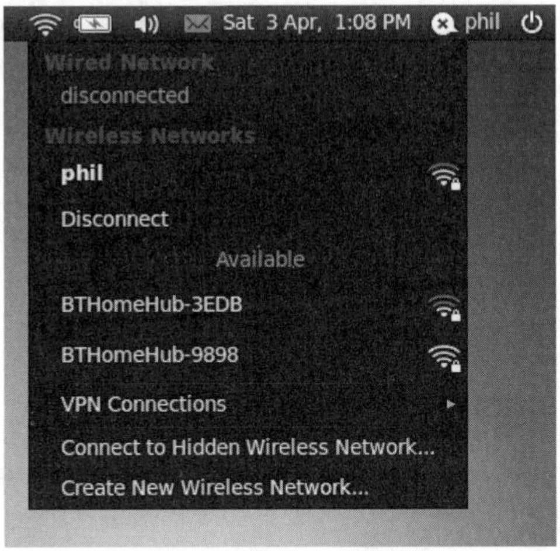

Figure 4-4: The Network Manager shows you available wireless networks and their signal strengths.

If you were not successful in making your wireless connection (the system will tell you whether that's the case), you have a few possibilities beyond the annoying noncompatible-card scenario. First, double-check to make sure your card is actually physically turned on. I know that sounds dumb, but I have been guilty of this oversight myself on numerous occasions. Many laptops have a key you can press to enable or disable the wireless card; on mine you have to press the function key (FN) and F2 at the same time.

Another, less common, possibility is that your network does not use DHCP, in which case you will have to manually input your connection settings as provided by your network administrator or service provider. Armed with that information, simply follow the steps listed in "Setting Up a Cable or Ethernet Connection for Providers Not Using DHCP" on page 47. Just be sure to use the Wireless tab instead of the Wired one.

If you still have no luck connecting wirelessly, the drivers may not be installed for your card, or Ubuntu may not support the card. You can try plenty of tricks to get things working, so head over to Chapter 21 and look for "Installing Drivers for Your Network/Wireless Card" on page 390.

Switching Off or Refreshing Your Wireless Connection

Sometimes you'll want to disconnect from a wireless network, such as when you use your laptop on an airplane or when you just want to connect to a different network, as you might when moving your laptop from one wireless hotspot to another.

To do this, click the Network Manager icon once to reveal the list of available wireless networks (that is, signals). In that list, click the **Disconnect** option below the name of the wireless network to which you are connected. Within a second or two, you will be disconnected.

If you want to turn off your wireless card (as you should do if you're boarding an airplane) and you don't have a physical way to do it, like a switch or a button, just right-click the Network Manager icon, and then deselect **Enable Wireless**. And if you want to turn that card back on again, just get back to that menu, and select **Enable Wireless** again.

Sometimes, your wireless card might lose its connection for no apparent reason, so it can be useful to refresh the connection (that is, turn it off and on again) to try to get it back. The quickest way to do this is to click the Network Manager icon and then click the name of your wireless network in the list. You'll be disconnected and then automatically reconnected.

If that doesn't work, try disabling and then enabling the wireless connection using Network Manager's Enable Wireless option, as described earlier. If you still have no luck, try turning the wireless card off and on again using a switch or button if you have one, or unplug it and plug it back in again. Finally, if nothing seems to be working, try restarting the computer.

Connecting with a DSL or ADSL Modem

How easy it is to set up your DSL or ADSL modem depends on the connector that it has. If it can be connected using an Ethernet cable, use that, and follow the instructions in "Setting Up a Wired Connection" on page 46; it'll be much easier than trying to use a USB cable! If you have a USB or internal modem, try the instructions in this section and hope for the best.

The first step is to check whether Ubuntu recognized your modem. Assuming it's already plugged in, click **System ▸ Preferences ▸ Network Connections**, and select the **DSL** tab. If a connection is listed in that window, your modem was recognized, and you can begin setting it up. If the list is empty, refer to *https://help.ubuntu.com/8.04/internet/C/modems-adsl-usb.html* to see whether there are any steps you can follow to get your modem working.

Select the connection by clicking it once, and then click **Edit**. Click the **DSL** tab of the Editing window that appears, and enter your username and password into the appropriate fields. Then enter your connection information (usually a phone number) into the Service box, and click **Apply**. Now, click the Network Manager icon on the top panel, and choose your DSL connection from the list. Network Manager will try to connect using your modem— if it's not successful, go back and try changing some of the settings to see whether you can get it to cooperate.

Setting Up a Dial-up Connection

Although much of the world is moving to high-speed Internet connections, many of you may still be using dial-up Internet connections, which means you need to have a traditional dial-up modem to reach beyond your box to the outside world. In case you broadband surf-gods have forgotten, modems are those wonderful machines that whistle, chime, screech, and spit whenever you dial up your Internet provider. I suppose you could think of them as noisy telephones in need of a good burp.

Now here comes the bad news—in the world of Linux, very few internal modems are supported, and for those that are, the setup process can be quite frustrating. The main reason behind this compatibility problem is that most built-in modems are software dependent, and the software they depend on is part of, or designed for, Windows. Such modems are thus called *Winmodems.*

Of course, the Linux community has been working on ways to deal with these Winmodem beasts so that they will work with Linux systems. Though support for the wide variety of Winmodem models out there is still rather spotty, things are better than before, so you might just luck out. My advice is to hold off on the wondering and worrying and just give your modem a try to see whether it works. If it does, then you're all set. If it doesn't, well, then you do have some options, and at least you haven't done any damage to your system.

With all that intro-babble out of the way, let's get down to the steps for setting up your dial-up connection. First, get the settings information you need from your Internet provider. Most providers aim their operations at Windows and often Mac users, and very few offer Linux support. Still, there is no technical reason for your Linux system not to work via their setup, so just nag and push them until they give you the information you want. After that, make sure your modem is connected to a live telephone connection—for example, the phone jack in your wall.

Now it's time to set up the connection. I'll use the GNOME PPP program to do all of the setting up here, but there's a caveat: It's not installed by default, and you need an Internet connection to install it! If you have access to some other Internet connection that you can use temporarily, connect to that, and use the Ubuntu Software Center to download and install GNOME PPP (see Chapter 6 to learn how to install software). The alternative is to use the pppconfig command, which is installed by default but is difficult to use. Find another computer and check out *https://help.ubuntu.com/community/DialupModemHowto/SetUpDialer/* for instructions if you have no alternative but to use pppconfig.

Assuming that you got GNOME PPP installed using a borrowed Internet connection, you can follow these steps to set up your modem:

1. Select **Applications ▸ Internet ▸ GNOME PPP**, after which GNOME PPP will appear.

2. Click **Setup,** and make sure you're looking at the **Modem** tab.

3. Click the **Detect** button to identify your modem. If you get a message saying that no modem was found on your system, then you're out of luck—the best you can do is ask for advice on the Ubuntu forums (*http://www.ubuntuforums.org/*) or try selecting items from the Devices drop-down list by trial and error.

4. How you change the rest of the settings depends on how your modem and ISP are set up, so select the defaults for now. If these don't work, trial and error is a potential way forward again.

5. Click **Close** to get back to the GNOME PPP window. Type your username and password, and enter the phone number provided by your ISP.

6. Click **Connect**. You should then hear your modem begin its dialing, spitting, and churning sequence as it makes the connection with your provider.

7. If you manage to get connected, you can start your browsing, emailing, or whatever else it is you do online. If you get an error message, there's little you can do but take a deep breath and click the **Setup** button to try tweaking your settings.

What to Do If Your Modem Isn't Compatible

Though it may not sound that way, what I've just described is pretty much a best-case scenario. What happens, however, if your modem and Ubuntu do not see eye to eye? Well, there are a few options. My first, more radical suggestion, is to dump your dial-up ISP and find a broadband provider that covers your local area. If that is not an option, then you have two ways to go. One is to try to geek around with your modem to see whether you can get it to work. This is a slightly more complicated process, but there are instructions at *https://help.ubuntu.com/community/DialupModemHowto*. If you are faint of heart or a novice user, you may find what the process entails to be a bit more than you're willing to deal with.

The simpler, although costlier, way to get your modem to work is to purchase a true hardware modem. *Hardware modems* are not software dependent, so they work with any operating system. You can think of them as telephones without a handset.

Such modems come in two forms: internal and external. As for the internals, the USRobotics models 56K V.92 Performance Pro Modem (internal slot) and 56 PC Card Modem (PC card slot, for laptops) are true hardware modems that are easily available and are said to work. You can check out the USRobotics site (*http://www.usr.com/*) for more information on these models, though checking the Ubuntu forums for suggestions is always a good idea. Perhaps the safest of all solutions is to buy an external dial-up modem. They come with either serial or USB connectors and sit in a box outside your computer. Because the modem doesn't use your operating system to operate, it does not tie up system resources while it's busy, which may result in a possible pickup in computer speed.

Linux support for USB modems can be patchy, so do your research before buying one. External serial modems are a safer bet since most of them should work with your system . . . if you have a serial port, that is. Modern computers rarely have them any more, so check to see whether you have one by looking at the back of your computer for a connector with little prongs in it (see Figure 4-5). If you are worried and are looking for a sure thing, Zoom Telephonics (*http://www.zoom.com/*) makes an external serial modem that is compatible with Linux, and the company says so right on its website. The USRobotics 56K V.92 External Faxmodem is also said to work, though I haven't tried this model myself.

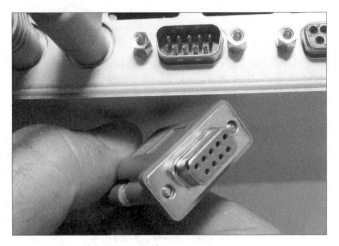

Figure 4-5: Serial port and connector

If you find another model that you think will do the trick, before you commit to it by slapping down the cash, do a Yahoo! or Google search with that modem's make and model number, along with the word *linux*, and see what search results you get. Of course, you can also try one of the Linux forums and ask about the modem make and model there. A lot of people are in the same boat, so you are sure to get plenty of opinions and advice.

Mobile (3G) Broadband Connections

Wireless networks, for all the convenience and freedom that they offer, still have quite a limited range. This won't be an issue if your computer never strays from within the general vicinity of your house or office, but it can get mighty inconvenient if you're on the road, miles from the nearest wireless-enabled coffee shop. This being the 21st century, there are, of course, ways around this limitation.

If you're a computer-equipped traveler, you've probably already come across mobile broadband technology, also known as *3G*. All you need to get a high-speed connection on the go is a 3G card (also inexplicably called a *dongle*), which plugs into your computer and connects you to the Net via a cell phone network (Figure 4-6). Ubuntu has pretty good support for most 3G cards right from the get-go, and the setup process is a snap:

1. Plug your 3G card or dongle into the computer; the New Mobile Broadband Connection Wizard should open automatically. If it doesn't, click **System ▶ Preferences ▶ Network Connections**, open the **Mobile Broadband** tab, and click **Add**.

2. The first page of the wizard has a drop-down list that should have the make and model of your 3G card displayed in it. If it says *Any Device* instead, your card may not have been recognized, so take a look at *https:// wiki.ubuntu.com/NetworkManager/Hardware/3G/* to see whether there are any steps you need to take to get Ubuntu to recognize the card.

3. Click **Forward**, select your country from the list, and then click **Forward** again.

4. Pick your mobile broadband provider from the list, and then hit **Forward**.

5. Now you need to select your broadband billing plan from the drop-down list (Figure 4-7). It's important that you choose the right plan to avoid being wrongly charged. If you don't see a plan that looks appropriate, choose *My plan is not listed*, and call up your broadband provider to ask what to put in the Access Point Name (APN) box.

6. Click **Forward**, check that all of the details look OK, and click **Apply**. You'll be taken to an Editing window where you can enter details such as your account PIN and password if needed.

7. Click **Apply**, and then close the Network Connections window to finish up.

Figure 4-6: A 3G mobile broadband card

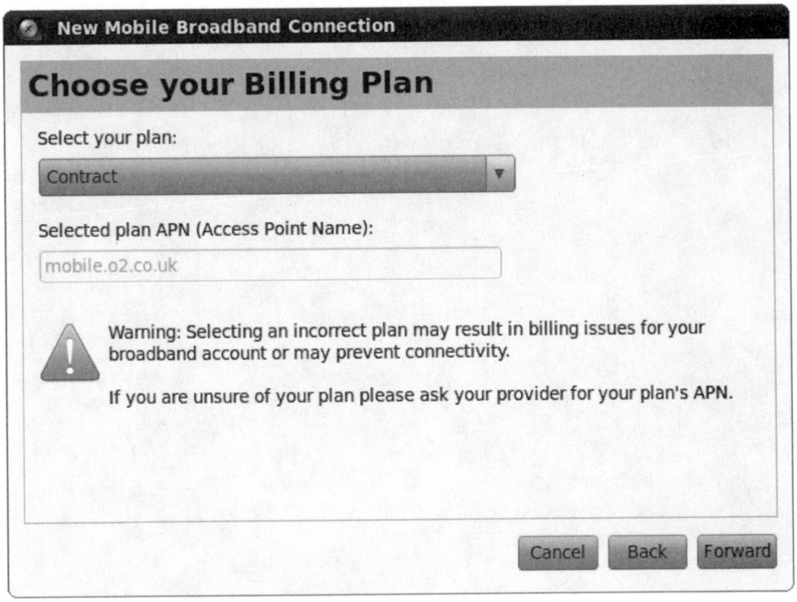

New Mobile Broadband Connection

Choose your Billing Plan

Select your plan:

Contract ▼

Selected plan APN (Access Point Name):

mobile.o2.co.uk

⚠ Warning: Selecting an incorrect plan may result in billing issues for your broadband account or may prevent connectivity.

If you are unsure of your plan please ask your provider for your plan's APN.

[Cancel] [Back] [Forward]

Figure 4-7: Choosing a broadband billing plan

To connect to mobile broadband, click the Network Manager icon on the top panel, and choose your broadband service from the list. Network Manager will spend a few seconds establishing the connection, after which you'll be notified that you're connected (or not, as the case may be). Disconnecting happens in just about the same way: Click the Network Manager icon again, but this time select the **Disconnect** item just below the name of your broadband service when the list pops up.

I'm Connected . . . So Now What?

Ideally you're cabled in, wired up, or otherwise happily connected to the Internet. (If not, take a look at Chapter 21 for some connection-troubleshooting tips.) That's great news, because now you can put Ubuntu through its paces by trying some of the interesting web-related software that comes preinstalled. Prime your clicking finger for action, and flip the page to see what life online is like as a new Linux user.

5

SLIPPING AND SLIDING

Exploring the Internet, Linux Style

Now that you have a working Internet connection, what can you do with it? The good news is that Linux can match anything that your previous operating system could do online, and in many cases it can do it faster or more easily. Ubuntu was born on the Web, so it should be no surprise that it comes with a very healthy suite of Internet-ready applications right out of the box.

In this chapter, you'll take a tour of Ubuntu's Internet software so you can start really getting a feel for what this Linux stuff is capable of. You'll begin with old stalwarts like the web browser and email client, tour briefly through instant messaging, and then head off in the more modish direction of Twitter and microblogging.

Firefox: Your Internet Browser

The default web browser in your Ubuntu system is Firefox, which is enjoying increasing popularity in not only the Linux world but in the Windows and Mac worlds as well. Chances are you are already a Firefox user, but if you are not, then you needn't worry—things work more or less the same in all browsers. That being the case, you should be able to use Firefox's basic features without any instruction. Of course, some of its features do distinguish Firefox from its competition, so I will mention those.

Controlling Browser Window Clutter with Tabs

Usually when you click a link on a web page, the new page opens in the same window. On some pages, links are coded so that the new page opens in a new, separate window, or maybe you occasionally opt for opening a link in a new window by right-clicking the link and then selecting the Open Link in New Window option. This can be very useful; however, once you have more than a few browser windows open, it gets sort of hard to find what you're looking for in all those open windows. It can also slow things down a bit.

This is where Firefox's tab feature comes in handy (so handy, in fact, that almost every other browser out there has copied it). To see how it works, try it yourself right here and now. Open your Firefox browser by clicking the launcher on the top GNOME panel (or selecting **Applications ▸ Internet ▸ Firefox Web Browser**); then search for the word *nyckelharpa* using Firefox's handy search box, which is at the top-right corner of the browser window (see Figure 5-1). By default, Firefox will perform searches for keywords entered in the search box using Google. You can, if you like, select other websites to search by clicking the colored *g* icon in the search box and then making your selection. Amazon.com, eBay, and Yahoo! are available, to name a few, and you can even add others. For now, however, let's stick to Google for our present search, by typing **nyckelharpa** in that search box. Once you've finished typing, press the ENTER key, after which a page of search results should appear in the main pane of the Firefox window.

One of the top results should be the American Nyckelharpa Association, and you are now going to open that page in a new tab, rather than in the same or a new window. To do that, right-click the link, and in the pop-up menu that appears, select **Open Link in New Tab**. You can, if you prefer, make things a tad easier and dispense with the pop-up menu selection step by simply clicking the link with the middle mouse button (or with both mouse buttons simultaneously) or by holding down the CTRL key as you click the link. Either way, the new page will appear in a new tab, while your original page of search results remains, ready and waiting in the other tab (see Figure 5-2). I am pretty confident in saying that, once you get used to this feature, you will wonder how you ever got along without it.

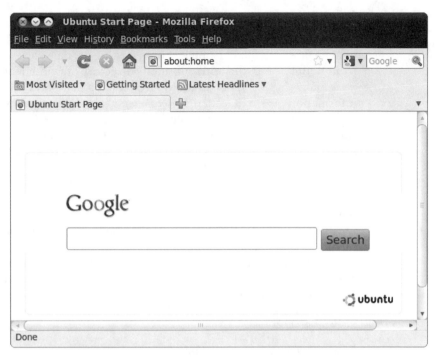

Figure 5-1: Performing a Google search from the Firefox search box

Figure 5-2: A link opened in a new tab in Firefox

Keeping Up-to-Date with Live Bookmarks

The Web is awash with all sorts of news and information, and it can be hard to keep tabs on it all. Personally, I hate missing my daily dose of offbeat stories from Boing Boing, the aptly subtitled "directory of wonderful things" (*http://www.boingboing.net/*). Fortunately, Firefox has a neat way of dealing with your information overload, called *live bookmarks* (also known as *RSS feeds*). These provide you with an automatically updated list of articles from any website that supports them. To see an example, click the **Latest Headlines** link underneath Firefox's address bar—it's a live bookmark for the BBC News website and should show you a long list of current news stories.

You can check whether a website has an RSS feed by looking in the address bar for an orange beacon symbol (like the one shown in Figure 5-3). If it has one, you're in business! Let's use Boing Boing as an example: Load *http://www.boingboing.net/* in Firefox, and click the beacon icon. You'll get a list of the most recent articles along with an invitation to subscribe to the feed in the box at the top of the page. Click **Subscribe Now**, and in the window that appears, click **Subscribe** to add the live bookmark to the same toolbar as the Latest Headlines link.

Figure 5-3: The beacon icon is displayed when a website has an associated RSS feed.

Some websites provide links to their RSS feeds rather than showing them in the address bar. If you find one of these links (it's normally called *ATOM* or *RSS/XML*), click it, and you should be taken to a list of articles with a box at the top, like in the previous example. From there, the steps for adding the feed to your bookmarks are the same.

Pop-up Manager

Firefox has a number of other useful features. One is its Popup Manager, which suppresses those annoying pop-up windows that often appear when you access a new web page. You can enable or disable this feature from the Preferences window (**Edit ▸ Preferences**) by clicking the **Content** icon in the top pane of that window and then checking or unchecking the **Block pop-up windows** box. You can also permit certain sites to provide pop-up windows (some pop-ups are not only useful but necessary for the correct functioning of a site) by clicking the **Exceptions** button to the right of that Block pop-up windows entry and inputting the web address for the site in question.

Multimedia Plug-Ins

One of the coolest things about Firefox is that it allows you to further expand its functionality by adding various extensions. The most commonly used extensions come in the form of *plug-ins*. These allow web pages to do much more than just display text and pictures—you'll often need a plug-in to watch videos or play games online. Three plug-ins are used far more widely than any others, so I'll concentrate on those here.

Flash

The most frequently used browser plug-in for any system is Adobe's Flash Player. Flash provides websites with all sorts of exciting multimedia effects and capabilities, and as a result, it is used by an ever-increasing number of sites. In fact, chances are you've probably seen numerous Flash-enhanced pages without even being aware of it. For example, if you've ever watched a video on YouTube, you've enjoyed the wonders of Flash.

How do you get the Flash Player plug-in? Well, all it takes is a few clicks and a working Internet connection:

1. Select **Applications ▸ Ubuntu Software Center** to open the Software Center.

2. Type `adobe flash` in the search box at the top right of the window.

3. In the list that appears, click the **Adobe Flash plug-in** item once. An Install button will appear (Figure 5-4).

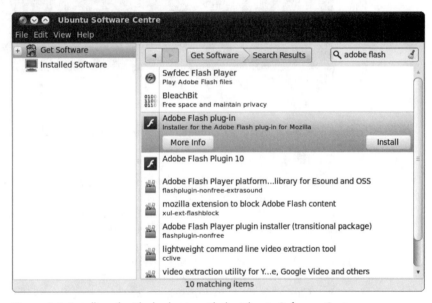

Figure 5-4: Installing the Flash plug-in with the Ubuntu Software Center

4. Click **Install**; then, if prompted, type your password, and click **Authenticate**. The plug-in will be downloaded and installed.

5. When the plug-in has finished installing, a green check will appear next to the Adobe Flash plug-in's icon in the list. Close the Ubuntu Software Center, and open Firefox (if it was already open, close it, and then start it up again).

6. To check that the plug-in is working, find a site that uses Flash. If you don't know of one offhand, try YouTube (*http://www.youtube.com/*). Once you have arrived at YouTube, click any video link you see. If Flash was installed successfully, a video should appear and start playing (Figure 5-5).

Figure 5-5: Playing a YouTube video after installing the Flash plug-in

Silverlight

A relative newcomer to the plug-in scene is Microsoft's Silverlight. It's less common than Flash but seems to be used on the websites of TV channels and major sporting events quite a lot. Unfortunately, Microsoft is a little behind the times, and it hasn't made Silverlight available for Linux yet. But never fear: An alternative, open source plug-in called Moonlight is available. To install Moonlight, follow these steps:

1. Open Firefox, and browse to *http://www.go-mono.com/moonlight/*.
2. Click the **Install** button on the Moonlight page, and scroll down to section 3, Download the plug-in.
3. Now, click the green down-pointing arrow. A narrow bar will appear at the top of the screen saying that the website was prevented from installing software.
4. Click the **Allow** button in the (usually black) bar, and a Software Installation window will pop up. Click **Install Now**, and wait for the plug-in to download.

5. Once that's finished, another bar will appear at the top of the Add-ons window. Click **Restart Firefox** to finish installing the plug-in (all of the pages that you have open will reappear when Firefox opens again).

6. Head over to *http://www.farseergames.com/waterdemo/*. If Moonlight was installed properly, you should now see a little boat bobbing around on the waves (Figure 5-6).

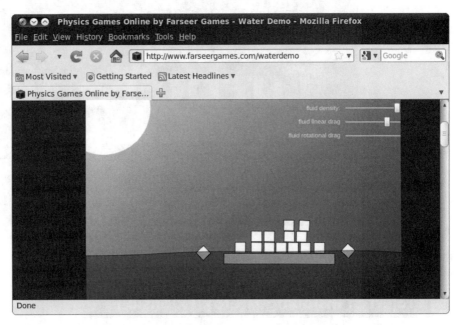

Figure 5-6: Checking that the Moonlight plug-in is working properly

Some Silverlight/Moonlight-enabled websites might require you to install extra plug-ins, especially if they are trying to display videos. If this is the case, yet another bar will appear at the top of the page, telling you that plug-ins are missing. Click the **Install Missing Plugins** button, and follow the onscreen instructions to install everything that you need.

Java

One last plug-in that you're likely to encounter is Java, which is used to run *Java applets.* A Java applet is a little application that you can run in your web browser, and they're commonly used for games and demonstrations. Ubuntu comes preinstalled with a Java plug-in called IcedTea, so there's no need to install anything extra. It's still a good idea to take a look at it in action, though, so head over to *http://www.turbotanks.com/.* An arcade "tanks" game should load if IcedTea is working properly (Figure 5-7).

Figure 5-7: Running the TurboTanks game in Firefox

Project 5: Installing Firefox Extensions

The plug-ins I covered earlier are near-essentials that pretty much everyone has installed, but hundreds of other, less vital extensions are available for Firefox too. These come in the form of *add-ons* and include all sort of things; many are quite functional, while others are just plain fun and goofy. They range from blog-writing tools and to-do lists to image viewers and travel guides. For this project, however, you will install a blog editor called ScribeFire (Figure 5-8) that allows you to write entries, log in to your blog, and upload your addition. All of this is available at the click of a button from an icon in the bottom-right corner of the window.

NOTE *If you don't have a blog but you'd like to give blogging a try, you can sign up for an account on a free hosting website, such as* http://www.blogger.com/, http://wordpress.com/, http://www.tumblr.com/, *or* http://www.livejournal.com/.

Figure 5-8: The ScribeFire extension installed in Firefox

5-1: Downloading and Installing the ScribeFire Extension

To get started with the process of installing any Firefox extension, you have to first find and download one. To do this, go to the Firefox **Tools** menu, and select **Add-ons**. The Add-ons window will then appear, showing you the extensions, themes, and plug-ins you already have installed. To add the ScribeFire extension, click the **Get Add-ons** button in the pane at the top of the window, after which Firefox will make some download recommendations that you can accept or ignore.

ScribeFire wasn't one of Firefox's recommendations at the time of writing, and chances are that it won't be when you open the Add-ons window either. This being the case, just do a search for *scribefire* in the search box (Figure 5-9). Once you find it, click the **Add to Firefox** button.

A Software Installation window like the one shown in Figure 5-10 will then appear. Just click the **Install Now** button in that window after it becomes active to start the installation.

Figure 5-9: Adding extensions in Firefox

Figure 5-10: Firefox gives you a preinstallation warning.

Once the installation process is complete, a message will appear in the Add-ons window telling you to restart Firefox. To do this, click the **Restart Firefox** button in the right-hand corner of that warning message (Figure 5-11).

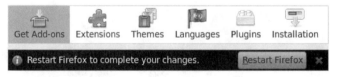

Figure 5-11: A message appears telling you to restart Firefox after the installation is complete.

5-2: Setting Up the ScribeFire Extension

When Firefox first starts up after you've installed the ScribeFire extension, you will see a small icon in the lower-right corner of the window. Just click that icon, and ScribeFire will appear as a resizable pane in the lower half of your current Firefox window. A ScribeFire Account Wizard will also pop up, asking for details about your blog. Follow the instructions to get it working with your blog.

Email with Evolution

Evolution is the default email program in Ubuntu, and it is probably best described as a better-groomed, spunkier clone of Microsoft Outlook (see Figure 5-12). It allows you to send and receive mail, make appointments, and keep a list of tasks. It can also filter junk mail, which is a necessity these days, and even synchronize with your PalmPilot, if you still have one of those. Also, if such things are important to you, it can connect to a Microsoft Exchange server.

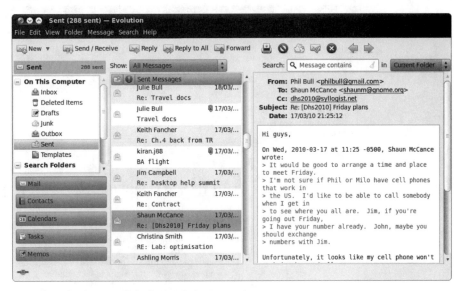

Figure 5-12: Ubuntu's default email client—Evolution

To start using Evolution, just click the envelope icon (called the *indicator applet*) on the top panel, and select **Set Up Mail**; or select **Applications ▶ Internet ▶ Evolution Mail**.

NOTE   *The Set Up Mail option will change to just plain Mail once you've entered your account details.*

When you first run Evolution, you will be greeted by a setup wizard, so have the account details you received from your email provider handy. These should consist of your POP host address for receiving mail, your SMTP host address for sending mail, and your mail password, which is very often different from your Internet logon password. Your mail password is not actually entered during the various wizard steps, so check the **Remember password** checkbox when filling in the POP details. When you first connect to your mail server, you will be prompted for your mail password, so you can type it at that time, and you won't have to deal with it again.

An Email Alternative: Thunderbird

Evolution is the most fully featured email software in the Linux world, but despite its obvious attractions and popularity, I prefer the more straightforward Thunderbird for my email chores. In contrast to the multifunctional Evolution, Thunderbird (Figure 5-13) is a more mail-oriented program that is very straightforward to use yet includes most of the most important email functions you've come to expect, such as junk mail filters. In fact, it is remarkably similar to Windows Mail in terms of appearance and handling. The fact that Thunderbird is also available in both Mac and Windows versions means that you may already be familiar with it.

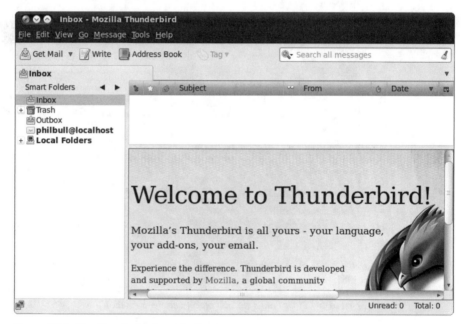

Figure 5-13: The Thunderbird email client

Thunderbird does not come bundled with Ubuntu, so if you want to try it, you will have to download it and install it yourself. Now that you have set up your machine to connect to the Internet, however, you can easily do this after going over the contents of Chapter 6 (OK, so I'm jumping the gun a bit again). Just do a search in the Ubuntu Software Center for *thunderbird*, click the **Mozilla Thunderbird Mail/News** item once, and click **Install** to install it. You may be asked to type the password for your Ubuntu user account, so do that and click **Authenticate**. Once it is installed, you can then run Thunderbird by selecting **Applications ▶ Internet ▶ Mozilla Thunderbird Mail/News**.

As I mentioned, both Evolution and Thunderbird are equally capable and possess essentially the same features in terms of mail handling. The difference is primarily a look-and-feel matter. Why not try both Evolution and Thunderbird and see which you like better?

By the way, if you find that you prefer Thunderbird to Evolution, you can add a panel launcher for it to make things easier on yourself when you want to run the program. Just go to **Applications ▸ Internet ▸ Mozilla Thunderbird Mail/News**, right-click that entry, and then in the pop-up menu that appears, select **Add this launcher to panel**.

Chatting with Your Friends via Empathy

Email is an extremely useful tool, but there's often quite a delay between sending a message and getting a response. What if you just fancy a quick chat? That's where *instant messaging (IM)* comes in. If you're not familiar with the concept, all you do is find your friend on an IM network and type a short message to them. Your message will show up on their screen in the blink of an eye. They can then reply to it, and you receive their reply just as quickly. So it continues, until you say goodbye and disconnect from the network.

There are lots of different IM networks out there, such as AIM, MSN/Windows Live, and Yahoo! Messenger. You can usually talk only to those people who are using the same network as you, and you'll need an *IM client* application to connect to any of them. Ubuntu comes preinstalled with a fully featured IM client called Empathy, which has the ability to connect to multiple networks at once.

Starting a Chat

For this section, I'm going to assume that you already have a user account on an instant messaging network. If you don't, you'll need to go to the network's website and sign up (most of them are free). Now that you have your account details ready, let's get Empathy connected to your chosen network:

1. Select **System ▸ Preferences ▸ Messaging and VoIP Accounts**. The Empathy Accounts window will open.

2. Choose **Yes, I'll enter my account details now**, and click **Forward**.

3. Select your IM network from the drop-down list at the top of the window, and then enter your account details (Figure 5-14). You'll normally need to enter your username and password.

4. Choose the **No, that's all for now** option at the bottom of the window, and then click **Forward**.

5. You'll be asked to enter your personal details. These are used to enable a feature that lets you talk to other people connected to the same local network as you—just enter them for now, choose a nickname, and click **Apply**. The Accounts window will disappear.

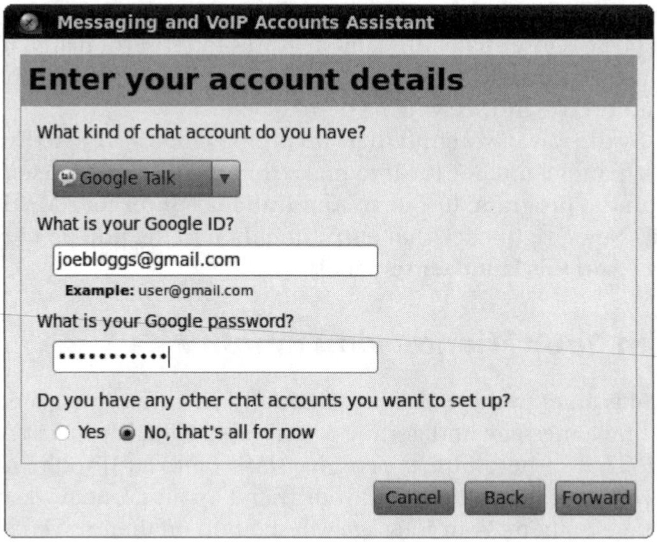

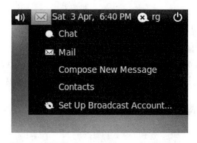

Figure 5-14: Entering your instant messaging account details

Your account should now be set up and ready to go, so let's take it for a test run. Click the envelope icon/indicator applet on the top panel, and choose **Chat** from the list (see Figure 5-15). An empty-looking Contact list will appear. To get online, choose **Available** from the drop-down list. If any of your IM contacts/friends/buddies are online, they'll be displayed in the main window. If nothing appears, try selecting **View ▸ Offline Contacts** in case all of your contacts are offline at the moment.

Figure 5-15: Accessing your chat account
via the indicator applet

If someone is online and available to chat, they'll have a green speech bubble icon next to their name. Double-click their name to start up a conversation. A new window will appear—type a message into the box at the bottom of the window, and then hit ENTER to send it (see Figure 5-16 for an example). Your messages, and those of your friend, will be displayed in the main part of the conversation screen. Ending a conversation is easy too—just close the conversation window.

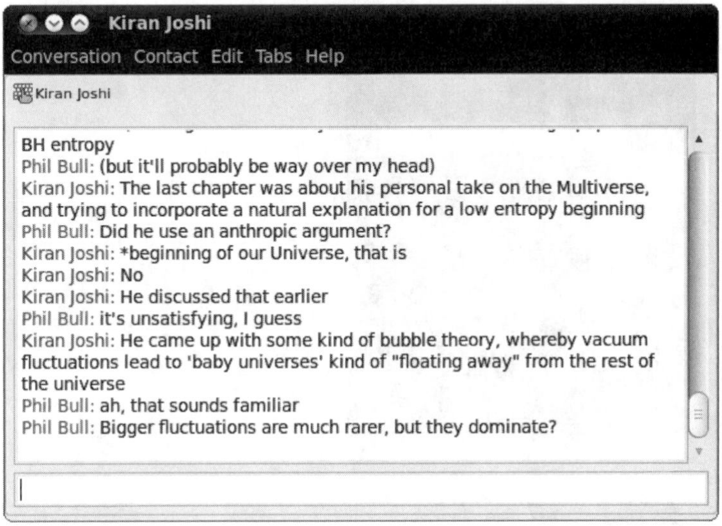

Figure 5-16: Chatting to friends using the Empathy IM client

I've only scratched the surface here. Empathy has lots of other features that you might want to try: You can send pictures and files to people, make phone and video calls, broadcast your location using *geotagging*, and even display your desktop on someone else's computer screen. Explaining all of this would probably take a whole chapter on its own, so instead I'm going to point you at Empathy's user guide, which should give you the lowdown on what else you can do and how you can do it. In any Empathy window, select **Help ▸ Contents**, wait a few seconds for the help window to pop up, and then look through the list of topics until you find something relevant.

Telling People When You Don't Want to Chat

Chatting is great, but very few people have the stamina to do it all day long. Once you've connected to an IM network, it can be annoying if people try to start conversations with you while you're busy. Fortunately, there's an easy way of letting everyone know that you don't want to be disturbed.

On the top panel you should see your username next to a speech bubble icon. If you're connected to an IM network, the bubble will be filled in with a solid color, which means that other people can tell that you're online. Click the speech bubble icon, and choose a different status (Away or Busy, for example) from the menu that pops up (Figure 5-17). Depending on the status you choose, other people either will be told that you're busy when they try to start a chat or won't be able to see that you're online at all. Peace and quiet, only a couple of clicks away.

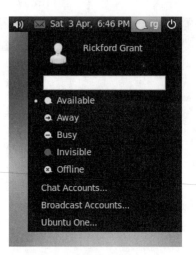

Figure 5-17: Changing your instant messaging status

Microblogging—Twitter and Friends

Blogging (writing an online diary/journal) is now a well-established Internet pastime. There are millions upon millions of blogs out there covering all sorts of subjects, from astronomy to economics to fluffy kittens. The quality of content varies wildly, but for the most part blog entries are typical newspaper-opinion-column types of pieces. So, what if you had a blog where you were forced to write everything you wanted to say in less than 140 characters? That is the idea behind microblogging: making frequent, very short, bulletin-like posts.

Twitter is the most well-known microblogging website (*http://www .twitter.com/*). People find all sorts of uses for Twitter: You can let your friends know what you're up to at the moment, receive breaking news, discuss popular topics with other users, write posts using your mobile phone . . . the list goes on. I just followed a Twitter conversation between a few of my friends who were watching a live hockey game. They sent messages every time something exciting happened, so I could follow the action textually, within seconds of it happening. News travels fast on Twitter.

Perhaps it's the sort of thing you need to try to appreciate, so if you don't have an account already, click the **Sign up now** button on the Twitter home page, and follow the instructions. Once you've done that, take a look around the website to see how things work. The basic idea is that you post messages (*tweets*) for your *followers* to see. People can choose to follow you by clicking a button when they view your user profile. You can choose to follow other people too—when you do this, all of their tweets will be displayed on your Twitter home page for you to read. Most people follow a few people and typically have a handful of followers themselves, but there are no restrictions on how many of each you can have.

Ubuntu's portal to the world of microblogging is called Gwibber, which was first mentioned in Chapter 3. Let's get it set up so you can see what it can do:

1. Select **Applications ▸ Internet ▸ Gwibber Social Client** to start Gwibber. Since this is the first time you've run it, the Accounts window will be shown, asking what sort of account you'd like to add.

2. Several types of account are available, but I'll use Twitter in this example. Select Twitter from the drop-down list, and click the **Add** button just below it.

3. A Twitter account screen will appear like the one in Figure 5-18. Enter your Twitter username and password, and then click the **Add** button on the right side of the window.

4. A new account will be displayed in the list on the left side of the Gwibber Accounts window. Click **Close** to finish adding accounts.

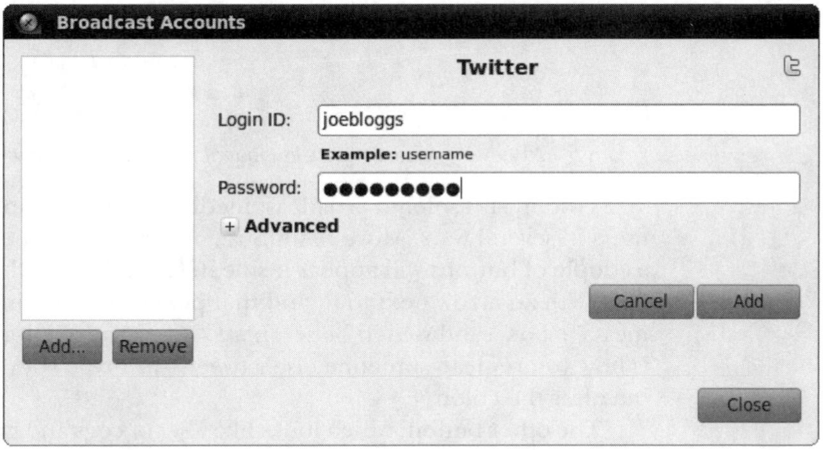

Figure 5-18: Entering your Twitter account details

Now it's time to get microblogging! Click the indicator applet (the envelope icon), and select **Broadcast** from the list that pops up. The Gwibber window will appear and should look something like the one in Figure 5-19. Tweets from other users are shown in the main pane. If there's nothing in there, you probably need to go to the Twitter site and start "following" some people—just click the **Follow** button on their profile page, and any posts they make will turn up for you to read in Gwibber.

To send your own tweets, type something into the message box at the bottom of the window: `Ubuntu is awesome`, for example. You're allowed a maximum of 140 characters per tweet, and the number of characters you have remaining is displayed in the bottom right of the box. When you're happy with what you've written, click **Send** to post the message for everyone to see. Do this as often as you like; you can tweet away all day!

Figure 5-19: Viewing recent tweets in the main Gwibber window

Twitter isn't solely a broadcast medium, and you can converse with other users in several ways. Move the mouse over a message in the main pane, and a couple of buttons will appear inside it. Click the one that looks like an envelope with an arrow next to it, and that person's username will appear in the message box, sandwiched between an @ sign and a colon (Figure 5-20). This is how you reply to someone else's tweet—just type your message as normal, but after the colon.

The other button, which looks like a set of cogs and gears, displays a menu when you click it (Figure 5-21). *Retweet* is an interesting option from that menu—click it, and you'll post a copy of the message for all your friends/followers to see. This is how Twitter users share links and spread news throughout the network. It's often the case that you hear about something cool from the friend of a friend of a friend, all thanks to these retweets.

If you're finished with Gwibber for now, just close the window. You can easily open it again by clicking the envelope icon, as you did earlier.

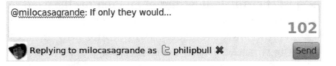

Figure 5-20: Replying to a tweet

Figure 5-21: Spreading interesting tweets using the Retweet option

Other Internet Applications

What I've covered thus far in terms of Internet applications is just the tip of the iceberg (might as well use that worn-out phrase before there aren't any icebergs left, right?). There are still more Internet applications that you might want to consider downloading and installing after you've completed Chapter 6, including Liferea (a stand-alone RSS feed reader) and Miro (an Internet TV browser). If this all sounds enticing, get those fingers of yours flipping—the mother lode awaits!

6

ROUNDING OUT THE BIRD

Downloading, Installing, and Updating Programs the Easy Way

One of the handiest things about Ubuntu is that it is equipped with a very simple-to-use application installation mechanism. The engine behind this is called Advanced Package Tool (APT), which allows you to easily download, install, update, and remove software packaged in DEB archives, or *packages*.

APT is a rather foolproof way of installing programs; nothing will go missing, since it automatically downloads and installs any files that the main application you are installing requires to run. Tracking down such files, called *dependencies*, proves to be a significant headache for most Linux users. The painful quest of finding and then installing this file or that, as well as any dependencies that those files themselves might have, has led to the missing dependency problem being referred to as *dependency hell*. APT makes that pretty much a thing of the past.

So, where does APT find all these files and applications? Well, the packages that APT searches for, downloads, and installs are located in a set of specific online repositories. These *repositories* are online servers in which a great number of applications, support files, and more are stored for use with your particular system. All of the files that originally came bundled with your system, including the system (kernel) itself and updates, when available, are stored there too. This is quite unlike Windows or Mac OS, where you normally need to buy a CD or download an installer file from a website to get new software.

The one thing about APT that some people, especially beginners, might consider a problem is that it is a command-driven application. This means you control it via commands in a command Terminal. Fortunately, Ubuntu has a number of different graphical frontends for APT that allow you to bypass the command line and make everything about as easy as you could ever hope it would be. In this chapter, you will be focusing on three of these frontends.

Project 6A: Installing Applications via the Ubuntu Software Center

By far, the easiest to use of the APT frontends is the Ubuntu Software Center. Being the most graphically satisfying of the frontends, it is especially useful when it comes to browsing for cool or handy applications. To get a feel for it, go to the **Applications** menu and select **Ubuntu Software Center**. The window that opens will look similar to Figure 6-1.

Figure 6-1: The Ubuntu Software Center

As you can see, items in the Ubuntu Software Center are categorized pretty much in the same manner as in the Ubuntu Applications menu. If you click any of the department icons in the main pane of the window, you will jump to a list of all the items available for that category. Applications that you've already installed are marked with a green check mark over their icons, while those that are not installed just display the plain icon. Not surprisingly, you will find that the installed items within each category mirror those in the relevant submenu of the Applications menu. To see a list of all your installed programs, click the **Installed Software** item in the pane on the left side of the window.

6A-1: Selecting Applications for Installation

The Ubuntu Software Center can install multiple applications simultaneously, so to give it a whirl, you can try installing a few interesting applications in this section. Let's start by selecting the very cool and decidedly useful address book application Rubrica (shown in Figure 6-2). To select Rubrica, click the **Office** department in the main pane of the window, scroll down the list of available applications, and double-click the **Rubrica Addressbook** item. A page containing information about Rubrica will be displayed. All you need to do now is click **Install - Free** and type your password if prompted. This will start the installation.

A progress indicator will appear on the page while Rubrica is downloaded and installed. Once the installation has completed, the Rubrica page will reload with a green check icon next to the word *Installed* to show that it was added to your computer successfully. That's all there is to it! Select **Applications ▸ Office ▸ Rubrica Addressbook** to start the program.

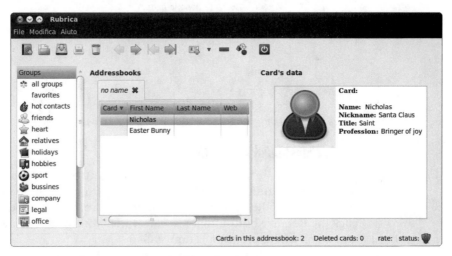

Figure 6-2: Rubrica—a very cool address book

6A-2: Searching for Applications

Next up is Sound Converter (which I'll talk more about using in Chapter 14). Scrolling through the list of programs can be tedious, so this time, try using the search feature: Type **Sound Converter** into the search box at the top right of the screen, and watch as the search results fly in. Sound Converter should appear at the top of the list of results, so select it and click **Install**. The installation will start like before—but this time, try clicking **Get Software** while the program is still installing.

All the installation magic will continue in the background, and you can still browse for other programs. No need to wait!

Finally, let's add a useful utility by the name of Sysinfo (Figure 6-3), which is a system profiler that can tell you all sorts of things about your computer. Just type **sysinfo** in the search box, click the **Sysinfo** search result that appears, and then click **Install** to add it to the installation queue. It'll be installed as soon as the Ubuntu Software Center has finished dealing with Sound Converter.

You can run the applications you've installed by going to the Applications menu and looking in the submenu that matches the Ubuntu Software Center "department" where you found the program—that would be Office for Rubrica, Sound & Video for Sound Converter, and System Tools for Sysinfo.

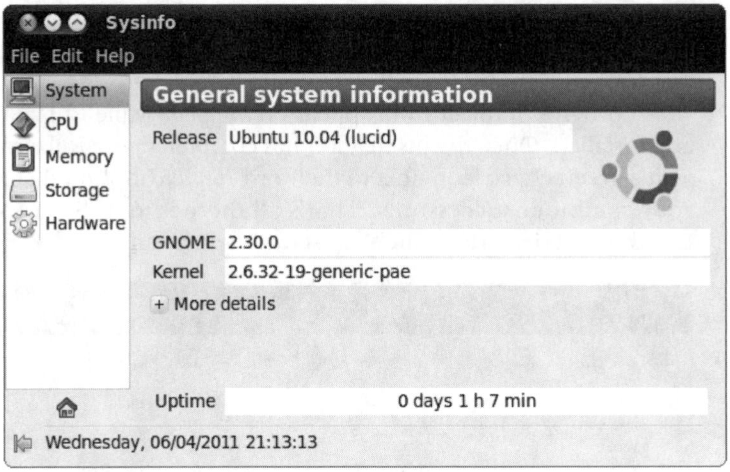

Figure 6-3: Keeping tabs on your system information with Sysinfo

6A-3: Uninstalling Applications

As you can see, installing applications via the Ubuntu Software Center is quite simple. And fortunately, it's just as easy to uninstall them. Navigate to (or search for) the program you want to remove, click it once in the list, and click the **Remove** button that appears. Enter your password again if asked, and watch as the program is uninstalled.

Performing System Upgrades via Update Manager

The second graphical frontend for APT that I'll cover in this chapter is Update Manager, which is used for updating your system. Updates are made available quite regularly and consist of newer versions of packages you already have installed. Most of the time a newer version will have been released because it fixes some security issue, but updates can also fix problems with software and introduce new features.

To get started, select **System ▸ Administration ▸ Update Manager**, and make sure that the Ubuntu Software Center isn't currently installing or removing anything (you can't use two APT frontends at the same time).

Once the Update Manager window appears (Figure 6-4), click the **Check** button to make sure the package information is as up-to-date as possible. You will then be prompted for your password. Type it, and after a short while, a list of all the available updates will appear in the Update Manager window.

Figure 6-4: Upgrading packages en masse via Update Manager

If there are any applications you don't want to upgrade, you can go through the list and uncheck the box next to their names. But for now, it's safest to just leave all the boxes checked. Either way, once you're ready, click the **Install Updates** button. The selected updates will then be downloaded and installed. Once the installation is complete, you will be notified in a separate window. Click **Close** in that window and in the Update Manager window to finish up. Depending on what you installed, another notification may appear telling you that you will have to restart your system in order for the changes to take effect. If so, it is best to be obedient and reboot.

How Often Should You Install Updates?

Ubuntu will check for updates every day, and the Update Manager window will appear on your desktop if it finds any. If this is happening too often and you find yourself being pestered by updates, select **System ▸ Administration ▸ Software Sources**. When the Software Sources window appears, select the

Updates tab (Figure 6-5), and under Automatic updates, change the Check for updates option to something else. Weekly updates should be fine.

You'll find a couple of other interesting options there too. If you select **Install security updates without confirmation**, updates will happen automatically, without any intervention from you. Alternatively, you can choose to have updates download in the background so they'll be ready to install immediately when Update Manager pops up.

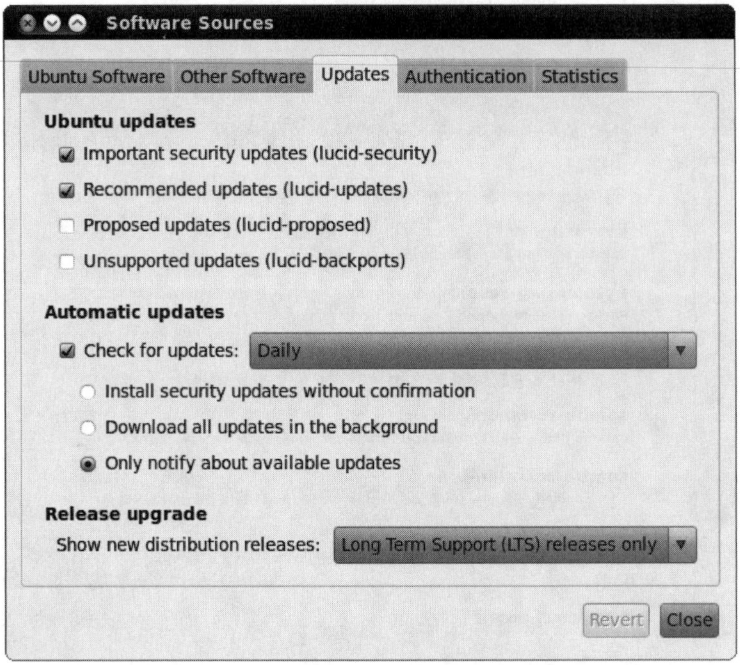

Figure 6-5: The Updates tab in the Software Sources window

If an Update Ruins Your Day . . . or System

Now, I don't want to worry you too much, but one thing about massive system updates is that afterward sometimes things just go all screwy, leaving you with all sorts of regrets and a mouthful of expletives just waiting to be uttered. This is a fact of life no matter what operating system you are using. It can happen in Windows, it can happen in Mac OS, and it can happen in Linux. Therefore, it is always a good idea to wait a bit before installing a seemingly major update and to check the user forums first to see whether there are any disaster stories about a particular update. Leaving a week between noticing an update and installing it should protect you from most rare mishaps, but there are no guarantees.

NOTE *To decide whether an update is "major," look for updates with* linux- *in their name* (linux-generic, *for example, as seen in Figure 6-6). These are important system packages and are the ones most likely to cause problems.*

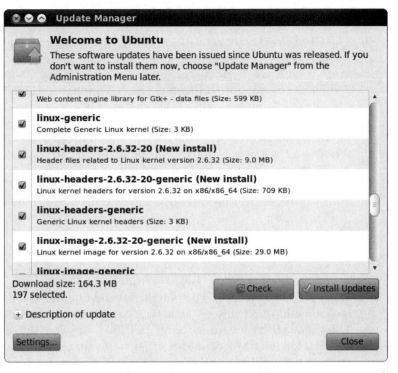

Figure 6-6: Updates with linux *in their name are usually important system packages*

If you install an update only to find that your system won't start up again, don't worry. All is not lost. In fact, nothing is lost . . . most likely. Just start up your machine again. If you have a dual-boot system, you will arrive at the GRUB boot menu, just like always. If you're not a dual-booter, you'll have to get to this menu by holding down SHIFT as soon as you start the computer. Don't let go of the SHIFT key until the GRUB menu appears (or Ubuntu starts, in which case you missed your cue, and you'll have to restart the computer and try again).

In the GRUB menu, you will see that you seem to have more than one Ubuntu system installed on your hard disk, which is true to some extent. For a short-term fix, you can take advantage of this by traveling back in time to the core system (the Linux kernel) that you had in place before your ill-fated upgrade. Just use your arrow keys to select a kernel that ends in a number lower than the highest (2.6.32-20 rather than 2.6.32-22, for example), press ENTER, and *voilá*, you are back to the system you have come to know and love. You'll have to do this each time you start up your machine, but at least you will have the chance to back up your valuable files before doing some research on the problem and trying again later.

With all this disaster and recovery talk, I hope I haven't scared you away from the idea of updating your system. After all, chances are great that nothing like this will ever happen to you. Still, it is good to know that if things do go awry, there is no need for panic. You've got backup.

Adding Extra Software Repositories

The Ubuntu software repositories contain more than 30,000 packages—enough to last a lifetime, or so you might think. But as it turns out, a whole world of software is waiting for you outside the official Ubuntu repositories, and it's not much more difficult to reach. Various individuals and companies compile small numbers of packages that are not available in Ubuntu into their own *third-party repositories*. These are typically free to access, if you can find them. All you need to do is tell APT to search for packages in one of these repositories as well as Ubuntu's, and you'll be able to get at the extra software.

Each repository has its own *APT line*. This is similar to a web address but contains extra information about the repository, which APT uses to figure out what sort of packages it contains. You'll need to get the correct APT line from the website of the repository you're trying to add, so let's pick an example to see how it works. Open Firefox, and head over to *http://www.getdeb.net/updates/Ubuntu/all#how_to_install*. GetDeb specializes in making packages for software that hasn't officially made it into Ubuntu yet. There should be some instructions on installing packages from GetDeb in a box at the top of the page, so skip to the second item in the list and find the APT line, which should look something like this: deb http://archive.getdeb.net/ubuntu lucid-getdeb apps. This follows the same format as all APT lines: the word deb, followed by a web address, followed by a couple of other words that specify which part of the repository should be checked by APT when it's looking for programs. Highlight the APT line, right-click it, and select **Copy** from the pop-up menu.

While you're in Firefox, you'll also need to grab the repository's *GPG key* (which I'll explain more at the end of this section). It should be linked to from the same website you got the APT line from; in the case of GetDeb, go to *http://archive.getdeb.net/getdeb-archive.key*; when the Opening getdeb-archive.key window opens, select **Save File**, and click **OK** to save the key file.

Now that you're in possession of these vital bits of information, adding the repository to your system is pretty straightforward:

1. Select **System ▸ Administration ▸ Software Sources**. Enter your password if asked, and then click the **Other Software** tab in the Software Sources window that appears.

2. Click **Add**. You'll be prompted to enter the APT line, so paste it into the box, and then click **Add Source** (Figure 6-7). A new entry should appear in the Other Software list.

3. Select the **Authentication** tab, and click **Import Key File**. Use the window that appears to find the *.key* file you downloaded earlier. (It's probably in your Downloads folder.)

4. Select the *.key* file by clicking it once, and then click **OK**. Check the list of trusted software providers to make sure that the GetDeb Archive Automatic Signing Key is now present, as it is in Figure 6-8.

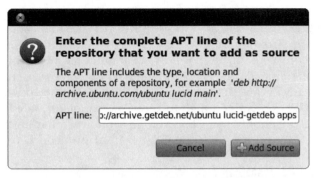

Figure 6-7: Entering the APT line for the GetDeb repository

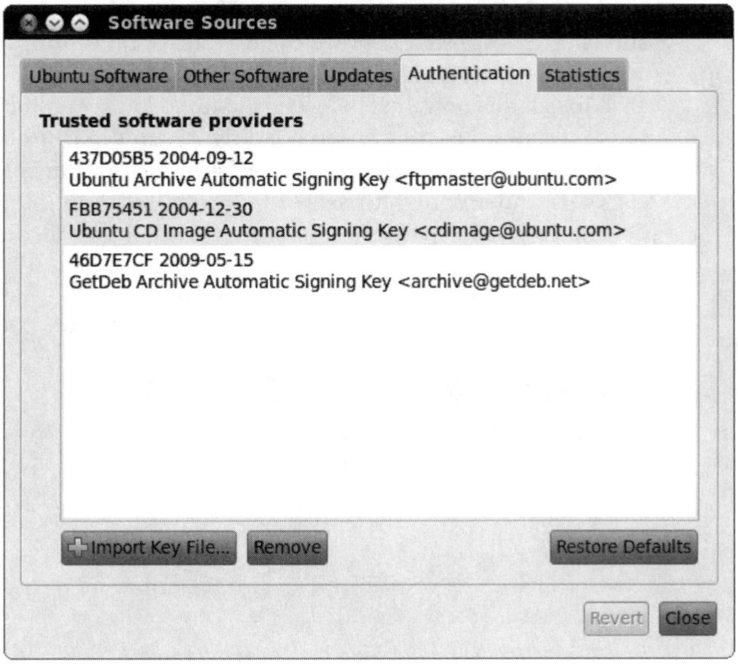

Software Sources

Ubuntu Software   Other Software   Updates   Authentication   Statistics

Trusted software providers

437D05B5 2004-09-12
Ubuntu Archive Automatic Signing Key <ftpmaster@ubuntu.com>

FBB75451 2004-12-30
Ubuntu CD Image Automatic Signing Key <cdimage@ubuntu.com>

46D7E7CF 2009-05-15
GetDeb Archive Automatic Signing Key <archive@getdeb.net>

Import Key File...   Remove   Restore Defaults

Revert   Close

Figure 6-8: Checking the list of trusted software providers to see whether the GetDeb key is there

5. Close the Software Sources window. You'll be told that the information about available software is outdated, so click **Reload** to fetch the most recent package information. It might take a little while to download.

6. Open the Ubuntu Software Center (or close it and then reopen it, if it was already open), and search for the program you wanted from the new repository. For instance, try searching for BookWrite, a fun little program to help you write your own novel. It should appear in the search results just like any other application, so you can install it in the usual way.

That was quite a few steps to go through, but that's all there is to it. It beats driving to your local computer store to buy a new program, eh?

One final note: Remember all that business about authentication and GPG keys? It was related to a security measure that checks whether the packages are from where you think they're from. (In theory, it's possible that someone could hijack a repository and put harmful fake packages in there.) If you don't add the GPG key, the Ubuntu Software Center will refuse to display any of the packages from the repository since it won't trust it. Having the GPG key isn't enough to keep you completely safe from nasty surprises, though. You should always exercise caution when using a third-party (that is, non-Ubuntu) repository; make sure it's trustworthy before you add it.

APT-URL: Installing from Websites

Now that you've added GetDeb to the list of available software repositories, you can take advantage of yet another APT frontend. Go to *http://www.getdeb.net/*, and click the **Apps** tab. Peruse the list of programs until you find something agreeable—I chose a time management application called *hamster-applet*—and click **Install this now**, just below its picture. Now you can click a link on a website to install software, without needing to visit the Ubuntu Software Center!

A Launch Application screen will appear with the apturl option selected—click **OK**, and enter your password if prompted. You'll then be shown a window that looks like the one in Figure 6-9; click **Install**, and wait as the usual downloading-and-installing activity carries on. When it's all over, hit **Close** in the window that appears, and go find your new program in the Applications menu (or wherever else it ends up). Quick and easy.

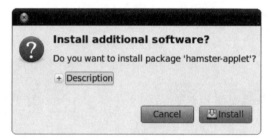

Figure 6-9: Installing a package from a website with APT-URL

Plenty of websites support APT links, but you won't be able to download software from them unless you've added their repository on your computer, like you did with GetDeb. If the link is for a program that is already available in the Ubuntu repositories, however, this can be installed as normal, without any further messing around in Software Sources.

Project 6B: Installing Software from a PPA: OpenSonic

Many Ubuntu enthusiasts catch the programming bug and decide to come up with their own software. There are all sorts of little programs out there that someone has written to scratch an itch of theirs, and plenty of them are available to you, for free, if you know where to get them. Luckily, most of them can now be found in personal package archives (PPAs) on Ubuntu's project website, Launchpad. PPAs are miniature software repositories and are an easy way for people to share their home-brewed software with others (emphasis on the home-brewed—sometimes software from PPAs doesn't work). You can find software in PPAs by visiting *https://launchpad.net/ubuntu/+ppas* and searching for what you want.

In this example, you'll see how to install OpenSonic, an open source remix of the classic Sonic the Hedgehog game (see Figure 6-10):

1. Type **lucid games** into the search box at *https://launchpad.net/ubuntu/+ppas*, and click **Search** to get underway.

2. The first search result should be Games (Lucid), so click that link, and look at the section titled *Adding this PPA to your system* on the page that loads.

3. Copy the bit that says ppa:falk-t-j/games—it's a shortcut that you can use to add this repository, instead of having to use the more cumbersome APT line. (You can still see the APT line by clicking the **Technical details about this PPA** link, if you're curious.)

4. Select **System ▶ Administration ▶ Software Sources**, and select the **Other Software** tab.

5. Click **Add**, and paste the PPA shortcut into the box provided. Then, click **Add Source**.

6. This time, the GPG key will be added automatically, so you can close the Software Sources window now.

7. Click **Reload** when prompted to update the package information, and then open the Ubuntu Software Center and install OpenSonic like you would any other package.

Figure 6-10: Playing OpenSonic

This is just an example—PPAs aren't only used by enthusiasts to distribute nostalgic games. Some Ubuntu developers use PPAs to make the latest versions of software available, albeit in an unofficial and untested manner. If a major new version of OpenOffice.org or Firefox comes out, for example, keep your ear to the Ubuntu forums (*http://www.ubuntuforums.org/*) to see whether someone has made the latest and greatest available through their PPA.

Project 6C: Installing DEB Packages Not Available via the Ubuntu Repositories: Skype

As you may recall, the applications you install from the various repositories via the Ubuntu Software Center are in the form of DEB packages. And although it might seem that these repositories contain just about every piece of software possible, certain packages, for one reason or another, will never find their way into a repository. Skype is one of these packages.

Skype, shown in Figure 6-11, is Voice over IP (VoIP) software that allows you to speak to other Skype users over the Internet, with the clarity of a regular telephone line. And the best part is, it doesn't cost anything—even if you call users overseas. Skype also offers paid services, such as SkypeOut, which allows you to call regular mobile and landline telephone numbers from your computer at a fraction of what it would normally cost from a regular telephone.

Figure 6-11: Skype

Although it is true that open source VoIP packages such as Ekiga Softphone are available in Ubuntu, they are not compatible with the much better known and more widespread Skype. Since it is very likely that the majority of people you know who are using a VoIP software package are using Skype, it only makes sense to use Skype so that you can easily communicate with them.

Because Skype is not available from the Ubuntu repositories, you will need to get it yourself from the Skype website (*http://www.skype.com/*). Once there, click the **Download** button, which will automatically take you to the download page for Linux versions of Skype. On that page, click the link for Ubuntu, and then click the **Save File** button in the window that appears.

Once the download is complete, you will find the Skype DEB package on your hard disk, probably in your *Downloads* folder. Double-click that package to open the Package Installer window (Figure 6-12). Click **Install Package**, after which you will be prompted for your password. Once the installation is complete, click the **Close** button in the window that appears and again in the Package Installer window.

NOTE *As is the case with all APT frontends, you cannot use Package Installer while another APT frontend is open. Make sure that Update Manager and the Ubuntu Software Center are closed before using Package Installer.*

Once all the pieces have been installed, you can run Skype by selecting **Applications ▸ Internet ▸ Skype**. If you find that you can't make calls or the sound doesn't work properly, take a look at *https://help.ubuntu.com/community/Skype/* for troubleshooting hints. Also, while we're on the topic of sound, remember that it is best to use Skype with a headset. Trying to talk with a stick microphone could cause feedback or echoes, because the microphone will pick up and transmit sounds from the speakers.

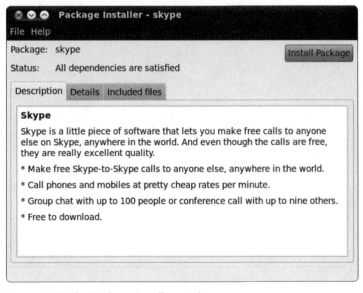

Figure 6-12: The Package Installer window

7

A TIDY NEST

File and Disc Handling in Ubuntu

 No matter which operating system you are using, you have to deal with files. Some people are very organized, placing every file in a logically named folder as soon as that file is saved for the first time. Then there are people like me, who save everything to the desktop until it is so full of junk that they can no longer make out the wallpaper, and only at that point do they start organizing in earnest (if placing all of those files in a single folder called *March17Cleanup* can be called organizing).

Of course, not only do files get stored on your hard disk, but they are also copied to and from CDs, DVDs, external hard disks, flash drives, and other storage media and devices. They are also often saved in archives, which are then compressed to reduce their spatial footprint, making them easier to send via email or to fit onto removable storage media.

With that introduction, you may have already guessed that in this chapter I will be dealing with file handling in Ubuntu, particularly in relation to the Nautilus file manager, which is at the heart of GNOME's file-handling capabilities.

Nautilus: Your File Manager

As I mentioned, the program that creates the file viewing and organizing interface on your system is called Nautilus, and it comes as part of the GNOME desktop environment. You may not have thought of an operating system's file manager as a program before, but in fact, that is what it is. (The Windows file manager is called Windows Explorer.) To take a look at Nautilus, just go to the **Places** menu, and select **Home Folder**.

When Nautilus opens to your home folder (shown in Figure 7-1), you will find that you can store your files thematically: *Documents, Downloads, Music, Pictures, Public, Templates,* and *Videos.* There is also another folder, titled *Desktop,* which, if double-clicked, will show everything you have stored on your desktop (a lot in my case; most likely nothing in yours). There is also another folder, called *Examples,* which contains sample files that give you an idea of what Ubuntu has in store for you.

You can create additional folders and files to your heart's content, so this preconfigured state of affairs is sure to change once you get down to really using your system. In fact, you will be making some changes in Chapter 8, which will make everything look a bit more lived in.

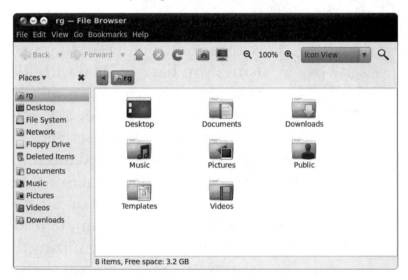

Figure 7-1: The contents of your home folder as viewed in a Nautilus window

The Side Pane

Nautilus has a lot of interesting features that deserve mention, and the most obvious of these is the side pane, which appears at the left side of the window. The side pane allows you to view a variety of information via selectable views. You can make your choices by clicking the drop-down menu at the top of the side pane (Figure 7-2).

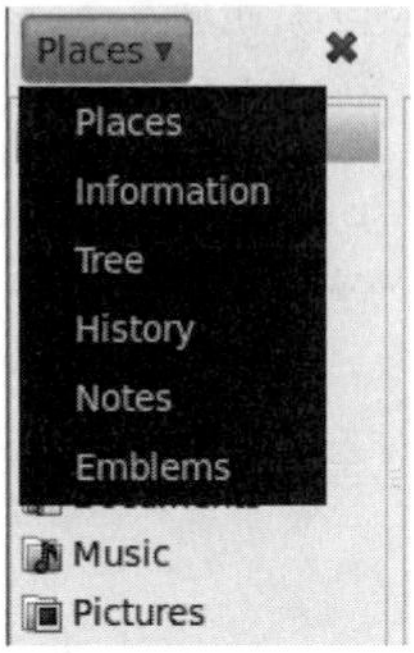

Figure 7-2: Selecting views for the Nautilus side pane

The default view in Ubuntu is Places, which is a sort of quick navigation tool. In Places you will find icons representing various data-storage locations available to your system, such as your home folder, desktop, full filesystem, any network shares you are connected to (more on that in a moment), and any removable storage media or devices you have in or connected to your system. Clicking any of these icons will show the contents of that location in the right panel of the Nautilus window.

There are, of course, other views, such as Tree, which provides you with an expandable hierarchical view of your filesystem, and History, which shows you where in your filesystem you have been most recently, much in the way the history function works in a web browser. There are still other views for you to choose from, a couple of which you will work with in Chapter 8.

Now You See It; Now You Don't

The side pane is a rather handy feature, but sometimes you may prefer to have more space to view the contents of your window and thus want to get rid of the pane temporarily. You can do this quite easily by clicking the little gray close button in the upper-right corner of the pane or by going to the **View** menu of a Nautilus window and then deselecting **Side Pane**. The check mark next to that entry will then disappear, as will the side pane. To get it back, just return to the **View** menu, and select **Side Pane** again. The check mark will then reappear, as will the side pane itself.

There is another way to hide the side pane that many people seem to stumble upon accidentally, usually resulting in a bit of unnecessary panic. If you look at the gray border at the right side of the side pane, you will notice that there is a small ribbed section in the center (see Figure 7-3). Dragging this ribbed section allows you to resize the width of the pane. What most folks don't realize straight off, however, is that simply clicking that ribbed section acts as a toggle to hide or show the side pane. When the pane is hidden in this way, the ribbed section still appears at the left border of the window, which is not true when the pane is hidden in one of the ways mentioned earlier.

So there it is—the side pane's little secret. No, it's not a particularly interesting secret, but it's one that should provide you not only with an added layer of convenience but also with some peace of mind.

Figure 7-3: Another way of showing and hiding the Nautilus side pane

File Handling in Nautilus

Since Nautilus is primarily a file manager, it only makes sense to get down to the business of using it at that level. Of course, most folks who use computers today are already familiar with the basics of drag-and-drop and a few other means of creating folders and copying, cutting, and moving files. But for those who are unfamiliar with one way or another of performing these essential procedures, I'll spell it all out. If you find this all a bit redundant, please bear with me for the good of the masses.

Creating, Naming, and Renaming Folders

Creating a folder is a simple enough task, and there are two ways of going about it. The easiest (in my opinion) is to right-click any empty space within a Nautilus window, and select **Create Folder** in the pop-up menu that appears.

If you prefer using menus over right-clicking empty space, you can instead start things rolling by selecting **File ▸ Create Folder**.

Regardless of where you made your Create Folder selection, a new folder with the name *untitled folder* will appear in the Nautilus window. The name box of the folder will be highlighted and surrounded with a black box, which means you can immediately give that folder a name by simply typing one— nothing to click or do other than that. Press ENTER, or click any open space in the Nautilus window to complete the job.

If you later decide that the name you gave your folder needs some tweaking or even a complete revision, you can rename it by right-clicking it and selecting **Rename** in the pop-up menu. Alternatively, you can click the folder once to highlight it and then select **Edit ▸ Rename**. After that, you can type the new name for the folder and then press ENTER, or you can click any open space in the Nautilus window to seal the deal.

Moving Files and Folders

Perhaps the easiest of all file manipulations you can perform in Nautilus is moving a file by means of drag-and-drop. I am pretty sure that anybody who has wielded a mouse is familiar with that particular move. There is another way of moving files and folders, however: cut and paste.

The easiest way of doing this is to right-click the file (or folder) you want to move and then select **Cut** from the pop-up menu (**Edit ▸ Cut** will also do the trick). At this point, it will seem as if nothing has happened, because the file will still be there, but don't worry.

After that, right-click any open space in the folder to which you want to move the file, and then select **Paste** in the pop-up menu. The file will then disappear from its original location and appear in its new one.

Can you use key combinations to do this? Sure. Simply follow the directions I just gave, but press CTRL-X to cut and CTRL-V to paste.

Copying Files and Folders

Based on the instructions I just gave, you can pretty well imagine the methods for copying files and folders, because they are essentially a variation on the same theme. Just right-click the file you want to copy, select **Copy** from the pop-up menu, right-click any open space within the target location, and then select **Paste**. Keystroke-wise, that would be CTRL-C to copy and, as before, CTRL-V to paste.

It is also possible to copy folders and files via the wonders of drag-and-drop, though this involves more hands than required for a simple drag-and-drop move; fortunately, the two you have will do nicely. Just press and hold the CTRL key while you drag the file or folder you want to copy to the target location. Be sure to release the mouse button and then the CTRL key (releasing in the opposite order will not work), and you will find a copy of the file in its new location.

Navigating in Nautilus

Navigating through your various folders and subfolders in Nautilus is quite straightforward. In fact, all is conceptually pretty much the same as what you are accustomed to in Windows and Mac OS. You can simply move into and out of folders through a combination of double-clicking folders and clicking the Back, Forward, and Up buttons.

Browsing with Breadcrumbs in Nautilus

In addition to the hierarchical view option provided in the side pane, another handy feature can make your navigation chores even easier: Nautilus's breadcrumb bar feature. As you wander ever deeper into your forest of folders, Nautilus will leave a trail of breadcrumbs (they look like buttons, actually) in the navigation bar for each folder you opened on the way to the one you are currently viewing.

Say, for example, that you have a folder called *gooseberries* inside a folder called *Dalarna* inside a folder called *SwedeStuff* inside a folder called *NordicStuff*, which itself is in your home folder. As you click your way to that *gooseberries* folder, starting by double-clicking the *NordicStuff* folder, Nautilus will display a button for that folder . . . and any folder opened before it. Take a look at Figure 7-4 to see what I mean.

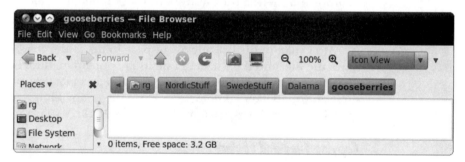

Figure 7-4: Breadcrumb navigation in Nautilus

As you can see, there is a button for each of the folders within the path from your home folder to your target: *gooseberries*. So what, right? Well, say you want to go back to the *NordicStuff* folder to open a file in which there's some text that you want to copy and then paste into a document within the *gooseberries* folder. That sounds like a minor pain, right?

Well, rather than goof around with the Back button, just follow the breadcrumbs! Simply click the **NordicStuff** breadcrumb button, and the contents of that folder will be there before you. Need to go back to *gooseberries*? Just click the **gooseberries** button. Back to *SwedeStuff*, you say? Just click the **SwedeStuff** button. All quite *fantastisk*!

Spelling It Out—Typing File Paths in Nautilus

If you prefer typing to clicking, you will be happy to know that you can navigate to a folder by typing its path. Just click the **Go** menu and select **Location** (keyboard shortcut lovers can press CTRL-L instead). A box will then appear in the location bar (Figure 7-5) showing the current location, which, in the case of my berried example, would be /home/rg/NordicStuff/SwedeStuff/Dalarna/ gooseberries. You can type the path to your target folder in that box and then press ENTER, after which the contents of the target folder will appear below in the main pane of the Nautilus window.

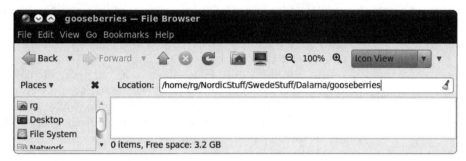

Figure 7-5: Typing the path to your target folder

Bookmarks Within Nautilus

With all this clicking away to deeply buried subfolders, it is worth mentioning another very handy feature of Nautilus: bookmarks. Yes, Nautilus lets you bookmark folders to which you have navigated. Although you are no doubt familiar with creating bookmarks for web pages that you frequent, you may be wondering why on Earth you would want to create bookmarks within your filesystem.

Well, imagine that you have a folder you need to use often, but it is even more buried away than my *gooseberries* folder in the previous section. Getting there would take an excessive number of mouse clicks, and all that clicking is bound to eventually give you a bad case of carpal tunnel syndrome. Although that is great for your doctor, it is most decidedly not good for you. Instead of maiming yourself, you could click your way to that folder once and then, in the Nautilus window, select **Bookmarks ▸ Add Bookmark**. After that, whenever you want to get back to that buried folder, you can just click the **Bookmarks** menu, and the folder will be right there waiting for you in the drop-down list.

Another handy thing about Nautilus bookmarks is that they also appear in Save As dialog boxes, such as when you save an OpenOffice.org document or download a file via Firefox. To use them in any such Save As dialog box, just click the **Save in folder** button, and you will find your bookmarks.

Understanding the Linux Filesystem

With all that path typing, navigating, and bookmarking you've just been learning, you should pretty much be able to figure out how to get from here to there in your home folder. Still, it is probably a good idea to know where your home folder actually is in the scheme of things, just in case you manage to get yourself really lost someday. To understand this, you should have a basic understanding of the Linux filesystem that, as you will find, is a bit different from what you were accustomed to in your previous operating system.

Unlike Windows, the Linux filesystem all stems from a single point called *root* and is represented by a solitary forward slash (/). Your own user account folder is located within a subfolder of root called *home*. This is represented as */home* or, to put it into words, the home folder within root. If your user account were to have the same name as mine, *rg*, the path to that folder would be */home/ rg*, or the *rg* folder within *home* within root. Whatever the name of your user account or the names of any other accounts you have on your machine happen to be, just remember that when you are lost, your folder, and those for all the other folks with user accounts on your machine, are located within the home folder. If you're a more graphically oriented person, the map in Figure 7-6 should help you.

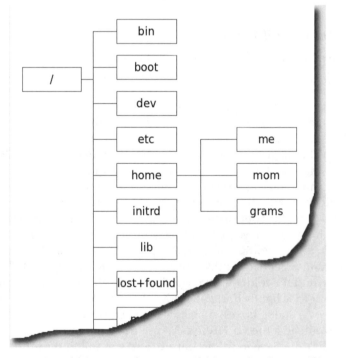

Figure 7-6: The location of your users' folders within the Linux filesystem

What's in All Those Other Folders?

Needless to say, there is more to the Linux filesystem than the root, home, and user account folders. Several other directories appear at the same level as home, though for the most part, you shouldn't be mucking around with them unless you know what you're doing. Fortunately, most of these folders are write protected, so you should be fairly well protected from yourself. Still, it is natural to be curious about what those other folders are there for, since . . . well, they're there. So, to satisfy your curiosity a bit, I'll do a little explaining.

In Ubuntu, four folders contain most of the applications on your system. The essential elements of your system are located in */sbin*. Other elements that need to be there, though they may not be used, such as commands and the like, are located in */bin*. Most of the applications that you actually think of as applications and use in a hands-on way are located in */usr*. Finally, there are some add-on applications, such as RealPlayer, that install themselves into */opt*.

Three other top-level folders that might be of interest to you are */etc*, */lib*, and */ media*. The first of these, */etc*, is the location of all the configuration files on your system. The second, */lib*, is the home of all of the libraries that are required by your system or applications installed on it. These libraries are the Linux equivalent of a Windows *.dll* file. Finally, */media* is where the contents of your various attached external media (such as USB drives and CDs) appear when present.

There are other top-level folders, but their purposes are a bit less straight-forward for the average Linux newbie and, to be honest, probably not all that interesting to you at this stage. Anyway, as I mentioned, there is no reason for you to be mucking around with any of these folders for the time being, because you can access the items located within them in different, and much safer, ways.

Using Nautilus as a Network Browser

Another handy Nautilus feature is its ability to function as a network browser. You can, for example, see what networks and shares are available to you on your home or office network by clicking **Network** in the side pane of the Nautilus window or by going to the **Places** menu in the GNOME panel and selecting **Network**. You can do the same from within a Nautilus window by going to its **Go** menu and selecting **Network**. Icons for any networks or computers on that network would then appear in the Nautilus window, like in Figure 7-7. From that window, you can then double-click your way to a share that you have permission to access, such as the *Shared Documents* folder of a Windows machine or the public folders of a Mac. By the way, in case you are wondering what a share is, I'll clear that up for you: A *network share* is a location on a computer, such as a folder, where other users on a network can access and save files. The *Shared Documents* folder on a Windows system is a good example. Other users on a network can copy files from and (usually) write files to the *Shared Documents* folder, whereas they cannot access any other part of the filesystem on that host machine.

If the share you are trying to open requires a username and password, you will be asked for those in a new window. Note that, in this case, the username and password you need to enter are those for the machine to which you are trying to connect—not the ones you're using in Ubuntu (unless the usernames and/or passwords happen to be the same, of course). You can then copy files to and from that share as if it were a folder on your own hard disk.

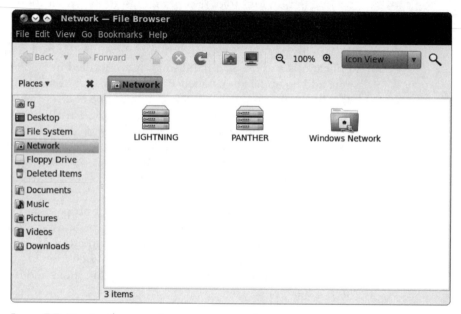

Figure 7-7: Viewing the computers on your network

In some cases, especially when trying to access shares on a Mac running OS X, the double-click method will not work. You will not be able to access any share on a particular machine, even if an icon for that machine appears in the Nautilus window. In such cases, double-click the icon for the machine you are trying to access and then, once open (to an empty window), select **Go ▸ Location**. A text box will appear in the location bar (just like in Figure 7-5) with the location of the machine you are trying to access already listed.

To that location, add a forward slash (/) followed by the username used on the target machine. For example, if the target machine is called *cowboycats* and the username is *mewtoyou*, the location would be smb://cowboycats/mewtoyou. You can also narrow things down to a particular folder on the machine, as long as you know the path to that folder, by adding to the path you've already typed; smb://cowboycats/mewtoyou/Documents, for example. If you prefer, you can type **smb://** and your Mac's IP address, which consists of a set of four numbers separated by periods. In the case of one of my machines, I would type `smb://192.168.0.100`. (You can find a Mac's IP address by going to the Mac's System Preferences, clicking **Sharing**, and then clicking **Windows Sharing**. The address should appear immediately below the service selection pane.)

NOTE *In case you are wondering, the* smb *at the head of that path stands for* server message block, *but to make things easier (and perhaps more useful in terms of your memory), you can just think of it as being short for* Samba, *which is software used by Unix-based systems (such as Linux and Mac OS X) in order to interact with Windows networks.*

Once you've made your way to the folder you want to browse on the networked machine you've connected to, it might be a good idea to use the bookmark function in Nautilus to bookmark that open share window. You can then easily access that share in the future by choosing the share's name in the Nautilus Bookmarks menu. Pretty cool, if I do say so myself.

Using Nautilus as an FTP Client

Not only does Nautilus allow you to browse and mount shares on local networks, but it can also act as a File Transfer Protocol (FTP) client, say when you want to change the files for your website on a remote server. To do this, go to the Connect to Server window (**File ▸ Connect to Server**), and then select **FTP (with login)** for the service type. Then type the information provided by your website host, and click the **Connect** button. An FTP Network Share icon will then appear on the desktop and in the side pane. Double-click that icon, type your password (for that account—not the one for your Ubuntu system, unless it happens to be the same) when prompted to do so, and then you will be able to view and add to the files you have there.

File and Folder Permissions Within Nautilus

As you make your way in the world of Ubuntu, you will find that occasionally you'll come across files or folders that are in some way locked, in terms of your being able to read them, being able to alter them, or both. These readability and alterability states are referred to as *permissions*.

Now, you may be wondering what the point of this permissions business is, so in order to help you understand, I will give you some examples of how it can be useful. Let's say you have some files that you don't want your spouse or kids to see—some bad poetry or a Christmas shopping list, for example. By denying read permission to those files or to a folder containing those files, no one would be able to sneak a peek unless they were savvy at changing permissions and had the permissions necessary to change permissions for those files or folders.

As another example, imagine you have a file that you have worked many hours on and have finally completed. To alleviate fears that you might accidentally ruin that file in some way, you could deny yourself write permissions. By doing this, you wouldn't be able to save any changes you make to that file.

You would be given the Save As option, but if you wanted to change the file itself, you would have to change the permissions. When you place such restrictions on a file or folder, a lock emblem appears on the icon for it, as shown in Figure 7-8.

Stay Outta Here   DO NOT TOUCH.txt

Figure 7-8: Nautilus tells you when permissions restrict your freedom of movement.

Changing File and Folder Permissions in Nautilus

To change file or folder permissions in Nautilus, just right-click the file or folder in question, and then select **Properties** from the pop-up menu. Once the Properties window opens, click the **Permissions** tab, and you will see who the owner of the file or folder is and what you and others are allowed or not allowed to do with it. As you can see in Figure 7-9, the options for folders and files are slightly different.

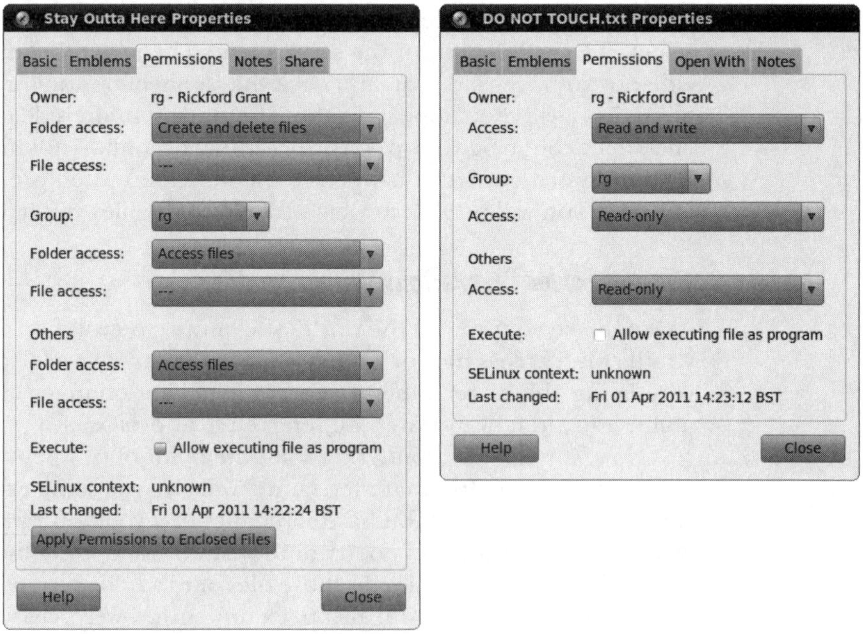

Figure 7-9: Changing permissions in a Nautilus Properties window for files and folders

You might find this permissions business a bit confusing, but it is really quite simple to understand. Permissions can be granted or denied to the *owner* of the file or folder (you), to a specified *group*, or to *others* (everybody else). Traditionally, these permissions are referred to as follows:

Read   Permission to view the contents of a file or folder

Write   Permission to alter the contents of a file or folder

Execute   Permission to run a program or script

Nautilus has tried to spell things out a bit more, as you can see in Figure 7-9. In general, however, you needn't worry all that much about setting permissions for your own files, because you are really the only one who has access to your user account. One possible exception you might run into is when you transfer files from CD to your hard disk. In this case, the files will be write protected, meaning you cannot alter the files until you change the permissions for them. You can change the permissions of such files in order to allow yourself to alter them by going to the **Owner** section of the Properties window and selecting **Read and write** in the menu next to the word *Access* (for files) or **Create and delete files** in the menu next to the words *File access* (for folders). Once you are done, click the **Close** button, and you'll be on your way.

Keeping Your Home Folder Private

Another exception to my you-don't-need-to-worry-about-permissions claim, and a potentially important one at that, is the state of permissions for your home folder, particularly when other people have user accounts on your machine. In Ubuntu, when someone logs in to their own account on your computer, they can click their way to your user folder and view its contents.

To remedy this situation—and thus protect the sanctity of your home folder, the privacy of its contents, and the peace of mind of its owner (you)— you can change the permissions of your home folder. Here's what you need to do:

1. Open a Nautilus window, and then click **File System** in the side pane. The contents of your entire hard disk will then appear in the right pane of the Nautilus window.

2. Look for and then double-click the folder named **home**. When the contents of the home folder you just clicked appear in the right pane, there should be only one folder there—your own folder, which will have the same name as your own username. For example, mine, as I mentioned earlier, is named *rg*.

3. Right-click your folder, and then select **Properties** in the pop-up menu.

4. In the *username* Properties window (mine says *rg Properties*), click the **Permissions** tab.

5. In the Permissions tab, go down to the Group and Others sections, and select **None** in the drop-down menus next to the words *Folder access*. Be sure to do this in both the Group and Others sections. When you're done, your window should look like mine in Figure 7-10. If so, click **Close**.

Figure 7-10: Changing the permissions of a home folder for privacy

Reading Data CDs and DVDs

Dealing with data CDs and DVDs in Ubuntu is quite simple, because everything is automatic. To read a CD or DVD with data on it, rather than music or video, place the disc in your drive, and a CD or DVD icon (they look the same) will automatically appear on the desktop and, if you have a Nautilus window open, in the side pane. You can double-click either of those icons, after which the disc's contents will appear in Nautilus. After that, you can copy files from the CD or DVD to your hard disk using standard drag-and-drop or copy-and-paste procedures.

When you want to remove the CD or DVD, just right-click the desktop icon for that disc or the icon for that disc in the side pane, and then select **Eject** in the pop-up menu. The disc will be ejected automatically.

Burning Data CDs and DVDs

Burning data CDs and DVDs in GNOME is extremely easy, as long as you have a CD or DVD burner hooked up to your computer! All you have to do is place a blank CD-Recordable (CD-R) or DVD (DVD-RW, DVD-R, and DVD+RW are all supported by Ubuntu) in your drive, making sure to select a media format supported by your drive, and a Blank Disc window will appear asking what you want to do. Just click **OK** to open Nautilus's CD/DVD Creator window, which as you no doubt notice looks pretty similar to other Nautilus windows, save for the colored band below the location bar and the Write to Disc button (Figure 7-11).

Figure 7-11: A Nautilus CD/DVD Creator window with files ready to be burned to disc

Once the CD/DVD Creator window is open, copying the files you want to burn to disc is pretty much a simple drag-and-drop maneuver. Just open a new Nautilus window, and drag the files you want to burn to disc from that window to the CD/DVD Creator window. If you prefer to do things in a decidedly Windows-esque fashion, you can select the files you want to transfer to disc by clicking each file once, holding down the CTRL key while doing so, for multiple selections. If you want to select multiple consecutive files, you can click the first file in the group, press and hold SHIFT, and then click the last file in the group, automatically selecting all the files in between. Once you've made your selections, release the CTRL or SHIFT key, right-click any of the highlighted files, and select **Copy** in the pop-up menu. After that, go back to the CD/DVD Creator window, right-click any open space, and then select **Paste** in the pop-up menu.

It is probably worth mentioning that the files you copy to the CD/DVD Creator window are not actually copied. Instead, what you see in the CD/DVD Creator window are essentially links pointing to the original files in their original locations. Thus, if you move one of the files from its original location before burning the contents of the CD/DVD Creator window to disc, the link won't work any more and the file won't be copied onto the disc. This isn't too much of a problem, since all of the other files will be put onto the disc correctly, but it is something worth being aware of.

Once you have copied all the files you want to burn to disc, click the **Write to Disc** button, after which a window (shown in Figure 7-12) will appear, telling you, among other things, how many megabytes of files you can still add to the disc (click **Cancel** to go back and add more if you want). Most people are happy to accept the default options (which are pretty sensible), so all that remains is to choose a more interesting name for the disc. However, if you'd rather not leave anything to chance, you can adjust the speed at which your disc will be burned (a slower speed means fewer chances for errors) by clicking **Properties** and picking a slower speed.

Once you are ready to burn the disc, just click the **Burn** button, and the CD/DVD Creator will do its work.

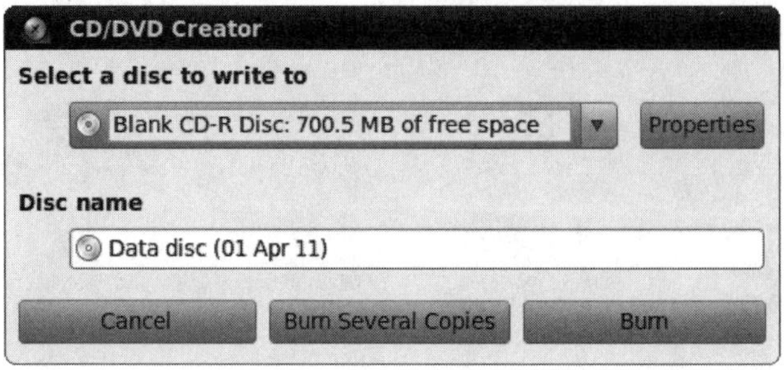

Figure 7-12: Setting options before burning a CD or DVD

NOTE   *If you intend to transfer the files to a Windows system, make sure you rename your files according to Windows naming conventions before you get down to the actual burning. In particular, avoid special characters and diacritics (such as umlauts and accents), and do not use the following characters, which are reserved for Windows system functions: / : ? * '' < > |.*

Once the burning gets under way, its progress will be shown in a new window, and when the job is done, you will be asked what you would like to do next. Assuming you are done with your disc burning for the day, click **Eject** and then **Close**.

In case you are wondering, the discs you burn in Linux *will* be readable in other operating systems.

Dealing with CD-RWs

CD-RWs are pretty much like CD-Rs except that they can be erased and then written to again. They are also quite a bit more expensive than CD-Rs and, generally, cannot handle faster burning speeds.

Using CD-RWs is much like working with CD-Rs. If the disc is blank, there is no difference in the process at all, which makes things quite simple. And, even if the CD-RW already has data on it that you want to replace with something else, the process is only slightly different.

One of these differences is that Nautilus will treat your CD-RW as a regular data disc rather than a blank one. This means that when you pop your disc into the drive, a regular Nautilus window will automatically open, rather than a CD/DVD Creator window.

To write to the disc, you will need to manually switch from the Nautilus window to a CD/DVD Creator window, which is easily done by selecting **CD/DVD Creator** in the **Go** menu of the Nautilus window opened for that disc. If you can't see a CD/DVD Creator option, click **Go ▸ Location** and type `burn:///` into the location bar (followed by ENTER) instead. Once you've done this, the window will become a CD/DVD Creator window. Now drag the files you want to burn to CD to that window; once you are ready to burn, click the **Write to Disc** button.

As is the case with regular CD-Rs or DVDs, a CD/DVD Creator window will appear. When you click the **Burn** button in that window with a used CD-RW in the drive, however, a slight difference occurs. At this point, a new window like that in Figure 7-13 will appear telling you that the disc seems to have files already written on it. Click the **Blank Disc** button in that window, and the CD/DVD Creator will erase the files already on the CD-RW and replace them with the new ones that you dragged to the CD/DVD Creator window. Not bad at all, eh?

Figure 7-13: Erasing a CD-RW with Nautilus

Burning ISO Images to Disc

When you download Ubuntu or other Linux distributions from the Internet, you usually download them in the form of one or more disc images, which are commonly referred to as *ISOs* because such files end in the *.iso* extension. An ISO is an image of a CD's file contents, which means that it is the CD minus the media itself. To put it another way, if CDs had souls, the ISO would be the soul of a CD; take away the CD's metal and plastic, and the remaining data would be an ISO.

Because it is impossible to download a physical CD over the Internet, the bodiless ISOs are the next best thing. For example, to get a working copy of Ubuntu from the Web, you usually need to download an ISO, which you then burn onto a blank CD in order to give the images their bodies back, so to speak. In the process, you create the working installation disc that you need to install Ubuntu.

Fortunately, burning an ISO to disc is a pretty simple chore. Just open a Nautilus window, and locate the icon for the ISO file you want to burn to disc. Right-click the ISO file, and in the pop-up menu that appears, select **Write to Disc**. Once you do this, the Write to Disc window will appear; just click the **Burn** button, and you'll be on your way.

Creating Your Own ISO Images

While on the topic of ISOs, it is good to know that you can create ISOs of your own. Of course, you're probably not going around creating your own Linux distros, but you might come up with a set of files that you need to repeatedly burn to disc now or in the future. To create your own ISO, follow the normal process for creating a data CD, but when the Write to Disc window (Figure 7-12) appears, select **Image File** in the drop-down menu below the words *Select a disc to write to*. After that, click **Properties**, which will open a new window asking for a filename for your new disc image. Give it a name, click **Close**, and hit the **Burn** button. In a very short time, you will have an ISO of your own creation.

Burning Multisession CDs

If you are coming from the Windows environment, you are no doubt familiar with multisession CDs. These are CDs on which data is added one session at a time. For example, you burn a few files to disc today and add a few more to the disc tomorrow and a few more files the day after that. Each time you burn additional files to the same disc, you are adding a session, which explains the name *multisession*. If that explanation seems a bit obtuse, you can basically think of them working like floppy disks (albeit with considerably more storage capacity).

Nautilus has basic support for multisession discs, but let's try something a little more specialized this time: Brasero, which is a more fully featured application that you can use for all of your disc-burning chores.

You can run Brasero from the **Applications** menu by selecting **Sound & Video ▶ Brasero Disc Burner**. In the main Brasero window that then opens, click the **Data project** button.

To burn the first session to a CD, drag the files you want to burn from Nautilus into the empty Brasero window (Figure 7-14), or click the **Add** button (which looks like a +) on the Brasero toolbar to browse for files manually.

When you have all the files in place that you want to burn, put a blank disc into the drive, choose a name for the disc using the box at the bottom of the screen, and click the **Burn** button. A Properties window will appear. In that window, check the **Leave the disc open to add other files later** box. (This is the step that sets up a multisession disc.) Once you've done that, click **Burn** to start the burning process. Brasero will eject the disc when the burn is complete.

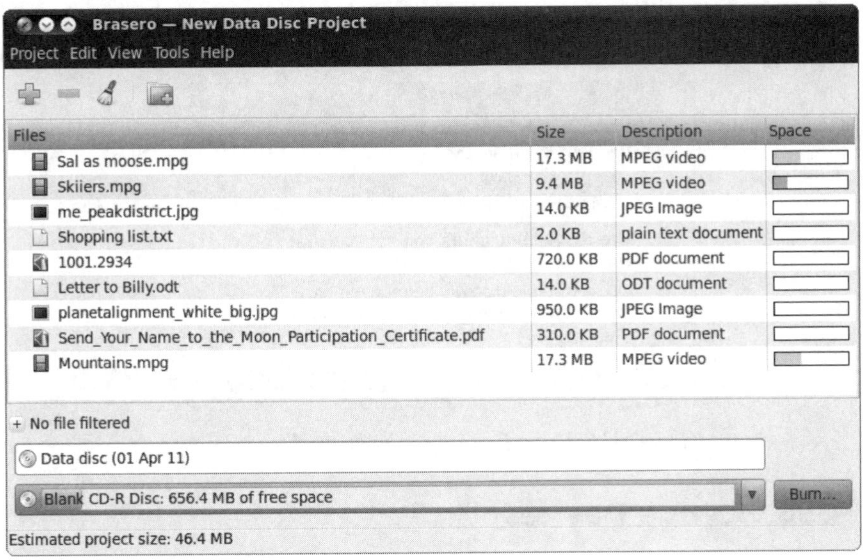

Figure 7-14: Using Brasero to create multisession discs

Burning Subsequent Sessions

Adding a new session to a multisession disc in Brasero is similar to the process used for creating the initial session. Here's what you do:

1. Run Brasero, and click the **Data project** button.
2. Insert your multisession disc into the drive, and when the drive stops spinning and you've gotten any Nautilus windows for that disc out of the way, click the **Import** button, after which the contents of your previous session will appear in the Brasero window.
3. Add files to the previous session, using either of the methods you used when creating the original session (via drag-and-drop or by selecting and clicking **Add**).
4. When you've added the files you want, click **Burn**. The process from then on out is exactly the same as it was for the first session. To add files in subsequent sessions, just follow the process outlined earlier yet again.

Duplicating CDs and DVDs

Now that you are familiar with Brasero, I'll introduce another of its features: CD/DVD duplication. To duplicate a disc, place it in the drive, start Brasero, and then click the **Disc copy** button. In the window that then appears (Figure 7-15), click the **Copy** button.

Brasero will begin copying your disc. When it's done, it will eject the disc and ask you to insert a blank one. A few seconds after you insert the blank disc, Brasero will automatically start writing to it. When the process is complete, the disc will be ejected. Nothing to it.

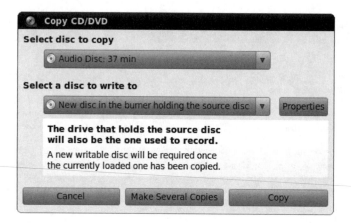

Figure 7-15: Using Brasero to duplicate discs

USB Storage Devices

Unless you have been under a digital rock for the past few years, you are no doubt well familiar with USB devices. Your printer is very likely a USB device, as is your scanner. And although your digital camera is not a USB device in the traditional sense, chances are that every time you connect it to your computer in order to transfer photos, you are doing so via a USB connector.

Among the most popular USB devices out there are those used for file storage. These include external hard disks, flash memory card readers, and the tiny, finger-sized devices known as *flash drives* (Figure 7-16). Flash drives are especially popular today and deservedly so: They are inexpensive, handy when you need to transfer large amounts of data, and pretty safe in terms of cross-platform (including Linux) compatibility.

Working with USB storage devices is really easy. Just plug the device into one of the USB ports on your computer. The LED on the device will do a bit of blinking while the system reads what's on it, and after that, a disc icon for that device will appear on your desktop. A few moments later, a Nautilus window will open, revealing the contents of the device. An icon for the USB device will also appear in the side pane of the Nautilus window. You can then copy files to and from the device using the drag-and-drop or copy-and-paste procedures I mentioned earlier in this chapter.

Once you are done and want to remove the device, right-click its desktop icon, and select **Safely Remove Drive** in the pop-up menu. (You can also right-click the icon in the Nautilus side pane and select the same option.) If there is any data that needs to be written to the device, the system will start writing. Once it's complete, the icon for the device will disappear from the desktop and Nautilus folder. Make sure that you always safely remove USB drives like this, rather than simply disconnecting them—otherwise, you risk losing data.

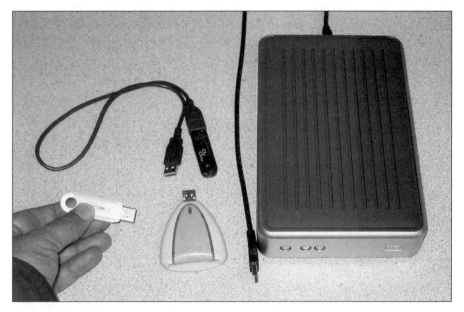

Figure 7-16: USB storage devices

Working with Bluetooth Devices

While we're on the topic of file handling, it is probably a good time to learn how to work with Bluetooth devices. As I mentioned in Chapter 3, if you have a Bluetooth adapter in your machine, either built in or plugged into a USB port, a Bluetooth icon will appear in the right half of the GNOME upper panel.

Pairing Devices

Before you can transfer files between your Bluetooth devices, you need to pair them. This is how you do it:

1. Click the Bluetooth icon in the top panel, and select **Set up new device**.

2. In the Bluetooth setup wizard that appears, click **Forward**.

3. Ubuntu will then search for Bluetooth devices in the vicinity of your computer. Once it discovers a device, that device will appear in the center pane of the window, as in Figure 7-17. Once the device you want to pair to appears, click it, and then click the **Forward** button.

4. In the next page of the wizard, a personal identification number (PIN) will appear (Figure 7-18). An input window should also then appear in the Bluetooth device you're trying to connect to. Input the PIN into that input box.

5. Assuming the pairing is successful, the final page of the wizard will then appear. Click **Close** to complete the pairing process.

Figure 7-17: Searching and selecting nearby Bluetooth devices in Ubuntu

Bluetooth New Device Setup

Device Setup

Please enter the following PIN on 'RG Phone':

948968

Cancel

Figure 7-18: The Bluetooth wizard provides you with a PIN to input into the device you're pairing to.

Sending Files by Bluetooth

To send a file by Bluetooth from your computer to another Bluetooth-capable device, click the Bluetooth panel icon, and select **Send files to device**. A window will then appear in which you can navigate to the target file. Once you have made your selection, click **Open**. The Select Device window will then appear (Figure 7-19). Select the recipient machine, and click **Send to**. Your machine will then begin transferring the file. If the recipient machine is set up to seek permission first before accepting a Bluetooth file transfer, you or the recipient will have to perform the appropriate action on the recipient machine before the transfer can be completed.

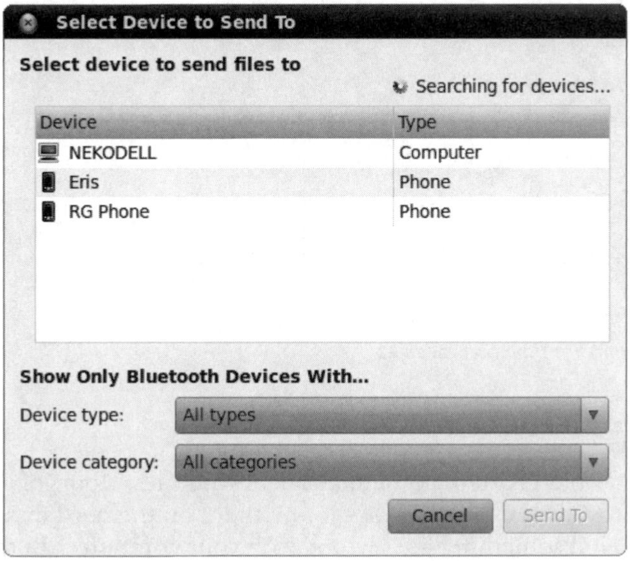

Figure 7-19: Selecting paired Bluetooth devices to receive sent files

Receiving Files by Bluetooth

To receive files via Bluetooth from another Bluetooth-capable device, you have to first set up your device to allow such transfers. To do this, click the Bluetooth panel icon, and select **Preferences**. In the Bluetooth Preferences window, click the device you want to set up, and then click **Receive Files**. A Personal File Sharing Preferences window will then appear. In that window, check the box next to the words *Receive files in Downloads folder over Bluetooth*. For your safety, select **Only for set up devices** in the drop-down menu button to the right of the words *Accept files*. Your window should then look like that in Figure 7-20. If so, click **Close**. Your machine will then automatically receive files sent to it via Bluetooth and save them to the Downloads folder.

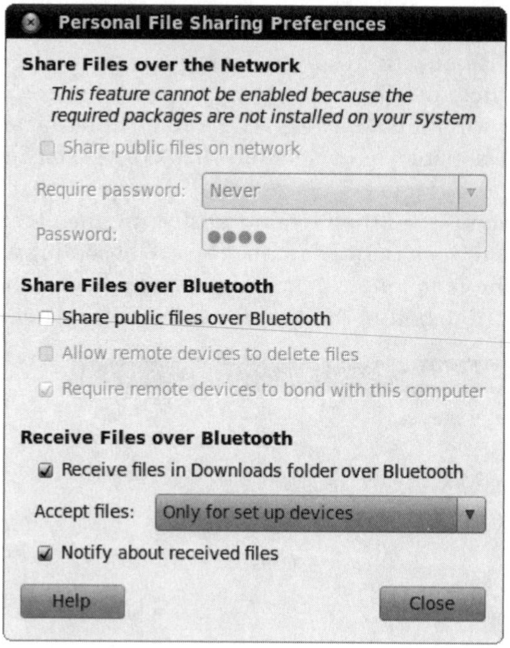

Figure 7-20: Setting up your system to receive files sent from other Bluetooth devices.

Backing Up Your Files

You've worked hard to accumulate all of your files. Hours of typing, hundreds of photos, piles of music CDs—it's all there on the hard disk. So, what happens to it if something goes wrong with your computer? In many cases the answer is, unfortunately, that all of the data is lost forever. To save you the pain of this experience, it's a great idea to make regular backups.

Plenty of backup utilities are available, but *Déjà Dup* stands out to me as being the easiest to use. Open the Ubuntu Software Center, and install the *Déjà Dup Backup Utility*. It'll put itself in the **System Tools** section of the **Applications** menu, so head over there and start it up.

Now is a good time to decide what you're going to use to store your backups. I have an external USB hard disk that does the trick, but you can use a USB flash drive, recordable CD or DVD, or even a web server. I wouldn't recommend putting your backups on the same computer, though. The best policy is to put some distance between the original files and the backups, so if there's a fire or some other disaster, you'll have at least one copy of them left intact. Make sure you have enough space for the backup too; regular CDs are only 700MB, but my *Pictures* folder alone weighs in at a whopping 4.3GB!

Connect, insert, or otherwise prepare your chosen backup device, and click the **Backup** button in Déjà Dup. A Preferences window will pop up like the one in Figure 7-21. Choose the location in which you'd like to save the backup files from the drop-down box. If you have sensitive files that you don't want anyone snooping around in, check **Encrypt backup files**.

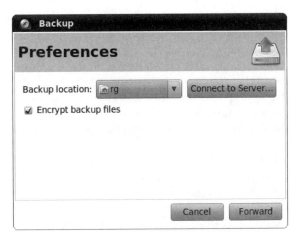

Figure 7-21: Choosing where to save the backup files in Déjà Dup

NOTE *If you want to put your backup files on a CD or DVD, you'll have to save them to a folder somewhere first and then copy that folder onto a disc using the burning software mentioned earlier this chapter.*

Hit **Forward,** and you'll be presented with the screen in Figure 7-22. Your first task is to decide what you want to back up, so check out the list labeled *Include files in folders,* which should have only your *Home* folder in it at the moment. This is a pretty sensible choice for most people, since absolutely all of your files should be in your *Home* folder. You can add and remove other items as you please using the buttons to the right of the list.

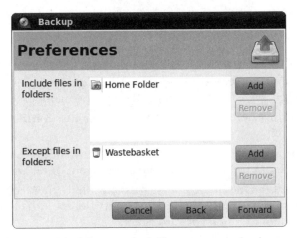

Figure 7-22: Selecting which files you want to backup

There's another list on that screen, labeled *Except files in folders.* You can use this to define any files or folders that you *don't* want to back up. Say, for example, that you wanted to back up everything in your *Home* folder except for your pictures—maybe you don't have space on your backup disk for all of them. All you'd need to do is to make sure that your *Home Folder* is in the *Include files in folders* list and your *Pictures* folder is in the *Except files in folders* list.

When you've chosen what to keep and what to ignore, click **Forward** again to get to the summary page. Check that everything looks hunky-dory, and click **Backup** to start the backup. If you chose to encrypt your backup, you'll be asked to type a password, so do this and click **Continue**.

Make sure you keep that password safe; otherwise, you won't be able to recover your backed-up files at a later date! A flurry of file copying will ensue and may last for some time if you have lots of files to back up. Once that's finished, click **Close**, and safely remove your backup disk (or whatever you have instead).

That should be it . . . for now. But remember, there's little point in backing up if you don't do it regularly, since you'll only be able to recover your older files (and not more recent ones) if something does go wrong. I make a backup about once a month, but I should probably do it more regularly than that. It's not much of a chore; when you next use Déjà Dup, it'll remember all of your settings from the previous backup. If you want to do something different, click **Edit ▸ Preferences** in the main window, and change the options there. You'll find options for automatically backing up as well; check the *Automatically backup on a regular schedule* setting in the Preferences window, and then choose how often you'd like the backup to happen. Click **Close**, and Déjà Dup should take care of the rest.

NOTE   *Canonical, the company behind Ubuntu, now offers an online backup service called Ubuntu One. Take a look at* https://one.ubuntu.com/ *for more information on that.*

Recovering from a Backup

Ideally you'll never have to recover your backup, but if you do, here's a quick guide:

1. Find your backup disk, hook it up to the computer, and start Déjà Dup.

2. Select **Edit ▸ Preferences,** and make sure that the disk is selected as the *Backup location.* Click **Close** to get back to the main screen.

3. Click **Restore,** and enter the password you chose for the backup if you encrypted it.

4. You'll be asked to choose which backup you want to restore. Choose the one that looks right (normally the most recent one), and click **Forward**.

5. If you want the files to be put back exactly where they came from, choose **Restore files to original locations**. Otherwise, you can choose a folder to restore them to. Click **Forward** again.

6. Glance over the summary to make sure everything looks OK, and click **Apply** to restore your files. There's a chance that you might have to reenter your encryption password, so go ahead and do so if asked.

7. Click **Close** once the restoration has finished, and check that the files have been put back correctly.

Everything should have returned to normal now. Phew!

Removing Unwanted Files

Remember all that talk of keeping a tidy nest at the start of the chapter? Well, now it's time to dust off your spring cleaning gear and give your home folder the once over.

The first stop is the Trash. Sometimes I'm surprised by just how much stuff accumulates here; I can go for weeks on end without emptying it. Luckily, this trash lacks the unpleasant odor of its real-world counterpart, so all that stands in your way is a quick check to make sure you didn't accidentally throw anything away. Click the Trash icon on the bottom panel, and when the window opens, click **Empty Trash** to delete all the files in there. They will be deleted permanently, with no way of getting them back.

Next up is something a little more sophisticated. If you're running low on hard disk space and want to know why (or just want to snoop around your files a little), select **Applications ▸ Accessories ▸ Disk Usage Analyzer**. When the window appears, click **Scan Home**, and wait for a little while as your folders are sized up. A colorful ring chart will appear, accompanied by a list showing where all your hard disk space is being eaten up. Hover the mouse over one of the colored segments on the chart to see what's taking up the most room, or double-click one of them to zoom in on a particular folder. After that, it's up to you to weed out the hard disk hogs: Click a folder in the left list, and choose **Move to Trash** to delete it.

Project 7: Creating and Extracting Compressed Files

Since I have been talking about file storage, it seems only fitting to wrap things up in this chapter by teaching you how to create and extract compressed files. In the Windows world, these are generally referred to as *Zip files*, while in the Linux world, *tarball* is the operative name. The Linux name, in case you're wondering, comes from the application that is used to create the archive for such files, Tar. Compressed archives are great for two reasons: They let you bundle a load of files together into one handy package, and they also squeeze all the files down so that they take up less space on your hard disk. If you've ever tried to email a bunch of files to someone, you know how useful this can be.

Anyway, to get some of the hands-on stuff down, you'll be creating a Windows/Linux/Mac–friendly Zip file and then extracting it. You can get down to business by opening a Nautilus window and creating a couple of dummy files to work with. Do this by going to the Nautilus **File** menu and selecting **Create Document ▸ Empty File**. A new file will appear in the Nautilus window, with its name highlighted. You can type a name for the file, such as the one I'm using: *dogwood*. Now repeat the process to create a second file. I'll be calling that one *violet*. Use something equally evocative for yours.

Now that you have two files to work with, you can create the compressed archive by following these steps:

1. Select the two files either by clicking your mouse to the side of the files and then dragging the cursor (with the mouse button still pressed) over both files until they are highlighted or by holding down the CTRL key and clicking each file individually.
2. Once both files are highlighted, right-click either one, and select **Compress** from the pop-up menu.
3. In the Compress window that then appears, type **blossoms** in the Filename text box, and then select **.zip** from the drop-down menu button to the right of that. Once everything looks like what I've set up in Figure 7-23, click the **Create** button, after which a compressed archive of your two files (*blossoms.zip*) will appear in your home folder.

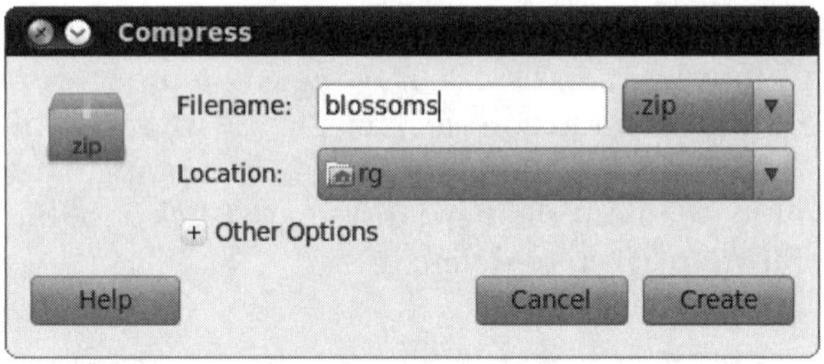

Figure 7-23: Creating a compressed archive

Now that you know how to put things together, let's get back to work and learn the equally simple task of ripping it all apart—well, OK, *extracting* it:

1. Drag the original *dogwood* and *violet* files to the Trash to get them out of the way.
2. Double-click the **blossoms.zip** file you've just created. A window showing the contents of the file will then appear (Figure 7-24).

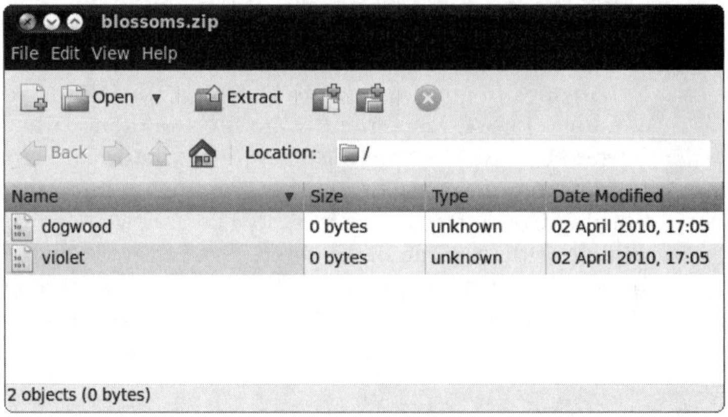

Figure 7-24: Extracting a compressed archive

3.   In that window, click the **Extract** button, after which another window, Extract, will appear.

4.   Click the **Extract** button in that window, and within a second (two at the most), you will find two new copies of *dogwood* and *violet* in your home folder.

Now you've created and extracted a compressed archive, which is in this case a Zip file. You can also create a compressed tarball in the future by following the same procedure (probably with real rather than dummy files), but when it's time to select an archive type, select *.tar.gz* instead of *.zip*. Other than that single step, it is the same creation and extraction process.

8

DRESSING UP THE BIRD

Customizing the Look and Feel of Your System

Before entering the world of Linux, I had used just about every desktop operating system around. Despite the differences among them all, however, one thing that I eventually suffered from in each case was a kind of visual boredom. I suppose you might call it GUI fatigue. It wasn't that I was tired of using a graphical interface; it was just that I couldn't help but get sick of looking at the same old icons, window borders, and color schemes. Of course, there were some changes that could be made, but it just wasn't possible to get around the basic look and feel without add-ons that demanded a price in terms of performance.

One of the features of Linux that pleased me to no end, and continues to do so, is that users can drastically change the look of things. I don't mean just the icons and backgrounds but *everything*, including the actual window borders and controls. Add to that the variety of graphical desktop environments and window managers available for Linux, and you have a totally customizable system. Is it any wonder that there are so many more Linux desktop screenshots on the Web than for any other system? If you don't believe me, just take a look at a site dedicated to Linux screenshots, *http://www.lynucs.org/*, and click the **Screenshots** link.

You may not be as fickle as I am in terms of the look and feel of your system, but you can learn to use and enjoy all the graphical customization power that Linux offers you as you work through this chapter.

Project 8A: Creating a New User Account

If you are reluctant to alter the look of your current setup, you can create a new user account and experiment with making the changes in this chapter when logged in to the new account. If you opt to go this route, your regular home environment will remain untouched, because look-and-feel customizations that are performed in one user account do not affect other user accounts. When you are all done with the project, you can then simply delete the new user account. Either way, it's up to you.

8A-1: Creating the Account

To set up a new user account, follow these steps:

1. Select **System ▶ Administration ▶ Users and Groups**.

2. Once the Users Settings window appears, click **Add**. If asked for your password, type it into the box, and click **Authenticate**.

3. In the Create New User window that appears (Figure 8-1), type a new username in the Short Name box; I'm using *graphika* for my example. In the Name field, you can type whatever you like; I'm using *Graphics Lover*.

4. Click **OK** to add the new user. A Change User Password window will appear.

5. The Set password by hand option should be selected. Type a password for the new user; you should put numbers and letters in the password to make it more difficult to guess. Retype the password in the Confirmation box to confirm your choice, and then click **OK**.

6. You'll be taken back to the Users Settings window (Figure 8-2). Select the new *graphika* account from the list on the left of the window, and then click the **Change** button next to where it says *Account type*.

7. In the window that appears, give yourself the ability to install software and perform other administrative tasks in the new account by selecting **Administrator**. Click **OK** to return to the main Users Settings window.

8. Click **OK**, and close the Users Settings window. The new account should be ready to use.

NOTE *Normally, the privilege to install software and perform other system-wide changes (Administrator) is not selected by default on new user accounts, since you probably don't want your kids, workmates, or anyone else with their own user account on your computer installing all sorts of weird stuff and screwing up your system settings. We need it here because we're going to be installing things, though.*

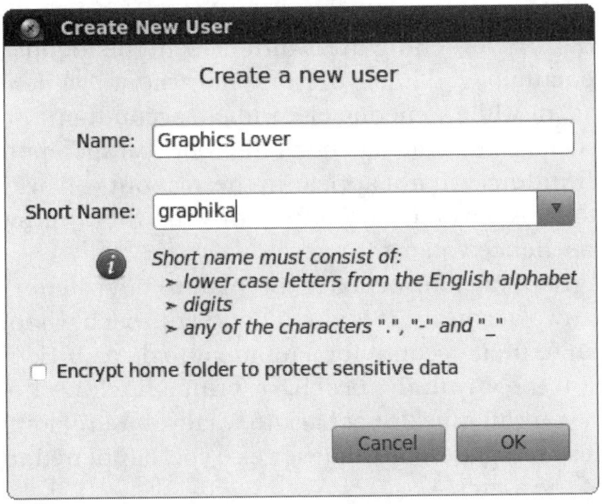

Figure 8-1: Creating a new user account

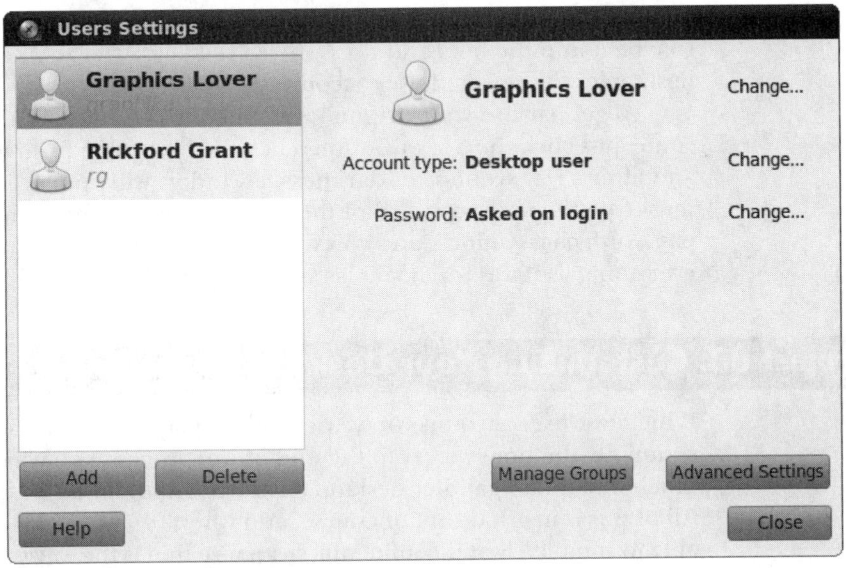

Figure 8-2: The new user account displayed in the Users Settings window

8A-2: Logging In to Your New Account

To use this new account, click the power button at the far right of the top panel, and click **Log Out**. A countdown will appear, but you can skip that; just click the **Log Out** button. After a few seconds, you will be back at the login screen. Click your new username in that window, type the password for the account, and press ENTER. You will soon be at the new, untouched desktop of your just-created user.

When you log out of a user account, all the programs you have running will be closed—if you were planning to use a different account for only a few minutes, it can be annoying to have to open everything again when you get back to the original account. Fortunately, there's an alternative: You can temporarily *switch users*. Switching users differs from the logout/login approach, in that you remain logged in to your original account while you log in to your other account (or while someone else with an account on your computer logs in to theirs). Going this route keeps all the windows and applications you have open. These windows will not appear in the account you are switching to, but they will be there, conveniently waiting for you, when you switch back to the account from whence you came.

This is a good way to proceed if you plan to be switching back and forth between your two accounts. It is also a good approach when, say, your child needs to log in to their account for a moment to do a quick email check, burn a CD to play on the way to the beach, or print a file for school. When your child is done, you can quickly get back to what you were doing without having to reopen files, web pages, or whatever else you happened to be dealing with at the time of the switch.

You can switch users quite easily by clicking the power button on the top GNOME panel and selecting the user account you want to switch to. After a few seconds you'll be asked for the password for the account you selected, so type it into the box, and press the ENTER key. After that, you will be at the desktop of the selected user account.

To get back to your original user account after going the switch-user route, just click the power button, click the username from which you came, and after a few seconds of darkness, a window will appear into which you must type the user password of the account you are returning to. Type your password, click **Unlock**, and you will be back at your original desktop, with everything as it was when you last saw it, open windows and all. Pretty cool.

Project 8B: Customizing Your Desktop Environment

Whichever user account you've decided to play with, you are now ready for action. By the time we get to the end of the process, you will have created a much wilder and gaudier desktop environment than you've ever seen before. All of this is in good fun, of course, and when you are done, you should be able to completely and confidently customize things the way you want on your own. So, let's go.

8B-1: Adding Emblems to Folders

One of the coolest things about Nautilus is that it allows you to add little folder-top icons called *emblems*. These emblems can graphically remind you what each folder is for, and they're not only for folders—you can add them to files too. The look of these emblems also changes when you change your desktop themes, so you're in for more visual excitement later in this chapter. For now, however, let's learn how to use them by adding one to the *Documents* folder. Open your home folder, right-click **Documents**, and then select **Properties** in the pop-up menu. When the Properties window appears, click the **Emblems** tab, and scroll down until you see the emblem called *Personal* (Figure 8-3). Click the checkbox next to it, and then click the **Close** button. The emblem should now appear on your folder.

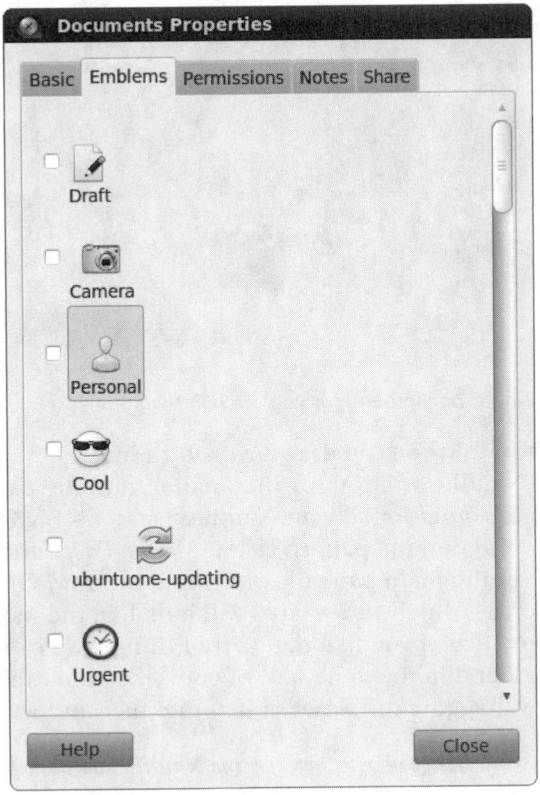

Figure 8-3: Choosing emblems for your folders

Now, for additional practice, try adding the Sound emblem to your *Music* folder. Just use the same steps as before, and substitute the appropriate items and entries. When you're finished, you should have a *Music* folder that is surrounded by musical notes—one is the emblem, the other is the folder's default icon. Not all folders have default icons, so that's when emblems really come in handy.

8B-2: Setting Window Backgrounds (and Emblems Again)

Once you've added those two emblems, your folders should look a bit spunkier (and you'll make those emblems look spunkier still later in the chapter). Nevertheless, the background of the Nautilus window is still plain and white. You need not stand for that if you don't want to; you can change it as well. To do so, just go to your home window, click the **Edit** menu, and select **Backgrounds and Emblems**. The Backgrounds and Emblems window will then appear (see Figure 8-4).

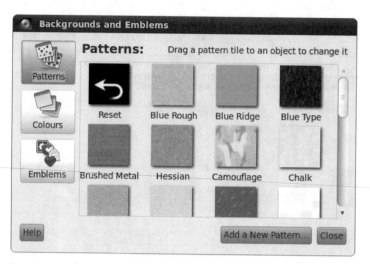

Figure 8-4: Choosing a background for your Nautilus window

From this window, you can drag any pattern into your home window, or into any other Nautilus window for that matter, and the pattern will then become the background for all your Nautilus windows. So, for experience's sake, scroll down to find the pattern called *Manila Paper*, and then drag it to the whitespace in the main pane of your home window. Once you've done that, the previously white window area will look like the wallpaper in a lawyer's office. Very nice, if you like that sort of thing. You can change it to a different background in the same way, of course, or you can go back to the default white by dragging the **Reset** swatch into the window.

NOTE   *If you prefer to use an image of your own for the Nautilus window background, you can do so quite easily. Just locate the image in a new Nautilus window, click it with both the left and right mouse buttons (or just the middle mouse button, if you have a three-button mouse), and then drag the image to any open space within the target window. When you release the buttons, select **Set as Background** in the pop-up menu that then appears.*

In addition to the buttons for pattern and color swatches, there is a third button in the Backgrounds and Emblems window called *Emblems*. Clicking the Emblems button reveals all the emblems you saw in Project 8B-1, thus providing you with another way to add them to your folders. This method is far handier when adding emblems to several folders or files in the same go.

To see how this works, click the **Emblems** button. Then drag the **Camera** emblem onto your *Pictures* folder and the **People** emblem onto your *Public* folder. The selected emblems will immediately appear on those folders, adding to the growing proliferation of icons in the window.

8B-3: Dolling Up the Side Pane (and Emblems Yet Again)

Now let's change the look of the Nautilus side pane. Keeping the Backgrounds and Emblems window open (if you already closed it, open it again), click the **Places** menu button in the Nautilus side pane, and select **Information**.

You can add a different background pattern to the side pane now as well, but for practice let's add a color instead. To do this, click the **Colors** button in the Backgrounds and Emblems window. The window will now be filled with swatches of color. Drag the **Grapefruit** swatch to your side pane, and it will turn from gray to, of all things, grapefruit (albeit a very dark and unusually colored grapefruit). You can also create a two-color gradation effect by adding yet another color. Drag the **Mango** swatch to the very bottom of the side pane (but still within the pane), and you should have a grapefruit-to-mango, top-to-bottom gradation within the pane. Of course, if you are not pleased with this tropical color set, you can get back to your original default gray panel by dragging the **Reset** swatch onto the area. When you're done, you can close the Backgrounds and Emblems window.

The side pane of your Nautilus window provides yet a third way to work with emblems. But before I let you in on this third (and last) way, let's add another folder to your home folder. Create a folder and name it *Finances*, which you can use to store files dealing with your relative worth in the modern scheme of things.

After you've created the new folder, go to the side pane, click the **Information** drop-down menu, and select **Emblems**. A list of emblems will appear within the side pane. Select the **Money** emblem, and drag it onto your *Finances* folder. Next, select the **Plan** emblem, and drag it onto the *Finances* folder too. Add even more emblems to it if you like—you should be able to fit about four on there before Nautilus decides to end the madness and prevent any more from being displayed. Your window should now look something like the one shown in Figure 8-5.

Once you are done, go back to the drop-down menu, and select **Places** to get everything back to relative normalcy again.

Even if it's not your cup of tea, you have to admit that your Nautilus window is definitely more colorful now. You can, of course, change it to look however you want, but I'll ask you to hold off on that a little while longer, because you are going to be doing some more playing around with it shortly.

8B-4: Changing the Desktop Background

Now that your home folder window is all gussied up (or gaudied up, depending on your aesthetic sense of things), you may think your desktop looks rather drab in comparison.

You can easily change the desktop background (often called *wallpaper*) by right-clicking any open space on the desktop and selecting **Change Desktop Background** in the pop-up menu. This will open the Appearance Preferences window, opened to the Background tab (see Figure 8-6).

Figure 8-5: Selecting emblems from the Nautilus side pane

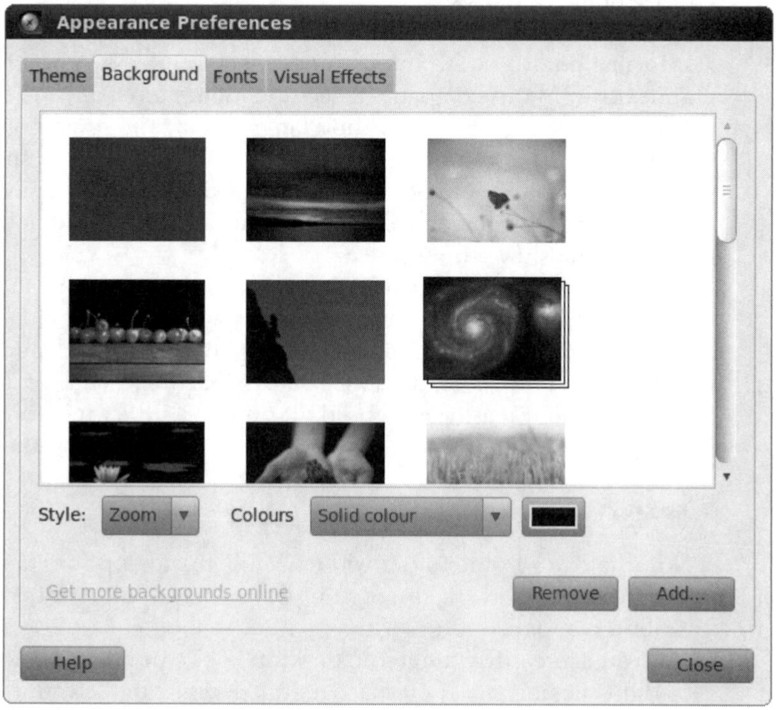

Figure 8-6: Changing your desktop background

Installing Additional Wallpapers

As you can see if you hover your mouse over it, the default wallpaper in Ubuntu is called *Ubuntu*. If purple blobs aren't your style, click any of the other wallpapers to immediately change the wallpaper on the desktop. There are quite a few to choose from, but maybe you'd prefer to use some images of your own. These could be photos from a digital camera, works of art you created on your computer, or just about anything you want to put there. In this case, however, you are going to venture out onto the Web to get and then install some wallpaper.

A number of sites provide free desktop wallpaper—two sites specifically geared toward Linux users are *http://www.gnome-look.org/* and *http://art .gnome.org/*, but you can get wallpaper from wherever you like. Astronomy Picture of the Day (*http://apod.nasa.gov/apod/*) is a particular favorite of mine. If you want to follow along using the same bigger-than-life-Tux wallpaper that I use here, however, go directly to the wallpaper image by pointing your web browser to *http://www.taiabati.com/linux/OLDindex.php/*, scrolling down the page a tad to the second TUX section, and then clicking the download button next to the image size that best matches your screen. When the picture appears in the browser window, right-click it, and then select **Save Image As**. In the Save Image window, give it an easy-to-remember name (*wall_TUX-2_1024 x768.png* may be exact, but it might prove a bit much to deal with after a while), or use the one I gave it, *mightyTux.png*, and click **Save**. If you prefer, you can download any wallpaper you like from wherever you like, as long as it is in a supported format, such as BMP, PNG, or JPEG. It's all up to you.

Once you've downloaded your wallpaper, move it from your *Downloads* folder into your *Pictures* folder. You may want to create a *Wallpapers* subfolder to keep things better organized, but that's up to you, too. After that, you can install the new image by going to the Background tab in the Appearance Preferences window and clicking the **Add** button. In the Add Wallpaper window that then appears, navigate to your new wallpaper, click it once to highlight it, and then click **Open**. The wallpaper will then appear highlighted in the Appearance Preferences window and will soon thereafter appear on the desktop (Figure 8-7). Once it does, click **Close** to complete the process.

Wallpaper from Internet to Desktop—Quick and Easy

It's also possible to almost automatically set an image from the Web as your desktop wallpaper by right-clicking that image within your web browser and then selecting **Set As Desktop Background**. A small window will then appear, in which you can preview what the download will look like onscreen (Figure 8-8). You can also adjust the position (tiled or centered, for example) and background color for your desktop in this window. Once you're done making adjustments, click the **Set Desktop Background** button. The image will then appear on your desktop, while the image file will be saved to a download location (your home folder, by default) with the title *Firefox_wallpaper.png*.

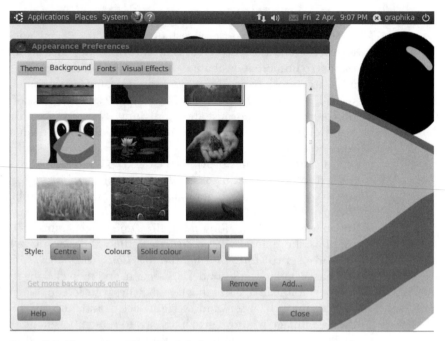

Figure 8-7: The newly wallpapered desktop

Figure 8-8: Selecting web page images as desktop wallpapers

8B-5: Hiding the Bottom Panel

You may have noticed that you can barely see the panel at the bottom of the screen in Figure 8-7. This is because the panel obscured the bottom of the new wallpaper, which irritated me. I went to the Panel Properties window by right-clicking some empty space in the bottom panel and selecting **Properties** in the pop-up menu. In the Panel Properties window, I clicked the **Autohide** checkbox and then clicked **Close**. The autohide function works just like it does in Windows or Mac OS X—the panel stays out of view until you move your mouse into the general vicinity of where it should be. You can make the same change if you like, but that is an aesthetic matter that I will leave up to you. Ah, the sweet taste of artistic freedom.

8B-6: Downloading and Installing the Art Manager (GNOME Art)

Searching the Internet for wallpaper to install can in itself be a rather fun adventure, but sometimes it can also feel like quite a chore. Fortunately for you, me, and all involved in such things, there is an even easier way: the Art Manager. The Art Manager, also known as GNOME Art, is a handy application that searches the *http://art.gnome.org/* site and downloads a list, with thumbnails, of all the wallpapers that are available there. It can also do this for the various window borders, controls, and icon theme sets that you can use in the following parts of this project. Using the thumbnail lists, you can easily download and install whatever you want—all without ever placing a cursor in your web browser. Needless to say, the Art Manager is decidedly cool!

Unfortunately, the Art Manager is not installed by default. However, after having gone through Chapter 6, you know how easy it is to download and install applications like the Art Manager. All you have to do is run the Ubuntu Software Center, search for *gnome-art*, and then install the Art Manager.

You can then run the Art Manager by selecting **System ▶ Preferences ▶ Art Manager**. The GNOME Art window will then appear with absolutely nothing in it. To put it to use and relieve that emptiness, select **Art ▶ Backgrounds ▶ GNOME**. (You can select **All** instead of GNOME if you like, but it will take longer to download the list of available wallpapers.)

Once you've made your selection, the Art Manager will begin downloading a list of all that is available for you at *http://art.gnome.org/*. It may seem like nothing is happening for a minute or so, but that is normal; just hang in there. It might take a few minutes to download previews of the backgrounds, but when it's done, you will see a list of thumbnails for you to choose from (Figure 8-9).

You can now install wallpaper by scrolling down until you find one that suits your fancy, clicking it once to highlight it, and then clicking the **Install** button. The Art Manager will then download and install it. After that, open the Appearance Preferences window, and choose the wallpaper you just downloaded as your desktop wallpaper. As I said before, the Art Manager is a very handy tool to have, especially since you'll be using it more soon within this project.

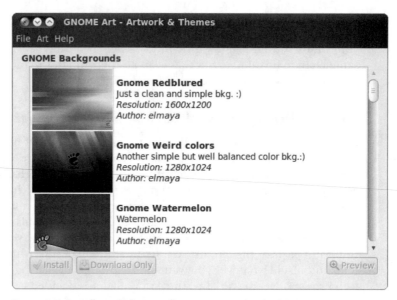

Figure 8-9: Installing desktop wallpapers using the Art Manager

8B-7: Changing Window Borders, Controls, and Icon Sets

Now we get to my favorite part of this journey through the world of digital cosmetic surgery—changing the way window borders and controls look in GNOME. The procedure is really quite easy. Select **System ▸ Preferences ▸ Appearance**. The Appearance Preferences window will open to the Theme tab, showing you a list of the themes that are installed on your system (see Figure 8-10). The default theme in Lucid Lynx is called *Ambiance*, but, as you can see, there are several others.

To get the hang of things, take a look at each of the themes listed by clicking them one by one. The changes will take effect immediately. Just clicking a theme will change your window borders, controls, and even, if you take a peek in your home folder, the icons. This is especially noticeable when you click Dust Sand or New Wave.

Each theme consists of a window border, a set of controls, and a collection of icons. It's also possible to mix and match these elements on your own. For example, let's say that you like the subdued look and color of the controls in Dust, but you prefer the window icons in Clearlooks and the borders in Dark-Room. Well, you needn't despair, because you can create a custom theme consisting of these three different elements.

To create your own mix-and-match theme, just click the **Customize** button on the Theme tab of the Appearance Preferences window. A new window will open, in which you will find five tabs: Controls, Colors, Window Border, Icons, and Pointer (Figure 8-11). From within each of these tabs, you can select the components you prefer. For now, let's first click the **Controls** tab and select **Dust**. Then click the **Window Border** tab, and select **DarkRoom**. Finally, click the **Icons** tab, and select **GNOME**.

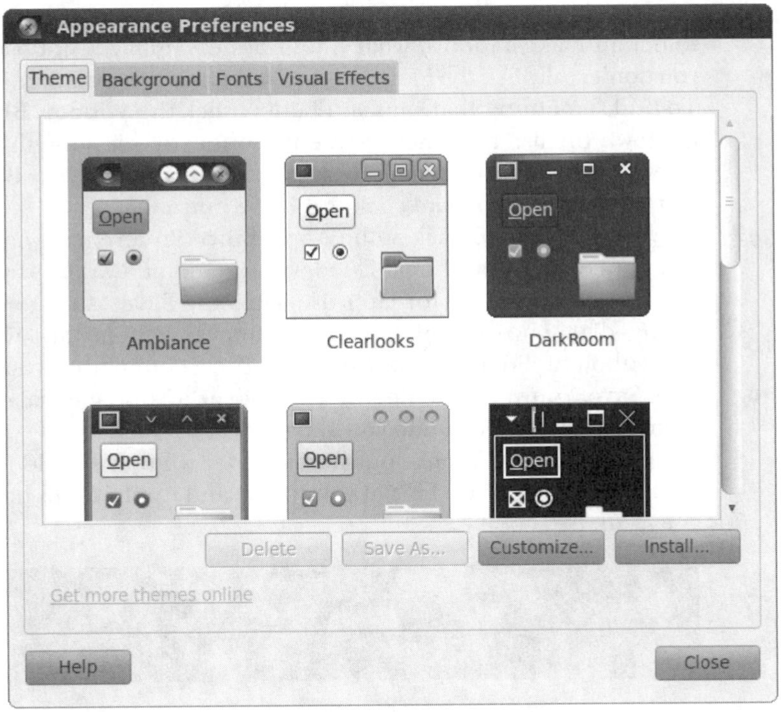

Figure 8-10: Selecting a theme in GNOME

Figure 8-11: Creating a custom theme in Ubuntu

Now keep the Customize Theme window open, but open your home folder and take a look at what you've done. Hmm . . . not bad. But, perhaps you don't really like the look of those DarkRoom window borders all that much. To find something that suits you better, click the **Window Border** tab again, go down the list, and click each entry until you see something you do like (New Wave seems to do the trick for me) and select that. Better? Now that you are satisfied, you can click the **Close** button.

You will now be back at the Appearance Preferences window, where you will notice your new theme listed with the name *Custom*. If you want to save this new combination for later use, click the **Save As** button. Doing so will open a dialog box in which you can name your theme and write a brief comment about it. So, name your theme, write a comment if you like, and then click **Save**. Your new theme will now appear in alphabetical order within the theme list under the name you chose.

Once that's all done, your home folder window should look like that in Figure 8-12 (and take a look at your panel and Applications menu while you're at it). Ah, très cool!

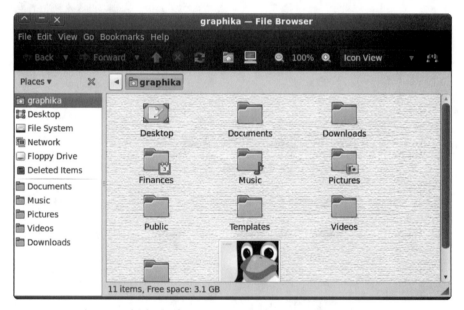

Figure 8-12: Changing the look of your system windows

8B-8: Installing Additional Window Borders, Controls, and Icons

If you are excited about this customization thing but you're not satisfied with the theme choices included with the system, you can download and install still other window borders, controls, and icons. To show you how to do this, I will walk you through creating a faux Mac theme, which will look fairly similar to the standard Aqua theme of Mac OS X, as you can see in Figure 8-13.

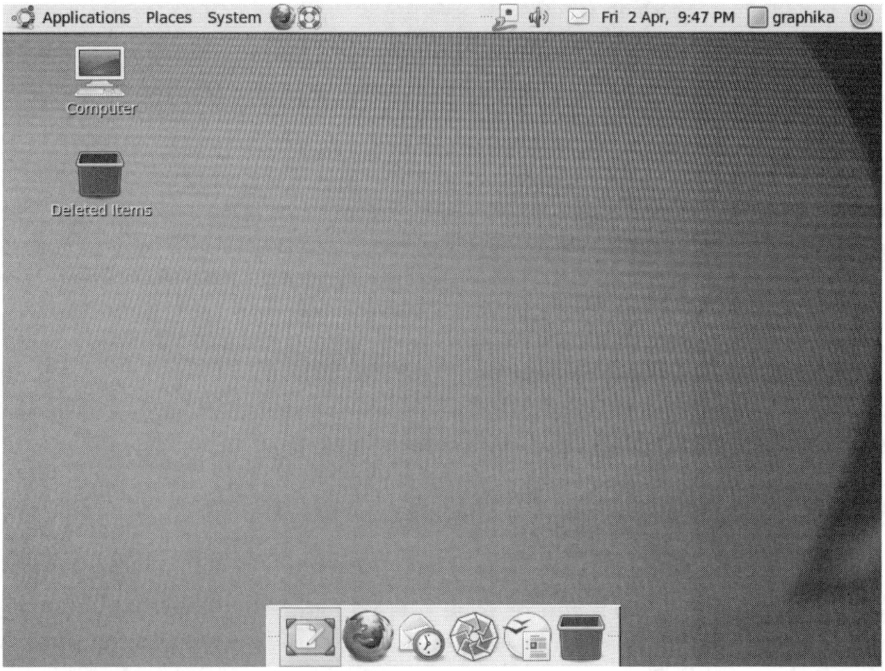

Figure 8-13: An "Aquafied" Ubuntu desktop

Getting and Installing the Files You'll Need

To get the files you'll need to do this, take the Art Manager for another ride. Once it is up and running, select **Art ▸ Backgrounds ▸ Other**. Once the list of available wallpapers appears in the Art Manager window, scroll down until you find one called *Real shoot*, install it by clicking the **Install** button, and then select and apply it on the Background tab of the Appearance Preferences window.

NOTE   *If the Art Manager does not automatically start downloading a list of available files when you make a selection from the Art menu, just restart the Art Manager and try again.*

Next, get a set of matching application control widgets and window borders by selecting **Art ▸ Desktop Themes ▸ Application** in the Art Manager. When the list is downloaded, look for a file called *Yattacier 3*, and install it. In the Appearance Preferences window that then appears, select **Yattacier 3** in the list on the Theme tab.

To round things up, let's add some new icons to the mix by returning to the Art Manager and selecting **Art ▸ Desktop Themes ▸ Icon**. Once the list has finished downloading, look for and install Snow-Apple. After that, it's basically a repeat of the previous step, but this time around, click the **Icons** tab in the Customize Theme window, and then select **Snow Apple**.

Finishing Touches

Well, things are certainly sort of Mac-ish now, but there is even more we can do to emphasize the effect. Open the Panel Properties window for your bottom panel by right-clicking a blank area of the panel and selecting **Properties** in the pop-up menu. In the **General** tab of that window, uncheck **Expand**, and then increase the size of the panel to about 54 pixels. When you're done, click **Close**, and then start adding launchers for the applications you use most. You might also want to remove the Workspace Switcher and the Window List to complete the effect. Right-click the little dotted or ridged bit immediately to the left of where the names of currently open windows are displayed and choose **Remove From Panel** to get rid of the Window List, and right-click any of the set of four boxes on the bottom panel and choose **Remove From Panel** to remove the Workspace Switcher.

NOTE *If you'd like a more OS X–ish Dock, plenty are available; try Avant Window Navigator, Cairo Dock, or Docky, all of which are available via the Ubuntu Software Center. You must have Visual Effects turned on (that is, set to Normal or Extra) on the Visual Effects tab of the Appearance Preferences window in order to use these.*

Once you're done, go to the top menu, and remove the two icons next to the System menu. After that, add a Window Selector applet so that you have some way to navigate through your open windows. You might also want to change the background in your home folder, since the warm tones currently there no longer match your new cooler configuration.

The transformation is now complete, but you can also add trash can and computer icons to your desktop by going on to Project 8B-10, after which your desktop should look something like mine back in Figure 8-13. You can stick with your new OS X–ish theme or switch to something else. For consistency's sake, I will switch back to the default theme now. By the way, if you do decide to keep the faux Aqua theme, remember to click the **Save As** button in the Appearance Preferences window and give the theme a name.

8B-9: Changing the Order of the Window Buttons

If you're used to Windows, you might be finding the order of the buttons at the tops of windows a little . . . weird. Instead of having your minimize, maximize, and close buttons at the top right of the window, Ubuntu puts them at the top left. I don't mind this layout so much, but if you're struggling with it, you'll be glad to know it's easy to change them to the right:

1. Press ALT-F2 to open the Run Application window.
2. Run the GNOME Configuration Editor by typing `gconf-editor` in that window and then pressing ENTER.
3. When the Configuration Editor window appears, click the small + next to *apps*, scroll down to *metacity*, and click the + next to that.
4. Click **general** in that expanded metacity section to display a set of options.

5. Scroll down to the *button_layout* option. It should be set to *close,minimize, maximize:* at the moment—this gives the order of the buttons (for example, the maximize button is the third one along) and the side of the window that they appear on (for example, all three are on the left side of the colon, so the buttons will appear on the left of the window).

6. To get the buttons into the familiar Windows order, click the *value* of the button_layout option to start editing it. Type `:minimize,maximize,close` in place of the old value.

7. Press ENTER to finish editing, and the window buttons in all your windows should switch sides immediately (as shown in Figure 8-14).

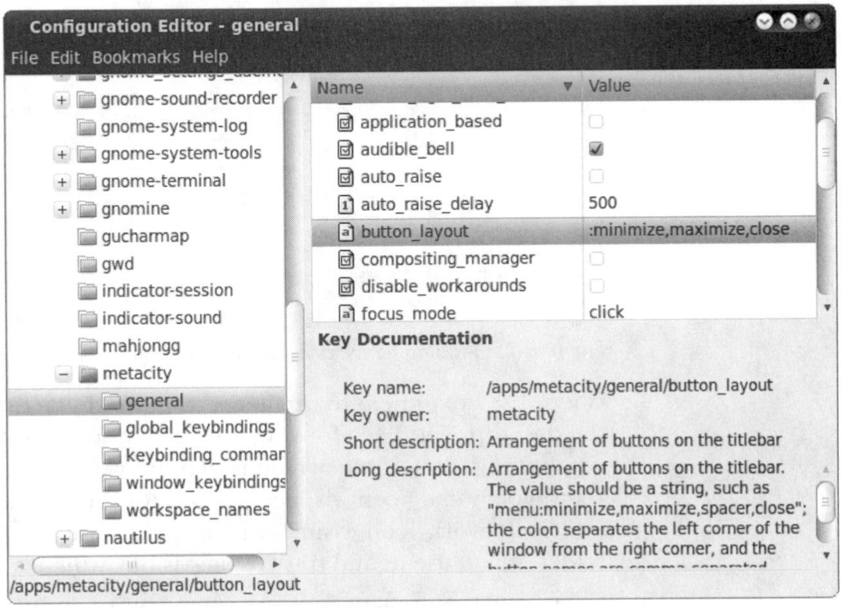

Figure 8-14: Putting the window buttons on the right side of the window

8B-10: Placing Home and Trash Icons on the Desktop

As you are already aware, unlike Windows, Mac OS X, or other Linux distributions, Ubuntu has a completely empty desktop upon installation. A lot of people advocate this approach because it discourages the permanent use of the desktop as a location to store files and program launchers. After all, as the argument goes, you don't place your trash can or file cabinet on the desktop in your office, do you?

All such logic aside, many people prefer to have their trash can, hard disk, and home folder on their desktops, thank you very much. If you are one of them, as I am, here's what you need to do:

1. Open the GNOME Configuration Editor, as you did in "Project 8B-9: Changing the Order of the Window Buttons" on page 138.

2. Click the + next to *apps*, scroll down to *nautilus*, and click the + next to that.

3. Click **desktop** in the nautilus section, after which the options for that item will appear in the right pane of the window (Figure 8-15).

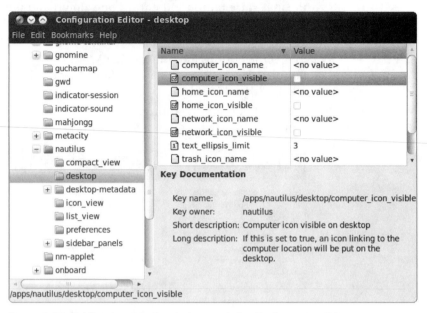

Figure 8-15: Adding icons to the desktop with the Configuration Editor

4. Check the boxes next to the items you would like to appear on the desktop. You have four unchecked choices to choose from: computer_icon_visible, which is like the (My) Computer folder in Windows; home_icon_visible, which is for quick access to your home folder; network_icon_visible, which is to create a link to your Network folder, if you use it; and trash_icon_visible, which is for you-know-what.

5. Check any that look useful, and when you're done, close the Configuration Editor.

8B-11: Stretching Desktop Icons

A pretty cool feature in the GNOME desktop is stretchable icons. This allows you to make individual desktop icons any size you want, which can be not only aesthetically pleasing but also quite functional. For example, you could stretch one of your most commonly used launchers to make it easy to locate, or you could stretch the thumbnail of a photo file so that it appears as desktop art (see Figure 8-16).

To stretch a desktop icon, right-click the icon, and select **Stretch icon** in the pop-up menu. Four blue squares will appear at each of the corners surrounding the icon (as shown in Figure 8-17). Just click and drag any of those squares until the icon is the size you want. Once you are done stretching, click anywhere on the desktop, and the squares will disappear. If you have second thoughts and want to revert the icon to its original size, right-click it, and choose **Restore Icon's Original Size** from the menu.

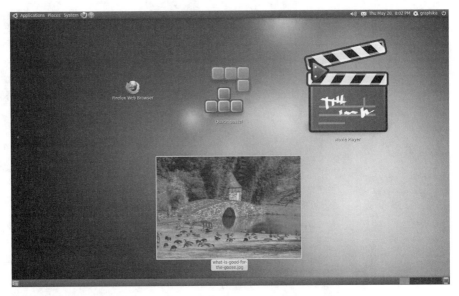

Figure 8-16: Desktop icons can be stretched to any size you want.

Figure 8-17: Stretching a desktop icon

8B-12: Doing It All Again!

Now that you're equipped with the necessary know-how to customize just about everything, it's time to say goodbye to *graphika* and start work on your own user account. Click the power button at the top right of the screen, select **Log Out**, and then click the **Log Out** button to get back to the login screen. Now, log in to your usual user account and begin the task of imposing your sense of style on the place. . . .

Font Feathered Frenzy: Changing Your Fonts

By now Ubuntu should be starting to feel a little more *you*; you've got your favorite desktop wallpaper, chosen the most appealing window borders, and added icons galore . . . so what else is there to tweak? Why, your fonts, of course! Most of the time you look at your computer screen will be spent reading, so it's only logical to want to spruce up the text too. To get started doing this, select **System ▶ Preferences ▶ Appearance**, which will open the Appearance Preferences window again. Click the **Fonts** tab in that window to see the options available to you (Figure 8-18).

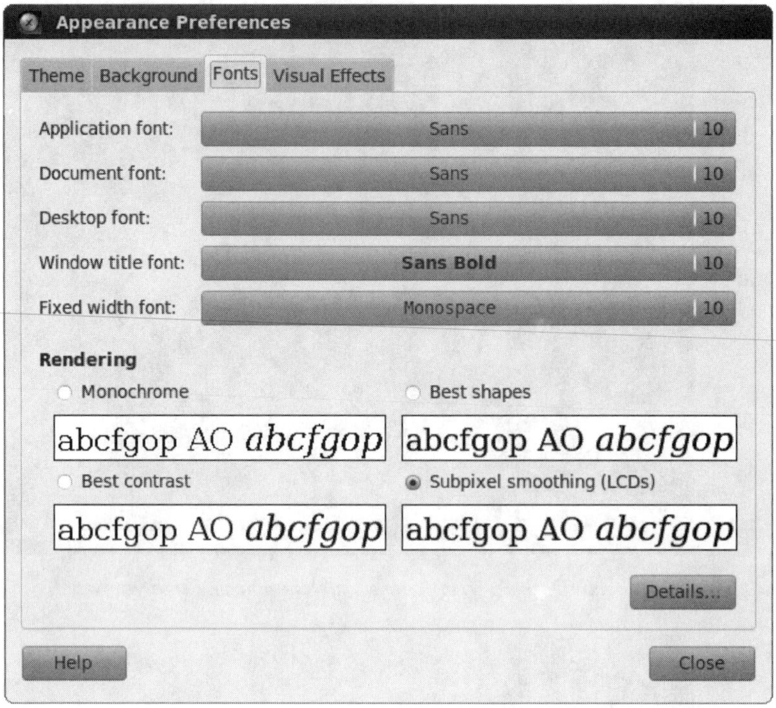

Figure 8-18: The Fonts tab

As you can see, you can specify font preferences in five categories: applications, documents, desktop, window titles, and the Terminal (fixed width font). To change any of these, just click the corresponding font button, and a Pick a Font window will appear. This lets you choose the font family, style, and size, and it will preview your current selection at the bottom of the window.

Once you click **OK,** the choices you make take effect immediately, so you will soon know whether you can live with them. Unlike the other aspects of customization, those choices could drive you stark raving mad. Sure, it is easy and fun to live with the gaudiest desktop imaginable, the wildest and most mismatched color scheme on the planet, and the goofiest icons ever to be seen by post-Neanderthal man, but if your font selections get too out of hand, watch out! You do have to be able to read the results, after all.

The fonts you see on your screen generally look quite smooth and clean. If you are using an LCD monitor, however, you may find that fonts will look even better if you select **Subpixel smoothing (LCDs)** in the Rendering section of the Font tab in the Appearance Preferences window. If you're not sure whether you need to do this, just give it a try to see whether you notice any difference. GNOME applies the changes immediately upon selection, so if you keep a window with text in it open behind the preferences window, you can easily see the effect of each of your selections as you make them.

Your Ubuntu system comes with a wide variety of very usable and, at least to my eyes, rather handsome TrueType fonts. However, these tend to be a bit on the conservative side of the aesthetic spectrum, and many users will want to add a few more distinctive fonts to the system repertoire. In my own case, I had this really cool idea of writing messages to my friend in old Scandinavian runes. (Of course, my friend wet-blanketed the idea, so it all came to naught. . . .)

You probably won't be interested in sending cryptic, runic messages to your friends, but you may want to print an award for an event using some sort of Gothic font, or you might be preparing a newsletter for the local chapter of your snail-breeders society and want to use a font that is round, bubbly, and slimy. Whatever your penchant, purpose, or desire, you will probably come to the point when you want to install some other TrueType fonts on your system, so in this project I'll tell you how to do just that.

How you install fonts depends on who is going to use them. If you have only one user account on your machine, the easiest way is to install the fonts locally, as described in "Project 8C-2: Installing Fonts Locally" on page 144. Locally installed fonts are ones that only you or someone logged in to your user account will be able to use. On the other hand, if you have more than one user account and want the fonts to be available to all the users on your machine, you'll need to install them globally—in this case, see "Project 8C-3: Installing TrueType Fonts Globally" on page 145.

8C-1: Getting the Font Files

The Internet is awash in free fonts. For this project, I will point you to the *http://www.fontfreak.com/* site, which has a very nice collection of fonts. Once you get to the FontFreak home page, click the **Fonts** link under the "FREE FONTS" heading on the left side of the page. The next page will ask you whether you want to download all the free fonts on the site in one single file; click **No thanks, I will download them one by one**. This will lead you to the main list of free fonts; browse through the various pages until you find one that is to your liking, and then click it. Which font you download is completely up to you, but be sure to choose the PC version, not the Mac version. You can do this by clicking the Windows icon at the bottom of the font page (next to where it says *Download*). When the download window pops up, choose **Save File** and click **OK** to save the font as a *.zip* file. To follow along with this project, download a couple of fonts—I chose Aajax Surreal Freak and Accidental Presidency.

When you've finished downloading, drag the font files from the *Downloads* folder (or wherever you saved them) to your home folder so it's easy to follow along with my instructions. Also, be sure to unzip your font files before going on to the installation steps. (Right-click each *.zip* file, and choose **Extract Here**.)

8C-2: Installing Fonts Locally

If you're the sole user of your computer, installing fonts locally will do just fine. To get started, you need to set up your system by providing it with a location to place your fonts. You will need to do this only the very first time. Here's what you must do:

1. Open your home folder, and, in that window, create an invisible fonts folder by selecting **File ▸ Create Folder**.

2. When the folder appears, name it *.fonts* (the period before the name means that it will be hidden).

3. Hide the new folder by clicking the **Reload** button. Your *.fonts* folder should no longer be visible. If this is the case, you can close the window—your setup was successful.

Now that everything is set up, let's continue with this project using one of the fonts you downloaded. After you've decided which font to use, follow these steps:

4. Choose the unzipped font file (its name probably ends in *.ttf*), and copy it by right-clicking and selecting **Copy**.

5. Press CTRL-L, or select **Go ▸ Location**. This will display the location bar in Nautilus.

6. In the location bar, type **~/.fonts**, and press ENTER. The ~ sign is a shortcut that means "my home folder."

7. You should be taken to the empty *.fonts* folder you just created, like the one in Figure 8-19. Right-click anywhere in the folder, and select **Paste** to copy the font into the folder.

Now that you have installed your font, you can give it a try in one of your applications, such as OpenOffice.org Writer. (Any running applications need to be restarted before the new font will appear in that application's font menu.)

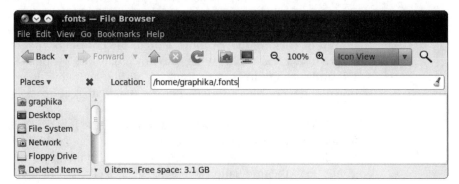

Figure 8-19: The empty .fonts folder

8C-3: Installing TrueType Fonts Globally

As I mentioned earlier, the font you just installed locally can be used only when you log in under your usual username. If, however, you want to install fonts that can be used by you and anyone else who has an account on your computer, the process is slightly different and will require a little "superuser" action. You can use the other font you downloaded for this part of the project.

The folder for globally installed fonts is in root territory, so you will need to open the file browser as superuser in order to install the fonts. *Superuser* is another name for the root (administrative) user. It's possible to run a program as root without switching to a different user account by using a system called sudo (more on this in Chapter 9), but since root can modify important system files, you shouldn't run a program in sudo mode unless you absolutely must.

Here are the steps for getting your font file into the global font directory:

1. Press ALT-F2, and then type `gksudo nautilus /usr/share/fonts/truetype` into the box that appears. Click **Run**, and type your password if prompted.

2. A File Browser window will open. Select **File ▸ Create Folder** to create a new folder; call it *MyFonts*.

3. Open a normal File Browser (Nautilis) window by selecting **Places ▸ Home**, find the *.ttf* font file you want to install, and copy it (for example, by right-clicking it and selecting **Copy**).

4. Switch back to the truetype File Browser window, open your newly created *MyFonts* folder, and paste the font file into it.

5. Be sure to close the superuser File Browser window—leaving it open is a recipe for disaster!

NOTE   *The gksudo command in Step 1 is the graphical environment version of the non-graphical sudo command that you will learn to use via the command Terminal in Chapter 9.*

Now you can test things by opening OpenOffice.org and looking for the font in the font menu. Remember that you will need to restart OpenOffice.org if it was already open when you installed the font.

Project 8D: Changing Your Login Screen

There's always a holdout. You may have gotten your desktop and windows looking just the way you like, but the screen that's displayed when you log in hasn't changed one bit—it's still the same old default theme, with the same old default background. It's time to give it a makeover.

The login screen, also known as the *greeter*, is shown to everyone who has a user account on your computer, so you might want to check with others before making some of the following cosmetic changes. If you're the only person who uses the computer, then ask yourself for permission and carry on.

8D-1: Beautifying the Login Screen

The software that displays the login screen is called GDM, and it has its own hidden user account on your computer. This might seem a little strange, but this is the way lots of Linux programs do things when they are shared between several users. What you need to do now is log in to this hidden user account and change the settings for GDM. Fortunately, it's a pretty straightforward process and doesn't even require you to log out of your own account:

1. Press ALT-F2 to open the Run Application window.

2. Type `gksu -u gdm dbus-launch gnome-appearance-properties` into the box, as shown in Figure 8-20.

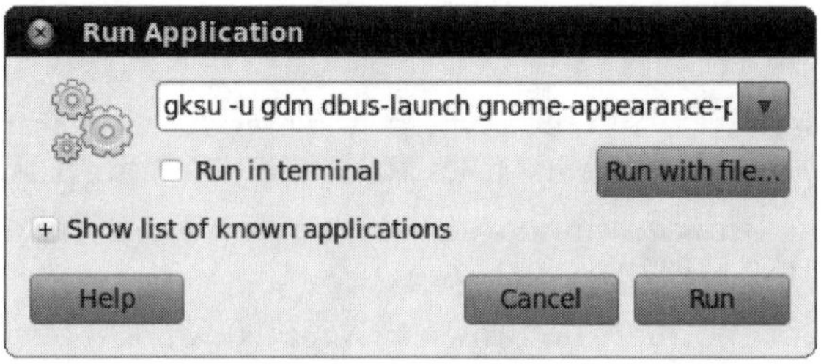

Figure 8-20: Typing the command into the Run Application window

3. Click **Run**. You'll be asked for your password, so type it, and click **OK**.

NOTE *Some extra icons might appear on your panel when you perform this step. Don't worry, they're harmless and will disappear when you log out and log back in again.*

4. The Appearance Preferences window should appear. This Appearance Preferences window works the same way as the one you used earlier in this chapter.

5. Use the Background tab to change the wallpaper that appears behind the login screen and the Theme tab to change how the login window looks.

6. When you're happy with your changes, click **Close**, and log out of your user account to get back to the login screen and inspect your changes.

Take a look at Figure 8-21 to see what you can do. I changed the background to a delicious-looking picture of cherries and the login window to the browny-orange Human theme, for a slightly more rural feel.

Figure 8-21: Changing the way the login screen looks

8D-2: Adding a Picture to Your User Account

Aesthetics aside, it's time to make things a little more *personal*. What better way to do this than by adding a picture to your user account? Select **System ▸ Preferences ▸ About Me**, and when the window appears (Figure 8-22), click the button that looks like a blank face. The Select Image window will appear—choose one of the stock images from the list, or use the pane on the left of the screen to find a picture from elsewhere (a passport photo, perhaps). Now, click **Open** to finalize your selection, and the picture will appear next to your username in the About Me window.

While you're there, fill out some of the other information if you like. It's not used for very much, but as anyone who has ever possessed a permanent marker knows, it can be fun to stamp your identity all over your things. When you're finished, close the About Me window. The picture you chose will be displayed next to your username on the login screen the next time you start the computer (as you can see in Figure 8-21).

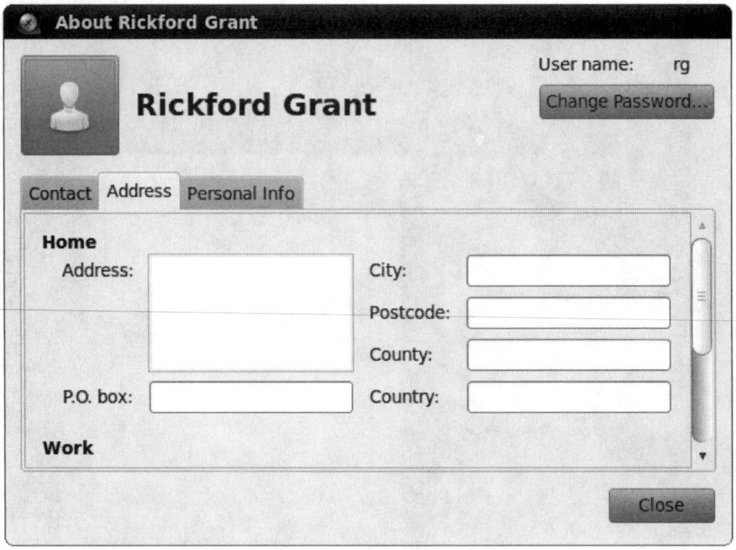

Figure 8-22: The About Me window

8D-3: Logging In Automatically

While you're tinkering with the login screen, it seems like a good idea to mention some of the other login-related options that you can change. Log in to your user account again, and select **System ▸ Administration ▸ Login Screen**. Click the **Unlock** button, and type your password to gain access to the settings in the Login Screen Settings window that appears.

If you're the only person who uses the computer, you can save time by having your user account automatically log in when the machine starts up. Select the **Log in as** option, and choose your username from the drop-down list (it should be selected automatically). If you're not the only user but you're the person who uses the computer for most of the time, there's also a setting to give other people a chance to log in before you're logged in automatically. Check **Allow 30 seconds for anyone else to log in first**, and change the amount of time you'd like GDM to wait before logging you in.

The last option in this window (the one talking about default sessions) can be used to switch between different *desktop environments*. As you know, Ubuntu uses the GNOME desktop by default, but you can install others like KDE and Xfce instead. That's a bit of a teaser for you would-be geeks out there—if you want to perform the ultimate customization and change the whole desktop environment, this is one of the settings you're going to need to change. Changing desktops is beyond the scope of this book, though, so I'm just going to leave it there! (If you're interested in trying a different desktop environment, you might find *https://help.ubuntu.com/community/FromUbuntuToKubuntu/* useful.)

NOTE   *If you're not keen on the sound that plays every time you log in, uncheck the* Play log-in sound *option in the Login Screen window.*

When you're happy with your changes, close the Login Screen Settings window, and restart your computer for the changes to take effect. Then, depending on which option you chose, either you'll be logged in straightaway or an Automatic Login button will appear and count down the seconds until it logs you in. In the latter case, you can stop the automatic login by selecting a different username.

Choosing a Screensaver

Screensavers used to be a must-have (and must-use) item for computer users who wanted to prevent damage (burn-in) to their monitors. Video display technology, however, has now advanced to the point where screensavers are no longer necessary. Nevertheless, screensavers are cool to look at, and plenty are available online to supplement the 15 that come installed by default. Right out of the box, the screensaver is set up to merely blank your screen after 5 minutes. However, you can also choose to have the various screensavers switch randomly every few minutes, or you can opt for a single screensaver that you especially like. You can change these settings by selecting **System ▸ Preferences ▸ Screensaver**, after which the Screensaver Preferences window (Figure 8-23) will appear.

NOTE   *If you'd prefer a screensaver with a more personal touch, choose the* Pictures *folder option from the list on the left of the window. This will display a slide show of all the photos in your* Pictures *folder when the screensaver is activated.*

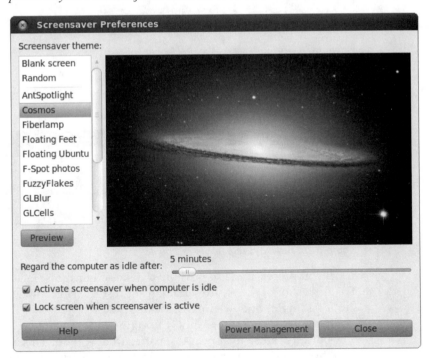

Figure 8-23: Setting screensaver preferences

Taking Screenshots

Now that you know how to make your Ubuntu desktop look a bit more like your own, you might want to share or record the results of your artistic endeavors, and taking screenshots is the way to do just that. The easiest way to go about this is by selecting **Applications ▶ Accessories ▶ Take Screenshot**.

The Screenshot application, shown in Figure 8-24, will appear. In this window you can decide whether you want to take an image of the whole screen, a section of the screen, or a selected window. You can also apply a delay before the screenshot is taken to give yourself some wiggle time. You can even add effects to your window shots, such as a drop shadow.

Figure 8-24: Taking a screenshot in Ubuntu

When you're ready, click Take Screenshot, and a window like the one in Figure 8-25 will appear. In that window, you can name the image and decide where to save it.

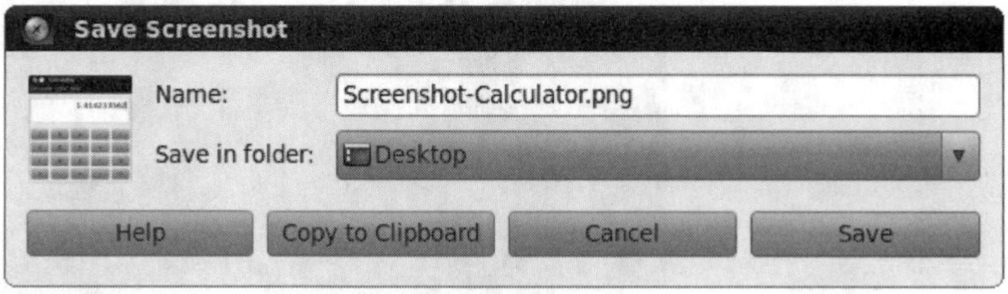

Figure 8-25: Saving a screenshot in Ubuntu

If you prefer, it is also possible to take screenshots via key combinations. To take a shot of the entire screen, just press the PRINT SCREEN key. To take a shot of a single window, press ALT-PRINT SCREEN.

If you try taking screenshots of single window, you may find that the window borders refuse to appear no matter what you do. This is not a problem with the screenshot mechanism but rather a side effect of your system's visual effects engine, Compiz, which I'll talk about more in the next section. One solution is to use the GIMP for your screenshot-taking chores (discussed in Chapter 13). Alternatively, you can just shut off Compiz: Select **System ▸ Preferences ▸ Appearance**, and click the **Visual Effects** tab in the Appearance Preferences window that appears. Once on that tab, select **None** (Figure 8-26); the change should take place almost immediately, and once it does, you can close the Appearance Preferences window and try taking your screenshot again.

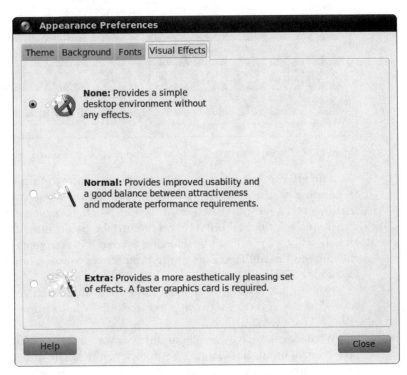

Figure 8-26: Shutting off Compiz using the Visual Effects tab

Customizing Visual Effects

Having learned how to customize your system using the more traditional tools at your disposal, it's time to let loose and have some fun with some of the newest customization tools the Linux world has to offer. Compiz, Ubuntu's visual effects engine, provides all sorts of wild and interesting visual effects for your desktop.

Compiz will be automatically enabled at startup only if you have a graphics card that supports its basic set of features. An easy way to tell whether Compiz has kicked in on your machine is to open any window (your home folder, for example) and then check to see whether that window has a drop shadow (see Figure 8-27 for an example). If it does, Compiz is at work.

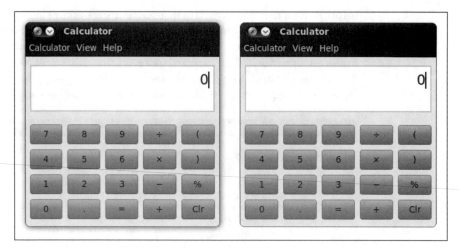

Figure 8-27: The window on the left has a drop shadow; the one on the right does not.

The effects that are active by default are really the tip of the iceberg. Depending on the capabilities of your graphics card, you will get the drop shadows and a few other bells and whistles, such as cooler window-opening transitions, but that's about it . . . on the surface, at any rate. If you like, you can kick the effects up a notch by selecting **System ▸ Preferences ▸ Appearance**, clicking the **Visual Effects** tab of the Preferences window, and finally selecting **Extra** in that tab.

I should warn you not to be freaked out at first when you try to move your windows and they start wiggling like jelly—that's one of the additional effects (Wobbly Windows).

Whatever the hardware capabilities of your system, if you really want to take control of all that Compiz has to offer, it is worth your while to install the CompizConfig Settings Manager (Figure 8-28), which you can get via the Ubuntu Software Center (search for *Advanced Desktop Effects Settings* and install it). Once it's installed, you can run it by selecting **System ▸ Preferences ▸ CompizConfig Settings Manager**.

Once the CompizConfig Settings Manager is installed, you can see everything Compiz is capable of doing, and you can pick and choose from those features as you see fit. Although most of what Compiz has to offer is essentially eye-candy (which is what this chapter is all about, after all), there are some functional utilities and extras. A favorite of mine is the Annotate tool, which allows you to write all over your screen while making presentations, brainstorming, or just flipping out (shown in Figure 8-29).

To activate the Annotate tool—or any other Compiz feature—open the CompizConfig Settings Manager, and check the box next to its name. To figure out how to actually use what you've enabled, click the name of the feature. This will open a tab showing its settings, including the keystrokes needed to initiate that feature (Figure 8-30).

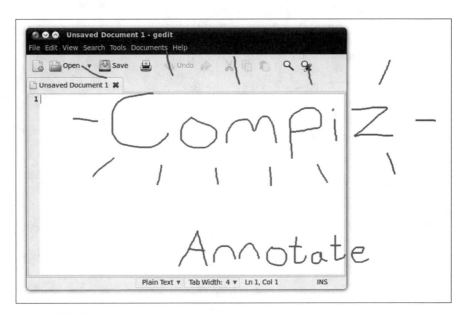

Figure 8-28: Taking control of Compiz's special effects

NOTE   *Some of the keys used for the default Compiz shortcuts may seem unfamiliar; of these, the most commonly used ones are the* Super *key (typically the Windows key on your keyboard) and* Button1 *(usually your left mouse button).*

Figure 8-29: Compiz's Annotate tool in action

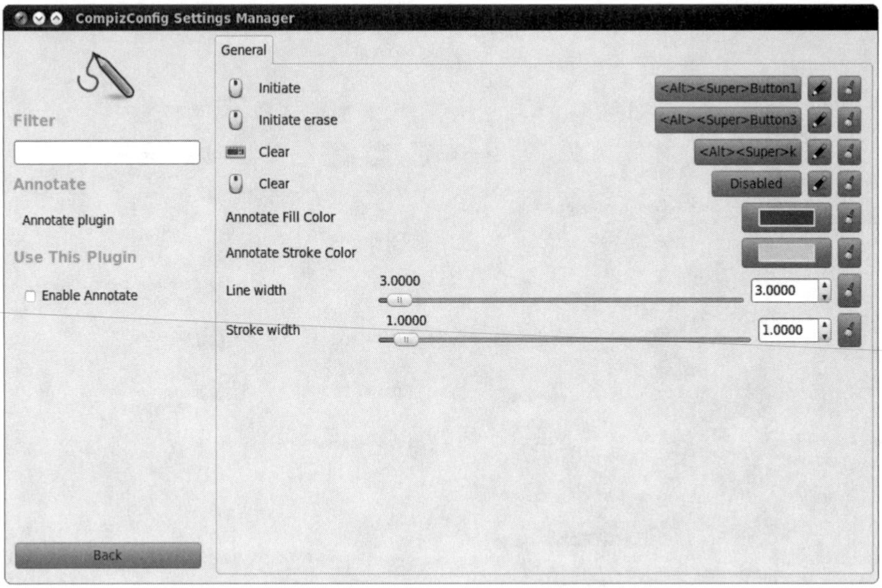

CompizConfig Settings Manager
General
Filter
Annotate
Annotate plugin
Use This Plugin
Enable Annotate
Back
Initiate
Initiate erase
Clear
Clear
Annotate Fill Color
Annotate Stroke Color
Line width
Stroke width
3.0000
1.0000
<Alt><Super>Button1
<Alt><Super>Button3
<Alt><Super>k
Disabled
3.0000
1.0000

Figure 8-30: Almost every Compiz feature has its own settings.

You can also edit the various keystroke combinations by clicking the button where the current keystroke combination is shown and then making your new choices in the Edit window that appears (Figure 8-31). When you're done with the settings for an individual feature, click the **Back** button in the lower-left corner of the CompizConfig Settings Manager window to go back to the main screen.

Edit Initiate
Enabled
Shift
Super
Ctrl
Alt
Button1
Cancel
OK

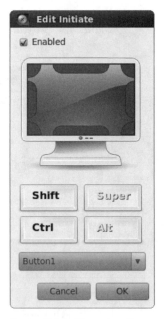

Figure 8-31: Changing the keystroke combination used to initiate a Compiz feature

9

SIMPLE KITTEN WAYS

Getting to Know the Linux Terminal and Command Line . . . and the Cool
Things It Can Do

 Many people shy away from Linux because
they envision it as a system for compu-geeks,
an environment in which you do everything
the hard way—by command line. In this era of graphical interfaces, the idea of typing commands to get
things done seems like a dreadful throwback to the
days of DOS, and that puts many people off, especially
those who remember what it was like in the "old days."

This reaction is fair enough, but it is not really an accurate reflection of
the reality of the Linux world. After all, most Linux users today utilize some
sort of graphical interface. They can, and often do, achieve all that they
hope to achieve through drop-down menus and mouse clicks alone. Many
are able to survive quite happily without ever once opening their Terminal.
The same could be true of you.

Be that as it may, there is still much to be said for the power and convenience of the command line. The fact that the command line can now be utilized within a graphical environment also makes it much less forbidding. The Terminal is just a tiny text-based island in a sea of graphical bodies (see Figure 9-1). Using the command line can be as pain-free as anything else you do on your system, and it can actually provide you with a little fun if you are willing to give it a try.

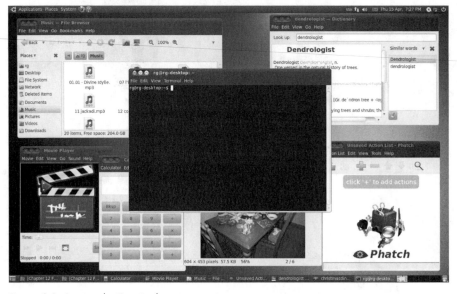

Figure 9-1: Putting the Terminal in perspective

Unfortunately, many guides to using the command line are written by hard-core command-line junkies, whose enthusiasm for what they see as a really good thing inadvertently makes what they write seem even more off-putting to the recent Linux immigrant or wanna-be.

For your sake, I will try to curb my own enthusiasm so as not to scare you right back to Chapter 6 and the more comfortable world of the Ubuntu Software Center. I will also try to help you keep things in perspective by teaching you, whenever possible, to use the command line as a complement to the various graphical tools that you have at your disposal, rather than presenting it as the sole way of going about things. Of course, I am not going to cover every possible angle in this regard—just enough to give you some exposure and experience and, ideally, make you feel at least a little more at ease with the command line. Who knows; could you actually come to think of using the command line as . . . fun? Well, I won't get too carried away.

Meet the Terminal

You can run the Linux command-line Terminal application in your Ubuntu system by selecting **Applications ▸ Accessories ▸ Terminal**. When the Terminal opens, it will, in all its simplicity, look much like Figure 9-2.

Figure 9-2: The Terminal application

As you can see, all it says is `rg@rg-desktop:~$`. In this case, `rg` is my username, `rg-desktop` is the name I gave my computer during installation, and the tilde (`~`) signifies that I am in my home folder. If it were to say `~/Music`, for example, it would mean that I am currently in the *Music* folder within my home folder. Of course, all this will be different in your case, because your username and computer name will be different. If your username is *frog* and your computer's name is *wetrock*, for example, the command line will say `frog@wetrock:~$`. If all this is sounding rather obtuse to you, just think of it this way: *username*@*computer_name*:`~$` in the Terminal is the equivalent of your home folder in Nautilus.

Typing in the Terminal is straightforward enough; you just type as you usually do. You can also delete and insert letters or phrases by using the DELETE and BACKSPACE keys and the arrow keys. For practice, try the following:

1. Type **I like strawberries so very much**.
2. Change `strawberries` to `cherries` (because cherries are, in fact, so much better). Just use your left arrow key to move the cursor in front of the first *s* in `strawberries`.
3. Tap your DELETE key as many times as necessary to erase the word `strawberries` (uh, that would be 12 times, methinks).
4. Type **cherries**, and then use your right arrow key to move the cursor back to the end of this meaningful sentence.

Now that you've completed this fascinating bit of typing practice, press the ENTER key. As you will almost immediately see, the Terminal's response to your efforts thus far is merely a dismissive `I: command not found`. Although you've typed a string of text that has meaning to you, it means absolutely nothing to your system. In fact, the system was so shortsighted that it could see nothing other than the first word you typed in the Terminal (`I`); and because `I` is not a valid command, the system had no idea what do to with it.

Some Goofy Yet Useful Fun with the Command Terminal

A rather cool thing about typing in the command Terminal is that it has what you might call *short-term memory*. Try it by typing the word **cherry** and then pressing ENTER. Ignoring the command-not-found message, go on and type **vanilla**, and press ENTER. Now type **gelato**, and press ENTER. So far, so dumb, right? Well, not really. Let's type everything we've typed thus far again, but this time let's do it with only one key.

Huh?

Yes, just press the up arrow key once, and what do you see? That's right—the last command you typed appears, which in this case would be gelato. Press the up arrow key again, and the command that you typed before that will appear—vanilla. One more time? Yes, cherry. And one more time for the grand finale . . . I like cherries so very much.

Considering what we have thus far, this may all seem a bit silly, but imagine that you're not typing goofy little words and instead have to deal with considerably longer strings, such as a simple copy command (which you'll learn about later in this chapter) like this:

```
cp Photos/mypics/stpierre/coastal/onthebeach1_27.jpg /home/frog/
photos_for_mom/stpierre
```

By typing that string, you are copying an image called *onthebeach1_27.jpg* from the *coastal* folder to another folder called *stpierre*. If you wanted to copy another photo in the *coastal* folder, *onthebeach1_16.jpg*, for instance, you could simply press the up arrow key once, use the left arrow key and DELETE key to move over to and delete the 27, and replace it with **16**. All in all, it would be much simpler and much faster. It would also help you avoid mistakes in typing. Not so dumb anymore, eh?

Nontoxic Commands

As you now know, all of this typing is easy enough, but to actually do something useful with your Terminal, you need to type commands—and there are more of them than you could ever hope or need to know. To get you started, we will begin with some commands that are easy to understand, nontoxic, and completely kitten-friendly.

$ whoami

There is no command as easy, safe, or even as seemingly useless as whoami. Rather than help those with multiple-personality disorders discover who they are at any given moment, the whoami command simply tells you which user is currently logged in. Try it by typing whoami after the $ and then pressing the ENTER key. Remember that commands are case sensitive.

The Terminal will now tell you the username of the person currently logged in. If you are logged in as *frog*, you should get frog as the answer to your command.

$ finger

If you enjoyed discovering who you are with the whoami command, then you might enjoy finding out even more about yourself using the finger command. You can use the finger command in a number of ways, but a very simple one is finding out about a particular user. Try this on yourself by typing **finger** and then your username. In my case, that would be **finger rg**. Once you've typed the command, press ENTER, and see what you get. You can see my results in Figure 9-3.

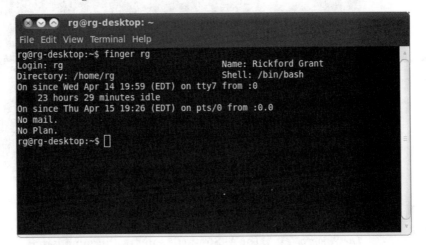

Figure 9-3: Output from the finger command

As you can see, my login name is *rg*, my real name is Rickford Grant, my home directory is */home/rg*, and I am using the Bash shell for typing my commands. I have been logged on since Wednesday, April 14, at 19:59 Eastern daylight time (EDT), and I've had my Terminal session open since Thursday, April 15, at 19:26. I have no mail or plan. It doesn't tell you my Social Security number or my mother's maiden name, but it is pretty cool, don't you think?

What Is a Shell?

As you noticed, I mentioned that the results of the finger command showed I was using the Bash shell, so you may be understandably wondering just what Bash is. Well, Bash (Bourne Again Shell) is one of the many shells that are used in Linux systems, and it's the one that happens to come with your Ubuntu distro (and most others, for that matter). A *shell* is a program that interprets the commands you type into the Terminal and delivers them, so to speak, to your system so that it can act upon them. I like to think of it as a command-handling subsystem, for which the Terminal acts as a graphical frontend.

What Is a Plan?

I also mentioned that the results said I had no plan, so you may also be wondering what that is all about. A *.plan* file is a small file kept in your home folder that other users see when they use the `finger` command on you. Traditionally, a *.plan* file contained information about where you were going to be or what you were working on. These days, however, most people use them to leave odd little messages, quotations, or whatever, much as they do in email signatures. Take a look at Figure 9-4 to see what happens after I add a *.plan* file to my home folder.

Figure 9-4: Output from the `finger` command with a plan

You can now see my plan, which is a quotation from Kurt Vonnegut's *The Sirens of Titan* (or Al Stewart's song by the same name, for that matter), though you can put anything you want in your own. You will get the chance to create your own plan file in Project 9A, so if this all seems fun to you, just hang in there.

Before moving on, I should mention that you can also use the `finger` command to do a little domestic espionage of sorts. Let's say your child, Chris, has a user account on your machine. Chris, who wants your permission to go to the movies, claims to have been hard at work on the computer all day writing a report for school. Having your doubts, you could type **finger chris** to see what the facts actually are. It may be a bit underhanded and rotten, but it works. It also works both ways; others can check up on you as well. You can try it by seeing when the last time you logged in to your graphika account was (assuming you created such an account in Chapter 8). Just type **finger graphika**, and then press ENTER.

You can even use the `finger` command to find out facts about people on other systems, providing their network's finger service is active and you know their email address. Typing something like **finger *username@hostname.com*** would do the trick. It's kind of cool but also kind of spooky, I suppose.

$ pwd

If you know who you are but aren't exactly sure where you are, pwd (print working directory) should come in handy. The pwd command tells you exactly where the Terminal is in your directory tree.

Let's say, for example, that my Terminal is in my personal home directory (which is actually called *rg*) in the system's home directory (which is actually called *home* and which is where all the user account directories are located) when I use the pwd command; I would, after pressing the ENTER key, get / home/rg printed to my Terminal. You should get similar results if you try it.

NOTE *The word* print, *in this case, has nothing to do with your printer; it merely means that the response will be printed to, or displayed in, the Terminal.*

$ df

Another safe and easy, but much more useful, command is df (disk filesystem). The df command tells you how much disk space you have used, as well as how much space you still have available, on each of the partitions on your various mounted disks. Try it by typing **df** and then pressing ENTER. Your output should look something like that shown in Figure 9-5 (depending, of course, on the size of your mounted disks and how they are set up).

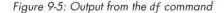

```
rg@rg-desktop: ~
File  Edit  View  Terminal  Help
rg@rg-desktop:~$ df
Filesystem            1K-blocks      Used Available Use% Mounted on
/dev/sda1             231812120   6146508 213890228   3% /
none                    1479036       240   1478796   1% /dev
none                    1483188       312   1482876   1% /dev/shm
none                    1483188        68   1483120   1% /var/run
none                    1483188         0   1483188   0% /var/lock
none                    1483188         0   1483188   0% /lib/init/rw
rg@rg-desktop:~$
```

Figure 9-5: Output from the df command

As you will notice, the sizes are given in kilobytes (KB) rather than the gigabytes (GB) and megabytes (MB) you are probably more used to, but there is a way around this. Many commands accept a *flag*, or *option*, to further fine-tune how the command performs. These flags are written directly after the main command and are preceded by a space and a hyphen.

In this case, you can try using the -h (human readable) flag to have your figures come out in the way you are most familiar with. Try this by typing **df -h** on the command line and pressing ENTER. The output should now appear in a more familiar format (see Figure 9-6).

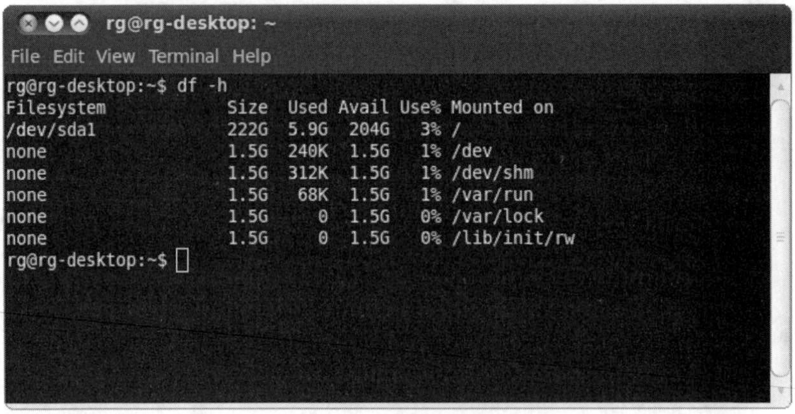

Figure 9-6: Output from the df command with the -h flag

$ ls

Another harmless but handy command is ls (list directory contents). The ls command shows you what is in your current directory. This is the nongraphical equivalent of double-clicking a folder in Nautilus to see what is inside. Try it by typing **ls** and then pressing the ENTER key.

If you've been following *my* commands so far, your results should list all of the folders in your home directory. You can also use the -R flag to show not only the list of files in the folder but also what is within the subfolders. Of course, you should have no subfolders in any of the folders you created in Chapters 7 and 8, so you can hold off experimenting with this for a while. Instead, try typing **ls -a** to see your invisible, or *hidden*, files.

$ calendar

I'll let you experiment with this one on your own. Just type **calendar**, and press ENTER to see the somewhat interesting results.

$ exit

The exit command is a simple one that allows you to exit the Terminal. Just type **exit**, and press ENTER. The Terminal window will close.

Commands with Some Teeth

The simple commands you have tried so far are all of the safe-and-sane, fire marshal–approved variety; they merely print information to your Terminal. Now you are going to try to get some real tangible results from the commands you use. These commands are also essentially safe and sane if you follow my instructions.

$ mkdir

You have already learned how to create folders by means of menus and your mouse, but you can also do this using the command line. The command is mkdir (make directory), and it is easy as pie to use (though I've never been quite sure how pie is easy).

To see how this command works and to work with the commands that follow, use the mkdir command now to create a folder called *command_exp* (for command experiments). All you have to do is type **mkdir command_exp** in a new Terminal window and press ENTER. The new folder should appear in your home folder, so go ahead and check to see whether it is there by clicking the home icon on your desktop.

OK, good, *bra, bueno!* Now let's create another new folder within that new folder—a *subfolder*, if you will. We'll call this one *sub*. So, just type **mkdir command_exp/sub**, and press ENTER. You can now take a peek and see whether the *sub* folder appears within the *command_exp* folder, if you like.

$ mv

The next command is the mv (move) command, but before you experiment with it, you need to create a dummy file—you need something to move, after all. You can do this by using another command—touch. To make the file—let's call it *expfile.txt*—go to the Terminal, type **touch expfile.txt**, and press ENTER. The new file will now appear in your home folder.

To move the file that you've just created, you will use the mv command, of course. Just type **mv expfile.txt command_exp/sub** (this tells the system which file to move and where to move it to), and press ENTER. The file will now be in your *sub* folder.

$ cd

Until now, you have been using the command line from your home folder. With the cd command, you can change your Terminal's location to another folder. This is a very handy command that you will be using quite a lot when doing the projects in this book. To take it out for a spin, let's get inside the *command_exp* folder by typing **cd command_exp** and pressing ENTER. If you've done this correctly, the prompt in your Terminal should now read *username@ computer_name*:~/command_exp$. If so, you can pat yourself on the back.

While you are there, you might as well try the ls command with the R (recursive) flag to see how that works. Just type **ls -R**, and press ENTER. Your Terminal should now show that you have a subfolder there called *sub* and a file inside that subfolder called *expfile.txt*.

That is all you really want to do in there for now, so to get back to your home directory, just type **cd** and press ENTER, which will take you back home, so to speak.

For future reference, it is worth noting a couple of other cd command shortcuts. If you are within a subfolder of a subfolder and want to move back a step (from */home/rg/peas/pudding* to */home/rg/peas*, for example), you can do so by typing **cd ..** (with a space between cd and ..) and pressing ENTER. You can also type **cd -** (with a space between cd and -) in order to get back to a directory where you were previously (from */home/rg* to */home/rg/peas/pudding*, for example).

$ cp

Being fickle, as humans are by nature, you might decide that not only do you want your *expfile.txt* file in the subfolder but that you also want a copy in your home directory, where it was in the first place. To copy *expfile.txt*, you can use the cp (copy) command.

To do this, the command needs to know where the file you want to copy is, what it is called, and where you want to copy it, which in this case is to your home folder. Normally you would type cp command_exp/sub/expfile.txt /home/ *username* to do this, but if you recall my mention of it near the beginning of this chapter, you can abbreviate the /home/*username* portion of the command string to ~/, which means the same thing and is an important tip to remember, because the tilde is frequently used in online instructions. Because reducing wear and tear on the fingers is always a desirable goal, type the following command, and then press ENTER:

```
cp command_exp/sub/expfile.txt ~/
```

Be sure to put a space between the file you are copying and its destination (in this case, between expfile.txt and ~/).

Once you've done this, you should have two copies of *expfile.txt*, one in your home folder and one in your *sub* folder. Go take a look to see the fruit of your endeavors.

$ rm

When you were a kid, you may well have experienced the joy of building a castle out of LEGO bricks and then the even greater joy of tearing the whole thing down (preferably by hurling D cell batteries at it). You will now embark on a similar move. The first tool in this nostalgic endeavor is the rm (remove) command, with which you can trash files.

The rm command, albeit very useful and easy to use, should be used with caution. Once you remove a file with this command, there is no going back— the file will not be placed in the Trash; it is gone for good.

To play it safe, let's try the rm command by getting rid of that new copy of *expfile.txt* that we just created in the home folder. The basic rm command structure consists of the command itself, rm, followed by the name of the file you want to remove. In this case, you want to remove the file called *expfile.txt* located in your home folder. Assuming your Terminal shows you to be home, remove the file by typing **rm expfile.txt** followed by a tap on the ol' ENTER key. The file will then be gone, and gone for good.

Now, double your pleasure by getting rid of the version of *expfile.txt* that is located in the subfolder *sub*. In this case, you need to specify where the file is because it isn't in the folder that the Terminal is in. Just type **rm command_exp/ sub/expfile.txt**, and then press ENTER. Oooh, very cool. Brings ya back, doesn't it?

$ rmdir

You will now continue the fun with the `rmdir` (remove directory) command, which is a bigger and more powerful version of the `rm` command.

You should use the `rmdir` command, like the `rm` command, with caution. There are no do-overs with `rmdir`. Once you remove a directory or folder with this command, it is gone for good.

To try this command, you can get rid of that *sub* folder you created. Type **rmdir command_exp/sub**, and press ENTER. The *sub* folder should now be gone. Finally, to round out the fun, use the `rmdir` command once more to get rid of the *command_exp* folder you created earlier. You've probably got it down by now, but just in case you don't, type **rmdir command_exp**, and then press ENTER.

$ chmod

In Chapter 7, you learned how to change file permissions via the Nautilus interface. This is without a doubt the easiest way to go about such things, but you might find times when it is easier to use the command-line approach.

The command for changing file permissions is `chmod` (change mode). To use it, just type the command followed by the permissions you want to extend to a file and then the location of the file itself. For example, let's say you copied a JPEG file, *mybirthday.jpg*, from a CD to the *personal* subfolder within the *Photos* folder on your hard disk, and the file is write protected. To change the file so that you have write permissions (meaning that you can alter the file), you would type the following and then press ENTER:

```
chmod 744 ~/photos/personal/mybirthday.jpg
```

To change the permissions of all the files and subfolders (and all the files within those subfolders) in one fell swoop, you can add the -R (recursive) flag to the `chmod` command. The command would thus be as follows:

```
chmod -R 744 ~/photos/personal
```

The number 744, by the way, extends read, write, and execute (run) permissions to you, the owner, but gives read-only rights to everyone else—a pretty safe choice when in doubt. If you want to figure out permission numbers for yourself, it is pretty easy. You are basically dealing with three number positions, each of which has eight numerical possibilities (0–7). The left slot represents permissions for the owner, the center slot represents permissions for the group, and the third slot represents permissions for others. The meanings of the numbers themselves are as follows:

7 Read, write, and execute permissions

6 Read and write permissions

5 Read and execute permissions

4 Read-only permissions

3 Write and execute permissions

2 Write-only permissions

1 Execute-only permissions

0 No permissions

Figure 9-7 points out the meaning of each of these numbers and what each number slot represents. In fact, if you don't mind a bit of simple addition, things are even easier to understand. To start with, remember that 1 = execute, 2 = write, and 4 = read. Add any of those numbers together, and you get the other permission combos. For example, 1 (execute) + 4 (read) = 5 (read and execute). As you can see, permissions aren't all that complicated.

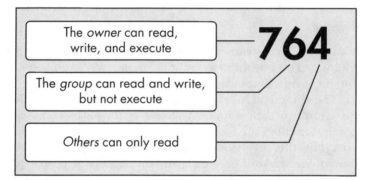

Figure 9-7: The meaning of permission numbers

Now if you're more of a letters than numbers sort of person, you'll be happy to know that there is another way to change permissions that is probably even easier. In this approach, you have to deal only with two groups of letters and the symbols + and -.

The first group consists of the following:

u User (owner of the file)

g Group (specified group of users)

o Others (anyone who is not the user or a member of the group)

a All (all of the above)

The second group consists of the following:

r   Read

w   Write

x   Execute

You might already be able to figure out how this is all going to work, but I'll spell it out just in case your intuition is worn out for the day. Let's say you want to change the permissions of a file (*butterhaters.txt*, for example) so that all users on your machine can read and write to it. After opening a Terminal window, you can make the change by typing `chmod a+rw butterhaters.txt` and pressing ENTER.

Oops! Just remembered that you don't want anyone changing the content of the file, eh? Well, to take back the write permissions for that file, you just need to type `chmod a-w butterhaters.txt` and then press ENTER. As you can see, the + gives permissions, while the - taketh away.

That's much simpler, you've got to admit.

$ sudo

When you ran the Ubuntu Software Center in Chapter 6, you were first asked to input your password before you could run the program. The reason for this, as I mentioned then, is that the Ubuntu Software Center installs the files it downloads in various folders throughout your system, almost all of which are write protected. By supplying your password, you are telling your system that you, as holder of the password, have the right to allow the Ubuntu Software Center to do that.

The command version of that same password-giving process is the sudo command. To perform an operation in a folder that is write protected, you would first type **sudo** and then the command you want to perform. For example, if you wanted to copy an icon image, let's call it *myicon.png*, to the globally located and write-protected *pixmaps* folder (*/usr/share/pixmaps*), you would type **sudo cp myicon.png /usr/share/pixmaps.**

After typing a command preceded by the sudo command and pressing ENTER, you will be prompted for your password. Once you type your password and press ENTER again, the command will be executed. I should mention that once you input your password, it will stay in memory for about five minutes. This means that you will not be prompted for your password when using the sudo command again within that time frame.

$ locate

Now that you are familiar with the sudo command, let's take it out for a spin by working with the locate command. The locate command is essentially a command-line alternative to the graphical Search tool found in the Places menu. Using the command is quite easy: Simply type the command followed by a space and the name of the file you want to find.

Before you can use this command, though, you will need to create a database of filenames for `locate` to use. This is where using the `sudo` command, along with yet another command, `updatedb`, comes into play. Just type **sudo updatedb**, and press ENTER. After you type your password when asked to do so, it will seem that nothing is happening for a while, but don't worry. As long as the cursor in your Terminal is blinking, progress is being made, and when your user prompt returns, you will have successfully created the database file. After that, you can use the `locate` command.

Oh, and in the future if you think that the process seems to be taking longer and longer, don't worry—it is. The more files and applications you add to your system, the longer it will take your system to catalog them all.

To take this new command for a test drive, let's look for the *openofficeorg3-writer.png* file that you worked with in Chapter 3. Just type the following, and press ENTER:

```
locate openofficeorg3-writer.png
```

Your results should look like those in Figure 9-8.

Figure 9-8: The results of a `locate` search

$ apt-get

Let's move on to a command that might seem a bit familiar to you: `apt-get`. Yes, this command is indeed a means of controlling the powerful package download and installation tool, APT, which I covered in Chapter 6. Although it might not be as pleasing to use APT via the command line as it is via the Ubuntu Software Center, doing so can come in handy. I'll cover the basics for you here.

Just for fun and to get a bit of nontoxic practice with `apt-get`, open a Terminal window, type **apt-get moo**, and press ENTER. The result of this endeavor, as you will see, is an example of another Easter egg lurking within your system (Figure 9-9). Useless, yes, but a safe first step in working with `apt-get`.

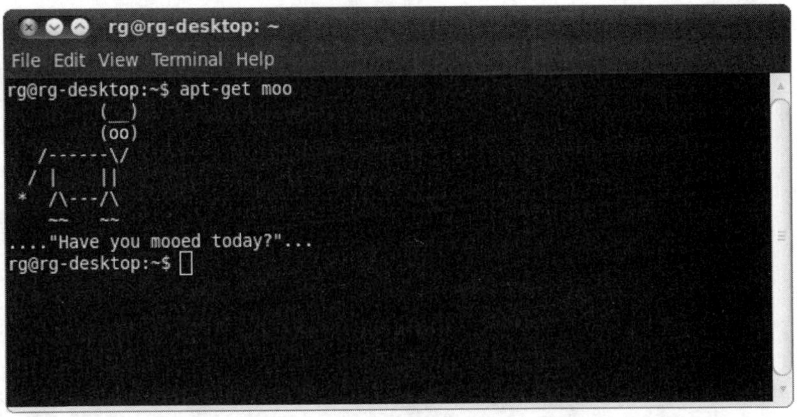

```
  ⊗ ⊙ ⊘    rg@rg-desktop: ~
 File  Edit  View  Terminal  Help
 rg@rg-desktop:~$ apt-get moo
          (__)
          (oo)
    /------\/
   /  |    ||
  *   /\---/\
      ~~   ~~
 ...."Have you mooed today?"...
 rg@rg-desktop:~$ ▯
```

Figure 9-9: Discovering an Easter egg via apt-get

To actually put the apt-get command to use, start by making sure to close any APT frontends you might have open, such as the Ubuntu Software Center. As I mentioned, you can run only one APT tool at a time. Once the coast is clear, you should always start out any operations involving apt-get with an update of the APT database so that you will be downloading the newest stuff. To do this, just type the command **sudo apt-get update**.

If you want to install a single package without heading over to the Ubuntu Software Center, you can do so by typing **sudo apt-get install** *package-name*. For example, if you want to download and install the Shufflepuck game clone, Tuxpuck, you would type **sudo apt-get install tuxpuck**. If you eventually get annoyed with Tuxpuck after having lost one too many times, you can uninstall it by typing **sudo apt-get remove tuxpuck**.

Finally, bearing in mind all the warnings offered in Chapter 6, if you want to upgrade your entire system via the command line, you can do so by typing **sudo apt-get dist-upgrade** (but only after doing a **sudo apt-get update** first).

$ aptitude

To wrap up this section, let's finish with an increasingly popular alternative to apt-get, called aptitude. One of the differences responsible for aptitude's popularity is that it is considered to have superior dependency handling to apt-get; in addition, it is arguably easier to use, because of its semigraphical interface (Figure 9-10). Because of this hybrid graphical interface, a lengthy discussion of how to use aptitude would take us from the main purpose of this chapter, which is learning to work with commands. That being the case, I will only briefly touch upon its use.

Start aptitude by typing **sudo aptitude** in a Terminal window and pressing ENTER. To install a package, you would click **Search** in the blue menu ribbon at the top of the window, select **Find** in the drop-down menu that appears, type the name of the package you are looking for in the search box, and then click **Ok** (Figure 9-11).

Figure 9-10: The semigraphical interface of aptitude

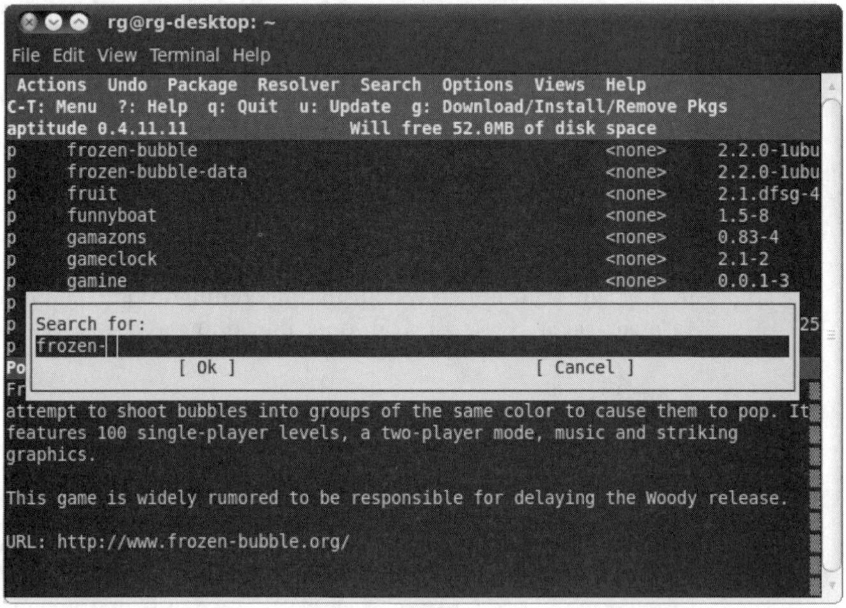

Figure 9-11: Performing a package search in aptitude

Back in the main aptitude screen, you would select the package you want, click **Package** in the blue menu strip at the top of the page, and then select **Install**. If you prefer, you can just press the + key after selecting the target package to accomplish the same thing. Your package should now appear in green text. You may select other packages to install at the same time in the same way. Once done, press G on your keyboard, and the download and installation process will begin. If you are first presented with a screen telling you that certain packages will also be installed or removed, read through that screen, and then press G again to move on to the actual installation.

It is also possible to use `aptitude` strictly in command mode in almost the same manner as apt-get, using pretty much the same arguments. To make sure the package lists that aptitude uses are up-to-date, you would start with the command **sudo aptitude update**. To install a package, such as the puzzle game Tangrams (aka gtans), you would type **sudo aptitude install gtans**. You would uninstall the package by typing **sudo aptitude remove gtans**.

A Couple of Other Biters You'll Be Using Soon

This is as good a place as any to introduce two more commands that you will be called upon to use in this chapter and elsewhere in the book: `ln` and `tar`. You needn't practice with these yet, because you will be using them very soon, but you might as well know what they are all about.

$ ln

You use the `ln` (link) command to create a link file that launches or activates another file located in a separate folder. This is very useful when trying to activate a file that is buried deep in the subfolder of a subfolder of a sub-folder somewhere on your hard disk. The command is very often used with the `-s` (symbolic) flag, which provides essentially the same thing as the short-cut you've come to know in Windows or the alias on the Mac.

The easiest way to use the `ln` command is to first use the `cd` command to change the Terminal's location to the folder where you want to place the link. Then you can type the `ln` command on the command line, followed by the path of the file to which you want to link. For example, let's say you want to put a link in your home folder for an OpenOffice.org Writer file of your autobiography called *myLife.odt*.

The file is pretty well buried in a nest of subfolders deep within your home folder: */home/username/Documents/personal/self/autobiography/myLife.odt*. To create the link, you would open a new Terminal window, type the following command string, and then press ENTER:

```
ln -s Documents/personal/self/autobiography/myLife.odt
```

Once you are finished, the link will appear in your home folder as an icon matching the original file in appearance, albeit sporting an arrow to signify that it is a link.

$ tar

In Chapter 7 you learned to create and extract archives, or *tarballs*, but did you know that you can also create and extract tarballs using the command line? The tar command is your key to doing this.

To create an archive, you would simply type **tar -cvf**, followed by the name the final tarball will be, and then the name of the folder or file you are trying to archive. For example, let's say you want to create an archive of your photos folder, and you want to call it *pics4pals*. In this case, you would type the following command and then press ENTER:

```
tar -cvf pics4pals.tar photos
```

As you no doubt noticed, there are some flags after the tar command in that string. The c tells the tar program to *create* a new archive. The v tells the program to be *verbose*, or, in other words, to tell you what it is doing in the Terminal as it is doing it. Finally, the f tells the program that what follows is the *file information*.

If, after creating the archive, you suddenly remember that there is one more file you want to add to the mix, you can use the -r flag to append the archive.

For example, to add a file called *cranky.png* to the archive, you would type the following and then press ENTER:

```
tar -rvf pics4pals.tar cranky.png
```

Of course, chances are that you will be doing more tarball extracting than creating, so you no doubt want to know how to do that. Fortunately, the process is pretty similar to what you use when creating the tarball. The main difference is in the first flag. Rather than using the tar command with the -c flag, you would instead use it with the -x flag, which tells the tar program to *extract* the specified archive. So if you want to extract a tarball called *spicyfood.tar*, type the following command, and press ENTER:

```
tar -xvf spicyfood.tar
```

What you have been doing thus far is creating and extracting archives, which are basically just collections of files. They are not, however, compressed. In fact, most tarballs you find will be compressed, and you can tell by the ending *tar.gz*. That *gz* means that the archive was compressed using the gzip program. Extracting a compressed tarball is just as easy as extracting a straight tar archive; all you have to do is add the -z flag, which tells your system to use the gzip program to decompress the archive. For example, if you want to extract a compressed tarball called *goosedown.tar.gz*, type the following command, and press ENTER:

```
tar -xzvf goosedown.tar.gz
```

Well, now that you know how to decompress and extract a gzipped tarball, you probably want to know how to create one. This is, again, little different than creating the tar archive itself; you would just add the -z tag to tell the program to use gzip to compress the folder. For example, to create a compressed version of your *Documentia* folder, which we'll call *tightdocs.tar.gz,* you would type the following and press ENTER:

```
tar -czvf tightdocs.tar.gz Documentia
```

It's worth mentioning at this point that you may also come across some files compressed with the bzip program. Such files are recognizable by some variation on the *.bz* or *.bz2* file extension. Dealing with these files should pose no problem, because the commands are almost identical to those for gzip. Just substitute -j for -z in the command string.

Compressing and Extracting Compressed Single Files

If you want to compress or decompress a single file, you don't really need to use the tar program at all, since its purpose is to create archives consisting of several files. You can instead use the gzip and gunzip commands directly. For example, to compress a file called *matilda.png,* you would type **gzip matilda.png** and press ENTER. The *matilda.png* file would then become *matilda.jpg.gz.* To decompress the file, you would type **gunzip matilda.jpg.gz** and press ENTER, after which the *matilda.jpg* file would be back to normal.

So, can you compress an archive you've already created with the tar command? Sure. For example, to compress the *spicyfood.tar* archive mentioned earlier, you would type **gzip spicyfood.tar**, and *voila*—you've got yourslf a compressed *spicyfood.tar.gz* archive. Pretty cool, don't you think?

Project 9A: Creating a Plan

Now that you have a bit of command experience, it's time to get some practice and put all those commands to good use. In this project, you'll start off easy by creating a *.plan* file, like the one mentioned earlier in the chapter.

The actual *.plan* file is a hidden file (as you can see by the dot before its name), which contains the plan or message that you add to that file. That message will appear in the output of someone's Terminal when they use the finger command to find out more about you. You may not need such a *.plan* file, but it is an easy enough way to get started working a bit more with commands and the Terminal itself, so let's give it a try.

To start out, you'll open the Terminal-based Pico editor to create the *.plan* file. To do this, open a Terminal window, type **pico .plan** (being sure to put a space between pico and .plan), and press ENTER. Your Terminal should now look a bit different, as you can see in Figure 9-12.

You will now be looking at your new, and totally empty, *.plan* file within the Pico editor. All you have to do now is type your plan or message. Once you've done that, press CTRL-X to exit the Pico editor, and it will ask you whether you want to save your work. You do, so type **Y**, after which you will be presented with a set of save options. You have already named the file *.plan,* as you can see near the bottom of the screen, so all you have to do is press ENTER. You will be back at your now-familiar user prompt in the Terminal window.

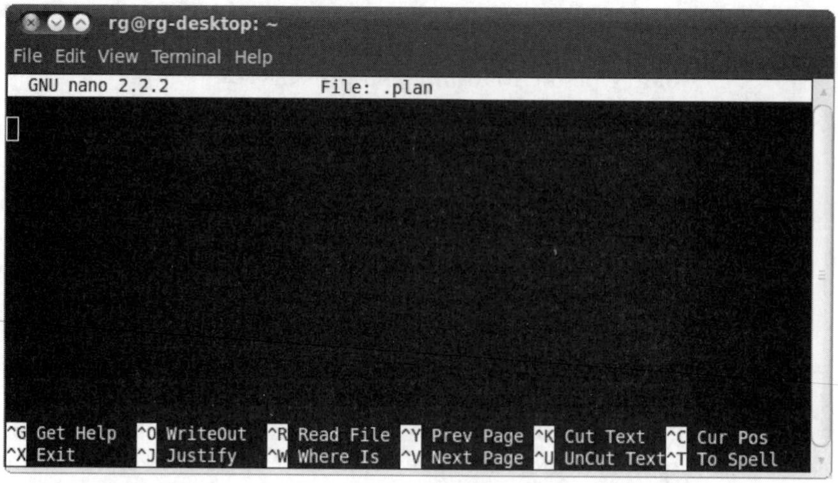

Figure 9-12: The Pico editor

To wrap things up, you want to change the permission of the new *.plan* file by typing `chmod 644 .plan` in the Terminal window and then pressing ENTER. The *.plan* file should now be in your home folder and readable (see Note below) by all, so go on and test your work by typing `finger username` and pressing ENTER. The message you entered in your *.plan* file should now appear in the results in place of the no Plan you found there earlier. If you want to change the contents of your *.plan* file later, just follow the same steps, and change the text when the *.plan* appears in the Pico editor.

NOTE   *The name of the* .plan *file is preceded by a period, which means that it is a hidden file. Thus, if you take a look in your home folder, you will not be able to see the file unless you have checked the* Show hidden and backup files *box in the Nautilus Preferences window.*

Project 9B: More Command Practice with pyWings

Now let's get some more experience with the Terminal by installing a simple, and admittedly kind of silly, oracle program called pyWings (see Figure 9-13). pyWings will give you cryptic guidance in response to whatever questions you may ask it.

To use pyWings, type whatever your confusion is in the input box, click one of the concern icons on the left (self, another, world), click one of the realm icons on the right (love, work, truth), and hit the big button that looks like half an eye. The oracle will then tell you what it has to say. As an example, I asked the oracle why I feel so down when the skies are so sunny, and I picked *self* as my concern and *truth* as the realm. Figure 9-14 shows the wisdom that was bestowed upon me.

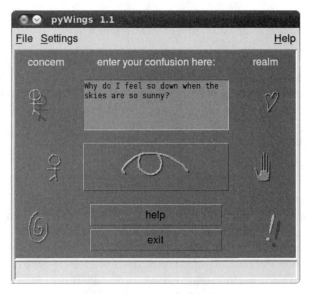

Figure 9-13: Seeking wisdom from pyWings

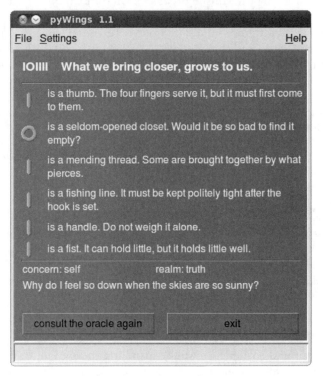

Figure 9-14: pyWings bestows its wisdom.

As you can see, the oracle told me, "What we bring closer, grows to us," which I will interpret as . . . well, I'm not sure what to interpret it as.

Hmmm.

pyWings was written in a programming language called Python, which actually creates scripts rather than true conventional programs. You will learn a little more about this distinction in later in the chapter, but one of the differences I can mention right off the bat is that you don't actually have to install pyWings; you are simply going to put it on your hard drive in your home folder and run it from there, more or less as is.

9B-1: Getting Ready for pyWings (Installing Tkinter)

As I mentioned, one difference between pyWings and most of the other applications you know is that pyWings is a Python script. To create a graphical interface for itself, pyWings uses a toolbox known as *Tkinter*, which is the de facto standard (though not the only) GUI toolbox for Python. Tkinter, however, no longer comes bundled with Ubuntu, so you will need to download and install it yourself. Fortunately, this is quite easily done.

Although it is possible to whip open the Ubuntu Software Center and install Tkinter by the simple means learned in Chapter 6, it seems more appropriate in this command line–oriented chapter to . . . yeah, you got it, use the command line. That said, open a Terminal window, type **sudo apt-get install python-tk**, and then press ENTER. When asked for your password, type it, and then press ENTER. APT will search the online repositories and find your file, along with anything else it requires to function properly. Once it is ready, it will ask you whether you want to continue. You do, so type **y**, and then press ENTER. When your username prompt reappears, you'll know the job is done, and you can go on to the next step.

NOTE   *If you prefer, you can perform this installation using aptitude instead, using the techniques we discussed earlier in the chapter.*

9B-2: Getting pyWings

You are just about ready to begin "installing" pyWings, but before you do, you need to get it from *http://sourceforge.net/projects/pywings/*. Once there, click the **View all files** button, and then download the file *pywings-1.1.tar.gz*. Then place the file in your home folder so that you can follow along easily with the rest of this project.

9B-3: Creating a LocalApps Folder for pyWings

As I mentioned earlier, you will be installing the pyWings program locally in your home folder. Installing a program *locally* means that you are installing the program and all its support and data files in your home folder. This makes things a bit easier, but it also means that the program will not be available to other users. It also means that if you're not careful, you might inadvertently delete it.

To make things a bit easier and safer for you, you are going to create a folder in your home folder in which to place pyWings and all other applications that you install locally on your machine in the future. You will, logically enough, call the folder *LocalApps*.

Let's make the folder using a command in order to get some more practice. Go to the Terminal, make sure you are in your home folder, type the following command, and then press ENTER:

```
mkdir LocalApps
```

9B-4: Extracting the pyWings Tarball

Now it is time to extract the tarball. You could do this by the double-click method you learned in Chapter 7, but since you're working with the command line here, let's use that instead.

To start, you're going to place the tarball in the same folder into which you extract its files. Usually this isn't necessary because the contents of most tarballs are already packaged in a folder of their own. By double-clicking the tarball to open it in File Roller, you can see whether things are packed in a folder or simply as a group of files. In the case of pyWings, it is the latter, so follow these steps:

1. Create a *pywings* folder by typing `mkdir pywings` and pressing ENTER.
2. Move the pyWings tarball into that folder by typing `mv pywings*.gz pywings` and pressing ENTER.

   You can see that in this step you used an asterisk (*) to save some wear and tear on your fingers. The asterisk is a wildcard character that in this case told your system to move any file beginning in *pywings* and ending in *.gz*. Fortunately you had only one item matching those criteria.
3. Move to the new *pywings* folder by typing `cd pywings` and pressing ENTER.
4. Now you get down to the process of extracting the tarball itself using the tar command. To do this, type `tar -xzvf pywings*.gz`, and press ENTER.

   Again, notice that you used the asterisk to save youself some keystrokes, though you could just as well have typed `-1.1.tar` in its stead.
5. Finally, type `cd`, and press ENTER to bring the Terminal back to your home folder.

9B-5: Moving the pyWings Folder to Your LocalApps Folder

The extraction process is now complete. Before going on to running pyWings, however, let's move it to the new *LocalApps* folder you created in Project 9B-3. To do this, type the following command, and then press ENTER:

```
mv pywings LocalApps
```

9B-6: Running pyWings

Now that you have pyWings in place and ready for action, let's start up the great oracle right now so that you can get a better perspective on how to deal with the aspects of life that trouble you.

In the Terminal, make sure you are in your home directory, type the following command string, and then press ENTER:

```
python ~/LocalApps/pywings/pywings.py
```

Since *pywings.py* is a Python script, rather than an application, you are calling Python's attention to that fact so that Python will know it needs to deal with that script. If all went according to plan, pyWings should be up and running and will soon be making you a wiser person.

9B-7: Creating a Launchable Link for pyWings

The method of running pyWings that you've just used works well enough, but it is a pain to open your Terminal and type that somewhat lengthy string every time you want to find out what fate has in store for you. Let's find a way to make things easier in the future.

To run an application from the Terminal, you generally type the name of that application, or, to put it more precisely, the name of that program's executable file; the application's name thus acts as a sort of command. For your system to recognize that command, however, the command (the executable file or a link to it) must be in a location where the system can find it. Whenever you run a command of any sort, your system checks a series of locations (most of which are *bin folders*, where executable files are located) to find that command.

You can easily find out where these locations are by typing **echo $PATH** in a new Terminal window and then pressing ENTER. As you will see, on your Ubuntu system, these locations are as follows:

/usr/local/bin	*/bin*
/usr/local/sbin	*/usr/bin*
/sbin	*/usr/games*
/usr/sbin	

NOTE   *The results of the echo $PATH command will not appear as they do in the easier-to-read chart shown here but, rather, in a single line divided by colons. The actual output shown in the Terminal is* /usr/local/sbin:/usr/local/bin:/usr/sbin:/usr/bin:/ sbin:/bin:/usr/games.

If the command you typed is in one of those locations, the program, or script, will run. As you no doubt know, however, pyWings is not in any of those locations. It is in */home/*username*/LocalApps/pyWings* and is thus, in a sense, out of your system's sight.

To remedy this situation, you could add the path of your pyWings script to the list of paths that the system checks for run commands, so as to make the system aware of your new application's existence. However, let's try another method that I think is easier. What you will do is create a link to pyWings, a sort of launchable alias, in one of the locations your system does check for commands.

To create this link, you will be using three commands: cd (to change directories), sudo (to give yourself write access to the destination folder), and ln -s (to create the link).

1. In the Terminal, type **cd /usr/games**, and press ENTER. This puts you in one of the folders your system searches when you enter commands.

2. Type **sudo ln -s /home/*username*/LocalApps/pywings/pywings.py pywings**, and press ENTER. (Note that there is a space between the words pywings.py and pywings at the end of that command string.)

    The pywings at the end of that command string is the name that you are giving the link; the name of the link thus becomes the command you will use to run the application. If you type nothing, the link will be called *pywings.py*, which would mean three more keystrokes for you every time you wanted to start the program.

3. Type your password when prompted to do so, and then press ENTER.

4. Type **cd**, and press ENTER to return the Terminal to your home folder.

9B-8: Running pyWings Again

Now that you have created the link, you should be able to run the pyWings program much more easily. To try it, quit pyWings (if it is still running), type **pywings** in the Terminal window, and press ENTER. Your personal pyWings oracle should appear again.

You've managed to cut down on the number of keystrokes required to run pyWings from the Terminal. However, if you are really into this pyWings thing and want to use it often, it will probably be handiest to add a launcher to your panel, a drawer, or the Applications menu.

To add a pyWings panel launcher, for example, right-click any open space in the panel, and select **Add to Panel**. When the Add to Panel window appears, click the **Custom Application Launcher** item, and click **Add**. In the Create Launcher window that appears, type **pyWings** in the Name section, anything you want in the Comment section (**Your Obtuse Guru**, for example), and, assuming you created a launchable link in Project 9B-7, type **pywings** in the Command section. For an icon, click the **No Icon** button, and then look around until you find an icon that suits your fancy. I like *gnome-eog.png* myself. Once you've made your selection, click **Add** in the Browse icons window, and then click **OK** in the Create Launcher window.

9B-9: Adding Emblems to Your LocalApps Folder

Now that pyWings is successfully installed and working, it is probably a good idea to add an emblem to your new *LocalApps* folder so that you don't inadvertently dump it in the Trash someday. You already learned how to do this in Chapter 8, so I won't give you the step-by-step instructions.

Project 9C: Command Practice Review with Briscola

If you want to reinforce the skills you've put to use in the previous project, why not go a bit Continental and try Briscola—a simple, yet very traditional, Italian card game (see Figure 9-15)? Unlike pyWings, which is a Python script, Briscola is a script of a different flavor, written in a scripting language called Tcl, which uses something called Tk to create its graphical interface.

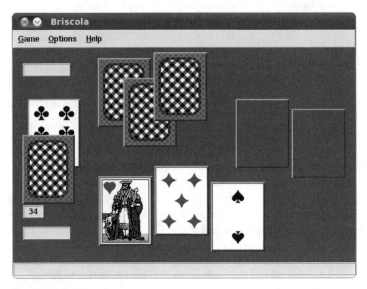

Figure 9-15: Briscola

9C-1: Getting Briscola

You are just about ready to begin "installing" Briscola, but before you do, you must get it. You can get Briscola by going to the project's home page at *http://www.rigacci.org/comp/software/* and downloading it in the traditional manner, but since we're working with commands, let's instead get Briscola by using a new command: wget.

To do this, just open a Terminal window, type the following command string, and then press ENTER:

```
wget http://www.rigacci.org/comp/software/briscola/briscola-4.1.tar.gz
```

NOTE *If you have any trouble downloading Briscola in this way, you can also download it from the site for this book:* http://www.edgy-penguins.org/UFNG/.

In your Terminal window, you will see wget in action as it connects to the site where Briscola is stored and then downloads the file. When it's done, you will find the Briscola tarball in your home folder.

9C-2: Extracting the Briscola Tarball and Renaming the Briscola Folder

Extracting the Briscola tarball is essentially the same process as that for pyWings; however, Briscola is already packaged within its own folder, so you won't have to create a special folder for it.

Although I am sure you now know the drill, I'll tell you again. Just open a Terminal window, type the following command, and press ENTER:

```
tar -xzvf briscola*.gz
```

A new folder, *Briscola-4.1*, will now appear in your home folder with all the Briscola files in it. To make things easier to deal with in the future, let's shorten the name of the folder to simply *briscola*. You already know how to do this via the right-click method, but this time around let's to do it via the command line. To do this, you use, perhaps surprisingly, the mv command followed by the name of the file whose name you are going to change, followed by the new name of the file.

Give it a go by typing the following command and pressing ENTER:

```
mv briscola-4.1 briscola
```

9C-3: Preparing the Briscola Script

Most applications that come in tarball form include a README file, which includes information on what you need to do to install and use the application. If you double-click the **README** file in the *briscola* folder in Nautilus, you will see that the "HOW TO START" section tells you to adjust the first line of the *briscola.tk* script to point it to your Tk shell, and to adjust the second line of the script to point to the directory where the various Briscola files are located.

To perform the adjustments as instructed in the README file, just follow these steps:

1. Find the Tk shell, called Wish, by typing **locate wish** in the Terminal window and pressing ENTER, and then note the location given on a piece of paper. You may get a number of locations in your search results, but the one you want is /usr/bin/wish.

2. Direct the Terminal to the *briscola* folder by typing **cd briscola** and pressing ENTER.

3. Use the Pico editor, which we used in Project 9A, to edit the *briscola.tk* file by typing **pico briscola.tk** and pressing ENTER. The *briscola.tk* file will appear in the Pico editor in your Terminal window.

4. Change the very first line of the *briscola.tk* file from #!/usr/local/bin/wish to #!/usr/bin/wish.

5. In the second line, change /usr/local/games/briscola to **/usr/share/games/ briscola**, which is where you will place Briscola in just a bit. Your editor window should now look like Figure 9-16.

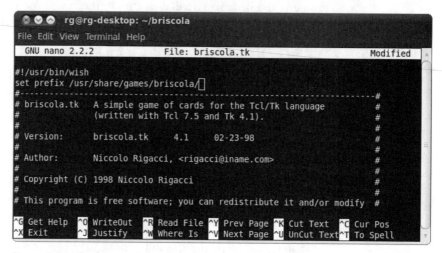

```
  😊 😊 😊   rg@rg-desktop: ~/briscola
File  Edit  View  Terminal  Help
   GNU nano 2.2.2                     File: briscola.tk                      Modified

#!/usr/bin/wish
set prefix /usr/share/games/briscola/
#--------------------------------------------------------------------------#
# briscola.tk    A simple game of cards for the Tcl/Tk language             #
#                (written with Tcl 7.5 and Tk 4.1).                         #
#                                                                           #
# Version:       briscola.tk     4.1      02-23-98                          #
#                                                                           #
# Author:        Niccolo Rigacci, <rigacci@iname.com>                      #
#                                                                           #
# Copyright (C) 1998 Niccolo Rigacci                                        #
#                                                                           #
# This program is free software; you can redistribute it and/or modify     #

^G Get Help   ^O WriteOut   ^R Read File   ^Y Prev Page   ^K Cut Text    ^C Cur Pos
^X Exit       ^J Justify    ^W Where Is    ^V Next Page   ^U UnCut Text  ^T To Spell
```

Figure 9-16: Configuring Briscola with the Pico editor

6. Press CTRL-X on your keyboard.

7. Type **y**, and press ENTER to save your changes.

8. Type **cd**, and press ENTER to return the Terminal to your home folder.

9C-4: Moving the Briscola Folder to a Global Location

You could move the *briscola* folder to the *LocalApps* folder and play it from there, as you did with pyWings, but this time around, let's do things a bit differently by moving the whole thing to global territory. This not only keeps it safe from any obsessive housekeeping tendencies but also allows all users on the same computer to play the game. You will need to use the sudo command to do this so that you can have write access in those protected folders.

To do this, just type the following command in the Terminal window, and press ENTER:

```
sudo mv briscola /usr/share/games
```

When you are prompted for your password, type it, and press ENTER.

9C-5: Creating a Launchable Link for Briscola

Even though you've moved Briscola to a global location, you still can't run it with a simple one-word command because the *briscola.tk* file is not in the system's command search path. Just as you did for pyWings, you will now create a launchable link for Briscola to solve that problem. Here are the steps:

1. In the Terminal, type `cd /usr/games`, and press ENTER.
2. Now create the link by typing `sudo ln -s /usr/share/games/briscola/ briscola.tk briscola`, and press ENTER.
3. Type `cd`, and press ENTER to return the Terminal to your home folder.

You can now easily run Briscola by typing `briscola` in the Terminal and pressing ENTER.

Can You Do the Same Thing with pyWings?

Sure. If you want to move pyWings to a global location, just follow the same procedure for moving the *pywings* folder and creating the link as you did for Briscola, making the necessary substitutions, of course. You will have to remove the previously created pyWings link, though, by typing the following command and pressing ENTER:

```
sudo rm /usr/games/pywings
```

After that, move the *pywings* folder to global territory by typing `sudo mv ~/ LocalApps/pywings /usr/share/games/pywings` and pressing ENTER. When prompted for your password, type it, and press ENTER. You can then create the launchable link by typing `cd /usr/games`, pressing ENTER, typing `sudo ln -s /usr/share/ games/pywings/pywings.py pywings`, and pressing ENTER once more.

Playing Briscola

As I already mentioned, Briscola is easy—about as easy a card game as there is. It is a trick-taking game, which means that you put out a card and then your opponent puts out a card, and the one who puts out the higher point-value card wins the hand, or *trick*. Points are awarded on the basis of the cards involved in that trick. The winner of the trick then goes on to *lead* the next trick, meaning that the winner puts out his or her card first the next time around. When all the cards are played, the points for each player are then tallied, and the player with the higher points wins. It's much simpler to do than it is to describe.

Want to Know More?

If you would like a more detailed set of rules for playing Briscola (and just about any other card game in the world), check out *http://www.pagat.com/*.

Project 9D: Compiling and Installing Programs from Source: Xmahjongg

Though it was far more common in the earlier days, *compiling programs from source* seems to be a phrase you still hear more in the Linux world than in any other. For the beginner, just the mention of compiling a program from source seems off-putting enough. The words *compile* and *source* seem to instill a sense of foreboding in the heart of the new user. That certainly was the case for me, anyway.

You can live long and prosper without ever bothering to compile anything on your system. You can move along quite happily with your system as is, or you can just install programs by means of the much more convenient Ubuntu Software Center. Still, once in the Linux world, you are likely to come across this installation method and may well become curious, especially if you move into the geekier side of the community.

So, What Is Source?

To get started, it is probably a good idea to understand what *source* is so as to help you to understand a bit about how a program actually gets from its primitive state on the programmer's computer to an up-and-running application on your machine. First the programmer writes a program in a programming language. You have probably heard of programming languages such as BASIC or C, and there are many others. What the programmer actually writes with such a language is a set of instructions called the *source code*, or *source*. Your computer, however, cannot actually understand any of that source on its own. It is as if the computer speaks ancient Greek, and the source code is all written in French. The computer therefore needs some sort of interpreter to help it out.

The various languages that programmers use are called *high-level languages*—they are relatively easy for programmers to read. The computer, on the other hand, only understands *low-level languages*, which are quite difficult for most mere mortal programmers to deal with. To convert the high-level language instructions to a low-level language, the computer needs some other program to translate.

If this translation process actually takes place while a program is running, the translator program is called an *interpreter*. Applications that run using an interpreter are usually called *scripts*. The pyWings and Briscola applications earlier in this chapter are examples of such script applications.

The problem with such scripts is that they can be slower than most of the applications you're familiar with—the computer must run an interpreter, interpret the source code, and run the actual application all at the same time. This is like having a French book translated into Greek by a live interpreter; it's very slow indeed.

As an alternative, most programs use a compiler instead of an interpreter. A *compiler* translates the high-level source code into low-level *machine code*, or *object code*, that the computer can understand before the application is actually run. Once this translation is done, the computer never has to bother with the high-level instructions again; it can merely read the translated version each time it runs the program. This is like having a translated version of a foreign book that you can read any time you want. Because computers can run compiled programs without simultaneously using an interpreter, compiled programs run faster than scripts. Most applications for all operating systems are, therefore, compiled.

The Basics

The actual process of compiling an application from source and then installing it is quite simple—a truly "one, two, three" bit of presto change-o. Basically, after extracting the source code from an archived file (usually in the form of a tarball), you would use the following commands to accomplish the task:

./configure   To configure a *makefile*, which provides instructions for the make command

make   To translate the source code into object code that the computer can understand

sudo make install   To give yourself write privileges in protected folders and then install the application

make clean   To tidy up the leftovers once the process is complete (to clean up the mess)

I know that sounds like a lot of commands, but as I always say, it is easier to actually do than it looks like on the page, so fear not.

9D-1: Installing the Tools You Need

Before doing anything else, you have to get your system ready to do what you're about to ask of it. Because Ubuntu is designed with the average computer user in mind, it does not come with the various applications and libraries you need to compile applications from source. Fortunately, however, everything you need to get the job done is available via the Ubuntu Software Center. To get ready for the work at hand in this chapter (and many other jobs you are likely to do on your own in the future), perform searches for and install the following packages:

- build-essential
- libgtk2.0-dev

9D-2: Downloading and Extracting the Xmahjongg File

To get some hands-on experience with compiling a program from source, you will be working with a game called *Xmahjongg*, which you can see in Figure 9-17. If you've tried the version of Mahjongg that comes with your Ubuntu distribution, you will notice that this one is much easier on your eyes and is a bit more colorful (check out the project site at *http://www.lcdf.org/xmahjongg/* to catch a glimpse of it in its full-color glory).

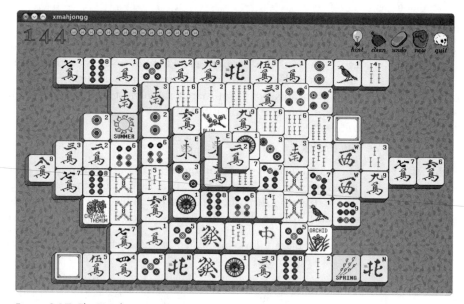

Figure 9-17: The Xmahjongg game

Xmahjongg is available via the Ubuntu Software Center, so it is not absolutely necessary to install it in the way you are about to, but doing so provides a perfect opportunity to learn how to compile a program from source. The amount of source code isn't all that great, so it won't take too much time to do, and it requires no tinkering.

To get started, you will first have to download the Xmahjongg source code. You can get this from the Xmahjongg project page at *http://www.lcdf.org/ xmahjongg/*. Download the tarball *xmahjongg-3.7.tar.gz*, or a newer version if there is one. Do not download any of the other file types available on that page.

If you prefer, you can instead download the Xmahjongg tarball by using the wget command that you learned in Project 9C-1. Just open a Terminal window, type the following command, and then press ENTER:

```
wget http://www.lcdf.org/xmahjongg/xmahjongg-3.7.tar.gz
```

Once you have the file on your hard disk, untar the *xmahjongg-3.7.tar.gz* file. You can do this either by using the command line, as you learned to do earlier in the chapter, or by double-clicking the file and dragging its contents into the appropriate folder. To make it easier for you to follow along with the directions I'll be giving you, be sure to place the untarred Xmahjongg folder in your home folder. Then you will be ready to roll.

Normally at this point, you would look through the folder to find some instructions for dealing with the package, just as you did earlier in the chapter for Briscola. In most source code packages, this information is included in an INSTALL file, like the one in the *xmahjongg-3.7* folder (Figure 9-18). To read the INSTALL file, just double-click it, and it will open in Gedit.

In this case, you can simply close the INSTALL file, because it prescribes the same steps I've listed next. However, in the future, when you install other programs from source, you will need to follow the instructions in the INSTALL files that come with the source files. However, with most INSTALL files, the instructions will match the process I am about to describe.

Of course, it may well happen that you take a look at the contents of the INSTALL file and start wondering what alien tongue it is written in. In cases when you have no idea what the INSTALL file is going on about, just look for a *configure* file in the package folder. If you find one, you should be able to follow the instructions in this project.

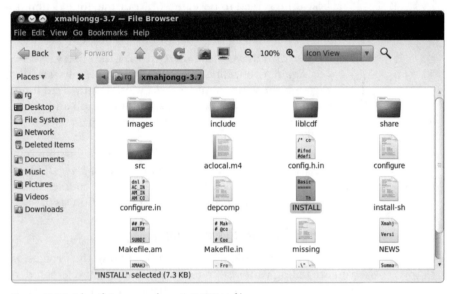

Figure 9-18: Identifying a package's INSTALL file

9D-3: Running configure and make for Xmahjongg

Now that you have downloaded and untarred the Xmahjongg tarball, installation is pretty standard. Here's what you need to do:

1. Open a Terminal window, and then move into the new folder by typing **cd xmahjongg*** and pressing ENTER.

    The next step is sort of a setup phase that runs the configure script in the *xmahjongg-3.7* folder. The configure script checks what files, compilers, and other things it needs, and then it searches your computer to see whether those things are there and, if so, where. Based on this information, it writes a file called a *makefile*, which is a set of instructions that will tell the make command in the subsequent step how to set things up specifically for your system configuration.

2. Configure the program by typing **./configure** and pressing ENTER.

   While you are running configure, you will see lots of odd and mysterious things flowing through your Terminal window; this is essentially a running account of what is going on, each step of the way. This can take a bit of time, but don't worry. As long as the mysterious text keeps flowing and you don't get an error message at the very end of the whole process, all will be well.

   When configure has done its thing, you will see your prompt again, and you can go on to the next step, which is the translation, or *compilation*, step. The make command reads the makefile created by configure to see how things need to be set up on your machine. Then it proceeds to call on the compiler to translate the high-level source code into low-level, machine-readable files that can be installed in the subsequent step.

3. To perform this translation, type **make**, and press ENTER.

   Again, you will be treated to even more mysterious text flowing through the window and a short wait, usually a tad longer than for the configure process. Once make has done its job and you see your prompt again, you are ready to install the program.

Up to this point, you have not changed your system in any way. All the changes thus far have taken place in the *xmahjongg-3.7* folder only—your system is still as pure as the day you started. Of course, all that is going to end right now when you perform the final installation step.

9D-4: Installing and Running Xmahjongg

Now you've come to the last step in this part of the process, make install. Here you are telling your system to install what you have created, or *compiled*, in the make step. Note that because installation takes place in permissions-protected parts of your system, you will need to add sudo to the command string to give yourself administrative privileges.

To perform the installation, type **sudo make install**, and press ENTER. You will then be prompted for your password. After typing it and pressing ENTER, the installation process will take place. Once your Terminal brings you back to your user prompt, Xmahjongg will be installed and ready to run. As a general rule, programs compiled from source do not automatically install a launcher in your Applications menu; you must instead run them by command. Although you can run a program for the first time by typing a command in the Run Application panel applet, it is better to run the program for the first time by typing the command in your Terminal window. If anything has gone amiss during installation, the Terminal will tell you what the problem is, whereas the Run Application method would just leave you wondering what's going on.

To run Xmahjongg, just type **xmahjongg** in a Terminal window, and then press ENTER. If everything goes as it should, you can then create a program launcher for Xmahjongg in your Applications menu, on the GNOME Panel, or in a panel drawer.

9D-5: Cleaning Up and/or Uninstalling Xmahjongg

Once you are done and everything seems to be working as it should, you would normally tidy things up in the Xmahjongg folder by getting rid of any unnecessary files. You can do this via the Terminal by using the `cd` command to go back into the Xmahjongg folder, typing `make clean`, and then pressing ENTER.

If you want to uninstall Xmahjongg, open a Terminal window, go back to the Xmahjongg folder by using the `cd` command, type `sudo make uninstall`, and finally press ENTER. The routine is essentially the same for any applications installed in this way, though as you might imagine, uninstallation isn't always as smooth a process as what I've just described (and it's definitely not as easy as it is via the Ubuntu Software Center).

The main reason for the uninstallation process being less than cooperative is that the `make uninstall` routine requires you to keep the original project folder, which means you have to keep a bit of clutter you normally wouldn't need to bother with. On top of this, some projects do not provide a `make uninstall` routine at all. This means that you have to keep track of where everything has been installed in your system and then remove each item using a series of `sudo rm` commands.

All that negativity aside, go ahead, have some fun, and put your command-line skills to the test. You'll have something to tell your grandkids about in the future.

Customizing the Terminal

The Terminal is a very simple application in terms of looks, though you can spice things up a bit if you're so inclined. Not only can you change the background and text colors in the Terminal, but you can even display one of your favorite photos as a background (as shown in Figure 9-19) or make the background transparent.

To change the Terminal background, go to the Terminal, and select **Edit ▸ Profiles**. When the Profiles window appears, select the profile you want to edit, which the first time out would be Default, and then click the **Edit** button. In the Editing Profile window that appears, click the **Background** tab, select **Background image** (Figure 9-20), and then navigate to the photo you want to use as your background by clicking the **Menu** button next to the words *Image file* and then finding the file in the Select Background Image window. When you've found the photo of your choice, click **Open**. Depending on the image you use for your background, you may find it rather difficult to see the text once your image appears in the Terminal. If so, try moving the slider under the words *Shade transparent or image background* in the Editing Profile window. If that still doesn't do the trick, click the **Colors** tab, deselect **Use colors from system theme**, and then try some of the preset Foreground and Background combinations from the menu button next to the words *Built-in schemes*.

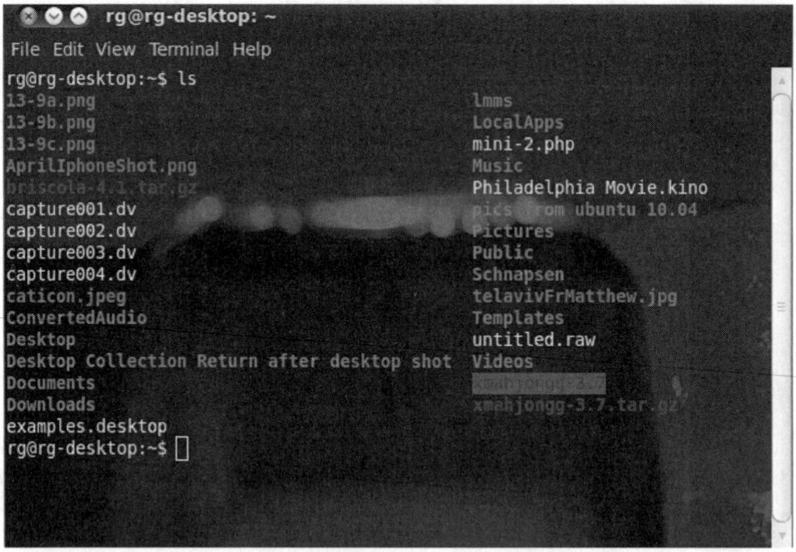

Figure 9-19: A Terminal window with customized background and font colors

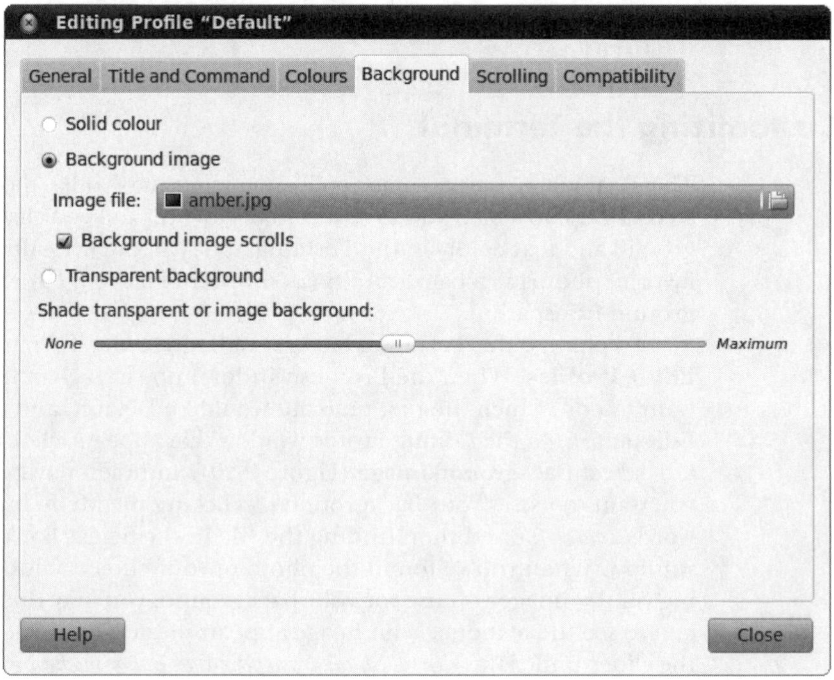

Figure 9-20: Customizing the Terminal window

If you just want to make the background transparent, go back to the **Background** tab, select **Transparent background**, and drag the slider to the right. You can also use the slider to adjust the shading of your background image if you choose to go that route.

Depending on the colors present in your background image or in your desktop wallpaper (if you've gone the transparent route), you may also want to change the font color for your Terminal to make things easier to see. To do this, click the **Colors** tab, deselect **Use colors from system theme**, and then make the appropriate font color selection.

Tabbed Shell Sessions in the Terminal

To wrap things up in this chapter, I thought I might mention one particularly convenient feature of the GNOME Terminal: tabs. Just as you can view multiple web pages in one Firefox web browser window through the use of tabs, tabs in the Terminal application allow you to have more than one shell session running at the same time without having more Terminal windows open (see Figure 9-21). This reduces the amount of desktop clutter and generally makes things easier to deal with. You can open a new tab within the Terminal by going to the Terminal and selecting **File ▸ Open Tab**.

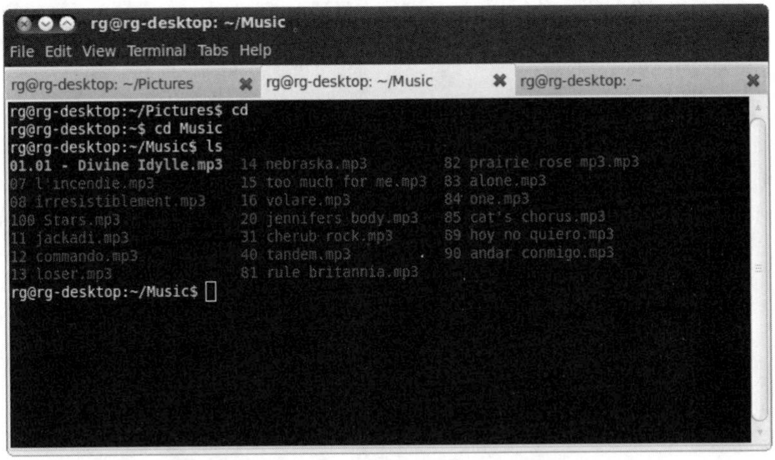

Figure 9-21: Running multiple shell sessions in tabs within the GNOME Terminal

10

GUTENBIRD

Setting Up and Using Your Printer and Scanner

 Two of the most common computer periph-
erals are printers and scanners. This only
makes sense, because it is those two tools
that turn a web-surfing, game-playing, music-
churning, number-crunching box of chips into a meaningful production tool—a virtual publishing house, if
you will. These two tools help your computer convert
digital information into hard copy (in the case of printers) and convert hard
copy into digital information (in the case of scanners). It is not surprising,
therefore, that these tools often come together these days in the form of mul-
tifunction printers.

In this chapter, you will learn how to connect these useful devices to your
computer, how to set them up, and how to use them. If you're more into working with your digital camera than with a scanner, you might want to sneak a
peek at Chapter 13; otherwise, put on your printer's smock, and read on.

Printers

Unless the only thing you use your computer for is playing games, listening to MP3s, or stopping doors on hot, breezy days, you will no doubt want to hook up your machine to a printer. Despite the paperless-office era that the personal computer was supposedly going to usher in, it seems that the computer's strength as a desktop-publishing and general work tool has made producing high-quality printed documents an even more attractive proposition than ever before.

Confirming That Your Printer Is Supported

Setting up a printer to work with your new system is a pretty easy task, and it seems that printer support in the Linux world gets better with each release. In general, support for Epson, Brother, Samsung, and Hewlett-Packard printers is good, while support for other makers and other printer types is a bit spottier (though improving).

If you really want to make sure your printer is supported, just try it by following the instructions in the next section. If you are thinking about buying a printer or are trying to decide whether to switch to Linux, go to *http://www.linuxprinting.org/*. On that site, you can check out the online database to see whether your printer is currently supported and, if so, to what degree. Listings for supported printers also include information on what drivers are best for your purposes. There is also a page of suggested makes and models, in case you're considering buying a printer with the intent of using it with your Linux system. Read this before making your purchase decision. You might also want to consult Ubuntu's list at *https://wiki.ubuntu.com/HardwareSupportComponentsPrinters/*.

Getting Ubuntu to Automatically Recognize and Set Up Your Printer

Printer handling in Ubuntu is pretty much a no-brainer, because Ubuntu automatically detects most printers. If you have a USB printer, connect it to your computer, and then power up the printer (vice versa should work just fine, too). Assuming Ubuntu recognizes your printer, and chances are it will, a small printer icon will appear in the upper-right panel while the system goes through its automatic setup routine. When it is done, a small notification bubble like the one in Figure 10-1 will appear, telling you that your printer has been recognized. There is nothing more for you to do in this case—your printer is set up and ready to roll.

It is also possible, however, that Ubuntu will recognize your printer but not find a driver that is an exact match for it. In this case, it will offer a substitute driver, and the autorecognition window will look slightly different from the one in Figure 10-1.

Sat 17 Apr, 3:29 PM
phil
Printer added
`Photosmart-C3100-series' is ready for printing.

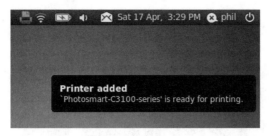

Figure 10-1: Ubuntu lets you know it has automatically recognized and configured your printer.

If you find yourself in this situation, it wouldn't be a bad idea to print a test page to see whether the substituted driver works as it should. You can do this by clicking **System ▸ Administration ▸ Printing** and then double-clicking your printer in the Printing window that appears. A Printer Properties window will open; make sure that *Settings* is selected from the list to the left of the window and then click the **Print Test Page** button (Figure 10-2). If the test page looks normal (something like Figure 10-3), things should be fine, and you can close the Printer Properties and Printing windows.

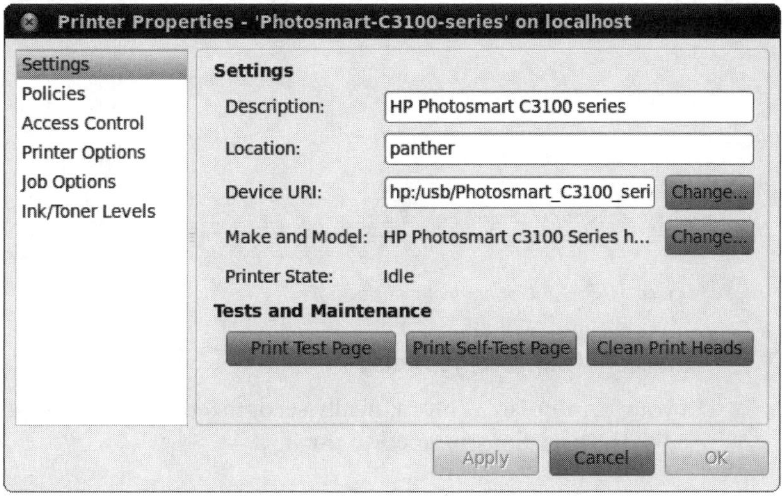

Printer Properties - 'Photosmart-C3100-series' on localhost
Settings
Policies
Access Control
Printer Options
Job Options
Ink/Toner Levels
Settings
Description:
HP Photosmart C3100 series
Location:
panther
Device URI:
hp:/usb/Photosmart_C3100_seri
Change...
Make and Model:
HP Photosmart c3100 Series h...
Change...
Printer State:
Idle
Tests and Maintenance
Print Test Page
Print Self-Test Page
Clean Print Heads
Apply
Cancel
OK

Figure 10-2: Printing a test page with your new printer via the Printer Properties window

If you have a printer that plugs into your computer's parallel port, autodetection and setup should also work if the printer was connected when you turned on the computer. If it was not, shut down your system and turn your computer off, connect your printer to the computer, turn on the printer, and then start your computer again. With luck, your printer should be recognized and set up automatically this time around. You can also try this same approach with a USB printer that was not recognized initially.

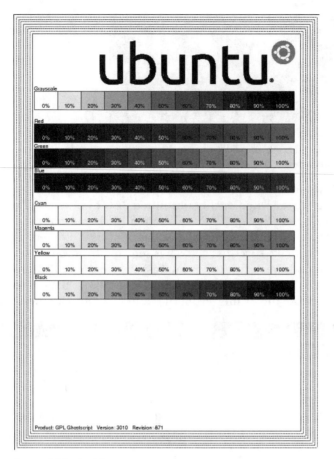

Figure 10-3: An Ubuntu test print page

Manually Configuring Printers

If your printer isn't automatically recognized, you can still set things up manually. Here's what you need to do:

1. Select **System ▸ Administration ▸ Printing**. A Printing window will appear, showing the printers that have already been recognized and/or configured.

2. Click the **Add** button, after which the system will show any new finds in a New Printer window (Figure 10-4).

3. Click the entry for your printer in the left pane of that window, and then click **Forward**.

4. The system will then begin searching for drivers for your printer and will identify the make of your printer in the next screen of the wizard. Check that the correct make is selected, and then click **Forward**.

5. On the next screen, your printer model should appear in the left pane, while the recommended driver will appear in the right pane (Figure 10-5). Click **Forward**.

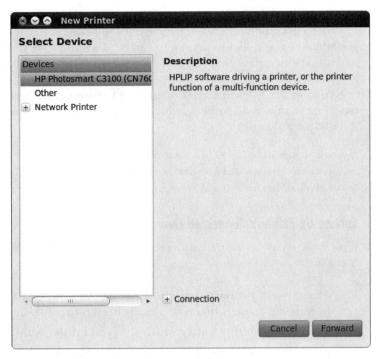

Figure 10-4: Setting up a printer manually

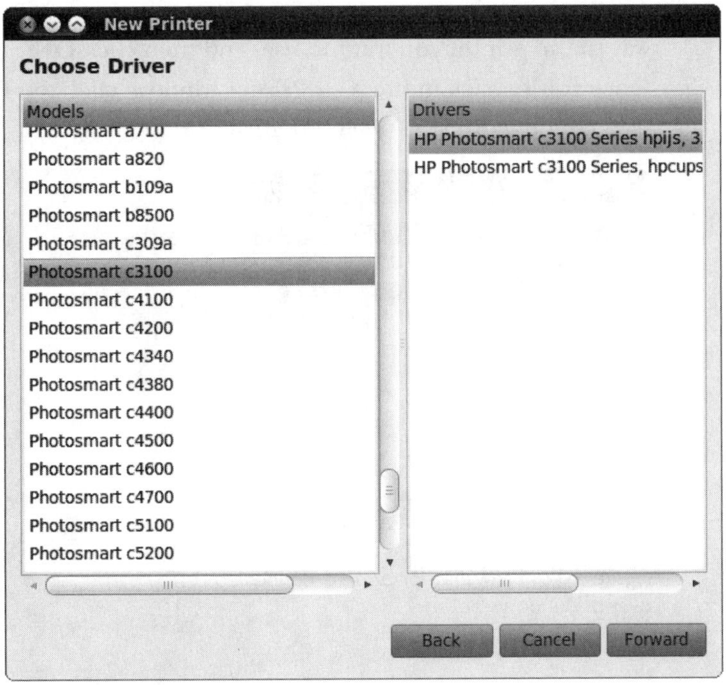

Figure 10-5: The printer setup wizard recommends which driver to use.

6. In the final screen of the wizard, fill in the blanks to suit your needs, and then click **Apply**, after which the wizard will close and you'll be asked whether you'd like to print a test page. To make sure that everything is hunky-dory, it is always a good idea to print a test page, so click **Yes**.

Your system will send a test document to your printer and let you know it has done so in a small window, which you can close. The printer should print the test page shortly.

NOTE   *If your test page didn't come out the way it should or if your printer wasn't configured automatically or correctly by the system, check out* http://www.linuxprinting.org/ *to see whether there are any special requirements or caveats for your model.*

Setting Up Printers Connected Over a Network

If you want to use a printer connected via a home or office network, just follow these steps:

1. Select **System ▸ Administration ▸ Printing**. A Printing window will appear, showing the printers that have already been recognized and/or configured.
2. Click the **Add** button, after which the New Printer window will appear.
3. Select **Network Printer ▸ Windows Printer via SAMBA** in the left pane of that window by clicking that entry once, and then click the **Browse** button in the top-right corner of the page.
4. In the SMB Browser window that appears (Figure 10-6), navigate your way to the printer you want to use, and then click **OK**.
5. Once you're back in the New Printer window, click the **Forward** button.
6. Now continue from Step 5 in "Manually Configuring Printers" on page 196.

Figure 10-6: Browsing for printers connected over a Windows network

For the Driverless Among You

As I mentioned, Linux does not yet have built-in support for some printers. For those of you who find yourselves with such printers, you can take a few routes in order to get things working.

Checking the Connections

You'd be surprised how many times I have triumphantly solved someone's printer problems by simply turning on the printer or wiggling or replugging the USB or parallel connectors. Printers that are powered down and/or that have loose connections are often to blame if the printer's model name fails to appear in the first page of the printer setup wizard.

If that approach fails, browse to *http://www.linuxprinting.org/*, because it is sometimes the case that Linux can support certain printers only if they are connected via the parallel port, even if they work via USB in other systems.

Trying Your Windows Drivers

If your printer came with an installation disc, you might want to see whether you can find a driver for it there. The driver on such a disc should end in *.ppd* (for "PostScript printer description"). To use one of these drivers, try adding your printer as described earlier, but when you get to the New Printer window where you select your printer's make, click the **Provide PPD file** option. Then try to locate the appropriate file by clicking the button that says **(None)** in the middle of the page. If you find your driver, click the **Forward** button, and then continue the printer setup.

Using Third-Party Drivers

Recently, more Linux printer drivers are becoming available. If you don't find your printer on that second page of the printer setup wizard, just try googling the make and model of your printer plus the word *linux*. In the past, for example, I had a laser printer that did not appear at *http://www.linuxprinting.org/*, so I googled the printer, *samsung+SCX4100+linux,* which led me to *http://www.driverstock.com/*, a site that provides free printer drivers for most operating systems, including Linux. On that site, I found not only the driver for my printer but also the driver for its built-in scanner.

You might also want to check the website for the manufacturer of your printer, because many now provide Linux drivers for a number of their printers. Brother, Lexmark, Hewlett-Packard, Canon, and Samsung do, to name a few. There is also a German company (*http://www.turboprint.info/*) that provides Linux drivers, albeit for a fee, for machines that are really hard to deal with and for high-quality graphics solutions.

If you happen to find and download a driver for your printer that does not come with its own installer, just follow the directions given for trying Windows drivers. Finally, don't forget to give the Ubuntu forums (*http://www.ubuntuforums.org/*) a try to see whether anyone there has any experience getting the printer in question to work on their system.

Trial and Error

Finally, there is always the old trial-and-error approach, which works on occasion. When setting up your printer via the wizard window, try choosing one of the other printer models and/or drivers available from your printer's manufacturer.

After you are done with the wizard, double-click the printer you added in the Printing window, click the **Settings** tab, and then click the **Print Test Page** button to see what happens. If nothing happens, click the **Change** button at the far right end of the Make and Model row on the Settings screen, select a different printer model and/or driver, and then, back on the Settings screen, click the **Print Test Page** button again. Repeat that process until something works. With any luck, something will . . . might . . . well, just give it a try if you're desperate.

Printing Details

Now that your printer is set up, you will no doubt want to start printing! This is an easy task, and it isn't very different from how it works in the Windows and Mac worlds, so you shouldn't need much explanation to proceed. In fact, printing in Ubuntu has become easier than ever, because all the settings you would normally want to toy with are all on their own tabs within the Print window that appears when you select Print in an application's File menu. I would even dare say that figuring out printing options in Ubuntu is now easier than it is in Windows or OS X.

You should be aware that the function of the tabs can vary depending on the application you happen to be printing from. For instance, the tabs you'll see when printing from the GIMP will be slightly different from those you will see when printing from Firefox. The General and Page Setup tabs will almost always be there, however. All that said, I'll give you an idea of some of the settings that are available within some of the Print window's tabs:

General   Printer selection, pages to print, number of copies, order of printing, collating

Page Setup   Pages per sheet, scaling, paper type, paper source, output tray

Options   Print frames, shrink to fit page, print background, headers and footers

Image Settings   Size, resolution, page positioning

Job   Print timing (now, later, at time), cover page

Image Quality/Advanced   Output resolution (DPI), printing speed and quality

Printing in OpenOffice.org

Occasionally, you will come across an application such as OpenOffice.org that has a slightly different way of handling printing. Fortunately, the differences may actually make printing in OpenOffice.org more Windows-like and thus easier for newbies from the Windows world to follow along with. As you can see in Figure 10-7, the main Print window for OpenOffice.org applications allows you to select the printer you want to use, the range of pages, and how many copies you want to print. You can access other options by clicking the Properties and/or Options buttons.

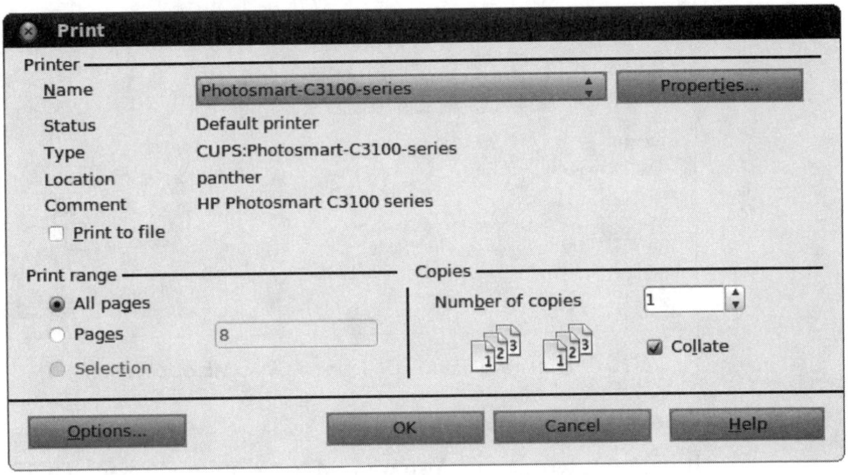

Figure 10-7: Print settings in OpenOffice.org modules

Printing to PDF

One of the nice features of Linux is that you can save most documents or web pages as PDF files. In some cases, such as in OpenOffice.org, you do this by exporting the document to PDF. In most other applications, however, you do it via the Print window, in which case you are said to be "printing to PDF." Whether you are *saving as* PDF, *exporting to* PDF, or *printing to* PDF, you are essentially doing the same thing: creating a PDF file of your document.

This is very handy, because it allows you to create documents that cannot be altered by others and yet can easily be read regardless of the word processor program or operating system the reader is using. Best of all, this feature, which you would have to pay a pretty penny for in the Windows world, costs you nothing, because it is built in to your system.

In most GNOME applications (and now in Firefox, too), you can print to PDF by going to the **File** menu of the application in question and selecting **Print**. When the Print window (Figure 10-8) appears, select **Print to File** in the list of printers, and make sure **PDF** is selected as the output format. Choose a name for the PDF file, and then click the **Print** button to save it.

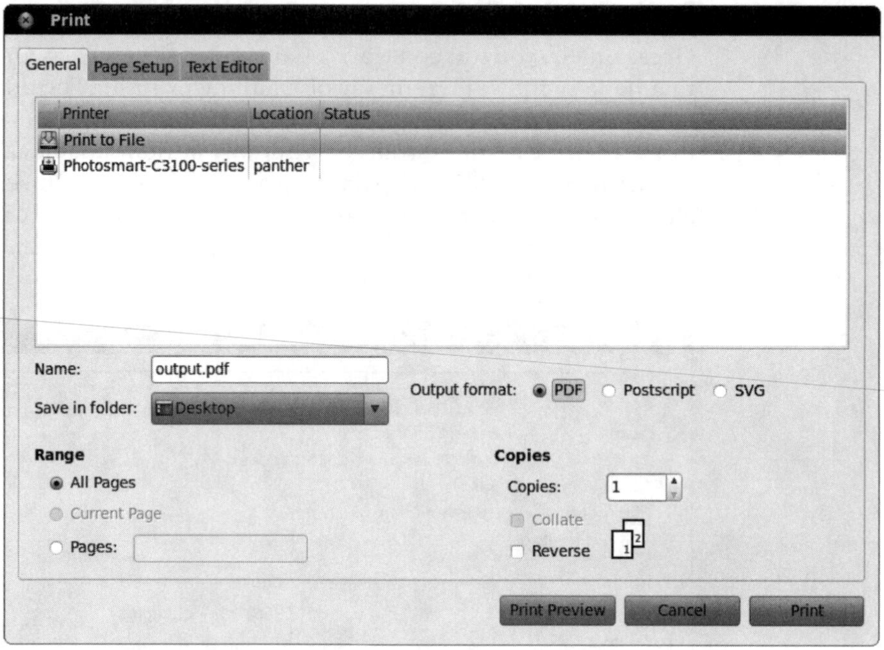

Figure 10-8: Printing a file to PDF in most GNOME applications

Canceling a Print Job

It happens to all of us. You wanted to print just 1 page of a 57-page document, but you accidentally started printing the whole thing. What can you do to save your ink and 56 sheets of paper? Fortunately, the solution is simple.

Once you've clicked the Print button and the print job is sent to your printer, a small printer icon will appear somewhere at the right end of the top GNOME panel (usually to the left of the other items there), as you can see in Figure 10-9.

Figure 10-9: A printer icon appears in the GNOME panel while printing.

Just click that icon once, and a window showing your current and queued print jobs will appear (as shown in Figure 10-10). Your errant print job will be listed in that window, so right-click the name of the job to select it, and then, in the pop-up menu, select **Cancel**. You'll be asked whether you really want to cancel the job; click **Yes**.

After you do this, the print job listed in the queue window will disappear, and your printer will stop printing. You can then close the print queue window. This is a very easy process that you may well find is more effective than what you've experienced in other operating systems.

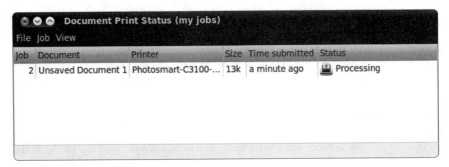

Figure 10-10: Canceling a print job via the print queue window

In some cases, things will be even easier, particularly if you installed your printer driver yourself by means of the installer that came packaged with the driver. In many such cases, the driver will provide its own progress window that will appear whenever you print a document. If so, you can simply click the **Cancel** button (or equivalent) in that window to cancel the printing job.

NOTE   *In some cases, you may have to clear your printer after canceling a print job. You can do this by turning your printer off, waiting a few seconds, and then turning it on again.*

Checking Ink Levels and Other Printer Maintenance Tasks

Printer ink (and toner) has a knack of vanishing at a rate of knots, so it's natural to want to check up on how your cartridges are doing. You might also run into problems with the printer, such as streaks on printouts or jagged lines that should really be straight, so it might be necessary to clean or align the print heads too. Unfortunately, there's no one simple method of doing this since every make of printer handles it differently. I'll just mention a few ways you can access these options for the most common brands:

HPLIP   This works only for Hewlett-Packard printers. Open the Ubuntu Software Center, and install HPLIP Toolbox. Select **System ▸ Preferences ▸ HPLIP Toolbox** to run it, and use the Supplies tab to check ink levels and the Actions tab to align and clean your cartridges.

Inkblot   This works for a number of Epson, Canon, and HP printers—check *http://libinklevel.sourceforge.net/#supported/* to see whether your printer is supported. Open the Ubuntu Software Center, install Inkblot, and then select **Applications ▸ System Tools ▸ Inkblot** to check your ink levels.

escputil   This works for some Epson printers and is worth a try if Inkblot doesn't support your model. Open the Ubuntu Software Center, and install *escputil*. Then, open a Terminal by selecting **Applications ▸ Accessories ▸ Terminal**. Type `escputil -i` (don't forget the space) and hit ENTER to display the ink levels. To clean the print head, type `escputil -c`.

If you have no luck with these utilities or if your printer's make isn't listed, you might still be able to access ink levels and maintenance functions using the manufacturer's own Linux driver, if one exists. Also, some newer printers allow you to check ink levels and align and clean cartridges using controls on the printer. When in doubt, check your printer's manual.

Scanners

Scanners are extremely useful and about as cheap a peripheral device as you can get. They allow you to take images or pages of text and input them, in digital form, into your computer—in much the same way as you would duplicate a document on a copy machine.

Even though scanners have been around for a relatively long time, support for them in Linux is still a bit spotty. Fortunately, this is changing for the better with every new Linux release. The backend—the hidden part of your system that handles scanner recognition and support in Linux—is called *Sane*. If you are wondering whether Linux will be able to recognize your scanner or if you are trying to figure out what type of scanner to buy, you can visit the Sane website at *http://www.sane-project.org/sane-mfgs.html/*.

There you will be able to see whether your scanner is supported or get tips about what scanner to buy. The page is pretty long, so you might want to use the Find function in your web browser (select **Edit ▶ Find** in Firefox) to search for your scanner model. As I have mentioned, you can also try the Ubuntu forums (*http://www.ubuntuforums.org/*) and ask for Ubuntu-specific recommendations there.

Scanning, No Questions Asked, with Simple Scan

Simple Scan is a new addition to Ubuntu's line-up of default applications, and it certainly lives up to its name—it doesn't take many clicks to get a document from scanner bed to computer screen. To run Simple Scan, make sure that your scanner is connected and switched on, and then select **Applications ▶ Graphics ▶ Simple Scan**. If you get a warning saying that no scanners were detected, skip to "Unrecognized Scanners" on page 207.

Assuming that your scanner has been recognized, you'll be presented with the screen in Figure 10-11.

It's pretty easy from here—select the type of document you're scanning (Text or Photo) from the drop-down menu next to the Scan button (the menu's icon is a small down-arrow), and then click **Scan**. Your scanner will roar into action, and, after a short wait, you'll be presented with a preview of the picture or document you placed on the scanner. You can crop and rotate the image by using the options in the Page menu or by right-clicking the preview. When you're happy with your scan, select **Document ▶ Save** to finish up.

One little tip: To change the resolution of your scans, select **Document ▶ Preferences**, and tweak the settings in the window that appears. Higher resolutions take longer to scan and take up more disk space, but lower resolutions can look terrible, so choose wisely!

Figure 10-11: Scanning with Simple Scan

Not-So-Simple Scanning with XSane

Simple Scan will be able to handle most of your scanning needs, but if you have some particularly complex scanning that you need to do, you can use XSane. XSane is a real monster of a scanning program, packed full of professional features and fine-tuning options (see Figure 10-12). Search for and install XSane using the Ubuntu Software Center, and then select **Applications ▶ Graphics ▶ XSane Image Scanner**. XSane will perform a search for an attached scanner. If it finds one, it will start up. If it doesn't, a window will appear that says "No devices available." If this happens, click the **Close** button, and skip to "Unrecognized Scanners" on page 207.

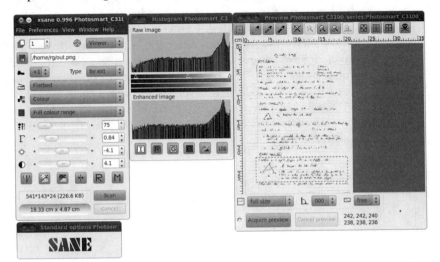

Figure 10-12: Scanning with XSane

To actually scan something, place your photo or document on the scanner bed, and click the **Acquire preview** button in the bottom-left corner of the XSane Preview window. Once the preview appears, use the selection tools to define the exact area you want to scan, and then choose your resolution and color depth settings in the main XSane window. When everything is ready, click the **Scan** button. Your scanned image will then appear in a Viewer window (as shown in Figure 10-13).

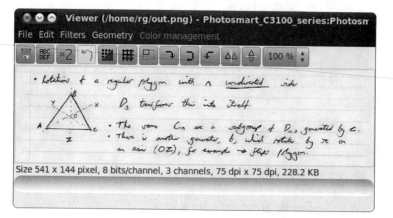

Figure 10-13: The results of your scan are displayed in a separate Viewer window.

In that window, you can perform some minor tweaks of the scanned image using the buttons and menu items provided and then save the image by selecting **File ▸ Save image**.

If you want to convert a scanned document into a text file, you'll first have to install the Gocr package using the Ubuntu Software Center. Gocr performs a process called *optical character recognition*, which tries to figure out what text the image contains by recognizing the shapes of individual letters. (It only works for typed text, not handwriting.)

Once Gocr is installed, scan your document into XSane as before. This time, click the second button from the left (the one that says **ABCDEF**) before you click **Save image**, and you will find that you can save the file as a text document now as well. The text recognition isn't perfect, so make sure you go over the text file to look for typos afterward.

XSane has plenty more tricks up its sleeve—visit *http://www.xsane.org/doc/sane-xsane-doc.html/* for information on what features are available and how to use them.

Unrecognized Scanners

If you receive a message telling you that no scanners were detected when you open a scanning program, your scanner may not have been recognized properly by Ubuntu. Here are a few things you can try to work around this:

- Install the *libsane-extras* package using the Ubuntu Software Center. This contains a handful of scanner drivers that aren't installed by default. Once it's installed, try opening your scanning program again to see whether it worked.

- Press ALT-F2 to open the Run Application window; then type `gksudo simple-scan`, and click **Run**, entering your password if prompted. This will start Simple Scan with root (administrator) privileges, a step that sometimes manages to raise the scanner from its slumber.

- If you still have no luck, check out *https://wiki.ubuntu.com/Hardware SupportComponentsScanners/* to see whether there are any special instructions that you need to follow, or ask for advice on the Ubuntu forums (*http://www.ubuntuforums.org/*).

Why Are My Scanned Images So Big?

To wrap up this section on scanning, let me address a question that seems to confuse a lot of people: Why does a scanned image on the computer screen seem so much bigger than its real-life counterpart? One of the first areas of confusion is that there is a general blurring of how the terms *pixels per inch (ppi)* and *dots per inch (dpi)* are used. Most applications use these terms interchangeably, and yet they aren't really the same thing. To make things simple, when you are talking about images on your screen, you are talking about *pixels* (the little squares that make up your screen image) per inch, and when you are talking about printer resolution, you are talking about *dots* (of printer ink) per inch.

Your computer screen generally has a resolution of 96ppi, while most modern inkjet and laser printers have a resolution range of 300 to 1200dpi, or sometimes even more. This means that a photo scanned at 96ppi, which looks just fine on your screen, ends up looking pretty lame when you print it. On the other hand, when you scan a picture at 300ppi, the image will look much better in your printout but will be gigantic if you display it "full size" on your screen. This is because there will be three times as many pixels per inch, so it looks three times bigger onscreen.

As an example, look at Figure 10-14, where you can see an identical image scanned at three different resolutions: 96ppi, 150ppi, and 300ppi. As you can see, the 96ppi image at the far left (measuring 5 by 6 inches—about the size of the hard copy itself) is the smallest, while the other two images are proportionally bigger (about 10 by 12 inches for the 150ppi image and about 22 by 25 inches for the 300ppi image).

Figure 10-14: The same image scanned at three different resolutions

Which Resolution Should I Use When Scanning?

Which resolution you use when scanning depends on a variety of factors, the most important of which is what you plan to do with the image when you're finished. When I look at Figure 10-14 on my computer screen, the smallest image looks best, the middle image looks OK, and the largest looks a bit odd, not as sharp as the other two. Basically, when scanning images for display on a computer—on web pages, for instance—it is probably best to stick with a ppi similar to typical screen resolutions or slightly larger: 96 to 150ppi.

When it comes to printing, a whole new set of considerations comes into play. First, there are the limitations of your scanner, since different models have different maximum resolutions. The resolution limits of your printer are also, naturally enough, a major consideration. For example, laser printers and inkjet printers have different characteristics; laser printers will generally produce better-quality images than inkjet printers, while inkjet output will be more greatly affected by the type of paper used than a laser printer will be. Of course, your printed output is not going to suffer if you scan your images at higher resolutions than those at which you plan to print them, but you will end up with a lot of files taking up too much disk space. Remember, *the higher the resolution of a scanned image, the greater the file size in terms of disk space.* If this is of concern to you, you can simply resize the images after you're done printing using an application such as the GIMP (more on that in Chapter 13), but if you would prefer not being so cavalier with your use of disk space from the get-go, you can follow these very general guidelines:

- If you are using a laser printer, scan at the same resolution at which you are going to print.
- If you are going to use an inkjet printer with photo-quality paper, scan at about 80 percent of your target printout resolution—about 240ppi for a 300dpi printout.

- If you are using an inkjet printer with regular paper, scan at about 65 percent of your target printout resolution—about 195ppi for a 300dpi printout.

Needless to say, these are just suggestions to get you started. What works best for you and your particular scanner/printer setup may be slightly different. Nothing works better than a bit of experimentation and trial and error. In this case, you can't really go wrong. Just give yourself some time, don't get frustrated, and, most importantly, don't wait until you desperately need to scan something before trying things—stay ahead of the game.

11

POLYGLOT PENGUINS

Linux Speaks Your Language

These days, almost all operating systems are multilingual, or at least capable of becoming so. This is true of Linux as well. Just open your web browser and, without performing any special installations, you can read pages in any European language, including those with Cyrillic alphabets, such as Russian. You can even view pages in Chinese, Japanese, Thai, Arabic, and Hebrew, to name but a few.

But the multilingual capabilities of Linux are much greater than this, and the way that it handles multilingual matters makes it quite easy to take advantage of these capabilities. As you will soon see, you can even set up your system to give you a totally foreign language environment, allowing you to function completely in the language of your choice. Add to this the ever-expanding number of free programs available for language study, and you have a truly meaningful language-learning tool.

Read-Only Language Support

If all you want is to be able to read web pages or documents written in a foreign language, you don't need to install any additional language support except in some rare cases. From the get-go, you will be able to view documents in just about any language you happen to throw at your system—it doesn't matter if it's Swedish, Italian, Chinese, Japanese, Arabic, Hebrew, Russian, Vietnamese, Armenian, or Thai. You will be able to read whatever you are linguistically capable of reading (see Figure 11-1 for an example).

Figure 11-1: A Japanese web page displayed in Firefox

Firefox usually automatically recognizes the language in which a web page is written and thus displays the page correctly. Sometimes, however, the author of the page may neglect to include the character coding for that page in the HTML, in which case Firefox, not knowing that the page is prepared in another language, will very often open it in the default language of your system. The result is a page in which you see nothing but odd combinations of symbols and letters that have no meaning. In this case, try changing the character coding in Firefox to the language encoding you believe the page to be in. Some languages employ more than one encoding scheme, so if you're not sure, give each one a try. You can make your choices by going to the Firefox **View** menu and selecting **Character Encoding**. From the submenu there, you can select the appropriate coding for the language of that page.

Typing Nonstandard Characters

Typing characters that are not standard in English, such as *é, ç, ß, ø, æ,* and *å,* can be done quite easily in Linux without any modifications. In most situations, you can do this by using the Character Map utility included in your system, which can be found at **Applications ▸ Accessories ▸ Character Map**. Upon running Character Map, a window like the one shown in Figure 11-2 will appear.

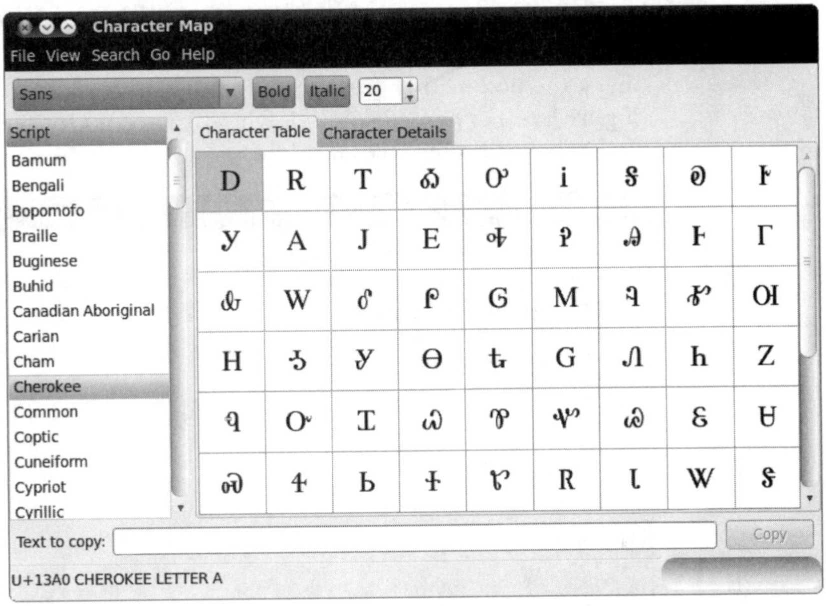

Figure 11-2: Inputting characters with the Character Map utility

To input the character you want, just select the language or character set in the left pane of the window, and then, in the right pane, double-click the character you want to input. The character will appear in the little input box next to the words *Text to copy* at the bottom of the window. Just click the **Copy** button, and then paste the character wherever you want to place it.

OpenOffice.org offers a method of its own that you can use. Click **Insert** in the menu bar, and then select **Special Character**. A selection window will open, and you can select the character you want there. Once you've done that, click the **OK** button, and the character will appear in your document, after which the selection window will close by itself. Double-clicking the character you want will also accomplish the same thing.

Using the Compose Key Option

If you need to type an accent or umlaut only once in a while and don't feel particularly keen on opening an application or going to a special menu to do so, using the *compose key option* for your keyboard is a good way to go. Basically this means you use one of the lesser-used keys on your keyboard in conjunction with six symbols (` , ' ~ " ^) to help in the creation, so to speak, of accented characters.

Before you can use this feature, you have to select which key you want to use as your compose key. For this example, I'll use the right ALT key, since most people don't use it much. Here's what you need to do:

1. Go to the **System** menu, and select **Preferences ▸ Keyboard**.

2. In the Keyboard Preferences window that appears, click the **Layouts** tab, and then click the **Options** button.

3. In the Keyboard Layout Options window, click the + button next to the words *Compose key position.*

4. Check the box next to the key you want to use as your compose key (Figure 11-3). Then close the Keyboard Layout Options window and the Keyboard Preferences window.

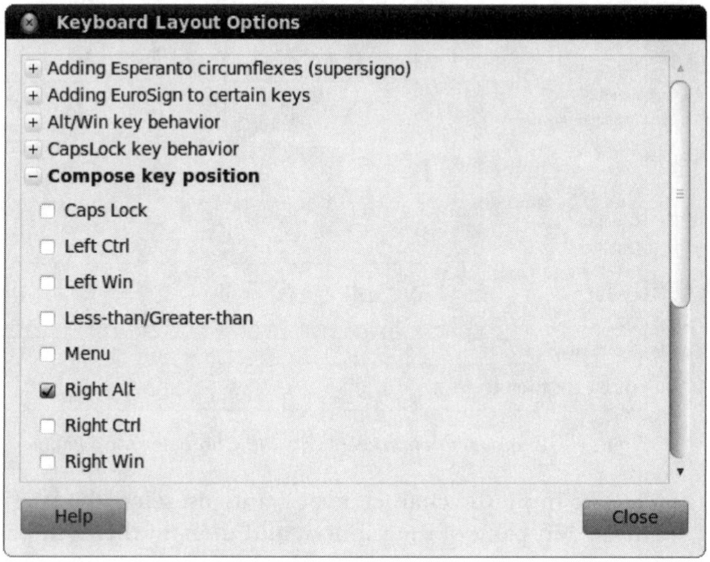

Figure 11-3: Selecting your compose key

Once you've done that, you can use your compose key to type those characters. Let's say, for example, that you wanted to type an umlauted *u* (that is, *ü*). While pressing the right ALT key (or whatever key you selected as your compose key), you would press ". Then you would release the right ALT key, press u, and *voilà*—you'd have yourself an *ü*! Here are some more examples:

á   right ALT + ' then a

ç   right ALT + , then c

è   right ALT + ` then e

ñ   right ALT + ~ then n

ô   right ALT + ^ then o

NOTE *These sequences are based on U.S. keyboard layouts. Combinations for other layouts may differ.*

Adding Keyboard Layouts

If you often type in a particular foreign language, it might be more convenient for you to add a whole new keyboard layout for the language or languages you use. For example, if you often type in Swedish and thus use the characters å, ä, and ö regularly, using the appropriate keyboard layout would be easier than repeatedly using the Character Map. This is even more true if you type in Greek, Russian, Serbian, Georgian, or any other language that uses a completely different alphabet. Of course, you will have to familiarize yourself with the keyboard layout, or *keymap*, for each language you choose, but this is a relatively easy task.

To add foreign language keyboard layouts to your system's repertoire, here's all you need to do:

1. Select **System ▸ Preferences ▸ Keyboard**.
2. In the Keyboard Preferences window, click the **Layouts** tab.
3. Once in the Layouts tab, click the **Add** button.
4. In the Choose a Layout window that then appears, select the keyboard layout you want to add, and when done, click **Add** (Figure 11-4).
5. Repeat Steps 3–4 to add other layouts (up to a maximum of four layouts).
6. When done, your window should look something like Figure 11-5 but with slightly different keyboard layout selections. Click **Close** to complete the process.

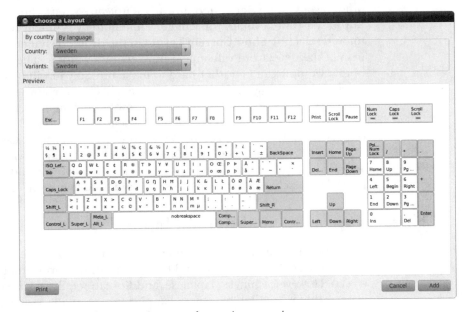

Figure 11-4: Selecting and viewing foreign-language keymaps

Figure 11-5: Viewing the active keyboard layouts on your system

After closing the Keyboard Preferences window, a keyboard layout indicator will appear in the upper-right corner of the top panel. The letters *USA* or *GBr* will appear, indicating that you are currently using your English language keymap. If you click that indicator, you will toggle between any of the other layouts you've activated. If you are not sure where the keys are located in your current keymap, you can get some help by right-clicking the indicator and selecting **Show Current Layout** in the drop-down menu, after which a map of the new layout will appear in a separate window. The keymap shown in that window can be rather hard to make out, so you will probably need to expand the window by dragging it by one of its bottom corners. You can also print a copy of the layout from this window by clicking the **Print** button.

If you just want to choose a single keyboard layout to replace your current one (such as British English instead of American English or German instead of Spanish), you can do so from the Keyboard Preferences window. Simply add the keyboard layout you want to use, and remove any additional layouts by clicking each one and then clicking the **Remove** button.

Chinese, Japanese, and Korean Input

For most European languages (and many other alphabet-based non-European languages), pressing a letter on the keyboard simply prints that letter to the screen. However, Chinese, Japanese, and Korean require a kind of conversion process that is handled by a special application (actually a set of applications) called an *input method editor (IME)*. Each of these languages has its own IME, and each is quite different because of the basic differences in the three writing systems.

Chinese

Although most people (at least those in the linguistic know) would think that Chinese would be the most complicated system, because the writing system consists of thousands of characters, it is in fact the simplest. The Chinese IME simply takes the Romanized keyboard input, known as *pinyin*, and converts it into Chinese characters, or *Hanzi*. For the IME, it is essentially a simple dictionary lookup task—big dictionary, simple IME. In the event that there is more than one character for the pinyin input, a list of possible candidates will appear, and the user can then simply select the appropriate character from that list. More recent Chinese IMEs also have predictive capabilities, by which they judge what you are trying to type on the basis of what you've typed so far (Figure 11-6). Although these more "intelligent" IMEs can be a bit squirrelly to use at first, they prove to be rather handy once you get the hang of things.

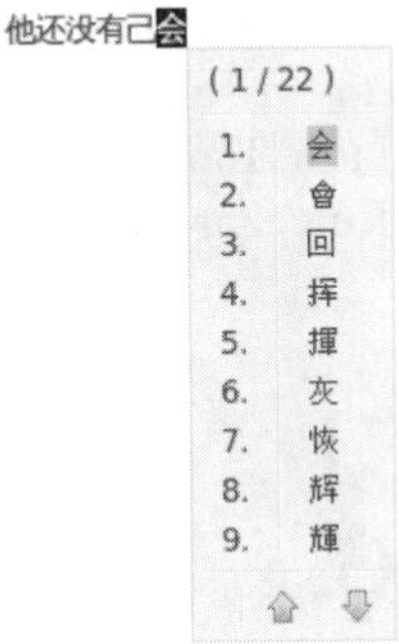

他还没有己会

(1 / 22)

1. 兹
2. 會
3. 回
4. 挥
5. 揮
6. 灰
7. 恢
8. 辉
9. 輝

Figure 11-6: Chinese IMEs can predict what you're going to write . . . kind of.

Japanese

The Japanese IME has a considerably more complicated task to perform, because it has three writing systems to deal with: *Kanji* (ideographic characters borrowed long ago from China), *hiragana* (the phono-alphabetic system used mainly for tense and case endings), and *katakana* (used mainly for words borrowed from other languages). Still, the standard input method for Japanese is primarily via the standard Roman keyboard layout, plus a few extra special-function keys. Thus, typing in Japanese is a two-step process whereby the IME first converts the romanized text into hiragana as it is typed and then converts it to appropriate Kanji, katakana, or hiragana elements after the spacebar is pressed.

You can see an example of these steps in Figure 11-7. In the first line, the IME has already converted the Romanized input on the fly. It has converted *rinakkusdenihongonyuuryokugamodekimasu* (which means *You can input Japanese in Linux*) to hiragana. When a line of hiragana is highlighted, it means that the line has not yet been converted beyond that. In the second line, however, the user has subsequently pressed the spacebar, which caused the IME to convert the hiragana string into the appropriate Kanji, hiragana, and katakana elements. The first word, *Linux*, has been converted to katakana text, because it is a borrowed word, while *Japanese input* has been converted to Kanji; the rest stays in hiragana.

りなっくすでにほんごにゅうりょくができます。

リナックスで日本語入力ができます。

Figure 11-7: IME conversions while typing in Japanese

Korean

The job of the Korean IME is again quite different from that of the Chinese and Japanese IMEs, because the language is written in a very different way. Korean is written either entirely in alphabetic letters, called *Hangul*, or in a combination of Hangul and ideographic characters borrowed from Chinese called *Hanja*. While the Hanja characters are essentially the same as their Chinese and Japanese counterparts, Hanzi and Kanji, the Korean phonetic alphabet, Hangul, has it own unique appearance, as you can see in the Korean word for Korea, *Hangug(k)*, in Figure 11-8.

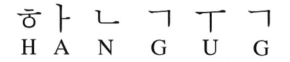

Figure 11-8: Korea (Hangug) *written horizontally in Hangul*

This seems simple; however, the representation is not quite correct, because Korean is very unique in the way that its alphabetic characters are put to the page. Unlike the usual side-by-side positioning of hiragana, katakana, and most other languages written with an alphabet, Hangul letters are grouped in pairs, triplets, or even quadruplets, which are written, as a general rule, clockwise. The IME, therefore, must take the input (usually based on a Korean alphabetical keyboard layout) while it is being typed, and it must adjust the size, spacing, and positioning of each of the letters as it puts them into appropriate clusters (see Figure 11-9).

Figure 11-9: An example of the clustering process in the Korean IME

Project 11: Setting Up Asian-Language Support

So, what do you do if, for example, you want to be able to type Chinese, Japanese, Korean, Hindi, Thai, or Nepali while still in your usual English environment? What if you want to be able to type all of those languages in the same document? Can you do it?

You bet.

There are actually several ways of going about this, but the default method in Ubuntu is the easy-to-use Intelligent Input Bus (IBus). IBus supports most Asian languages, including Chinese, Japanese, and Korean, and it provides a number of input methods for many of these.

11-1: Selecting Input Method Modules

The first thing you will need to do to use IBus is select the appropriate input modules for the language(s) you want to input. To do this, go to the **System** menu, and select **Preferences ▸ IBus Preferences**. A window will then appear asking you whether you would like to start the IBus daemon. Click **Yes**, after which yet another window may appear telling you what to do if you cannot get IBus to work. Click **OK** in that window. (Fortunately, these two windows will appear only when you first start IBus.) The IBus Preferences window will then appear. Click the **Input Method** tab.

NOTE *A daemon is a program that runs in the background, unbeknownst to the average user, providing a system with added functionality. In the case of IBus, that added functionality is the ability to input complex character sets.*

On that tab, click the **Select an input method** drop-down button, select the input method you require, and then click **Add**. The input method you just added will then appear in the main pane of the window beneath the default method, English. Repeat the process for any other input methods you want to add. When done, your window should look like a variation on what you see in Figure 11-10, depending on which languages you actually select. When you're done making your selection, click the **Close** button.

Figure 11-10: Selecting complex character input methods in IBus

As you will notice when selecting input methods, some languages, such as Chinese, have a number of methods to choose from (as shown in Figure 11-11). To give you some quick help, I will suggest appropriate choices for the student or casual user of Chinese, Japanese, and Korean.

- For simplified Chinese standard pinyin input support, select **Chinese – py**.
- For traditional Chinese zhuyin/Bopomofo input support, select **Chinese – bopomofo**.
- For Japanese input support, select **Japanese – anthy**.
- For Korean input based on the standard English keyboard, select **Korean – romaja**.

For those studying or teaching Chinese, you might also want to select **Chinese – pinyin**, which allows you to easily type the Chinese words in Roman letters with tone markings, as shown in Figure 11-12. Just type each character phonetically in pinyin followed by the character's tone number (type *zhong1 guo2* for China, for example), and then the diacritic tone markings will appear above the Romanized output. Very handy.

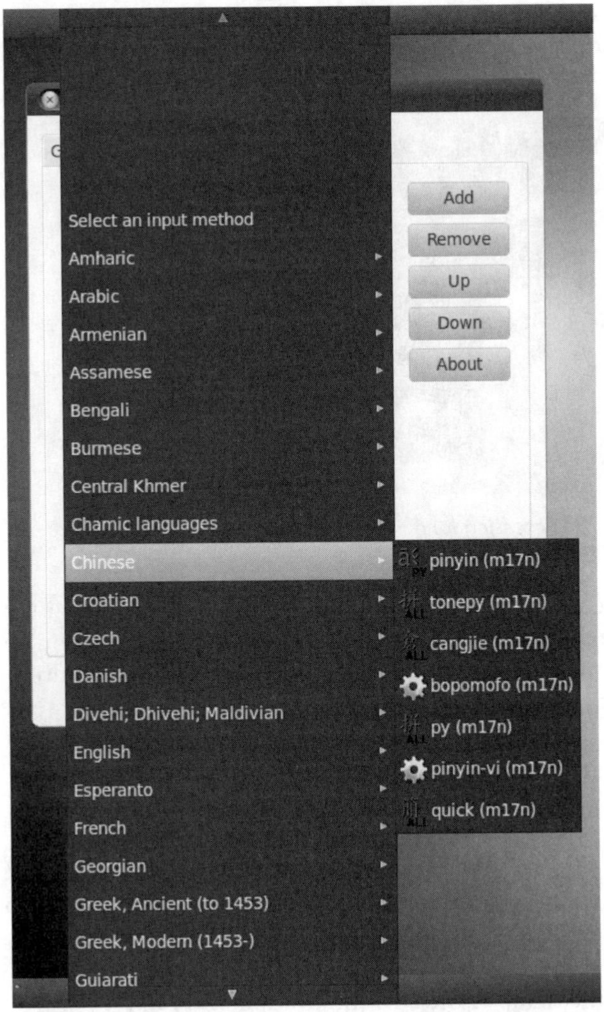

Figure 11-11: Some languages have more than one input method to choose from.

Nánníwān hăo dìfāng

Figure 11-12: IBus lets you easily show pinyin character readings with tone markings.

11-2: Typing Asian Languages with IBus

Once you have chosen your input methods and closed the IBus Preferences window, a small icon that looks like a mini keyboard will appear to the right of the volume controller in the top panel. If you click that panel, you will see all the available input methods listed in the drop-down menu that appears (as shown in Figure 11-13). To put this menu to use, you'll need to open an application that allows text input. To try things, let's use gedit (**Applications ▸ Accessories ▸ gedit Text Editor**).

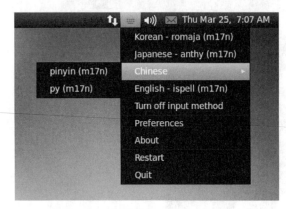

Figure 11-13: Accessing language input methods
from the IBus Panel applet

Once gedit appears, select the input method you want to use from the IBus panel applet. An input palette for the language you've selected will appear in the bottom-right corner of your desktop (Figure 11-14). You can now start typing in gedit using the input method you've selected.

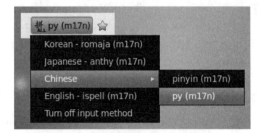

Figure 11-14: The IBus input palette

To switch from one input method to another, there are three options. First, you can go to the IBus Panel applet and change methods from the menu options. Second, you can make the change from the input palette: Clicking the name of the current input method will reveal a menu from which you can choose an alternative method (Figure 11-15). Finally, you can switch between methods with hotkey combinations: CTRL-spacebar toggles IBus on and off, while ALT-SHIFT-L switches you from one input method to the next.

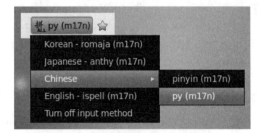

Figure 11-15: Switching between input methods
from the IBus input palette

Setting Up IBus to Automatically Start Up When You Log In

As you probably recall from when you first opened the IBus Preferences window, you have to start up IBus each time you log into your system. If you use IBus a lot and would thus prefer forgoing this extra step, you can easily set up your system to start it automatically when you log in. All you have to do is select **System ▸ Administration ▸ Language Support**.

In the Language tab, select **ibus** in the drop-down menu button next to the words *Keyboard input method system*, as shown in Figure 11-16. When done, close the window. The next time you log in, IBus will automatically start up and be ready for action when you need to use it.

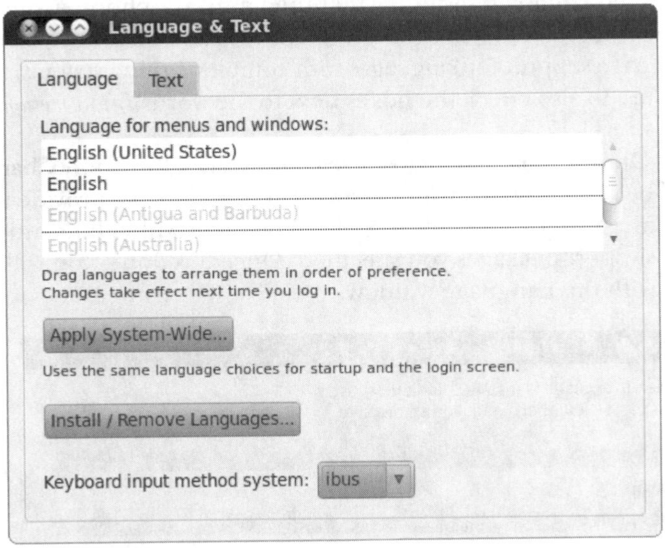

Figure 11-16: Setting up your system so that IBus automatically starts at login

If IBus still does not start up automatically the next time you log in, try adding it to your system's list of startup applications. To do this, select **Preferences ▸ Startup Applications**, and in the Startup Applications Preferences window, click the **Add** button. In the Name box type **Ibus**, and in the Command box type **/usr/bin/ibus-daemon -d**. When done, click **Add**, and then close the Startup Applications Preferences window.

Viewing Your System in Another Language

One of the many things that originally attracted me to the Linux world was being able to install language support for languages other than English and come up with a whole new system in a different language. On one of my machines, I have installed support for Chinese, Japanese, Swedish, and my default, English. With just a simple logout and a few more clicks, I can log back in with an interface in a totally different language. I can have a Chinese, Japanese, or Swedish system whenever I want.

This is very useful if you're in an environment where not everyone shares the same native language. At my former university, for example, where my Japanese and Chinese students sometimes used my computer, the additional language support allowed them to log in using their own language. It's even pretty handy if you are studying a foreign language and want to give yourself as much exposure as possible to it. All in all, it is a very useful feature.

Taking advantage of this feature in the GNOME environment is very easy. Basically all you have to do is install a group of support files for each language you want to add to your system. You can do this by going to the **System ▸ Administration ▸ Language Support**, after which the Language window will appear. In that window, click the **Install/Remove Languages** button. In the Installed Languages window that then appears, choose from the various languages available by checking the appropriate boxes. If you are installing language support for languages with complex writing systems, such as Japanese, be sure to also check the boxes next to the words *Input methods* and *Extra fonts* (Figure 11-17).

Once you have made your selections, click the **Apply Changes** button. You will be prompted for your password at this point, so provide what is required, and the Language Support tool will begin downloading and then installing the support packages you specified. Once it is done, you will be notified and left with the Language window.

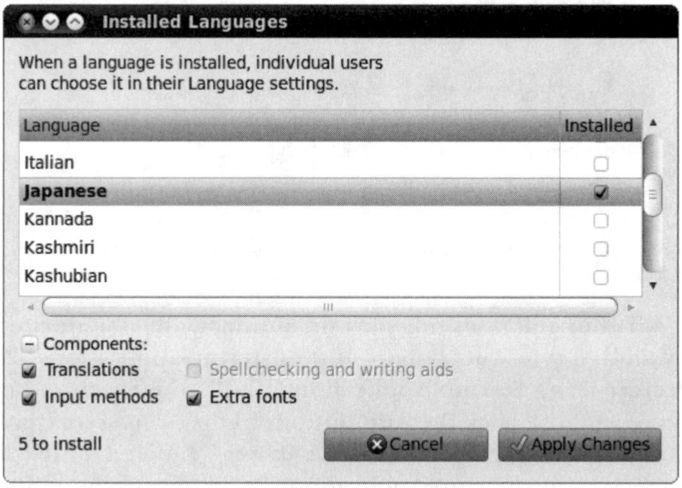

Figure 11-17: Selecting additional languages to install

Once you have installed support for the additional languages you want, you can choose to have your system open in a different language environment by using the Language window (**System ▸ Administration ▸ Language Support**). In the language tab of that window, select the language you want to use when you next log in, and drag it to the top of the list (Figure 11-18). For languages with complex input systems, you can also select your input method of choice, such as IBus, in the menu button next to the words *Keyboard input method system*. You can then close the window, log out, and then log in again, after which your system will appear in the language you chose.

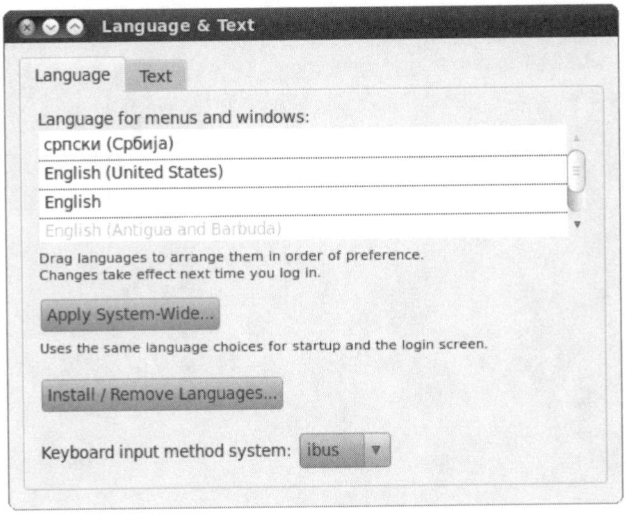

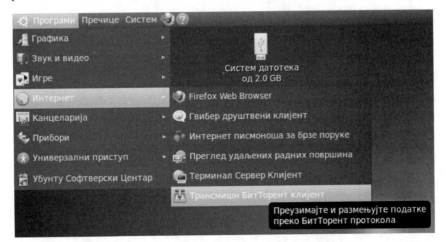

Figure 11-18: Selecting the language in which you want your
system to appear when you next log in

If you prefer, you can instead make these login choices from the login
screen. Once you click your name in the list of users, a set of menus will appear
in a panel at the bottom of the screen. Choose the language you want to use
from the Language menu in that panel. If the language you want is not there
and you know that you installed it, select **Other**, and then select the language
you are looking for in the window that appears. Once done, click **OK**, and
then proceed to log in normally.

Your startup process will then continue, and everything will progress as it
usually does. Depending on what language you've chosen, once your desktop
appears you will be in another linguistic world. Your menus, applications,
and even the little tips windows that pop up when you run your mouse over a
panel icon will all be in the newly selected language (Figure 11-19).

Figure 11-19: The Applications and Internet menus shown in Serbian

12

PENGUINS AT WORK

Getting Down to Business in Linux

I have to admit it, when I think about the joys of computing, I tend to think of the more hedonistic, self-indulgent areas like gaming, music, and graphics. Still, as is the case for most computer users, what I usually end up doing on my computer is work, and writing this book falls into that category.

Fortunately, Linux can get down to business and do it as well as the next OS. I think it's safe to say that you are missing nothing and are probably gaining quite a bit in terms of home and office productivity programs in the world of Linux. In this chapter, I'll walk you through the Linux offerings in this department.

OpenOffice.org

Whether they should be or not, people are quite obsessed with office suites, even though most people seldom need more than a word processor. The de facto standard among office suites is Microsoft Office, which is available in both the Windows and Macintosh worlds. Of course, because it is a Microsoft product, you can be quite sure that no Linux version is available.

Fortunately, Linux does have an exceedingly capable office suite in the form of OpenOffice.org, which is, incidentally, also freely available (as in *free*) in Windows and Mac OS X versions. OpenOffice.org is not some lightweight sour-grapes substitute for the Microsoft Office–less Linux world; it is a full-featured contender, and in some cases, OpenOffice.org is a clear winner.

OpenOffice.org Applications

The entire OpenOffice.org office suite consists of a number of application modules, and the most commonly used ones come bundled with Ubuntu. These include a word processor (Writer), a spreadsheet (Calc), and a presentation creator and player (Impress), all of which you can find by selecting **Applications ▸ Office**. In addition, there is a very handy vector drawing program (Draw), which you'll find by selecting **Applications ▸ Graphics**. The database module (Base) and the mathematical formula editor (Math), though no longer packaged with Ubuntu, are still available as separate downloads via Ubuntu Software Center (by searching for and marking *openoffice.org-base* and *openoffice.org-math*, respectively).

Since giving full and detailed instructions on how to use each of these applications would take up an entire book (and there are entire books on the subject), I will simply introduce each module to you.

Writer

As I mentioned earlier, the word processor is the office application that the majority of users turn to most often. Fortunately, OpenOffice.org Writer is a good one (see Figure 12-1). It is chock-full of features and can read and save Microsoft Word files. Like Word, it will even let you save your documents as HTML files so that you can easily change your documents into web pages.

As I said, Writer is a very straightforward word processor, so I won't go on about it, but if you would like an introduction to using Writer (or the other OpenOffice.org modules), check out the various tutorials and other resources available at *http://support.openoffice.org/*.

Calc

Calc is the OpenOffice.org spreadsheet application, and it is similar to Excel in terms of capabilities and general layout (see Figure 12-2). It can also, quite importantly, read and save Microsoft Excel files.

Since most people who use spreadsheets generally understand what they are all about and, after a bit of poking around, can figure out how to use them, I won't go into any sort of primer about using Calc. However, because there are many others who don't see any need to even try using spreadsheets, I will mention a few of the simpler tasks that can be done with Calc, in the hope of enticing some of you into trying it.

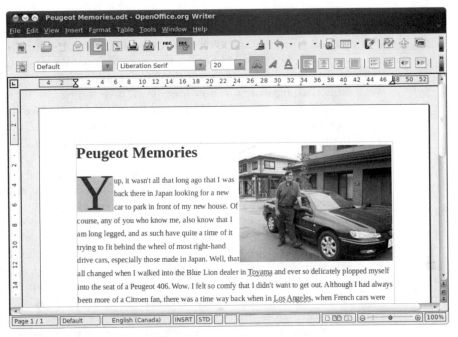

Figure 12-1: OpenOffice.org Writer

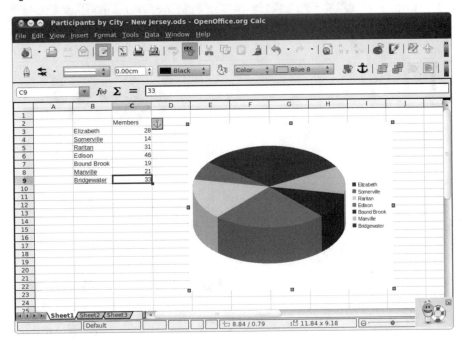

Figure 12-2: A graph created in OpenOffice.org Calc

Most people who don't use spreadsheets think of them as sort of giant calculators used for computing uncomfortably large sets of numbers, such as payrolls (which was the original purpose of such applications). That's right, of course, but spreadsheets can be used for everyday tasks too, such as projecting household budgets, calculating grade point averages (by teachers or students), figuring out how long it will take you to save up for your trip to Hungary, or even comparing the seat heights for the four or five motorcycles you are trying to choose among. And when doing any of these minor mathematical tasks, you can easily create graphs in order to make all the abstract numbers speak to you visually.

If numbers are just not your thing, you can still use Calc for creating lists of information, such as birthday lists, class rosters, shopping lists, address lists . . . whatever. You can even have Calc put the lists into alphabetical order, sort them by date of birth, and so on. Everyone eventually seems to find some use for Calc, so don't ignore it entirely.

And if you are still not convinced that Calc has a place in your life, you might at least find some amusement from an Easter egg hidden within the program, which allows you to play a Space Invaders clone called Star-Wars (Figure 12-3). Just type `=GAME("StarWars")` into any cell in Calc, and press ENTER. The instructions are in German, but it should be easy enough to figure out how to play even if you don't remember any of your high-school Deutsch.

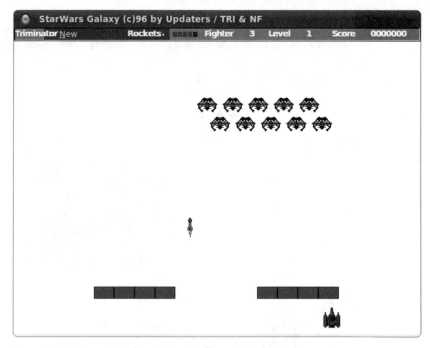

Figure 12-3: Space Invaders in OpenOffice.org Calc? Yup.

Impress

Impress is OpenOffice.org's answer to Microsoft's PowerPoint, with which it is compatible. It allows you to create attractive slides for use in presentations and also allows you to create notes or handouts to accompany them. Although these features make Impress quite handy in business and education settings, you may not find as much value in it as a home user.

Draw

More useful to the home user is OpenOffice.org Draw. Although Draw isn't great for creating true graphics in the artistic sense, it is very useful for creating flowcharts, organizational diagrams (such as seating arrangements for wedding receptions or conferences), or any other document in which you want a bit more control over the placement of text and graphics (especially when the two are combined), such as fliers, awards, diagrams, and newsletters. In this sense, Draw can be used quite effectively as a simple page layout program, as you can see in Figure 12-4.

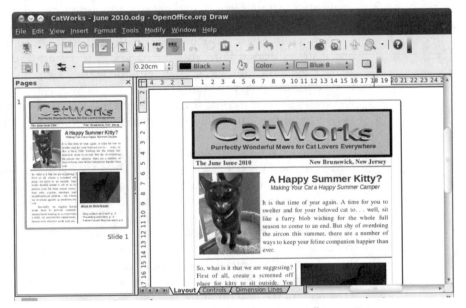

Figure 12-4: A newsletter created (and displayed) in OpenOffice.org Draw

Microsoft Office and OpenOffice.org File Compatibility

Although I mention the point throughout this section, it is worthwhile to reemphasize that OpenOffice.org can read and write Microsoft Office files. This compatibility is quite good, though tables sometimes prove slightly problematic.

To read Microsoft Office files, all you need to do is double-click the file in question, and it will open in the appropriate OpenOffice.org module. When saving files within OpenOffice.org to use within earlier versions of Microsoft Office, however, you must save them into the appropriate format, because OpenOffice.org will otherwise save files into its native format (*.odt* for Writer documents, *.ods* for Calc documents, and *.odp* for Impress documents) by default, and only the most recent versions of Office can deal with these files.

To do this when saving a file, click the small + next to the words *File type* in the Save window, and select the appropriate Microsoft Office format from the list of available file formats that appears below—choose **Microsoft Word 97/2000/XP** for a Writer document, for example.

OpenOffice.org Features

The three main applications in OpenOffice.org (Writer, Calc, and Impress) are quite similar to their pre–Office 2007 equivalents in Microsoft Office (Word, Excel, and PowerPoint), so switching to the OpenOffice.org applications should be relatively easy if you were weaned on those versions of Microsoft Office.

If you don't have any experience with Microsoft Office, you should still find it straightforward, because the basic layout is pretty intuitive. And if you are lacking in the intuition department, the built-in Help files are pretty good, too. To further help you along, the Tips system works just like tool tips in the Windows and Mac worlds. (In case you aren't sure what I'm talking about, *tool tips* are those little yellow boxes that pop up to tell you what a button or menu item does when you place your mouse over that button or menu item.) Another cool and useful help feature is What's This, which is a more detailed version of the Tips system. If you select **Help ▸ What's This**, your cursor will turn into a little question mark. Move that question mark cursor over almost any item in the OpenOffice.org interface, and you'll find out what it does rather than just what the item is called.

Despite all the straightforwardness I am speaking of, a few interface items will most likely be unfamiliar to you. That being the case, I will briefly discuss those items. I'll be using the word processor, Writer, as I describe these things, so if you want to run OpenOffice.org while following along, Writer might be a convenient starting point for you too.

Getting to Know the Buttons

Although you should be able to figure out what most of the buttons on the OpenOffice.org toolbars do, a few buttons are common to all OpenOffice.org modules and deserve a bit more explanation.

Export to PDF

The Export to PDF button is situated to the left of the two printer buttons (Print and Page Preview). You can use this button to *export*, or save, your document as a PDF file.

Hyperlink

 Clicking the Hyperlink button, the button to the left of the Table button, opens the Hyperlink window, from which you can assign links to specified documents—not only to web pages but also to documents on an individual computer and even targets within that document. Although a hyperlink on a web page is something we have all come to take for granted, the idea of hyperlinking between text documents sounds like a pretty radical concept. It is, in fact, a rather old one that has been around since before you or I even heard of the Internet.

Navigator

The fourth to the last button in the top row (the one that looks like a star-burst) is the Navigator button. Clicking this button (or just pressing the F5 key) opens the Navigator window (see Figure 12-5), which is a pretty cool navigational feature that comes in handy when working with lengthy or otherwise complex documents.

The Navigator allows you to easily bounce back and forth between pages in a document or even between elements therein, such as sections, links, and so on. Let's say you have a document with lots of illustrations in it (like this chapter), and you want to jump directly from graphic to graphic. In this case, you would double-click the word *Graphics* in the main pane of the Navigator window and then click the jump buttons (the odd little buttons to the left of the page number selector) to begin jumping.

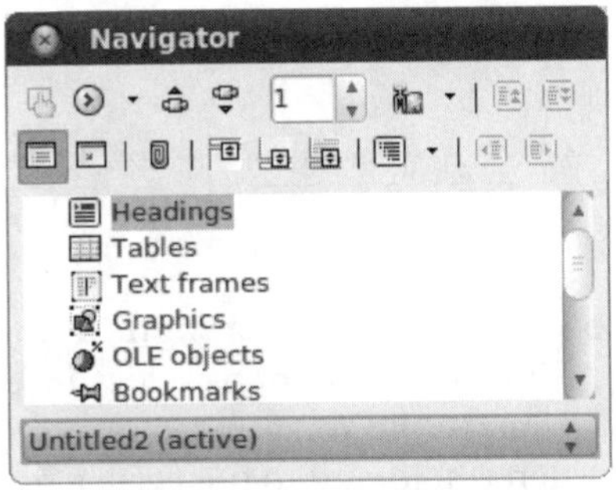

![Navigator window screenshot showing Headings, Tables, Text frames, Graphics, OLE objects, Bookmarks list with Untitled2 (active)]

Figure 12-5: The Navigator window

If you are dealing with a document containing various heading levels, such as all of the chapters in this book, you can also use Navigator to switch among those levels. Say you've decided to add a new main heading at the last minute to a document you've been writing. You thus need to drop all of the headings you had before down a notch; the former main heading becoming a subheading, and so on. By double-clicking the word *Headings,* the text of all the headings you have listed in the document appears. You can then select a heading in that list and click the Demote Level button (that's the one at the far right of the second row of buttons) to move it down a level.

Gallery

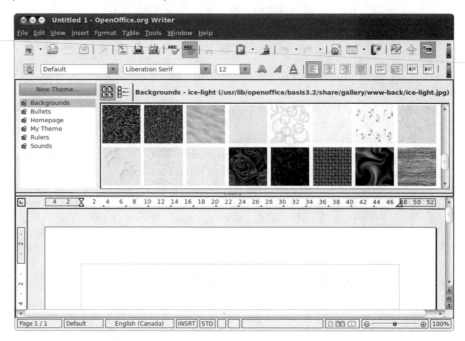

To the right of the Navigator button is the Gallery button. By clicking this button, the Gallery, a library of graphical elements for use in your documents or web pages, will appear in a separate pane at the top of your document window (see Figure 12-6). The elements within the Gallery range from various types of lines to buttons to colored three-dimensional doughnuts, and you can even add items of your own.

Figure 12-6: The Gallery

Inserting a graphic into your document is a simple enough task even when not using the Gallery. All you need to do is select **Insert ▸ Picture ▸ From File** and then locate the image file you want to insert. It can be handier to use the Gallery, however, when you intend to use certain graphics frequently. Once in the Gallery, your graphics are always only a click or two away and can be conveniently viewed in the Gallery browser window.

The collection of artwork that comes with OpenOffice.org is mostly geared toward building web pages, but other clip art is available elsewhere. For example, you can find a great collection online at *http://www.openclipart.org/*. Everything there is in the public domain, so it is all free to use. Be sure to check out the "Game baddie" collection—it's one of my favorites.

Adding these (or any other) graphic files to the Gallery is relatively easy to do. First you have to create a new category (called a *theme*) for each group of images you want to add. To create a Gallery theme of your own, just click the **New Theme** button in the Gallery window. This will open the Properties of New Theme window, where you should give your theme a name. Once you've done that, click the **Files** tab and then the **Find Files** button, which will open the Select Path window. From there you can navigate to the folder in which you are storing your clip art, photos, or other graphics. Once you have found the folder, click the **OK** button, after which a list of all the files in that folder will appear in the Properties of New Theme window.

From this window, you can easily add images to your new Gallery theme by clicking the name of each image you want to add (you might want to make sure that the box next to the word *Preview* is checked to make things a bit easier) and then clicking the **Add** button. Once you have done that, a copy of the image will immediately appear in the Gallery browser in your theme, where it will remain for future use (Figure 12-7). When you are done adding images to your new theme, click the **OK** button, after which the Properties of New Theme window will close, revealing your new theme and its contents. To use one of the images in the Gallery, just right-click the image you want to insert into your document, choose **Insert**, and then select **Copy** or **Link** in the pop-up menu.

If you're more of a convenience-oriented type, you will be happy to know that you can use the Ubuntu Software Center to download and install a significant portion of the clipart available from *http://www.openclipart.org/*. Just search for and install *openclipart-openoffice.org*. After the somewhat lengthy download and installation process is complete, restart OpenOffice.org (if it is running), and click the Gallery button. Your new collection will all be there!

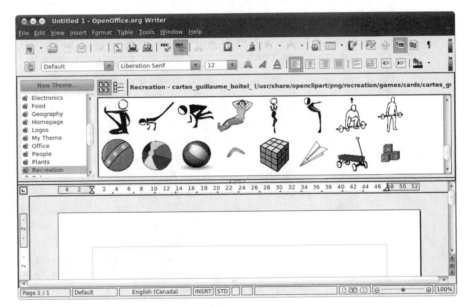

Figure 12-7: Viewing clip art and your own collections in the Gallery

Styles and Formatting

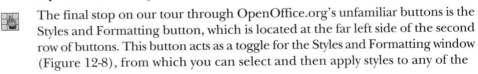

The final stop on our tour through OpenOffice.org's unfamiliar buttons is the Styles and Formatting button, which is located at the far left side of the second row of buttons. This button acts as a toggle for the Styles and Formatting window (Figure 12-8), from which you can select and then apply styles to any of the various elements within your document. Oh, and if you just can't take your hands off the keyboard for a moment to fiddle with the mouse, you can also open the window by pressing the F11 key.

Figure 12-8: The Styles and Formatting window

To give you an example of how convenient using styles can be, imagine that you are typing a bibliography page for some document you've prepared. You typed each entry as you might any paragraph, as in the following:

```
Smythe, W. (2004). Reconsidering the need for speech
between non-human interlocutors beyond the age of seven. The
Journal of the Society of Elves, Faeries, and Garden Gnomes,
20 (2), 125-147.
```

Like most paragraphs you type, the entry is formatted as a first-line indent, which is fine and dandy except that you want a hanging indent, which is the norm for bibliography entries. Rather than messing around with tabs or margins to get things the way you want, all you have to do is click your mouse anywhere within the paragraph and then double-click the **Hanging indent** entry in the Styles and Formatting window. After that, as if by magic (though you know better), the transformation is made:

```
Smythe, W. (2004). Reconsidering the need for speech between non-
    human interlocutors beyond the age of seven. The Journal of the
    Society of Elves, Faeries, and Garden Gnomes, 20 (2), 125-147.
```

You could follow the same procedure for each of your other entries or, with Hanging indent selected, click the **paint can** button in the Styles and Formatting window, after which your mouse cursor, when placed over the document, will appear as a paint can. Click in any other paragraph in your bibliography, and that entry, too, will be formatted in the new style. The process is essentially the same when applying different styles to any other document elements.

One thing that might annoy you when using the Styles and Formatting window is that it can be a pain at times, floating around as it does. It has a tendency to get in the way of your text no matter where you put it. Sure, you can toggle it on and off, but if you're using it a number of times within the same document, this can be get old too.

A happy compromise is to dock the Styles and Formatting window into the main document window. You can do this by dragging the Styles and Formatting window to the top-left or top-right corner of the document work area. When an outline of the Styles and Formatting window appears around the in-document portion of the window (as you can see in Figure 12-9), release the mouse button. The Styles and Formatting window will now appear as a pane on the side of the document window (Figure 12-10).

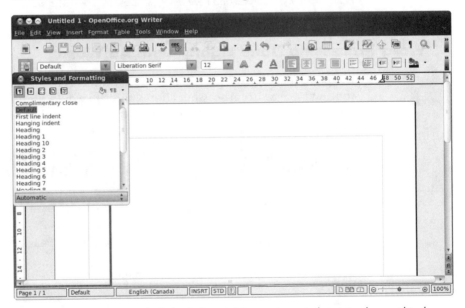

Figure 12-9: Preparing to dock the Styles and Formatting window into place within the main document window

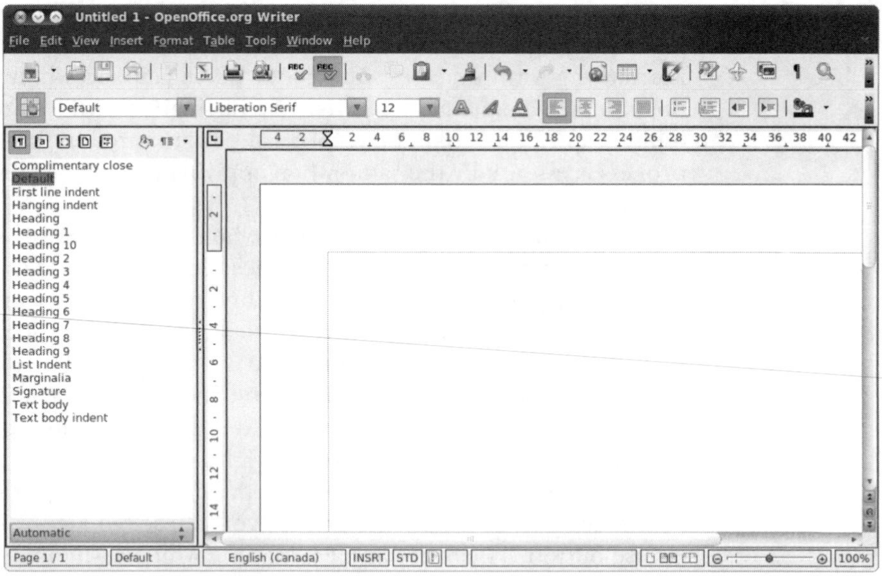

Figure 12-10: The Styles and Formatting window in place as a pane within the main document window

Word Processing Done Lightly with AbiWord

If OpenOffice.org's Writer is a bit more powerful than what you need for your everyday word processing chores and you would prefer something that pops up as soon as you click the launcher, then you might want to consider giving another word processor, AbiWord, a try (Figure 12-11).

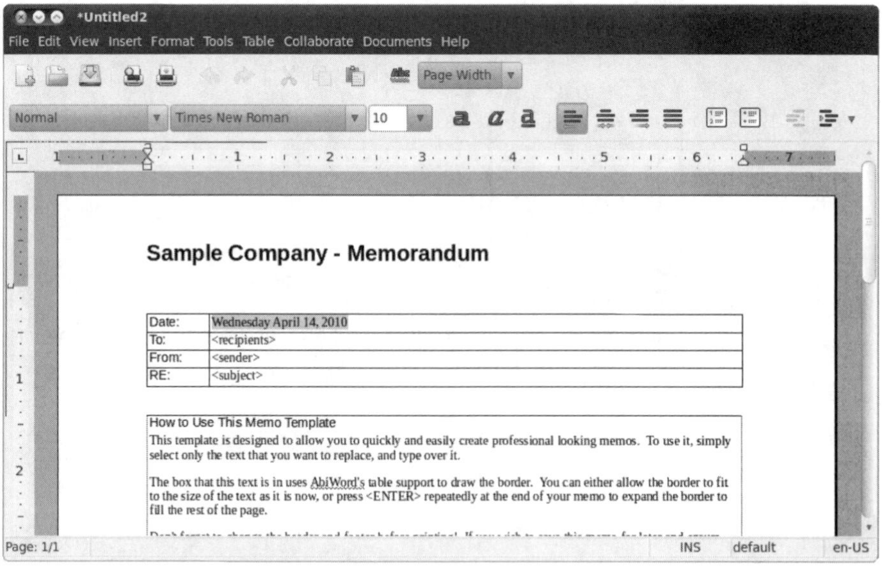

Figure 12-11: The other Linux word processor—AbiWord

AbiWord has a very straightforward and easy-to-use interface, which you should be able to figure out without much, if any, help. It also has a couple of rather interesting features, such as its autoresize function, which magnifies the onscreen document size (fonts, images, and everything) or shrinks it as you increase or decrease the size of the program window. And in case you're wondering, AbiWord can save and read Microsoft Word DOC files and save documents as PDF files.

You can easily install AbiWord via the Ubuntu Software Center by performing a search for *abiword*. Once you have AbiWord installed, you can run it by selecting **Applications ▶ Office ▶ AbiWord**.

Some Other Cool Productivity Apps

In addition to the more traditional office applications, a number of other applications are either included with or available for your system that can be grouped together under the "productivity" label. I will introduce a few of those to you here.

Sticky Notes

Mac users will be well familiar with the digital version of the now ubiquitous little yellow Post-it-like notes called Sticky Notes (Figure 12-12) that come as part of the GNOME desktop. GNOME's Sticky Notes is a panel applet that you can add to your own panel by right-clicking any open panel space and then selecting **Add to Panel** in the pop-up menu that appears. When the Add to Panel window appears, click **Sticky Notes**, and then click the **Add** button. Close the Add to Panel window by clicking **Close**. You will then be ready for note-taking action.

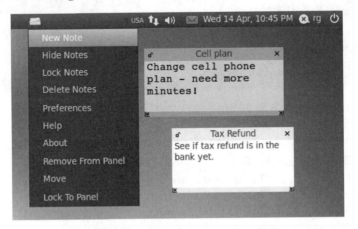

Figure 12-12: GNOME's Sticky Notes

Tomboy

If Sticky Notes just doesn't cut it for you and your more dramatic note-taking needs, then perhaps you will find yourself better served by another application that comes with your system, called Tomboy (Figure 12-13). Like Sticky Notes, Tomboy also works as a panel applet, but it is a bit more full featured, albeit without making any claims to stickiness. Instead, the various notes you create can be viewed by selecting them from the menu that appears when you click the Tomboy panel applet. All in all, it's a very handy approach.

What really gives Tomboy its bragging rights, however, is its search and hyperlink functions. These allow you to search for entries within your entire Tomboy note library and create hyperlinks that connect text in one note to another linked note. In fact, Tomboy will automatically create a hyperlink whenever you type a word that matches one of your existing note headings. To make matters even more exciting (or at least more useful), Tomboy, by means of its plug-ins feature, allows you to export notes to HTML or print them, either as hard copy or as PDF docs.

If you'd like to try Tomboy, start it by selecting **Applications ▶ Accessories ▶ Tomboy Notes**, after which Tomboy will appear in the top GNOME panel.

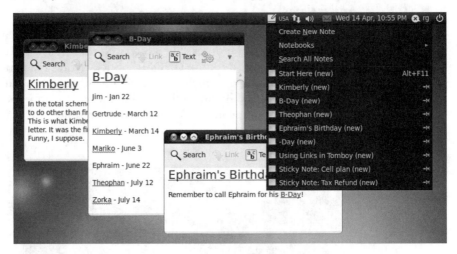

Figure 12-13: Notes taken seriously—Tomboy

GnuCash

If you are familiar with the personal financial management software Quicken, then you might be interested in GnuCash, which is the Linux world's best-known offering in the personal finance arena. It reads Quicken and Intuit QIF files, which makes things even nicer should you be making the transition from another operating system. Unfortunately, unless you live in Germany, you cannot use GnuCash for online banking. But as the GnuCash folks themselves say, don't blame them; blame your bank.

To install GnuCash, just do an Ubuntu Software Center search for *gnucash*, and then install both *gnucash* and *gnucash-docs*. Once these are installed, you can run the application by selecting **Applications ▸ Office ▸ GnuCash Finance Management**.

Scribus

To round things out, we come to a open source desktop publishing application, Scribus (Figure 12-14), for those times when OpenOffice.org Writer and Draw just don't cut it. Scribus is designed to produce commercial-grade output, with support for professional publishing features, such as CMYK colors, PostScript handling, and creation of color separations, to name but a few.

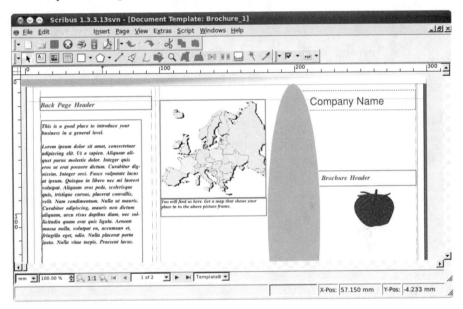

Figure 12-14: Scribus

You can download and install Scribus by doing an Ubuntu Software Center search for *scribus*. Once the installation is complete, you can run the application by selecting **Applications ▸ Graphics ▸ Scribus**.

13

BRUSH-WIELDING PENGUINS

Linux Does Art

Now that you know you can get down to business in Linux, it is time to don that beret of yours and address the artistic side of things. Yes, Linux does art, and as you will soon find out, a good number of programs on your system allow you to create and manipulate graphic files. These days, however, there is perhaps nothing as important to most users' graphical repertoires as their digital cameras, so that is where we'll begin.

Project 13A: Importing Images from Digital Cameras

Although scanner support for Linux can prove a bit spotty, support for digital cameras is practically a worry-free affair. In fact, if Ubuntu can't figure out what kind of camera you have, it just treats it as if it were an external hard drive or flash drive plugged into your computer's USB port. And even if your camera doesn't seem to communicate with your computer when connected directly, you can still transfer your images to your hard disk by removing the memory card from your camera, inserting it into a USB flash memory card reader, and plugging that reader into one of your computer's USB ports. In that case, your system will mount the card reader as if it were an external drive (which is pretty much what it is), thus allowing you to copy the images to your hard disk. Of course, you can use this method even if your camera works just fine with Ubuntu—some people find it to be the easiest way to deal with things, anyway.

13A-1: Importing Images from Camera to Computer Somewhat Automatically via F-Spot

When you connect your camera to your computer via a USB cable, put your camera in play mode, and power it on, Ubuntu will usually automatically recognize it and open a window that asks how you want to import the photos on the camera. To import the photos via F-Spot, accept the default selection in the drop-down menu button, Open F-Spot (as shown in Figure 13-1), and then click **OK**. After that, here's what you need to do:

1. In the window that appears, you will see thumbnails and filenames of all the photos on your camera. By default, all the images are selected. However, if you prefer to copy only some of the images, you can do so by holding down the CTRL key and clicking the desired images, as shown in Figure 13-2.

2. Once you've made your selections, click the **Target location** button, and choose where to copy your photos. Your *Pictures* folder, or a subfolder within it, might be a logical spot.

3. You can also tag the photos you are about to import by checking the **Attach tag** box and then selecting the desired tag from the menu button to the right. I'll talk more about tagging in Project 13B-2.

4. Finally, click the **Copy** button.

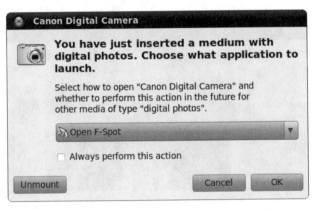

Figure 13-1: Ubuntu recognizes your camera and asks you how to proceed.

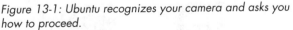

Figure 13-2: Selecting which photos to import from your digital camera via F-Spot Photo Manager

5. F-Spot will then begin the copying process, showing its progress in a separate window. When the download is complete, the words *Download Complete* will appear within the progress bar of that window. Click the **OK** button. You can now view your images within the main F-Spot window (Figure 13-3).

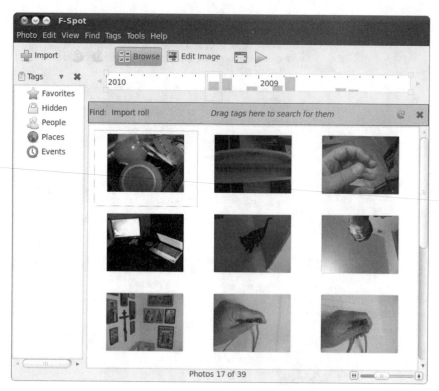

Figure 13-3: Viewing your imported digital camera images in F-Spot

13A-2: Transferring Images from Camera to Computer via Nautilus

As I mentioned, you can also use Nautilus to import photos from your camera. The process for doing this starts pretty much the same as I discussed in Project 13A-1, albeit with a slight twist. Here's how you do it:

1. Plug your camera into one of your computer's USB ports, and put your camera into play mode. Within seconds, a window like that in Figure 13-1 will appear. In that window, select **Open Folder** in the drop-down menu button instead of the default *F-Spot*, and then click **OK**. A Nautilus window will appear revealing the contents of your camera's storage card. An icon for your camera will also appear in the side pane of that window and any other open Nautilus window (Figure 13-4) and on your desktop as a double-clickable launcher.

2. Double-click your way through the folders on your camera until you find the photos you want to import.

3. Drag and drop or copy and paste the images from your camera to any logical spot in your home folder.

4. When you're done with your transfers, either click the eject icon next to the entry for your camera in the left pane of a Nautilus window or right-click the icon for your camera on the desktop, and select **Unmount**. The icon for your camera will then disappear from the side pane and desktop. Or, easiest of all, just turn off your camera, and both the desktop and Nautilus instances of your camera should automatically disappear.

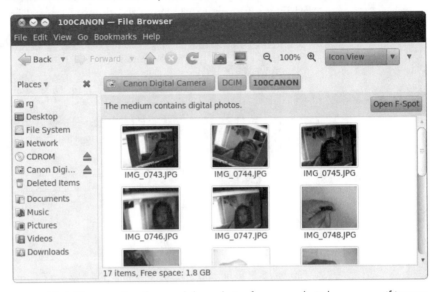

Figure 13-4: You can also drag and drop photos from your digital camera as if it were a USB drive.

Project 13B: Working with Digital Images in F-Spot Photo Manager

F-Spot not only imports images from you camera to computer but also acts as a handy photo-organizing, browsing, viewing, and editing tool. And working in conjunction with Evolution, the default email software in Ubuntu, F-Spot allows you to easily send images via email (**File ▸ Send by Mail**) without fiddling around with attachments. You can run F-Spot by selecting **Applications ▸ Graphics ▸ F-Spot Photo Manager**. Note that the first time out, you will be asked to select the folders that hold the images you want to import into F-Spot.

13B-1: Exporting Images to Online Albums and Galleries

A very cool feature of F-Spot is that it allows you to export images to numerous online gallery or album sites, such as Flickr and Picasa, much like Windows Live Photo Gallery. Exporting an image to an online gallery or album is pretty simple, and I'll use a Picasa web album for this example. Here's what you need to do:

1. Select the photos you want to place into your online album by holding down the CTRL key and clicking each photo once.

2. In the main F-Spot window, select **Photo ▸ Export to ▸ PicasaWeb**, after which an Export window like the one in Figure 13-5 will appear.

Figure 13-5: Exporting images to online galleries via F-Spot

3. The first time out, you will need to click the **Add** button at the top of the window (to the right of the word *Gallery*) to set things up so that F-Spot can access your online gallery.

4. In the small window that appears, type the username and password for your online album/gallery service (not your username and password for Ubuntu). Click **Add** in that window when you're done.

5. You can also decide which of your online albums you want to add the photos to by clicking the drop-down menu in the Album section. Or, if you want to create a new album, click the **Add** button to the right of that menu, provide a title and description in the small window that appears, and then click **Add**.

6. Once back in the Export window, click the **Export** button.

F-Spot will then start uploading your images to your online gallery site, letting you know what it's doing in a progress window. Once done, your web browser will open to your online gallery page, revealing your newly uploaded images. You can toggle this post-export automatic browser opening feature by checking or unchecking the **Open album in browser when done uploading** box in the Export window (Figure 13-5).

13B-2: Organizing Your Photo Collections with Tags

As your photo collection grows and grows, it can get rather tough to sort things out and find exactly what you need. Fortunately, F-Spot has a few ways of making this easier to deal with, one of which is the timeline slider, located immediately above the thumbnail-viewing pane, which allows you to locate images by year and month.

An additional and interesting way of organizing things is by using *tags*, which allow you to identify images thematically. Applying tags and using such tags to narrow down your photo searches is pretty easy to do.

First, to apply tags to your images, just drag the appropriate tag icon from the left pane of the F-Spot window directly onto the image you want to tag. You can place more than one tag on a picture. Once you have added the tag, a small version of the tag icon will appear below the image, as you can see in Figure 13-6.

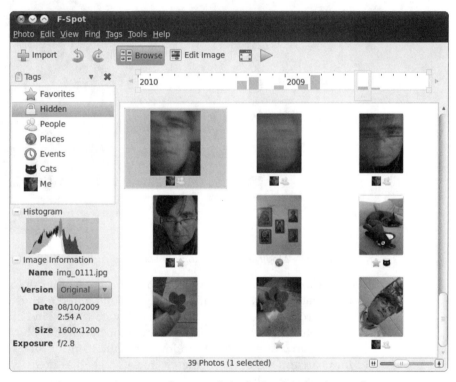

Figure 13-6: Using F-Spot's tags feature to help deal with hefty photo collections

The number of preset tags is rather limited, but you can add your own by selecting **Tags ▶ Create New Tag**.

Give your tag a name in the Create New Tag window that appears, and click **Create**. The new tag will then appear in the left pane of the F-Spot window, albeit without an icon. There are two ways to add an icon. One is to simply the drag the iconless tag to a photo you want to tag with it, after which a mini-thumbnail of that image will become the icon for the tag.

The other approach is to right-click the new tag and select **Edit Tag** in the pop-up menu. In the window that appears, click the iconless button next to the word *Icon*, and then select one of the predefined icons in the window that appears. You can also use this approach to edit the photo of an automatically created tag, which allows you to determine exactly what portion of a picture you want to use as the icon for that tag (Figure 13-7).

Figure 13-7: Modifying the portion of photo used as an icon tag in F-Spot

Searching for images by tag is perhaps even easier than adding the tags to the images in the first place. Let's say you wanted to find all of your images that were tagged as *Events*. You would first go to the **Find** menu and select **Find Selected Tag**. A find bar will then appear directly above the thumbnail-viewing area of the F-Spot window. Drag the icon for the Events tag to that find bar, and almost immediately images tagged as *Events* will appear in the thumbnail area below. Sweet.

Getting Arty with the GIMP

The Windows and Mac worlds may have Photoshop, but the Linux world has the GIMP (see Figure 13-8). Although arguably not as powerful as Photoshop, the GIMP is a capable contender, which may explain why it has been ported to both Mac and Windows. The GIMP allows you to create bitmap graphics and, quite importantly, retouch or completely doctor image files.

With the GIMP you can get rid of red-eye in your digital photos, airbrush out unwanted shadows (or even facial blemishes), give your image a canvas texture, change a photo into an oil painting, and even add a bell pepper here and there—with drop shadows no less.

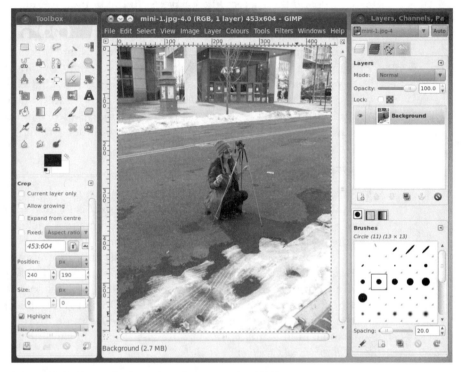

Figure 13-8: Manipulating a digital image in the GIMP

Because not everyone needs or uses the power of the GIMP, the powers that be unfortunately decided to no longer bundle it on the Ubuntu Desktop CD, thus freeing up space for more frequently run applications. Pity though that might be, you can still install the GIMP via the Ubuntu Software Center. Just do a search for *GIMP*, and then install it as you would any application, as you learned to do in Chapter 6. Once installed, you can run the GIMP by selecting **Applications ▸ Graphics ▸ GIMP Image Editor**.

Using the GIMP to Resize Images and Convert File Formats

Like F-Spot, the GIMP is also a very handy tool for resizing images. You can do this by simply right-clicking an image opened in the GIMP and then selecting **Image ▸ Scale Image** in the pop-up menu. This will open the Scale Image window, where you can set the new size of the image.

The GIMP is also an excellent tool for converting images from one file format to another. You can, for example, open a bitmap (*.bmp*) file and save it as a PNG (*.png*) file, save a JPEG (*.jpg*) file as a GIF (*.gif*) file, and so on.

Although this can also be done with other graphics applications, the GIMP supports an extremely wide variety of file formats, and it even lets you save an image file as a compressed tarball, which makes it a true file conversion king.

To perform a file conversion, just right-click an image opened within the GIMP, and then select **File ▸ Save As** in the pop-up menu. You can make the same selection from the File menu if you prefer. Either way, the Save Image window will then appear. In that window, you can specify the new file format by replacing the original file extension in the Name box at the top of that window with the extension for the format you want to convert the image to. If you're not sure what formats are available to you, click the small arrow to the left of the words *Select File Type (By Extension)*, and then choose from the options in the pane that appears below. To save a work in progress, use the GIMP-native XCF format so that you can continue working on the image later.

Learning More

It is lots of fun to learn to use the GIMP by just playing around with it for a while. To get you started, most of the fun stuff is located in the Filters menu of any image window. Of course, you should make a backup copy of any file you are planning to experiment with before altering it.

If you prefer working through manuals and tutorials over just learning by goofing around, you can download and install the GIMP User Manual via the Ubuntu Software Center by searching for *gimp-help-en* and then installing **Documentation for the GIMP (English)**. Once it is installed, you can access the manual from within the GIMP from the Help menu. You can also view the manual online at *http://docs.gimp.org/en/*, and you can find a series of tutorials at *http://www.gimp.org/tutorials/*.

Phatch Photo Batch Processor

While the GIMP and F-Spot are quite capable in terms of handling the vast majority of your photo-organizing and editing chores, they lack an easy-to-use batch file conversion method that allows you to apply various conversions to a group of files at the same time. For example, let's say you want to convert 100 of your photos so they look like black-and-white snapshots with white borders, are 50 percent smaller than the originals, have a similar thematic filename, and are saved in *.tiff* rather than *.jpg* format. Applying all these changes one by one would be excruciating—fortunately, Phatch comes to the rescue! (See Figure 13-9.)

You can download and install Phatch via the Ubuntu Software Center by doing a search for *phatch*. Once installed, you can run it by selecting **Applications ▸ Graphics ▸ Phatch PHoto bATCH Processor**.

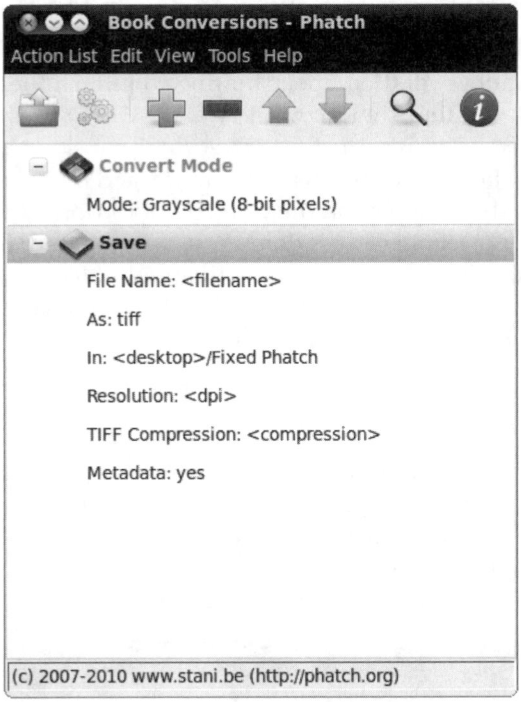

Figure 13-9: Batch photo file conversions with Phatch

Using Phatch

Using Phatch is easy, and actually quite a bit of hocus-pocusy fun. However, its interface might not be obvious for a first-time user. With that in mind, here is a brief rundown on how to use Phatch:

1. Click the + button in the main Phatch window, and the Phatch actions window will appear.

2. In that window, select the action (conversion) you want to apply to your photos, and click **Add**. Repeat this process for any other actions you want to apply.

3. Once you have added all the actions you want, click each action in the main Action List, and enter the appropriate parameters for each action (size, file format, size of border, output location, and so on).

4. If the actions are not listed in the order you want them to occur, click the action you want to move, and then change its position using the up and down arrow buttons.

5. Once everything is ready, save your Action List with a meaningful name so you can use it again if need be, and then select **Tools ▸ Execute**.

6. In the window that appears, click the **Browse Folder** button to find the photos you want to convert, and then click the **Batch** button.

7. Another window will then open showing you which files will be acted upon. Click **Continue** in that window.

Phatch will then perform the conversions listed on your Action List in the order listed. It will show you the progress of its work, and then a small window will appear telling you it's done. You can then find the new converted copies of your original photos in the destination folder you chose. If you failed to choose a destination folder, the newly created conversions should appear in a *Phatch* folder on your desktop.

gpaint

If the GIMP comes across as a bit overwhelming for you or if it seems to be overkill for your simpler tasks, you might want to try an application known as gpaint (or GNU Paint), which you can download and install via Ubuntu Software Center (search for *gpaint*). As you can see in Figure 13-10, gpaint is similar to Windows Paint and MacPaint, and just as simple.

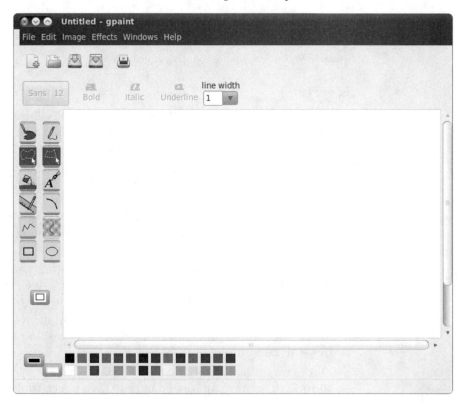

Figure 13-10: Art done simple—gpaint

Once you have installed gpaint, you can run it by selecting **Applications ▸ Graphics ▸ GNU Paint**.

Inkscape

The GIMP, like other so-called paint programs, creates bitmap images in various file formats. These are images in which the location and color of every single pixel is recorded. The image is essentially a collection of dots, or *pixels*. The file you create is a rather hefty map of these pixels, and this map tells your system where everything in your image is supposed to go when it is displayed or printed.

Drawing programs, on the other hand, create vector images, which are actually collections of mathematical formulae representing the various shapes in your image. This may sound rather unimportant to you, but such drawings have advantages in certain cases. One of these advantages is that vector image files take up less space on your hard disk than bitmaps. Another, and perhaps the most important, advantage is that shapes in vector images retain their smooth edges when the images are enlarged. A smooth circle created as a bitmap, for example, would begin to show jagged edges ("the jaggies") when enlarged to any extent, while the same circle in a vector image would remain smooth and round no matter how much you increased its size.

If you're interested in giving a drawing program a go, then try Inkscape (see Figure 13-11). To download and install it, do a search in the Ubuntu Software Center for *inkscape*. Once it is installed, you can run it by selecting **Applications ▸ Graphics ▸ Inkscape**.

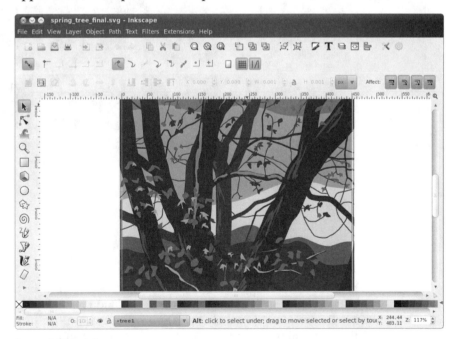

Figure 13-11: Inkscape

If you would like to learn how to use Inkscape, go to the Inkscape home page at *http://www.inkscape.org/*. Be sure to click the **Galleries** link on that page to see examples of what you can create with the program, such as the image shown in Figure 13-11, which is from *http://plurib.us/svg_gallery/*.

Project 13C: Installing Picasa

It wouldn't be right to dedicate a whole chapter to Linux's graphical capabilities without mentioning one of the newest entries in the Linux application arena—Picasa. Those of you coming from the Windows and Mac worlds are no doubt familiar with this very popular image-viewing, organizing, and editing application from Google, and you will no doubt be pleased to discover that it is available for Linux. Picasa is not an open source application, which may cause some Linux diehards to turn away, but it is free, feature rich, nice to look at, and decidedly cool (Figure 13-12). It also gives you easy access to various online photo blogs, photo finishers, and product providers, such as PhotoStamps, Shutterfly, Kodak, and even Walgreens.

Figure 13-12: Picasa

13C-1: Downloading and Installing the Picasa Package

Picasa is free, and getting it is relatively easy—just point your browser to *http:// picasa.google.com/linux*, and click the **Download Picasa for Linux** button. Once on the download page, click the appropriate download link (that would be the one under *For Debian/Ubuntu i386* if you're using the disc in this book).

After the download is complete, locate the Picasa DEB package on your hard disk, and double-click it. Click the **Install Package** button in the Package Installer window that appears. Provide your password if prompted for it, and then click **OK** to begin the installation. When the installation process is complete, you will be notified in the installation progress window. After that, you can close both that and the Package Installer window.

13C-2: Running and Setting Up Picasa

Once Picasa is installed, you can run it by going to the **Applications** menu and selecting **Graphics ▸ Picasa ▸ Picasa** or **Other ▸ Picasa** (the location varies, even with difference user accounts on the same computer!). The first time you do this, you will be greeted by a warning window telling you that Picasa can be integrated with GNOME so that whenever you hook up a digital camera to your computer, GNOME will run Picasa in order to handle the photo importation process. Make the choice you feel most comfortable with, after which another window about Picasa/Firefox integration will appear (click **OK**), and then finally a Picasa License Agreement window will appear. Agree to what you're asked by clicking **Next** and then in the next screen **I Agree**.

Picasa will then scan your desktop and home folder for images and add any images it finds to its library.

Working with Picasa should be very straightforward, but if you want to find out more, check out *http://picasa.google.com/linux/*. On that page, you will find a basic overview, links to more Linux-specific information (including FAQ and forum pages), and a Picasa Getting Started Guide.

A Few Other Graphics Apps to Consider

In addition to the graphics applications I have covered in this chapter, there are still more available. You can grab all of them via the Ubuntu Software Center. Although you can experiment with what's available, I will point out a few others worth noting. If nothing else, these applications will give you an idea of the breadth of stuff out there waiting for you.

gThumb Image Viewer

In earlier editions of Ubuntu, an application called gThumb (Figure 13-13), handy for use in photo-handling chores, used to come preinstalled. Some folks wish it still did. It has almost all the same features as F-Spot and a few of its own (such as creating original web album pages and some limited batch conversion capabilities). That said, it all really boils down to whether you prefer F-Spot or gThumb (or even Picasa, for that matter). They're all free and easy to use, so try them all to see which you like. If you do, install gThumb via the Ubuntu Software Center by searching for *gthumb*. Once installed, run it by selecting **Applications ▸ Graphics ▸ gThumb Image Viewer**.

Figure 13-13: gThumb

Blender

Perhaps one of the most impressive open source applications available today is Blender. Blender (Figure 13-14) is a professional-level 3D modeling, animation, and rendering program. It is rather complex, but that is the source of its power and popularity (it comes in versions for just about every operating system out there). If you would like to find out a bit more about Blender before taking the time (and disk space) to install it, go to *http://www.blender3d .org/*. Find it via the Ubuntu Software Center by searching for *blender*; once the program is installed, you can run it by selecting **Applications ▸ Graphics ▸ Blender (fullscreen)** or **Blender (windowed)**.

QCad

Another open source application that has found its way into almost all operating systems is QCad (Figure 13-15). QCad is a 2D computer-aided design (CAD) program with which you can create technical drawings such as room interiors, machine parts, or even musical instruments. (I've seen a plan for a Nyckelharpa done on QCad!) To find out more, go to the project home page at *http://www.ribbonsoft.com/qcad.html/*. Search the Ubuntu Software Center for *qcad*, and install the application. Once it is installed, you can run it by selecting **Applications ▸ Graphics ▸ QCad**.

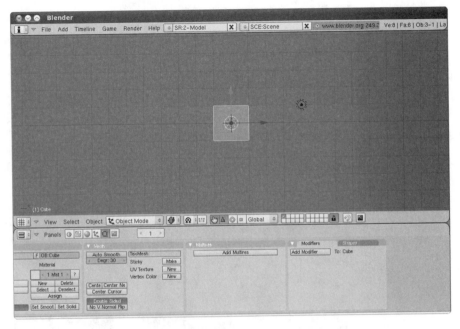

Figure 13-14: Blender

Figure 13-15: QCad

Tux Paint

To wrap things up, let's turn to an application for the kids (or the kids within us) and have a look at Tux Paint. With its big colorful buttons and fun and funky tools, Tux Paint, shown in Figure 13-16, is an application that your children can handle and enjoy. The best of Tux Paint's features (at least in my opinion) are its stamps, of which there is a good variety—everything from apples to seahorses and euro coins to boot! Oh, yes, and it talks to you. Click a duck stamp, and not only will you hear a voice say "duck," but you will also hear the "quack quack" we've come to associate with our green-necked friends. Search the Ubuntu Software Center for *tuxpaint*, and, once installed, launch it from **Applications ▸ Education ▸ Tux Paint**.

Figure 13-16: Tux Paint

14

TUX ROCKS

Music à la Linux

It's now time to move on to the audio side of things. Yes, Linux does indeed rock, and in this chapter you will find out about those musical talents that your system possesses. You will learn how to rip CDs, create MP3 and Ogg Vorbis files (files that you can recognize by their *.mp3* and *.ogg* filename extensions), add album cover art, change file tags, play music files, and burn files onto audio CDs that you can play in any CD player. You'll also learn how to play a variety of audio streams. If you're interested in learning how to work with your iPod, iPhone, or other digital media device, or how to convert audio files from one format to another, well, you'll have to wait until Chapter 15.

Audio File Formats

Before we go any further, it is probably best to discuss the various formats in which audio data can be stored on your computer. For the longest time, the de facto standards have been WAV (created by Microsoft/IBM and using the

.*wav* extension), AU (from Sun/Unix and using the .*au* extension), and AIFF (from Apple and using the .*aiff* extension), all of which are uncompressed formats. Files saved in these formats are, therefore, exceedingly large, with an average WAV file of CD-quality music weighing in at about 10MB per minute. To put that in perspective, back in 1988 my first Macintosh had a 40MB hard disk—more space than I thought I would ever need but not enough space to store a WAV file of Nirvana's "Come as You Are."

As computers underwent their evolution into the multimedia machines they are today, it became clear that something was going to have to be done about those disk-space-devouring audio files. Audio compression formats were thus developed. These compression formats work, to oversimplify things a bit, by cutting out the portions of a sound signal that the human ear cannot hear—sort of a dog-whistle approach. The most widely known and embraced of these audio compression formats is MP3. Audio files encoded in MP3 format can end up being as little as one-twelfth the size of the original WAV file without any noticeable loss in quality.

Another audio compression format that was developed was Ogg Vorbis. Ogg Vorbis was a product of the open source community, so, unlike MP3, which has always been used under the shadow of yet-to-be-exercised patent rights, it was free of patent and licensing worries from the get-go. Because of that and the fact that it was the equal of MP3 in terms of quality and performance (if not, as many claim, better), Ogg Vorbis became the darling of the Linux community.

As you work with ripping audio files in this chapter, you are sure to notice yet another encoding option—FLAC. Free Lossless Audio Codec (FLAC) is an encoding format that, unlike the MP3 and Ogg Vorbis formats, does not remove any audio information from the audio file during the encoding process. The downside of this is that FLAC provides space savings of only 30 to 50 percent, which is much less than the 80 percent neighborhood achieved by MP3 or Ogg Vorbis. The upside, of course, is that the FLAC files should be equivalent to CDs in terms of quality.

Given that retention of audio quality, FLAC becomes an ideal choice if you are not satisfied with the audio quality provided by Ogg Vorbis or MP3 files. It is also a good choice if you want to create both Ogg Vorbis and MP3 files . . . or if you just don't know which one you want to work with yet. In such cases, you can just rip the file and encode it in FLAC format. As I mentioned earlier, once you get to Chapter 15, you will learn how you can convert the FLAC file later, when you know what you want or need.

Project 14A: Installing MP3 Support for Audio Apps

All that talk about Ogg Vorbis and FLAC aside, there are still many people who like or need to deal with MP3 files. You may, for example, already have numerous MP3 files ripped from your music collection, or you may enjoy listening to one of the many Internet radio streams that are broadcast in MP3 format. Unfortunately, MP3 playback and encoding support is not included in Ubuntu because of licensing concerns. Even if you plan on using the Ogg Vorbis format in your future ripping and encoding endeavors, installing MP3 support is a good idea so as to cover all your audio bases. It's also a very easy process.

The easiest way to install MP3 playback support is to double-click an MP3 file that you have on your hard disk. A window will appear, asking whether you want to search for the plug-ins necessary to play the file. Click **Search**, after which another window will appear, showing you what you need to install (Figure 14-1). Check both boxes in that window, click the **Install** button, and in the confirmation window that then appears, click **Confirm**. You will then be asked for your password, so provide it, and then just wait until the process is complete. Once done, you'll be able to play not only your MP3 audio files but also MPEG and WMV videos.

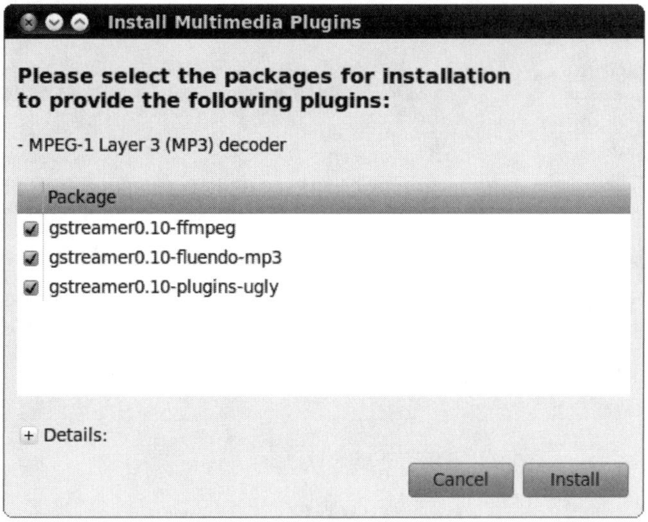

Please select the packages for installation to provide the following plugins:

- MPEG-1 Layer 3 (MP3) decoder

Package
☑ gstreamer0.10-ffmpeg
☑ gstreamer0.10-fluendo-mp3
☑ gstreamer0.10-plugins-ugly

+ Details:

Cancel   Install

Figure 14-1: Ubuntu helps you find the plug-ins you need.

If you prefer, you can download and install these plug-ins quite easily via the Ubuntu Software Center by doing a search for *gstreamer* and then installing *gstreamer0.10-ffmpeg* (GStreamer ffmpeg video plugin), *gstreamer0.10-fluendo-mp3* (Fluendo mp3 decoder GStreamer plugin), and *gstreamer0.10-plugins-ugly* (GStreamer extra plugins).

As for MP3 encoding support, which enables you to rip CDs and create your own space-saving MP3 files, well, things aren't so automatic. But it's not much of a chore, either, because all you need to do is use the Ubuntu Software Center to search for and install *gstreamer0.10-plugins-ugly-multiverse*. If you also want to give yourself AAC encoding ability, you should install *gstreamer0.10-plugins-bad-multiverse* as well. You will then be ready for action, as described in the next section.

Rhythmbox—Your Audio Player

The main audio player in Ubuntu is called Rhythmbox (see Figure 14-2), which seems to function pretty much like a simplified version of Apple's iTunes application. It's a relatively easy-to-use audio player that, despite some quirkiness in its early stages, has developed quite a following in the Linux world. To run Rhythmbox, just go to the **Applications** menu and select **Sound & Video ▸ Rhythmbox Music Player**.

Figure 14-2: The Rhythmbox audio player

Adding Songs and Albums to the Rhythmbox Library

If you are familiar with Apple's iTunes, then you should understand the Library in Rhythmbox too, because it is essentially the same concept. Rhythmbox should automatically import everything you have in your *Music* folder without any extra work on your part. If you prefer to add songs to the Rhythmbox library manually, you can open the preferences window (**Edit ▸ Preferences**), click the **Music** tab, and then uncheck the **Watch my library for new files** box. After that, you can add new albums to your Rhythmbox Library by going to the **Music** menu, selecting **Import Folder**, and then navigating to the folder for the new album you want to add. If you want to add a number of albums by the same artist, just navigate to and select the folder for that artist instead. If you want to add just a single audio file, you can also do that—select **Music ▸ Import File**, and then navigate to the song in question.

If you are not the navigating type, you can also add files and folders by other means. The simplest way is to drag the folder or song you want to add to the Library into the right pane of the Rhythmbox window. You can also add a song to the Library directly by right-clicking the file and selecting **Open with ▸ Open with Rhythmbox** in the pop-up menu that appears.

Ripping Audio CDs with Rhythmbox

Like iTunes, Rhythmbox also allows you to rip songs directly from a CD; convert them to Ogg Vorbis, MP3, or other audio formats; and then add the ripped tracks to its music library. The steps are as follows:

1. Open the Preferences window (**Edit ▸ Preferences**), click the **Music** tab, and select the encoding format you want to use (Ogg Vorbis is the default). Once you're done, click **Close**. Unless you change encoding formats often, you won't have to do this more than once.

2. Select your audio CD in the left pane of the Rhythmbox window.

3. Click the **Copy to library** button in the upper-right part of the Rhythmbox window. The ripping and encoding process will then begin, and the progress will show in the bottom-right corner of the Rhythmbox window. Once done, the ripped songs will automatically appear in the Rhythmbox Library.

NOTE   *If you have not installed the* gstreamer0.10-plugins-ugly-multiverse *package, the MP3 option will not appear in the Output Format menu.*

Browsing the Rhythmbox Library

The Rhythmbox Library, which you can make visible by clicking **Music** in the left pane of the Rhythmbox window, is a collection of all the music you add to it. This can prove to be a bit unwieldy as your collection grows. Fortunately, Rhythmbox has a nice browser function, like the one in iTunes, that can be toggled on and off by clicking the **Browse** button, shown in Figure 14-3. This function allows you to see lists of the artists and albums in two separate panes above the main Library list. If you click a specific artist in the Artist pane, a list of albums by that artist will appear in the right pane. You can then double-click one of the albums in that right pane to play it. If you want to play all the albums you have by that artist, just double-click the artist's name in the left pane. All in all, it's a very handy feature.

Figure 14-3: The Browse button in Rhythmbox

If you want to add a layer of categorization to the browser, you can do so by adding a Genre pane. To do this, just go to the **Edit** menu, select **Preferences**, select the **General** tab of the window that appears, and then select **Genres, artists, and albums**. After clicking the **Close** button in the Preferences window, you will have a three-pane browser in Rhythmbox (Figure 14-4).

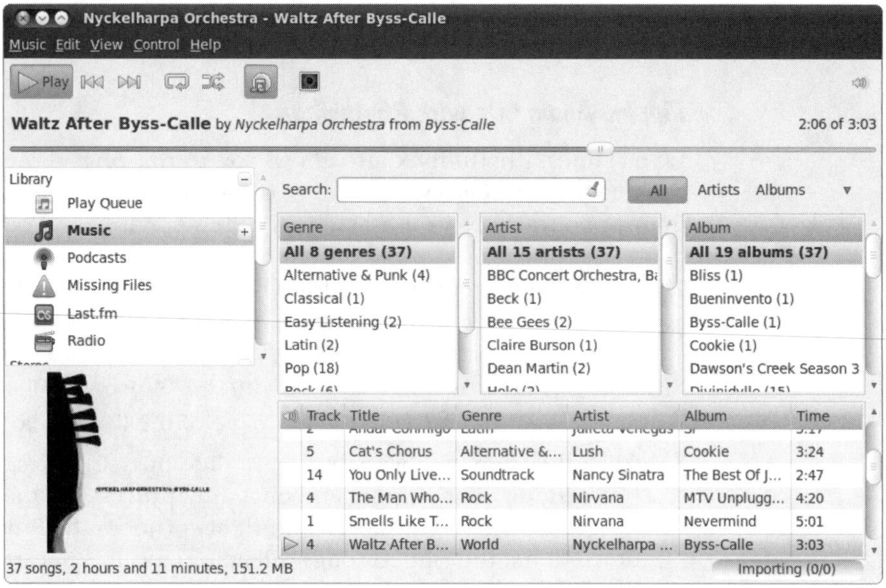

Figure 14-4: The Rhythmbox browser with expanded categorization

Creating Playlists in Rhythmbox

Of course, you can tailor things even further to match every situation and your every mood. There are days, after all, when you're feeling a bit too ethereal for Adam Lambert (and thank goodness for that). To prepare for such moments, you can create *playlists*, which are lists of songs to be played in a predetermined order. Just think of each playlist as an all-request radio station . . . where all the requests are your own.

To create a playlist in Rhythmbox, select **Music ▸ Playlist ▸ New Playlist**. When the Playlist icon appears in the left pane of the Rhythmbox window, type a name for the list, and then add the songs you want by simply dragging them from the Library pane to the Playlist icon. The songs themselves will remain in the Library, so you aren't really moving anything—just creating aliases.

You can also create *automatic playlists*, which are lists that automatically scan the Library for songs that match your creation criteria. You could choose to create a list for the all the songs in your Library by a particular artist or of a specific genre. To do this, just select **Music ▸ Playlist ▸ New Automatic Playlist**. A window will appear in which you can specify what the list is to contain. You can even specify how many songs you want in the list.

Once you've created your lists, you can play one by clicking the list once and then clicking the Play button near the top of the window (or by just double-clicking the list).

Online Music Stores via Rhythmbox

While iTunes only has the iTunes store, Rhythmbox provides you with options, all of which can be accessed from the left pane in the Rhythmbox window under the Stores heading. Two of these stores, Jamendo and Magnatune, provide music released under Creative Commons or open license by independent artists. The other store is the Ubuntu One Music Store, which provides music by major artists from the 7digital catalog. The songs sold there are free from the digital rights management (DRM) limitations found in many songs purchased from other online stores.

Other Cool Features in Rhythmbox

Rhythmbox includes a few cool features worth noting. In addition to being able to manage podcasts, it also supports displaying album cover art. As you can see in Figures 14-2 and 14-4, whenever you play a track in Rhythmbox, the album cover art for that track is automatically downloaded and displayed in the lower-left corner of the window (assuming that Rhythmbox can find the cover online).

Another cool feature has to do with lyrics. To use this feature, you must first activate it by selecting the **Edit** menu and selecting **Plugins**. In the Configure Plugins window that appears (Figure 14-5), check the **Song Lyrics** box, and then click the **Close** button. After that, go to the **View** menu, and select **Song Lyrics**. Rhythmbox will then search the Internet for the lyrics to the track you are currently playing and display them in a separate window (Figure 14-6).

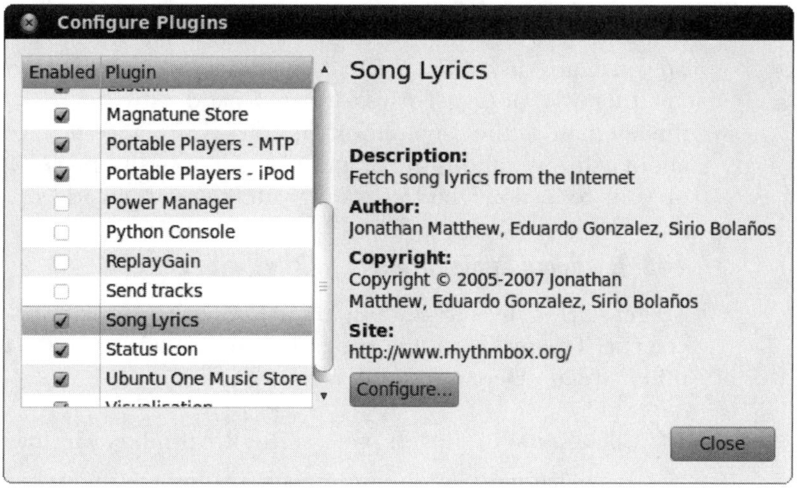

Figure 14-5: Activating Rhythmbox's lyrics function

Finally, if you are an iTunes user and attached to a bit of visual stimulation while playing your tunes, Rhythmbox can now satisfy you with a visualizer of its own. To activate it, go to the **View** menu and select **Visualization** (you can turn it off in the same way). The right half of the Rhythmbox window will then be filled with the wild, swirling shapes and colors of psychedelia that you've come to know and love.

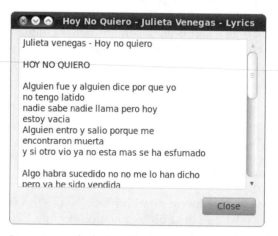

Figure 14-6: Rhythmbox displays the lyrics to the track currently playing.

Project 14B: Listening to Streaming Media with Rhythmbox

In addition to allowing you to play audio CDs or the music you have stored on your hard disk, Rhythmbox also allows you to play Internet radio streams in either MP3 or Ogg Vorbis format. To add a stream, click the **Radio** icon in the left pane of the Rhythmbox window—you will come face to face with only about a dozen stations the first time around. In this project, I will try to fatten up your collection a bit by showing you how you can add streams on your own.

14B-1: Adding Radio Streams to Rhythmbox

To get started, let's try adding FIP, a French music station specializing in the eclectic. The process for adding FIP is essentially the same for adding any other stream. Here are the steps:

1. Click **Radio** in the left pane of the Rhythmbox window.
2. At the right end of the button strip below the menu bar, click the **Create new Internet Radio Station** button (the one that looks like a little red radio).
3. In the window that then appears, type `http://www.tv-radio.com/station/fip_mp3/fip_mp3-128k.m3u/`, and click **Add**.
4. Double-click the new entry for your stream to play it.

The only problem with what you've just done is that the title of the stream appears in the Rhythmbox window as the URL you typed in, and the genre, for its part, appears as *unknown*. Needless to say, this isn't all that handy a way to have things, especially once you have more than a couple of streams listed and have to go wading through them to figure out what is what.

Remedying this state of affairs is a simple process. Just right-click the stream, and select **Properties**. In the window that appears, change the content of the Title and Genre boxes so that they represent something more meaningful to you. As you can see in Figure 14-7, I used *Radio France – FIP* for the title and *Eclectic* for the genre.

Figure 14-7: Changing a stream's title and genre properties in Rhythmbox

14B-2: Adding Additional Radio Streams to Rhythmbox

Now that you've had a taste of what Rhythmbox does with radio, you may well be hungry for more. Ah, but where do you find these radio streams? For the largest collection of MP3 streams, go to *http://www.shoutcast.com/*, find a stream that seems interesting to you, right-click the **Tune In!** button for that stream, and then select **Copy Link Location** in the pop-up menu. After that, paste the URL in the URL box of Rhythmbox's New Internet Radio Station window, and click **Add**. You can then double-click the stream in the right pane of the Rhythmbox window to play it.

Creating Audio CDs

All this talk about encoding and listening to MP3 and Ogg Vorbis files on your computer is fine and dandy, but there are no doubt times when you would like to have your songs on a plain audio CD that you can play while you slog your way to work on the New Jersey Turnpike or the Ventura Freeway. Luckily, this is easy enough to do, and there are a couple of ways to go about it.

Burning Audio CDs with Rhythmbox

For Rhythmbox users, the easiest way of going about things is to do it all from within Rhythmbox. To do this, first create a playlist with the songs you want to burn to CD, and then click the **Create Audio CD** button. A confirmation window will appear, asking you whether you want to create the CD you've just set out to create. You no doubt do, so click the **Create** button, and copies of your tracks will be created in WAV format. When that process is complete, you will be prompted for a blank CD, so pop one into your drive, click **OK**, and the burn process will begin. When it's done, the progress window will vanish, and your new audio CD should pop out of your drive. Simple.

Burning Audio CDs with Brasero

Another way to create "play-anywhere" audio CDs from your ripped MP3 and Ogg Vorbis files is with Brasero, which we first discussed in Chapter 7. To go this route, place a blank CD in your drive (and close the Nautilus window that pops up to handle it), and then select **Applications ▸ Sound & Video ▸ Brasero Disc Burner**. When Brasero appears, click **Audio project**. Now add any mix of songs (in any mix of audio formats) to the blank area of the window. You can do this by navigating to the songs you want in the left panes and then clicking the **Add** button (or just dragging the files to the right pane). You can also drag files from any open Nautilus window to the right pane of the Brasero window.

As you add songs to the Brasero window, a bar at the bottom of the window will show you how much more space you have available on the disk (Figure 14-8). Keep an eye on that so as not to queue up more than your disk can hold. Once you are ready, just click the **Burn** button, and then click **Burn** in the setup window that appears after that. A progress window will appear, and once the burn is complete, Brasero will let you know and eject your disk. You can then take the disk, plop it in your car stereo or wherever else you want to play it, and enjoy the results.

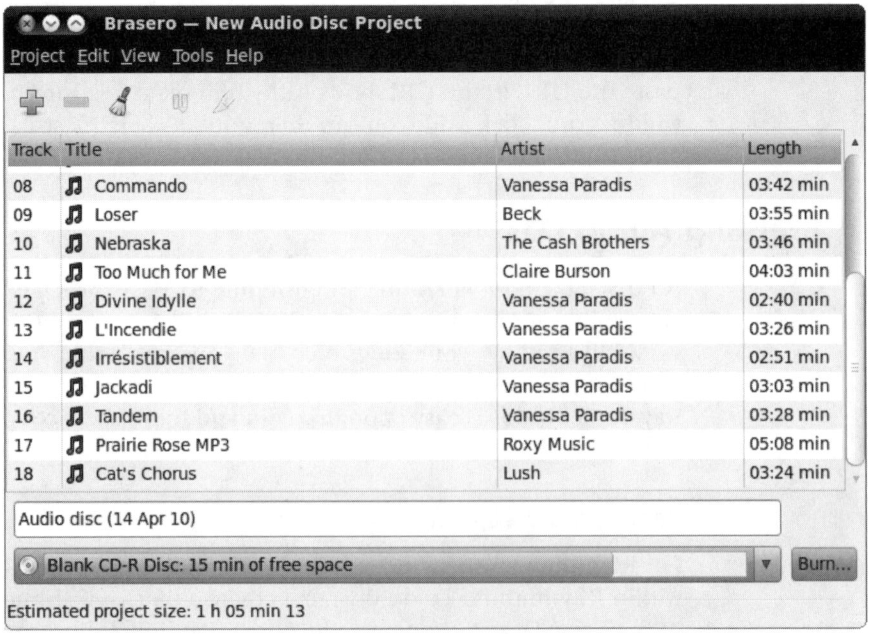
Brasero — New Audio Disc Project
Project Edit View Tools Help
Track Title Artist Length
08 Commando Vanessa Paradis 03:42 min
09 Loser Beck 03:55 min
10 Nebraska The Cash Brothers 03:46 min
11 Too Much for Me Claire Burson 04:03 min
12 Divine Idylle Vanessa Paradis 02:40 min
13 L'Incendie Vanessa Paradis 03:26 min
14 Irrésistiblement Vanessa Paradis 02:51 min
15 Jackadi Vanessa Paradis 03:03 min
16 Tandem Vanessa Paradis 03:28 min
17 Prairie Rose MP3 Roxy Music 05:08 min
18 Cat's Chorus Lush 03:24 min
Audio disc (14 Apr 10)
Blank CD-R Disc: 15 min of free space
Burn...
Estimated project size: 1 h 05 min 13

Figure 14-8: Preparing to burn an audio CD with Brasero

Now that you know how to play MP3 Internet broadcast streams, it is time to help round out your system a bit by installing RealPlayer 11 (Figure 14-9). Although not as common as in the past, RealMedia streams are still widely available on the Internet. You can also use Real-Player to play RealVideo streams, when they're available.

Figure 14-9: RealPlayer 11

14C-1: Downloading and Installing RealPlayer

Installing RealPlayer in Ubuntu, once a hit-or-miss sort of minor pain, is now easier than it's ever been before, so you can rest easy as you go through this project. Here's what you need to do:

1. Open Firefox, go to *http://www.real.com/realplayer/linux/*, and click the **Download DEB Installer** link.

2. In the window that then appears, accept the default option, Open with Gdebi Package Installer, by clicking **OK**.

3. A Package Installer window will soon open showing you what you are about to install. Click the **Install Package** button, and then provide your password when prompted.

In a few seconds, RealPlayer and all the dependencies your system requires to run RealPlayer will be installed. When the process is done, close the Package Installer.

14C-2: Setting Up RealPlayer and Testing Your Installation

Once Real Player 11 is installed on your machine, you will need to go through the final setup steps and then test it all. You can start by selecting **Applications ▸ Sound & Video ▸ RealPlayer 11**. A simple setup wizard will appear, which you will have no trouble with on your own, because all you really have to do is click the button in the bottom-right corner of the window a few times. Once you have completed the wizard, the RealPlayer window will appear.

You can test your installation of RealPlayer by making your way to a website with RealAudio content, such as *http://www.notmuch.com/*. Click the link for any file you want to play, after which a window will appear asking you what to do with the file. Accept the default, */opt/real/RealPlayer/realplay (default)*, by clicking **OK**. RealPlayer will then open, playing the stream you chose.

Other Cool Audio Apps

The applications I have covered so far are only a taste of what Ubuntu has in store for you in its repositories. You can start by browsing through the offerings listed in the Ubuntu Software Center. Try them, keep them if you like them, or remove them if you don't. After all, it doesn't cost you anything in Linux.

To give you a starting point, I will mention a few applications that I think might be worth investigating.

Alternative Players

If the music players that I've covered in this chapter have whetted your appetite for more, you are in luck—there are plenty of others, as a browse through Ubuntu Software Center's Sound & Video category will reveal. Check out Exaile, Banshee, Audacious, and Listen to get started. Oh, and as you'll find out in Chapter 16, if you haven't discovered it already, the Totem video player that comes with your system also doubles as an audio player. Wow.

Streaming Music with Streamtuner

If you are an Internet radio junkie, there is probably no application as useful to you as Streamtuner (Figure 14-10). Streamtuner is, as its name implies, an online radio stream tuner. It works by downloading lists of available streams from a variety of sources, which you can then easily browse. When you find something you like, just select the stream, click the **Tune in** button, and the stream will open in the player of your choice. The default player for most streams is Audacious, so when you download Streamtuner, the Ubuntu Software Center will also automatically download Audacious, which is a pretty cool audio player. You can, however, switch the default player for Streamtuner playback by going to its **Edit** menu, selecting **Preferences**, and then in the right pane of the Preferences window, changing the default applications for playback by typing the command for the application you want to use. This is usually the name of the application in all lowercase letters. For example, if you want your playback to be from Totem, you would click **Listen to a .m3u file**, scroll to the right, and change `audacious %q` to `totem %q`.

You'll also be happy to know that you can rip the streams you are listening to (and even those you aren't listening to) and save them as MP3 files. To record a stream from within Streamtuner, just right-click the target stream, and select **Record** in the pop-up menu.

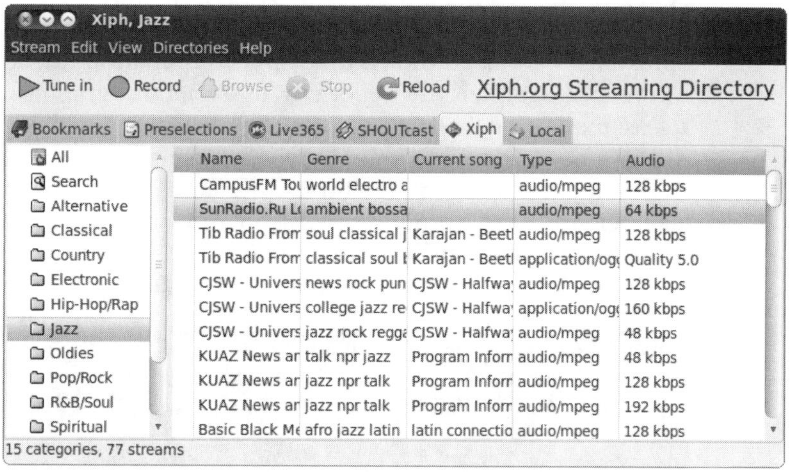

Figure 14-10: Browsing Internet radio streams with Streamtuner

EasyTAG and Audio Tag Tool

For the true audio geek, these two applications allow you to alter the tags of your MP3 and Ogg Vorbis music files. EasyTAG is the more full-featured of the two, but Audio Tag Tool (Figure 14-11) has a friendlier user interface. Give 'em both a try and see what you think. Search the Ubuntu Software Center for *easytag* or *tagtool*, install one or both, and then locate either by selecting **Applications ▸ Sound & Video**, and then making the appropriate choice in the submenu.

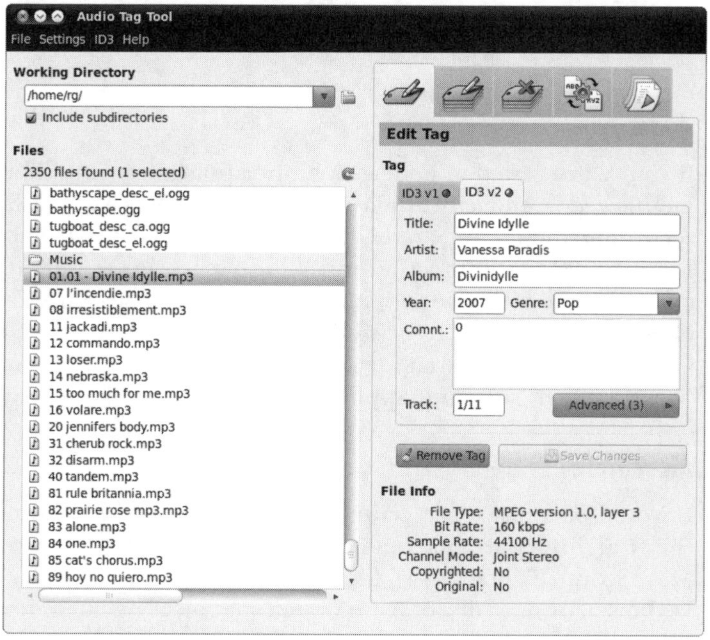

Figure 14-11: Editing MP3 and Ogg Vorbis file tags in Audio Tag Tool

LMMS

Linux MultiMedia Studio (LMMS) is a combination tracker/sequencer/synthesizer/sampler with a modern, user-friendly, graphical user interface—at least that's what the LMMS home page suggests. I can't swear to how easy it is to use, because I don't know much about apps in this genre. But there is a lot of hoopla about it in the Linux world, and it sure looks cool, as you can see in Figure 14-12. It sounds really cool too (try the demos once you install it). Search the Ubuntu Software Center for *lmms*, install the program, and run it by selecting **Applications ▸ Sound & Video ▸ Linux MultiMedia Studio**.

Figure 14-12: Creating music with LMMS

Audacity

If you're interested in podcasting, one application you will find repeatedly mentioned is Audacity. Audacity (Figure 14-13) is a multiplatform audio recording and editing application that is frequently used not only in the Linux world but in the Mac and Windows worlds as well. It allows you to cut and paste bits of sound, raise pitch, increase speed, add echo and other effects, and . . . well, all sorts of other neat stuff. Get it via Ubuntu Software Center by doing a search for and then installing *audacity*. Audacity will then be available by selecting **Applications ▸ Sound & Video ▸ Audacity**.

MuseScore

It would be a pity to wrap up this music chapter without mentioning the straightforward and very capable music notation program, *MuseScore*. MuseScore (Figure 14-14) allows you to create sheet music, either by mouse, keyboard, or midi device, with up to four voices per staff. It also allows you to play back the compositions you've put to the page. This is a great feature for folks like me, who can't read music but find themselves wanting to figure out

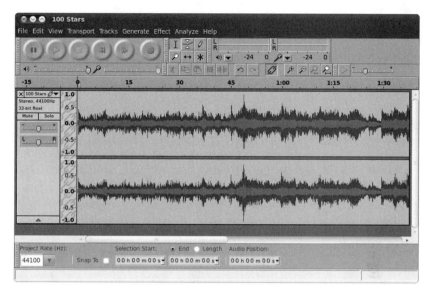

Figure 14-13: Audio recording and editing with Audacity

a melody based on its score. Just copy the notes to a page in MuseScore, click the play button, and your theretofore elusive melody is there before your ears (as well as your eyes). Install MuseScore from the Ubuntu Software Center by searching for *musescore*, and then run it from **Applications ▸ Sound & Video ▸ MuseScore**.

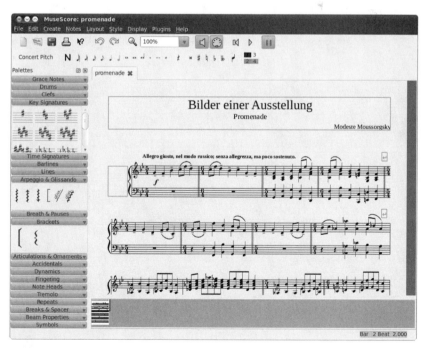

Figure 14-14: Putting notes to paper with MuseScore

15

PLUGGIN' IN THE PENGUIN

Working with Your iPod, iPhone, and Other Digital Media Devices

With all the talk in the previous chapter about ripping, encoding, and playing back audio files, you may be wondering whether Ubuntu will allow you to transfer any of those files to your digital media devices, such as your MP3 player or cell phone. Well, you will be happy to know that using your device on your Ubuntu system is quite easy—easier than ever before. No longer do you have to mess around with mount and unmount commands or edit system tables, and if you don't know what I'm talking about, consider yourself lucky. Just plug in your device, and Ubuntu will do the rest.

Knowing Your Limits

Assuming you downloaded and installed the recommended audio codecs mentioned in Chapter 14, you shouldn't encounter any problems handling music or podcasts on your digital media device in Ubuntu. Even if you didn't install them, Ubuntu should automatically help you find the necessary items if you try to play a file it doesn't support out of the box. Nevertheless, not all formats will work with equal degrees of comfort or success—it depends on your device and the file format's compatibility with Ubuntu. As a general rule of thumb, most players will be able to handle MP3 files and unlocked AAC (*.m4a*) files. Check your device's manual for specifics about other file formats (or just give them a try).

As far as Ubuntu goes, it can work with all the file formats mentioned with the exception of locked AAC files, but you will learn how to deal with this later in the chapter.

NOTE   *Although working with your digital media devices in Ubuntu has become increasingly simple, it is still a relatively new procedure. It is always worth approaching things with a bit of caution by making sure to have backups of the files on your device before working with it on Ubuntu.*

Mounting and Ejecting Your iPod or iPhone

Working with your iPod or iPhone is an extremely simple process. Basically, just plug it in via a USB connector, and Ubuntu will mount the device so you can access it. An icon for your device will then appear on the desktop (Figure 15-1) and in the left pane of any Nautilus window you happen to have open. Two of those what-do-you-want-me-to-do-with-this-stuff type of windows that appear when you insert a music CD or DVD into your drive or connect a digital camera to your machine via USB cable—one for the music and podcasts on your device and one for the photos (also shown in Figure 15-1)—will also appear, usually one directly above the other. By default, Ubuntu will point you to Rhythmbox for music-handling chores and to F-Spot for photo handling, both of which will be discussed later in the chapter. Click **OK** in each window to accept Ubuntu's choices.

To "eject" your iPod or iPhone, either right-click the desktop icon for the device and select **Eject** or, from a Nautilus window, click the eject button next to the icon for your device in the side pane of the window.

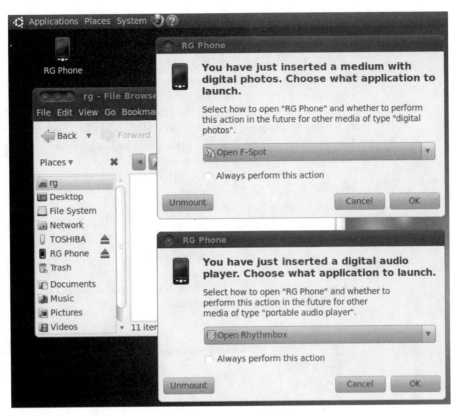

Figure 15-1: Ubuntu instantly recognizes your iPod or iPhone.

(Not) Auto-updating Your iPod or iPhone

With the simple instructions as to how to use your iPod or iPhone with Ubuntu out of the way, it's worth thinking about a couple of other things. Most important of these is the device's auto-updating settings. When you enable auto-update on your iPod or iPhone via iTunes, the function is set up within the device itself. You can use your iPod in Windows, Mac OS, or Linux—or all of them interchangeably. If you set up your iPod to auto-update songs and playlists, however, you are leaving yourself open for trouble unless you have exactly the same music collection on all of your machines.

The reason for this is simple. Although iTunes allows you to add files to your iPod, it does not allow you to copy files from it. The auto-update feature is thus strictly a one-way street. This means that whenever you hook up your auto-update–enabled iPod to an iTunes-enabled computer, iTunes will automatically add the tracks in its library to your iPod; more frighteningly, it will remove any tracks from your iPod that are not present in that machine's iTunes library. I learned this the hard way when I took my wife's loaded iPod to work and plugged it into my office Winbox with its completely empty iTunes library. When I brought the little Podster back home to her with nothing at all on it, well . . . what ensued wasn't pretty.

Make sure to disable your iPod's auto-update function before bringing the device into the Linux world. To do this, connect your iPod to your Mac or Windows machine, and open iTunes. In the left pane of the iTunes window, click your iPod in the Devices section, and then in the **Summary** tab in the right pane, check the box next to the words *Manually manage music* (or *Manually manage music and videos* in video-capable iPods), as shown in Figure 15-2. Next, if you have a photo-capable device, repeat nearly the same process for your photos by clicking the **Photos** tab in the right pane and then unchecking the box next to the words *Sync photos from.*

Figure 15-2: Disabling the auto-update function on your iPhone/iPod in iTunes

Working with Android-Based Phones

Although the iPhone continues to be the king of the smartphone hill, it now has some strong competition from phones running Google's Android operating system. Fortunately, working with your Android-powered device in Ubuntu is quite simple, and it's only slightly different from working with an iPhone or iPod. Basically, this is the process:

1. Connect your computer and Android-powered device using the USB cable that came with it.

2. A "USB Connected" notification should appear on the notification bar at the top of your phone's screen. Drag down the notification bar, and then touch **USB Connected**.

3. A dialog box should then appear on your phone asking you to either mount or cancel the connection. Touch **Mount**.

NOTE *Because there are different versions of the Android system in service today, it is possible that the details of the process described here might be slightly different from that for your phone. You should still be able to follow along.*

As with the iPhone, iPod touch, and photo-capable iPods, two windows will then appear asking you whether you want to run Rhythmbox to handle your music files and F-Spot for your photo files. An icon for your device should then appear on your desktop and in the side pane of any Nautilus window (Figure 15-3).

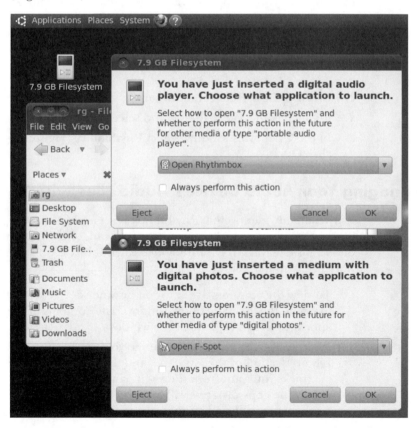

Figure 15-3: Ubuntu recognizes your Android-powered device and provides you with a number of ways to work with it.

To "eject" your Android device, either right-click the desktop icon for the device and select **Eject** or, from a Nautilus window, click the eject button next to the icon for your device in the side pane of the window. On your phone, then drag open the notification tray, and touch **Turn off USB storage**. In the dialog box that then appears, touch **Turn Off**.

Working with Other Digital Media Players and Cell Phones

Although the iPod may be the most popular digital media player out there and the iPhone holds the crown in the smartphone market, they are by no means the only games in town. As I have already shown, Android-based phones are also quite popular, and there are still other devices, ranging from simple $15 USB MP3 players to the Linux-based Palm Pre cellular phone.

How to work with these devices in Ubuntu can vary by device, but for the most part, they should work either in the same manner as an iPod or Android device or in the same manner as a USB data device. The Palm Pre, which uses a Linux-based operating system, works in Ubuntu in the same way as the iPhone, while the $19 generic MP3 player I bought at Office Depot acts like a USB thumb drive. The simplest way to see how your device will work is to connect it to your computer via a USB cable. If windows asking you how to deal with the device do not appear, open a Nautilus window to see whether you find an icon for the device there. If so, you can work with your device using the tried-and-true drag-and-drop method. You can also use Rhythmbox to work with the audio files on your generic device by doing the following:

1. Create a *Music* folder if there isn't one already on the device.
2. Right-click the **Music** folder, and select **Open with Other Application**.
3. In the Open with window, select **Rhythmbox** (Figure 15-4), and then click **Open**.

Managing Your Audio Device's Audio Files with Rhythmbox

As I've already mentioned, Rhythmbox is set as the default application for iPhones, iPods, Android-powered devices, and, one way or another, any other music players in Ubuntu. Once Rhythmbox is up and running, things work pretty much as they do in iTunes.

- To view the contents of your iPod or other device, click the icon for the device in the left pane of the window. The contents of the device will then appear in the right pane of the window.

- To copy a song from your library to your device, just click **Music** in the Library section of the left pane, and then drag the artists, albums, or single tracks you want from the right pane to your device's icon in the left pane. The copy progress will be shown in a progress bar in the lower-right corner of the Rhythmbox window (Figure 15-5).

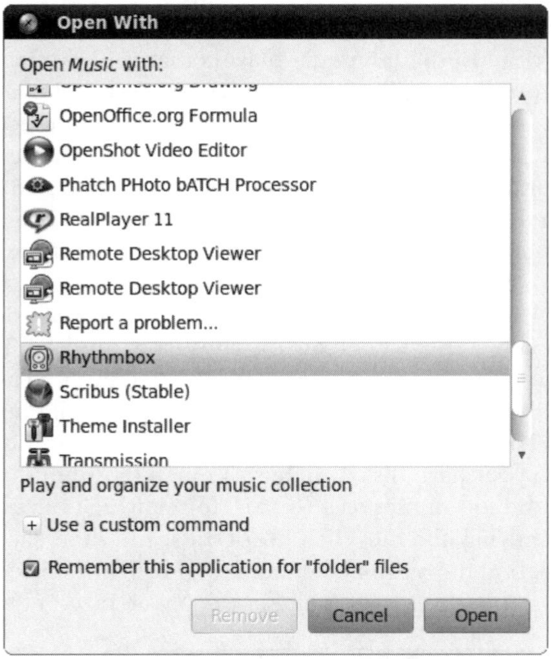

Figure 15-4: Selecting Rhythmbox as the application to use when working with the audio files on your generic MP3 player

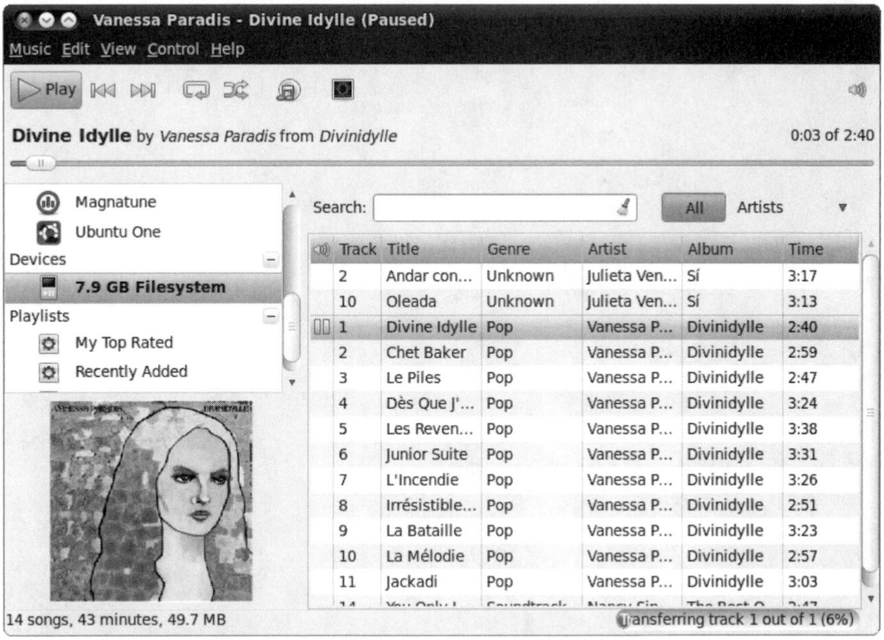

Figure 15-5: Adding songs to your digital audio player via Rhythmbox

Copying Songs from Your Audio Device to Your Hard Disk

One feature of most digital media players that isn't available in iTunes (at least not without the installation of a special freeware plug-in) is the ability to copy songs from your iPhone/iPod to your hard disk (or even to an external USB drive). Luckily, Rhythmbox allows you to do this quite easily.

To copy music from your iPhone/iPod, Android based phone, or other digital media device with Rhythmbox, select the tracks you want to export (hold down the CTRL key to make multiple selections, or use the tabs to select whole artists or genres if you like), and drag the selected items to your desktop, music folder, or wherever you want them. The only catch with this seemingly simple approach is that when copying files from an iPod/iPhone, you end up with files on your hard disk with funky filenames, such as *ZPAD.m4a* or *ATDT.mp3*, rather than the name that appeared on your iPhone/iPod or within Rhythmbox. This means you'll have to rename the files once they have been transferred to your hard disk, which isn't much of a chore unless you're dealing with lots and lots of files or if you just forget which file is which. In case of the latter, right-click the file, click **Properties**, and then click the **Audio** tab, where you will find the original filename (Figure 15-6). Once you know it, click the **Basic** tab, type the correct name in the Name box, and then click **Close**.

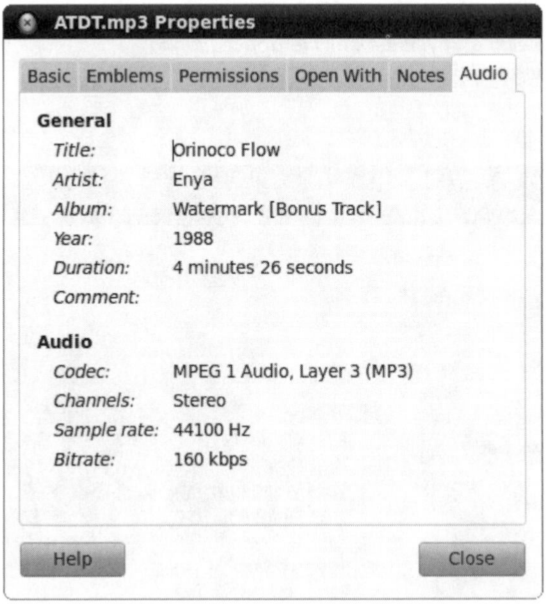

Figure 15-6: Finding the file properties of a mislabeled audio file

Ejecting Your iPod or Other Digital Device from Within Rhythmbox

When you're done working with your iPod or other digital device in Rhythmbox, you can eject it either by clicking its entry in the left pane of the Rhythmbox window and then clicking the **Eject** button near the top of the window or by right-clicking its icon in the left pane and selecting **Eject** in the pop-up menu that appears. If Rhythmbox is closed, this right-click-to-eject approach also works from within a Nautilus window or with the desktop icon for a mounted device.

Problems Writing to Your iPod

If you have an iPod (iPhones and iPod touch not included) that you were last using in conjunction with a Mac, you may find that although you can read the files on your iPod, you cannot write files to it. It is most likely that your iPod is formatted in Apple's native HFS+ filesystem, although this in itself is not a problem. The problem is that HFS+ formatted iPods have journaling enabled. *Journaling* is an HFS+ feature that acts to protect the filesystem from damage due to power surges, power failures, or hardware breakdowns.

As fate would have it, however, the Linux kernel doesn't deal well with journaling-enabled, HFS+ formatted devices. Fortunately, the tweak to fix this is quite simple, and it isn't even particularly geeky: You just have to disable journaling on your iPod.

Disabling journaling on an HFS+ formatted iPod is a very easy task if you have a Mac nearby. Just plug your iPod into a Mac, close iTunes when it automatically opens, and then run Disk Utility (in the Utilities folder within the Applications folder). When Disk Utility opens, select your iPod (by name) in the left pane of the window, press the OPTION key, and then choose **Disable Journaling** in the **File** menu. After a moment, journaling on your iPod will be disabled without any loss of data. If you connect your iPod to your Linux machine again, you will be able to use it more or less like normal.

Working with Photos on Your Digital Device

As I already mentioned, if your phone or digital device is photo-capable and Ubuntu automatically recognizes it, you will be led to F-Spot Photo Manager, just as you are when you hook up your digital camera to your Ubuntu machine. In the same way, F-Spot takes stock of what you have on your device and then allows you to copy photos to your hard disk.

As you can see in Figure 15-7, you first select the photos you want to copy to your hard disk, add a tag if you like, and then click **Copy**. After the photos are copied to your disk, they will appear in the main F-Spot window (Figure 15-8), from which you can work with them as you see fit.

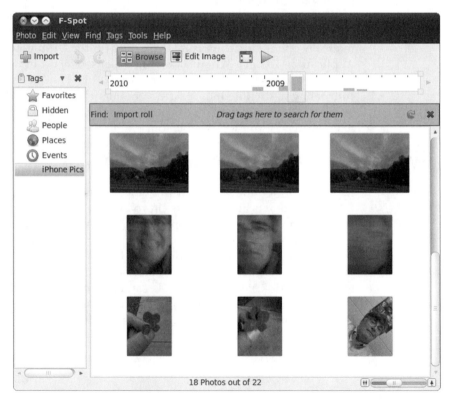

Figure 15-7: Importing photos from your iPhone/iPod or other digital device with F-Spot

Figure 15-8: F-Spot lets you organize the photos you've downloaded to your hard disk.

Converting Audio File Formats

As I pointed out at the beginning of the chapter, there may be some points of incompatibility when it comes to certain audio file formats, your hardware, and Ubuntu. Fortunately, SoundConverter (shown in Figure 15-9) makes it easy to convert Ogg Vorbis files to MP3 format, or vice versa. It can also convert AAC files to MP3 or Ogg Vorbis format, if that is of interest to you. Because SoundConverter does not come bundled with Ubuntu, you will have to install it. To do so, just run the Ubuntu Software Center, search for *soundconverter*, and install the application.

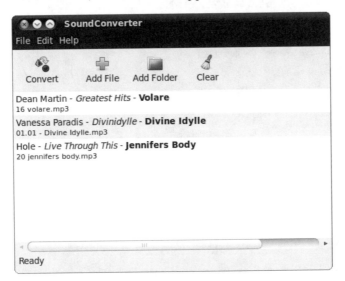

Figure 15-9: Converting audio file formats with SoundConverter

To use SoundConverter, just select **Applications ▸ Sound & Video ▸ Sound Converter**. Once SoundConverter starts, add the songs you want to convert to the main pane by clicking either the **Add File** or **Add Folder** button. You can also drag audio files from your *Music* folder (or wherever else you store them).

Once you've chosen the files to convert, you need to choose which format to convert them to. You can do this by selecting **Edit ▸ Preferences** and then making your choice in the Preferences window (Figure 15-10). While you're there, it is also a good idea to tell SoundConverter to place your converted files in a location other than the folder where the original files are stored. Doing this prevents having to deal with duplicates in Linux audio playback applications that automatically scan your *Music* folder, such as Rhythmbox. You might also want to check the **Create subfolders** box to keep things organized.

Once you have set things up and are ready to convert, click **Close** in the Preferences window, and then click **Convert** in the main window. SoundConverter will then begin doing its stuff.

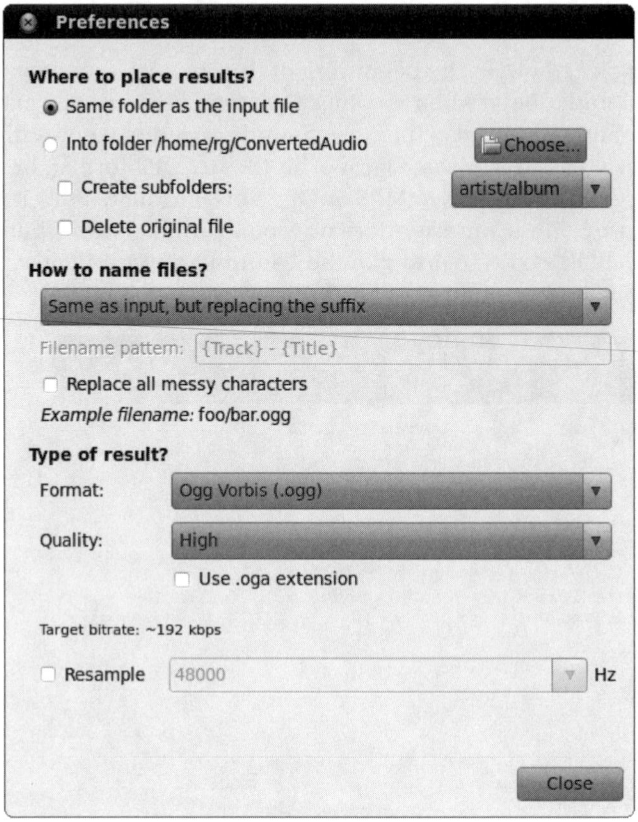

Figure 15-10: Setting conversion preferences in SoundConverter

Playing Locked AAC (M4P) Files

If you purchased music from the iTunes Store before Apple did away with digital rights management (DRM) in its music, chances are you are in possession of some locked AAC files, which you can recognize by the *.m4p* extension. These files can be played only on registered machines through iTunes. As you might have already discovered, you cannot do much with such files on your system as is. All you will get when you try to play one is an error message and an option to have Ubuntu search for the missing plug-in. Accepting that option is the easiest way to get the support you need to play such files within Ubuntu.

Once you accept, Ubuntu will search for the plug-in and necessary support files. Once Ubuntu finds them, it will show the result of its search in a new window (Figure 15-11). Click **Install** to continue. When the process is complete, you will be able to play previously locked AAC files on your system. If Rhythmbox was running while the installation process was taking place, however, you will need to restart it before it will be able to handle the files.

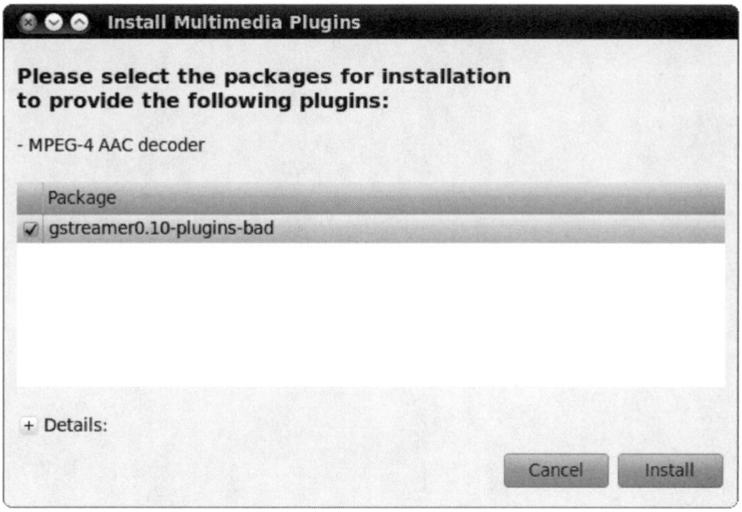

Figure 15-11: Ubuntu lets you know what plug-ins it finds to allow you to play locked AAC files.

Linux on Your iPod?

One thing you might notice if you do a Google search on using your iPod with Linux is that it is possible to actually replace your iPod's Apple-designed operating system with a form of Linux. Now, I am not advocating that you do this (and I most certainly have not done so myself), but some folks are interested in geeking around with whatever gadget they have in their hands. If you're such a person or if you're just curious, check out *http://www.ipodlinux.org/,* or the even more popular Rockbox (*http://www.rockbox.org/*), which also runs on a number of other, non-Apple, devices.

Working with . . . Your iPad?

Apple's newest offering, the iPad, has been on the shelves only a short time, and yet Linux enthusiasts are already trying the iPad out with Linux machines. Reports are that the iPad "mostly" works as of the current version, Ubuntu 10.04. If you want to see how the iPad works with your Ubuntu-powered PC, just connect the two by USB cable, and play around to see how it goes. Just remember that you're doing so at your own risk.

16

COUCH PENGUINS

Video and DVD Playback in Ubuntu

 Now that I've covered much of what Ubuntu can do in terms of audio, it's time to turn your attention to what is arguably the second most important of its talents in the CNN/MTV-era world: video. Ubuntu is quite capable in terms of video playback, allowing you to view video files you download from the Internet or from your digital movie camera, video CDs (VCDs), DVDs, and some Internet video streams. It even allows you to download movies from your digital video camera and then edit them.

DVDs

Your system allows you to play DVDs; however, due to licensing concerns, playback is limited to unencrypted discs by default. Unfortunately, this rules out a vast majority of the DVD movies you buy or rent at your local video shop and leaves you with a rather limited choice of movies that you can play on your computer. Given the limited offerings in the unencrypted DVD world, you will no doubt want to enable your system to play the encrypted variety.

Project 16A: Installing Support for Encrypted DVDs

As I already mentioned, Ubuntu does not allow you to play encrypted DVDs from the start. For you to watch such DVDs (and that would be the vast majority of them), you need to install a whole bunch of stuff, most crucially, the package *libdvdread4*. Fortunately, if you installed the audio support files I mentioned in Chapter 14, you're halfway there. If you didn't install them or if you just want to double-check, start by running the Ubuntu Software Center, and then make sure you have those files and a few useful others installed. If anything is missing, install it. Here's what you need to have:

- *gst-plugins-base*
- *gstreamer0.10-plugins-good*
- *gstreamer0.10-plugins-ugly*
- *gstreamer0.10-plugins-bad*
- *gst-ffmpeg*
- *libdvdread4*

Now you've come to the final and essential step required for this project. For this task, you're going to have to turn to the trusty ol' Terminal (**Applications ▸ Accessories ▸ Terminal**). Once the Terminal is open, type the following command, and then press ENTER:

```
sudo apt-get install libdvdread4
```

With just about any other application, you would be done at this point, but libdvdread4 requires you to also run an installation script that comes with it in order to fully get the job done. To run the script, go back to the Terminal, type the following, and then press ENTER:

```
sudo /usr/share/doc/libdvdread4/install-css.sh
```

Once the Terminal returns you to the user prompt, the process will be done. Try putting a DVD in your drive—Totem should open and start playing the DVD. (You'll learn more about Totem soon.) If it doesn't work, open the Ubuntu Software Center, and check to make sure all the support plug-ins listed earlier are installed. If everything is there, go back to the Terminal, and perform the last two steps again.

Can I Play Foreign DVDs?

Your computer can play DVDs of any broadcast standard (NTSC, PAL, or SECAM) and of any regional encoding. This is a better setup than the DVD player you have hooked up to your TV, because the vast majority of stand-alone DVD players in the United States (I would venture to guess 99.9 percent) do not allow you to play anything other than Region 1 NTSC discs (NTSC being the broadcast standard in the United States and what its televisions are designed to display, while the DVD region is 1). This information is usually provided on the back of DVD packages (see the examples in Figure 16-1), though the packaging for most discs produced for the U.S. market does not include it.

Figure 16-1: Examples of regional encoding labels on DVD packages

Despite the wonderful everything-goes nature of your computer in terms of DVD playback, there is a serious caveat to bear in mind. Depending on the manufacturer of your DVD drive, you will be able to switch back and forth between DVDs of differing regional encodings only four or five times. After that, the drive will be locked into the regional encoding of the disc you were playing at that time . . . *forever*. This is unrelated to your operating system—it is strictly a hardware matter. The only exception to this region-lock rule are those DVDs labeled *Region Free* or *ALL* (sometimes inaccurately labeled as *Region 0*), which can be played on any DVD player in any region and thus do not register as a regional encoding switch when you plop one of them in your computer's DVD drive.

If your drive does eventually lock into one regional encoding, especially one for which you have few DVDs, there is some good news. That news comes in the form of Videolan's *libdvdcss2*, the library that is included in the libdvdread4 package you installed in Project 16A. The libdvdcss2 library allows you to play back encrypted DVDs. In addition to that primary function, *libdvdcss2* also, in theory, allows you to play back DVDs from multiple regions even if your DVD drive is already locked into one region. It does this by performing a cryptic attack (to use Videolan's term for it) on your drive until it can find the disc key for that drive. Of course, this process of cryptic bombardment can take several minutes, so it is not the optimal way of going about things. It's better than being stuck, though. Whether this process of bypassing regional encodings is legal remains a subject of debate, so if you are concerned about such things, you should do a little research.

Totem Movie Player

The default video player in Ubuntu is Totem, which, as you can see in Figure 16-2, has a very simple interface that makes using it equally simple. You can run Totem by selecting **Applications ▸ Sound & Video ▸ Movie Player**. You can also run it, as you have just learned, by simply placing a DVD in your drive, because Ubuntu is set up to run Totem any time you do so.

Figure 16-2: Totem movie player

Using Totem to Play DVDs, VCDs, and Other Multimedia Files

As I already mentioned, you can play a DVD in Totem by simply placing your DVD in the drive, after which Totem will open and begin playing your movie. If you've got a copy of *Red Detachment of Women* on VCD that you're aching to watch, you can do so in the same way. Just pop the VCD in your drive; Totem should start up and begin playing it.

Not only does Totem play DVDs and VCDs, but it can also play MPEG files, and because you installed that big cocktail of packages I keep going on about, it can play WMV files too. You can play such files by either double-clicking them directly or going to the Totem **Movie** menu, selecting **Open**, and then navigating to the video file you want to view.

Totem as an Audio Player?

You may have noticed while on the Display tab of the Preferences window that there was a Visual Effects section. Well, those visual effects aren't for the videos you play but rather are visualizations to accompany your audio files when played via Totem (Figure 16-3). Yes, Totem not only does video but also does audio. In fact, it is, somewhat oddly, the default audio player for Ogg Vorbis and MP3 files in Ubuntu. Just double-click one of those files, and sure enough, Totem will be the application that pops up, blasting your ears out with your favorite melodies. Of course, you can also play such files from the Totem **Movie** menu by selecting **Open** and then navigating to the songs you want to play. If you have a CD in your disc drive, you can even use Totem as a CD player by going to the **Movie** menu and selecting **Play Disc 'Audio Disc'**.

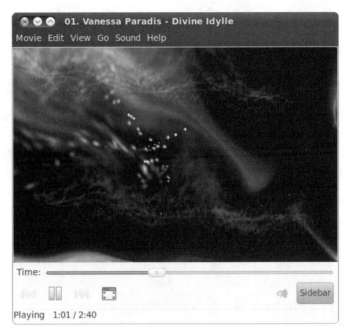

Figure 16-3: Totem as an audio player

A Couple of Other Cool Totem Features

Totem has a couple other cool features that you might like to know about. One is its ability to perform screen captures of whatever video you happen to be viewing at the time. Just select **Edit ▶ Take Screenshot**, and you've got yourself a screen capture—a still image taken from a video file.

Another feature worth mentioning is Totem's Sidebar. As you no doubt noticed, at the bottom-right corner of the Totem window there is a Sidebar button. If you click that button, a new pane will open at the right side of the Totem window. In that pane you can select and listen to BBC podcasts; search for and watch YouTube videos (Figure 16-4); and load, create, and save playlists. You can select from among these various functions from the drop-down menu button at the top of the Sidebar.

The playlists you create can consist of any combination of supported video or audio files, thus providing you with the whole multimedia banana. Any time you play a file in Totem, that file appears in the Playlist pane, but you can also add items to the list by simply dragging the files there from your desktop or any Nautilus window.

Figure 16-4: Viewing YouTube videos in Totem

An Alternative to Totem: VLC Media Player

Although the Totem video player has made great strides since it first appeared, some users find it somewhat temperamental and quirky. Luckily there are alternatives, like the VLC media player. VLC (Figure 16-5) is a very capable alternative player and is also available on Mac and Windows platforms. Like Totem, it also handles audio files as well as video and audio streams, including YouTube.

Figure 16-5: VLC media player at rest and at play

Download and install VLC from the Ubuntu Software Center, and once installed, run it by selecting **Applications ▸ Sound & Video ▸ VLC media player**. To View DVDs with VLC, insert a DVD into your drive, select **Open VLC media player** in the drop-down menu button in window that appears, and then click **OK**.

Editing Digital Video with PiTiVi

Digital video cameras have become increasingly common in recent years, and still digital cameras (and even phones!) have also become more impressive in terms of their video-handling capabilities. In addition, more and more people are sharing their video creations on YouTube—it's fair to say that home digital video is just about ubiquitous. Linux support for video processing is also catching up, though it's not quite 100 percent there.

Ubuntu's default video editor is called PiTiVi (Figure 16-6). You can run it by going to the **Applications** menu and selecting **Sound & Video ▸ Pitivi Video Editor**.

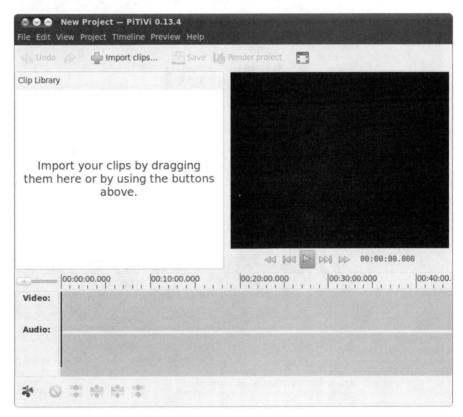

Figure 16-6: PiTiVi video editor

As you will immediately see, PiTiVi lacks the bells and whistles of applications like iMovie or Windows Live Movie Maker. It really is little more than a movie editor, allowing you only to trim and combine video clips. Some of its greatest limitations are its inability to capture video from digital video cameras or video streams, its inability to apply transitions or effects to videos, and, to top it all off, its inability to add titles to videos. Although these features are promised for the future, the fact that they are not available now makes the decision to bundle PiTiVi with Ubuntu a rather peculiar one.

Limitations and peculiarities aside, the actual editing process in PiTiVi is relatively straightforward. First you start a new project and decide its name and settings (**Project ▸ Project Settings**). Then you add files to that project, either by dragging and dropping from your home folder to the PiTiVi window or by clicking the **Import clips** button and then selecting the files you want to add via the Import a clip window that appears. The files, now called *clips*, will then appear in the Clip Library pane of the PiTiVi window. From that pane, you can drag the clips you want to work on to the timeline below and then split the clips, delete the embarrassing or boring bits out, and combine files (Figure 16-7). Be sure to save your project as you go along.

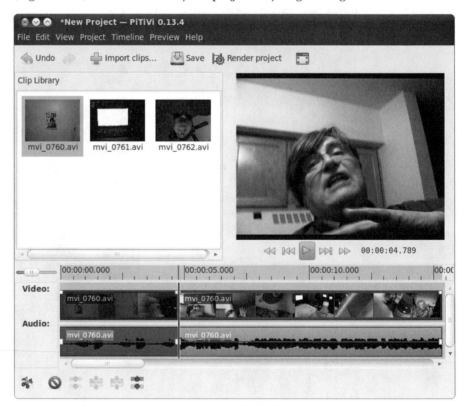

Figure 16-7: Editing video with PiTiVi

Once done with your editing, you can produce your new film by clicking the **Render project** button, after which a Render project window will appear. In that window, click the **Choose File** button, and then give your new film a title in the Choose file to render to window. This will be the name of the actual file that will be produced. Once done, click **OK**, and then click the **Render** button. The progress of the rendering process will be shown in the Render project window, and when it is done, the words *Rendering Complete* will appear. You can then close the Render project window and PiTiVi as well. Be sure to save your project when prompted to do so.

For more detailed information on using PiTiVi, have a look at the user manual, which is available from the PiTiVi site at *http://www.PiTiVi.org/*.

Project 16B: Capturing Digital Video with Kino

When you want to transfer a digital image or a digital video from your digital still camera to your computer, you just have to download it from camera to computer. When you want to transfer a video clip to your computer from a digital video (DV) camera that saves its data on tape or from a video stream, however, there is no way to simply drag it from one place to another. You have to capture the video stream to disk while you play it, and to do that you need some sort of software solution. This is usually found in the form of the system's video editor; however, as I mentioned in the previous section, Ubuntu's bundled video editor, PiTiVi, is not yet capable of doing this. This means you will have to install another editor, and the old-time favorite for this is Kino (Figure 16-8).

Figure 16-8: Another digital video editor, Kino

16B-1: Installing Kino and Setting Up Your System

The first and easiest step is to download and install Kino. Just go to the Ubuntu Software Center to do this. Once installed, you can take a look at Kino by selecting **Applications ▸ Sound & Video ▸ Kino**. At this point, you can use to Kino to work with video files you already have on your hard disk and start capturing video. If, however, your camera connects to your computer via a FireWire (IEEE 1394) connector, you must perform a few steps the first time around so your system can recognize the connection:

1. Connect your camera to your computer using the FireWire cable that came with (or you were forced to buy for) your camera.
2. Turn on your DV camera in play mode. Once you've done this, the *raw1394* module will appear in your system's */dev* directory, though you won't see any indication of this up front.
3. After a few seconds, turn off your camera, but leave the cable connected.
4. Open a Terminal window, type **cd /dev**, and press ENTER.
5. In the same Terminal window, change the permissions of the *raw1394* module so that everyone on your machine can read and write to it by typing **sudo chmod a+rw raw1394** and pressing ENTER.
6. Type your password when prompted, and then press ENTER.

If all goes without a hitch, you will be returned to your user prompt without any other messages appearing in the Terminal. You can then close the Terminal window.

16B-2: Capturing and Editing Digital Video with Kino

Once you have gone through the preparatory steps I've just mentioned, you are ready to capture video from your camera. To do this, connect your camera to your computer (if it isn't already connected), turn on your camera to Play mode, and then start up Kino. Once Kino is open, click the **Capture** tab to the right of the playback pane.

Now you can use the playback controls located below the playback pane. These control buttons actually control the functions of your camera. Start by clicking the **Rewind** button until you get to the beginning of the video segment you want to capture. Once you get there, click the **Play** button, after which the video on your camera will play back within the Kino window. When you reach the point at which you want to start capturing, click the **Capture** button just above the play back controls in the Kino window. Kino will then start capturing your video to disk (in your home folder by default) and show you what it is capturing in the main pane of the window (Figure 16-9). To keep things easy to manage, the captured video stream will be split into several files, the number of which depends on the length of the video played.

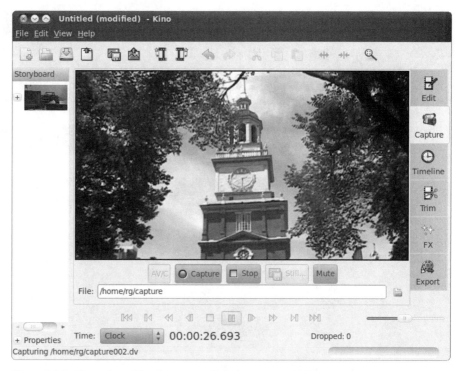

Figure 16-9: Capturing video from your digital camera with Kino

When you get to the point where you'd like to stop capturing, click the **Stop** button. You can then view the captured video by clicking the **Edit** tab and then using the playback controls at the bottom of the playback pane. You can also view the video in Timeline view (as shown in Figure 16-10) to navigate between the various segments of the video: Click the **Timeline** tab, click the segment you want to view, and then use the playback controls below the playback pane.

If you feel like getting a bit arty, you can also try the effects available in Kino (some examples of which are shown in Figure 16-11) by clicking the **FX** tab and then playing around with the various effects in the drop-down menu below the words *Video Filter*. Make your choice, and specify the segment you'd like to convert (or at least experiment with) by typing the beginning and ending frame numbers in the boxes below the word *Overwrite*. To see the results of the filter without saving the changes to disk, click the **Play** button. If you decide you want to convert the segment to keep the effect, click the **Render** button, and Kino will create a new file of just that segment. You can also double-click those files (as well as the original captures) to view them in Totem, which is better suited to viewing videos than Kino.

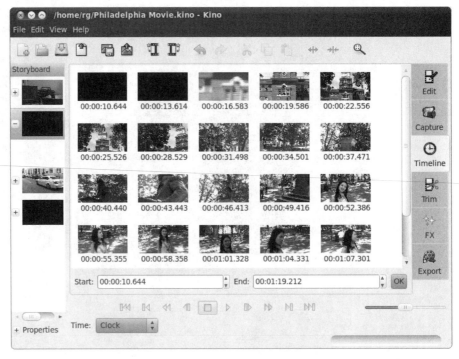

Figure 16-10: Kino's Timeline view

Figure 16-11: Examples of Kino's video effects, before and after

Other Video Apps

I've covered the main video applications in Ubuntu, but there are still others that you might want to consider, all of which are available via the Ubuntu Software Center. If you are interested in yet another alternative video/DVD player, you can try GNOME MPlayer, which has long had quite a significant following because of its ability to handle numerous video formats.

Another cool application for video streaming enthusiasts is Miro Internet TV (Figure 16-12), which allows you to easily search, download, and play online video streams. Just perform an Ubuntu Software Center search for *miro*.

If you have a webcam, you might also want to try an application called Cheese, which allows you take pictures and videos from your webcam and add cool graphical effects. Camorama is yet another webcam viewer/capture application to think about.

If you're looking for an alternative to PiViTi and Kino, try Avidemux. One very handy feature makes it worth having, even if you don't use it as your main video editor: It can rip audio tracks from video files. You can get Avidemux from the Ubuntu Software Center. Be sure to install the GTK+ version (not the Qt one).

For those of you interested in ripping DVDs, you might try DVD:Rip, AcidRip DVD Ripper, or the less daunting to figure out Thoggen DVD Ripper. You might also be interested in DVD95 and the more highly configurable K9copy, which are the Linux world's answers to DVDShrink. These applications allow you to rip dual-layer DVDs (DVD9) and compress the output so that it will fit on a single-layer blank DVD disc (DVD5). For creating your own DVDs from scratch (like you would with iDVD), a few applications are worth considering: DVD Styler, QDVDAuthor, and Bombono DVD.

Figure 16-12: A video streaming enthusiast's dream: Miro

17

FEATHERED FLIPPERS

Linux Gaming

Many people hate to admit it, but games are a big attraction to almost everyone at the helm of a personal computer. Even those who deny being gamers often find themselves caught in the act of rapping off a quick round of solitaire between work projects. As a Linux user, you will most likely find that one of the most common questions you will be asked about Linux by users of other operating systems is, "What games does it have?" Well, although there might not be as many games in the Linux world as there are on Planet Windows, Linux still has plenty to choose from. In fact, most Linux distributions come bundled with a number of games.

Ubuntu, for example, comes with the games AisleRiot Solitaire (a collection of more than 80 solitaire card games), gbrainy (a collection of puzzles, memory trainers, and brain teasers, shown in Figure 17-1), Mahjongg (a tile-matching game, similar to the one introduced in Chapter 9), Mines (the Linux world's answer to Minesweeper), Quadrapassel (a Tetris clone), and Sudoku. Many other free games are available via the Ubuntu Software Center (and other sources), some of which you will learn about in this chapter.

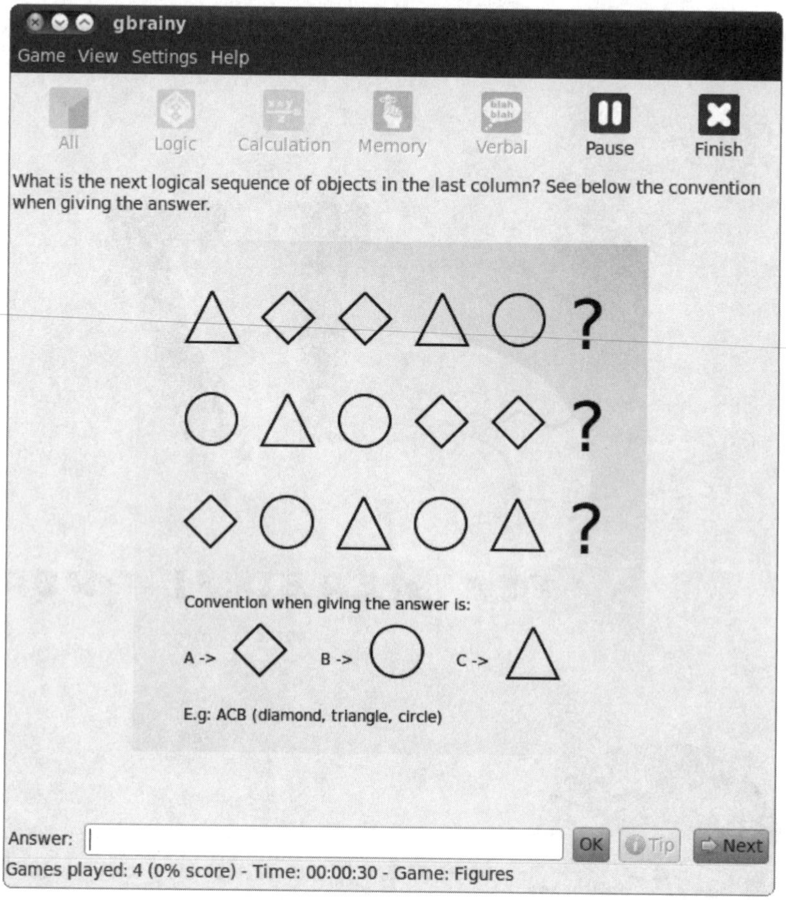

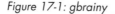

Figure 17-1: gbrainy

Project 17A: Expanding Your Game Collection via the Ubuntu Software Center

Expanding your gaming repertoire is quite easily done via the Ubuntu Software Center. In this project, you'll be plugging in a few gaming holes by installing some classic Linux games. The steps in this project are basically a review of what you learned in Chapter 6, so there will be no challenging work involved—just fire up the Ubuntu Software Center and click away.

17A-1: Installing Missing GNOME Games

The standard GNOME collection of games includes a number that were not included in Ubuntu 10.04 for the sake of space. These include several traditional favorites, such as the puzzlers Tetravex (Figure 17-2), which you can think of as a triangular form of dominoes, and Klotski (Figure 17-3), which is a challenging block-moving exercise. The collection also includes Same

GNOME (a GNOME version of the Japanese marble-matching game Same Game), Tali (an ancient Roman form of poker played with dice), Iagno (a GNOME clone of Reversi), Nibbles (one of those old-fashioned snake games), Five or More (a matching game based on the old Windows game Color Lines), Robots (a weird little "classic," in which you run around avoiding robots), Blackjack, and Chess.

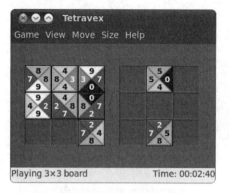

Figure 17-2: Tetravex

Figure 17-3: Klotski

These games come bundled as a single package called *GNOME Games*. To download and install the package via the Ubuntu Software Center, just search for *gnome-games*, and then install it. Once the installation is complete, the games will appear in the **Games** section of the **Applications** menu.

17A-2: Installing Some Linux Classics: Frozen Bubble, Tux Racer, and Pingus

Several other games might be called Linux classics, either because they're Linux originals or because they are penguin-themed, in honor of Linux's cuddly penguin mascot Tux. One of the most well-known and well-liked of these is Frozen Bubble (Figure 17-4). Frozen Bubble qualifies as the ultimate Linux classic: It was written for Linux, it's Linux (penguin) themed, and Linux versions are always released first. It has since been ported to Mac OS, Windows, and even iPhone and Android systems, but Frozen Bubble's soul is pure penguin.

Figure 17-4: Frozen Bubble

The objective of Frozen Bubble is simple: Clear the screen by matching like-colored bubbles, and move on to the next level. This may sound boring, but never fear—you'll be hooked in no time.

To get Frozen Bubble, search for *frozen-bubble* in the Ubuntu Software Center, and install it. You can then run Frozen Bubble by selecting **Applications ▸ Games ▸ Frozen-Bubble**.

Another Linux-themed game you might be interested in is Extreme Tux Racer (Figure 17-5). It's a rather odd (but fun) race-against-the-clock sort of game, in which you guide Tux as he slides down a long, icy mountain trail. You should be aware, however, that unless you have an accelerated graphics card, Extreme Tux Racer will run painfully slowly. If you're not sure whether your computer can handle it, just give it a shot and see for yourself—it's free, after all!

To install Extreme Tux Racer, search the Ubuntu Software Center for *extreme tux racer*, and install it. It will appear in the Games menu.

Unlike Extreme Tux Racer, Pingus (Figure 17-6) is a game that has no special graphical requirements. It's a maze game, based on the old classic Lemmings. Your goal is to lead your group of adorable little penguins safely to the end of each level, without letting them be dashed to bits on the dangerous obstacles awaiting them. There are 22 playable levels included with the game, and if you're feeling adventurous, you can try playing some of the untested levels—there are more than 200 of them! For instructions on playing these extra levels, visit *http://pingus.seul.org/faq.html/*.

To play Pingus, search the Ubuntu Software Center for *pingus*, and install it. You'll find it right where you would expect, in the Games menu.

Figure 17-5: Extreme Tux Racer

Figure 17-6: Pingus

3D Games

Most of the games I've mentioned so far are a little, well . . . two-dimensional. Sure, 2D games can be fun—I've certainly lost a significant portion of my life to Sudoku—but they don't have the excitement factor that you get from shooting hordes of aliens or crashing a high-powered sports car into a wall. Unfortunately, games designers have traditionally neglected Linux to concentrate on the significantly larger Windows market, so up until a couple of years ago there were few Linux-friendly 3D games to choose from. As the penguin has grown in popularity, however, people have started to take notice, and more Windows games now come with a Linux version.

The open source gaming community has come on leaps and bounds too, and there are some really high-quality games now. In this section I'll run through a few of my favorites, after first making sure that your computer can handle the strain of 3D graphics.

Checking for Hardware Acceleration

To play 3D games, you need a graphics card that can handle *hardware acceleration*. Without hardware acceleration, your computer's processor has to try to do all of the fancy graphics rendering itself (a task for which it just isn't designed), so your games end up running at a snail's pace, if at all. Most modern graphics cards have some hardware acceleration support built in, but whether it is enabled will depend on the state of the Linux driver for your card. You can find out how good 3D support is for your graphics card at *https://wiki.ubuntu.com/ HardwareSupportComponentsVideoCards/*.

If you just want to know whether you have the minimum level of acceleration required to play games, then open a Terminal (**Applications ▸ Accessories ▸ Terminal**), type `glxinfo | grep rendering`, and press ENTER. (That vertical line is the "pipe" symbol and can normally be inserted by pressing SHIFT and \ on your keyboard.) If you get a message telling you that glxinfo isn't installed, use the Ubuntu Software Center to install *mesa-utils* and then try again.

If hardware acceleration is enabled, you'll see `direct rendering: Yes` appear in the Terminal. That's good news, because it means you can skip to the next section and sink your teeth into some three-dimensional gaming goodness.

If you received the message `direct rendering: No` instead, you'll need to install different graphics drivers if you want hardware acceleration to work. See "Games/Compiz Don't Work: Installing Accelerated Graphics Drivers" on page 394 for instructions.

NOTE   *Many of the default graphics drivers for Linux can't handle* anti-aliasing, *which is the feature that removes jagged edges from graphics, making them look smoother and more life-like. If you can't live without anti-aliasing, you should also see Chapter 21 for information on installing a better graphics driver.*

Shooting Games

Like many people, my first real 3D gaming experiences were with first-person shooter (FPS) games. In fact, I still have a soft spot for Doom, arguably the granddaddy of all FPSs. What could be more fun than battling endless waves of hellish monsters in a military outpost on Mars? Nothing!

Doom looks a little dated nowadays, but if you have similarly nostalgic thoughts of this classic game, you'll be pleased to know that a version is available for Ubuntu. It's called Freedoom (Figure 17-7), and you can install it from the Ubuntu Software Center (like all the games in this section).

Figure 17-7: Freedoom

The gameplay in Doom may have aged gracefully, but the graphics sure haven't. If pixilated blobs are failing to intimidate you, why not try something a little smoother, in the form of Nexuiz (Figure 17-8)? In terms of gameplay, Nexuiz feels quite similar to Unreal Tournament—you collect a wide array of weapons and power-ups as you run around dimly lit levels, shooting at opponents of varying levels of (artificial) intelligence. As with most deathmatch-style games, the aim is generally to be the last one alive, but there are other game modes, like "capture the flag." There's also an online multiplayer option if you're finding that the computer-controlled opponents aren't providing enough of a challenge.

Tremulous (Figure 17-9) is another popular open source FPS, although its gameplay also contains elements of real-time strategy. You play online, taking the side of either humans or aliens. As you work to destroy the opposing team, you build structures and collect power-ups to gain as much of an advantage as you can. It can get quite involved, so I recommend that you read the notes at *http://www.tremulous.net/* before you begin playing.

Figure 17-8: Nexuiz

Figure 17-9: Tremulous

Plenty of other FPSs are available: AssaultCube, Warsow, and Alien
Arena immediately spring to mind. Check out the **Games ▸ Arcade** section in
the Ubuntu Software Center to see what else you can find.

Strategy Games

I enjoy first-person shooters, but my reaction times aren't quite up to scratch. If the thought of running around a virtual world and shooting at things leaves you feeling cold (or clumsy), perhaps a strategy game is more your style. There are plenty of these waiting to be discovered in the Ubuntu Software Center, but I thought I'd mention a couple of good ones here.

Warzone 2100 (Figure 17-10) is broadly similar to the Command and Conquer series of games. You start off on a battleground with a small collection of vehicles, which you must command to build a base and defend it from enemies. Once your base is in good shape, you can build new units and send them to attack your foes. Your opponents are doing the same, however, so battles can turn into subtle tactical affairs, where your ability to launch successful attacks must be balanced against the limited availability of resources and the constant threat of your base being destroyed.

Figure 17-10: Warzone 2100

If you're struggling to find the time to mastermind an entire military campaign, perhaps Wormux (Figure 17-11) will be more your kind of thing. It's a clone of the popular Worms game, which sees you in command of a small team of heavily armed worms (or, in the case of Wormux, open source mascots like the Firefox fox) scattered around an oddly shaped landscape. You take turns, using your overstocked arsenal to remove opponents from the map in elaborate ways before they can do the same to you. It's definitely worth playing, if only for the interesting sound effects. . . .

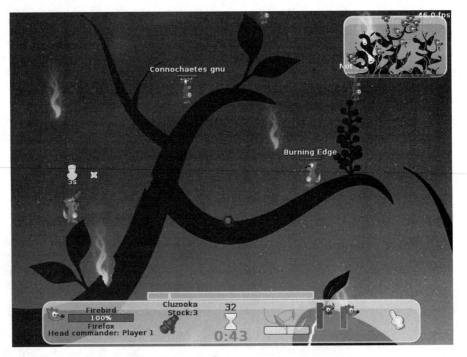

Figure 17-11: Wormux

Simulators

Waging war isn't everyone's idea of escapism, which is why an extensive collection of simulation games are available for Linux. I've tried to cover as many bases as possible in this section, but as always, you should peruse the Ubuntu Software Center if you don't see anything here that appeals to you.

When I think of simulation games, my mind immediately jumps to Sim City, the venerable city-building game. As the mayor, you're in charge of running your city: You plan construction work, build and maintain transport links, and set budgets and taxes. Throw the odd natural disaster into the mix, and you have a challenge on your hands! The Linux equivalents of Sim City are LinCity-NG and OpenCity. I prefer LinCity (Figure 17-12)—the graphics seem friendlier and more cartoonish—but you should try both and decide for yourself. The original Sim City game is available too, if you don't mind playing a game with old-fashioned graphics. Just search for *Micropolis* in the Ubuntu Software Center (it was renamed for legal reasons).

The hardcore flight simulator enthusiasts among you will want to take a look at FlightGear (Figure 17-13). The focus is definitely on realism, with all sorts of cockpit controls and aircraft for you to play with. If you really want the full experience, there's even an Earth-sized online multiplayer map to fly around. If you're not already in possession of a pilot's license, then it might be a good idea to read the manual before you play; you can find it at *http://www.flightgear.org/Docs/getstart/getstart.html/*.

Figure 17-12: LinCity-NG

Figure 17-13: FlightGear

A little less serious than FlightGear is Torcs, a motor racing game (Figure 17-14). It's a pretty standard track racer, where you speed around a circuit against computer-controlled opponents. It has a good choice of cars, tracks, and race styles, and more are available on the Torcs website at *http://torcs .sourceforge.net/*. If off-road racing is more your style, take a look at the Trigger rally game. It's not as well developed as Torcs, but it makes for a change.

Figure 17-14: Torcs

If you'll permit me to stretch the definition of "simulator" just a little, there's also a neat rockstar simulator called Frets on Fire (Figure 17-15). The gameplay is very much like Guitar Hero, but with one major difference: You use your keyboard to play notes rather than a guitar-shaped controller. However, if you don't mind doing a little tinkering, you can get your Guitar Hero controller to work with Frets on Fire. (See *http://fretsonfire.wikidot.com/using-guitar-hero-controller/*.) Plastic guitar or not, it's an addictive game.

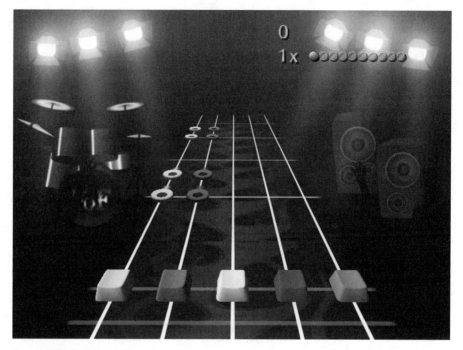

Figure 17-15: Frets on Fire

Even More 3D Games—Beyond the Ubuntu Software Center

I hope you've found something agreeable among my recommendations so far, but it's hardly an exhaustive list. In fact, hundreds of games will run on Ubuntu that haven't made their way into the Ubuntu Software Center yet.

PlayDeb (*http://www.playdeb.net/*) is a good source of extra games. Everything on PlayDeb is available through its own Ubuntu-friendly software repository, so you'll be able to install its games through the Ubuntu Software Center once you've added the PlayDeb repository to your list. See "Adding Extra Software Repositories" on page 86 for full details—the APT line that you need is deb http://archive.getdeb.net/ubuntu lucid-getdeb games.

In the next chapter, I'll also explain how you can run Windows games in Ubuntu using Wine. Indeed, this is how many people enjoy big commercial titles that don't have Linux versions: Guild Wars, Spore, and Call of Duty are just a few examples of games that can be run flawlessly in this way. If this sounds like your sort of thing, Project 18C-3 will be of particular interest to you—a neat little app called PlayOnLinux (Figure 17-16) can be used to handle most of the fiddly configuration stuff that is often required to get less-well-supported games running under Wine.

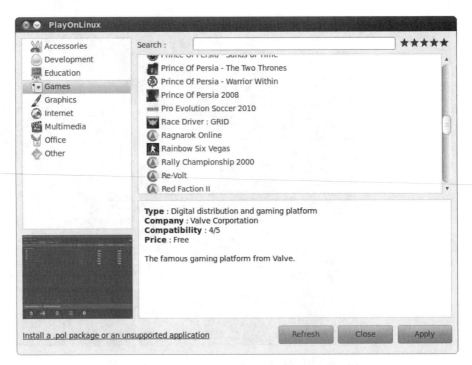

Figure 17-16: PlayOnLinux, displaying a list of some of the Windows games it supports

Project 17B: Installing a Java-Based Game: Schnapsen

As you can see from all the games discussed thus far in this chapter, the Ubuntu Software Center is a great one-stop shop for most Linux games. As you have also learned, however, there are also many games beyond those in the Ubuntu Software Center. These include the games you worked with in Chapter 9 that were written in scripting languages, such as the Python-based pyWings and the Tcl/Tk–based Briscola, but it just wouldn't be right to leave out games written in what might be considered the mother of all scripting languages—Java. In this project, you'll learn how to install the Java Runtime Environment and how to install and run the Java-based version of a classic Austrian card game: Schnapsen.

17B-1: Installing the Java Runtime Environment

To run Java-based applications, or *scripts*, you need to first install the Java Runtime Environment. You can do this via the Ubuntu Software Center by searching for and installing *openjdk java 6 runtime*. The whole set of Java packages is pretty hefty in terms of download weight, so don't get freaked out if it seems to take longer than usual. When the process is complete, close the Ubuntu Software Center, and move on to the next part of the project.

17B-2: Getting and Extracting Schnapsen

Once you've installed the Java Runtime Environment, you need to run a Java application in order to see it at work. The application you'll be installing is one I had been searching for ever since I moved to the world of Linux, a 20-card Austrian card game called Schnapsen, shown in Figure 17-17.

To get started, you will need to download and extract Schnapsen. Here's what you need to do:

1. Open your web browser, and go to *http://projects.hagru.at/tjger/en/*.

2. On that page, click the **Schnapsen** link in the left frame.

3. In the right frame, click **Schnapsen.zip**.

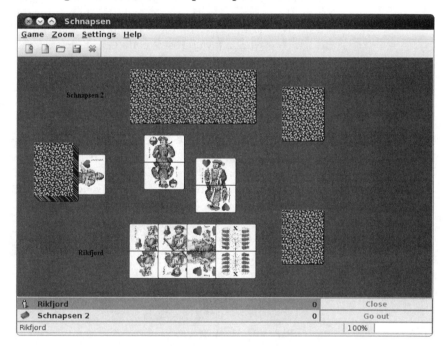

Figure 17-17: A Java version of the Austrian card game, Schnapsen

4. In the Opening Schnapsen_1.00.zip window that then appears, accept the default, *Open with Archive Manager*, by clicking **OK**.

5. When the Archive Manager window appears, click the **Extract** button, which will open the Extract window.

6. In that window, click the **Create Folder** button, and create a folder within your home folder called *Schnapsen*.

7. Click the **Extract** button in that window, and when the extraction process is complete, quit Archive Manager.

17B-3: Running and Anglicizing Schnapsen

Now that Schnapsen is in your home folder, it's time to run it. Open a new Terminal window, and then do the following:

1. Move into the new Schnapsen folder by typing **cd Schnapsen** and pressing ENTER.

2. Type **java -jar Schnapsen.jar** (be sure to place a space between java and jar and use a capital *S* at the beginning of *Schnapsen*), and press ENTER. Schnapsen will soon appear, after which you can start playing . . . if you speak German.

In case you're wondering, here's what you did in that last line: The first part of the command string, java, calls the Java Runtime Environment into action; the -jar flag after that tells Java that you are going to be running a JAR file, which is what a Java script is called; and the last part is the actual file you are going to run, Schnapsen.jar. (In the future, if you choose to run other Java-based applications, just follow the same pattern: java -jar *application_name*.jar.)

3. To switch the interface into English, go to the **Einstellungen** menu, and select **Sprache ▸ Englisch**.

4. If you are not familiar with the German card faces and suits (referred to as Traditional in this game), you can switch them over to the French suits you probably know (diamonds, hearts, spades, and clubs) by going to the **Settings** menu and selecting **French** in both the **Cards' set** and **Trump sign** menus (Figure 17-18).

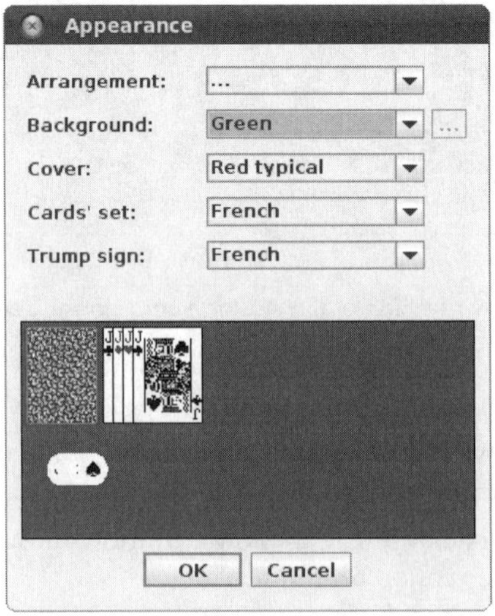

Figure 17-18: Switching from German to French suits and card faces in Schnapsen

You are now set to play. There are some basic rules in the Help menu, but you can also learn the rules of Schnapsen (and any other card game in the world) in greater depth at *http://www.pagat.com/*. Have fun!

Online Gaming

With all this talk of installing games, it's easy to forget that there are many games that you don't have to install at all. Numerous websites allow you to play games online for free, as long as you have the proper browser plug-ins installed. (See "Multimedia Plug-Ins" on page 62 for help installing plug-ins.) For example, check out *http://www.popcap.com/* and *http://gametrick.net/* for some great online time-wasters. You can also play any of the games found on Facebook or other social networking sites, such as Farmville and Mafia Wars, without ever leaving the comfort of your Ubuntu desktop.

Searching for More Games

There are lots of other great games for Ubuntu that I haven't covered, but rest assured that they're out there. Some are available as DEB files, and can be installed in the same way you installed Skype in Chapter 6. A good example is SDL Hana, a Linux version of the Japanese flower card game Hanafuda (Figure 17-19), which is available from *http://savannah.nongnu.org/pr/sdlhana/*.

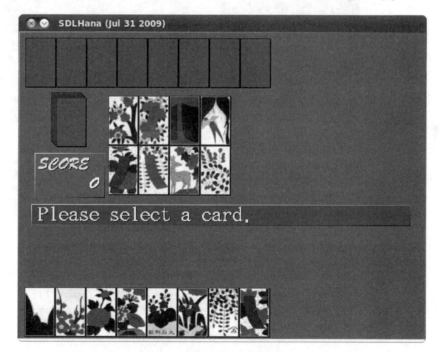

Figure 17-19: SDL Hana

Still more are available from the Ubuntu Software Center: Some of my old-time favorites include the Serbian Pac Man clone, Njam; and the Czech maze game, Fish Fillets NG, in which you guide two fish through all sorts of cumbersome, but very attractive, underwater locations.

There's plenty more available on the 3D side of things, too. In the beautifully designed Yo Frankie! (Figure 17-20), you play an evil sheep-throwing squirrel called Frank, who runs through idyllic landscapes being chased by unfriendly animals—kids (and aesthetes) will love it. You can also lose yourself in the Balazar role-playing game, with plenty of magic and monsters to keep you company; fly a space fighter in 4D in Adanaxis (yes, they managed to squeeze an extra dimension in there, sort of); and race go-karts, penguin-style, in SuperTuxKart (Figure 17-21).

Of course, you can just see what else there is in store for you by browsing the Ubuntu Software Center's Games category. There's a whole world of games out there, so enjoy the search.

Figure 17-20: Yo Frankie!

Figure 17-21: SuperTuxKart

18

PENGUINS AT THE GATES

Working with Ubuntu in a Windows World

Despite the rapidly growing popularity of Linux, it's still very much a Windows world. If you're anything like me, you'll often find yourself working with people who use Windows, so it's important to know how to make Ubuntu happily coexist with Microsoft's ubiquitous OS. Fortunately, Linux is just about the most accommodating operating system available and has no problems sharing files, reading Windows disks, and so forth. In fact, your Ubuntu programs probably support a wider range of file formats than their Windows equivalents; on more than one occasion I've tried to open a file in Windows, failed, and then booted into Ubuntu where I could open it effortlessly.

Of course, sharing files with others may not be your only Windows-related worry, especially if you're a dual-booter. Plenty of people decide to run both Windows and Linux on their computer, so it pays to know how you can minimize the bureaucracy involved in switching between the two. If you kept Windows for the sole purpose of running a specific application and you can't find a Linux-compatible equivalent to it, perhaps you can save the effort of dual-booting altogether and simply install the program directly onto Ubuntu. I told you Linux was accommodating . . . it'll even adopt Windows programs as its own!

Over the course of this chapter, you'll learn how to make the most of your double operating system setup: You'll install some Windows fonts, install some Windows programs, and share files on a Windows network. And if that isn't quite enough Windows for you, you'll even see how to run Windows (in a window!) in Ubuntu. You might want to sit in a dark room for this one—if you're not tired of windows already, you will be by the end of the chapter!

Project 18A: Accessing Files on Your Windows Partition (for Dual-Booters)

If you decided to dual-boot with Windows when you installed Ubuntu, then you'll have a partition lurking somewhere on your hard disk filled with your Windows files and programs (see Chapter 2 if you need a refresher on how partitions work). You can access files on Windows by *mounting* the partition from within Ubuntu. When you mount a partition, the files are made available to you through Nautilus (and other programs)—mounting is just Linux's way of recognizing a partition and preparing it for use.

18A-1: Mounting Your Windows Partition

Mounting your Windows partition in Linux used to be a bit of a chore, but that isn't the case anymore (at least not in Ubuntu). In fact, all you have to do is open a Nautilus window and click the Windows partition in the side pane.

You will most likely find at least two hard disk icons in the side pane, so it is possible that you won't be sure which one your Windows partition actually is. Just remember that your Linux partition is represented by the hard disk icon named *File System*. Things aren't so simple for the Windows partition, unfortunately. It could be labeled *OS* (as shown in the side pane in Figure 18-1) or with the size of the partition followed by the word *Media* (for example, if your Windows partition is 80GB in size, it might appear as *80GB Media* in the left pane). Or, it might be something else entirely. Guess which one it is, if necessary—it won't hurt if you get it wrong.

Now that you know which disk icon is which, it's time to get mounting! Just click the icon for the Windows partition in the Nautilus side pane. An Authenticate window may appear; type your Ubuntu password, and click the **Authenticate** button if it does. A new window showing the contents of your Windows partition will then appear.

NOTE *If you hibernated rather than quit Windows, you will most likely receive a "Cannot mount volume. You are not privileged to mount this volume." error message when trying to mount your Windows partition. Some hibernated Windows partitions cannot be safely read-write mounted in Linux, because adding new files while Windows is hibernated could seriously confuse it when it starts up again. To get full access to the drive, be sure to shut Windows down rather than hibernating.*

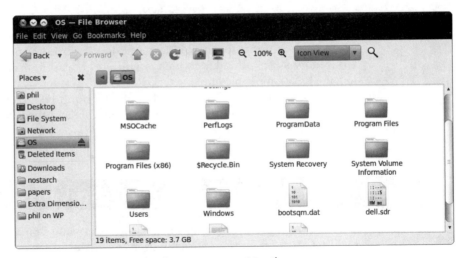

Figure 18-1: Mounting a Windows partition in Nautilus

18A-2: Unmounting Your Windows Partition

You can unmount your Windows partition immediately after finishing your work with it, or you can just wait until you shut down your system, whereupon it will be automatically unmounted. Before you can unmount it yourself, you must first make sure that none of your programs is accessing files or folders on the partition. Nautilus and the Terminal are the usual suspects, so before unmounting, close any Nautilus or Terminal windows that are browsing that partition. Once you've done that, click the little eject icon next to the Windows partition in the side pane of a Nautilus window (Figure 18-2), or right-click it and select **Unmount**.

Figure 18-2: The Windows partition "OS"
in the Nautilus side pane, complete with
eject icon

Accessing a Linux Partition While Running Windows

Viewing your Windows files in Ubuntu isn't too stressful, as you have no doubt just found out. But what about going the other way and getting Windows to recognize your Linux partition? Unfortunately, Windows isn't too helpful in this respect—it can only view FAT or NTFS-format partitions and has no built-in support for the ext format normally used by Linux. As such, if you need access to your Linux files in Windows, it's probably easiest to create a separate FAT partition to be shared between both operating systems (see Appendix C). Hmmm, not exactly convenient.

An alternative is to add support for Linux partitions into Windows by installing some extra software. Unfortunately, the state of such software is pretty dire: Support for the old-fashioned ext2 format is pretty good, but Ubuntu uses ext4 nowadays, which is a different beast entirely. As far as I can tell, the best that people have managed to do is to get an ext4 partition mounted in Windows in read-only mode. Although you won't be able to add new files to the partition, at least you'll be able to see what's in there and copy them into Windows. See *http://www.soluvas.com/read-browse-explore-open-ext2-ext3-ext4-partition-filesystem-from-windows-7/* for an example of how you can do this.

Project 18B: Installing Microsoft Windows Core Fonts

Like it or not, the computing world is still pretty much a Microsoft world, and that means the vast majority of users, even Mac users, are using Microsoft fonts. That being the case, it is inevitable that you will have to deal with documents using fonts such as Georgia, Verdana, Times New Roman, and Courier, to name a few. Of course, your system can substitute the fonts it has for those used in the document. But for you to see things precisely as they were intended and to allow others to see your documents the way you intended, it will behoove you to install those Microsoft core fonts on your own system.

Fortunately for you, there are two ways to get these fonts. One is to download and install them via the Ubuntu Software Center, while the other, for those of you with a dual-boot setup, is to simply copy them from your Windows partition. In the former case, all you need to do is install the Microsoft Core Fonts package using the Ubuntu Software Center. This is the older set of fonts from Windows XP, so installing this package won't get you any of the swishy new fonts that are bundled with later Windows versions. When the installation process is complete, your new Microsoft fonts will have been successfully installed and made ready for immediate use by every user account on your machine.

If you're a dual-booter, you can copy the fonts directly from your Windows installation. This has the advantage of getting all your Windows fonts into Ubuntu, even the newer ones (if you have Vista or Windows 7 installed). Here's what you need to do:

1. Mount your Windows partition, as described in "Project 18A: Accessing Files on Your Windows Partition (for Dual-Booters)" on page 324.
2. Open the Windows partition in Nautilus, and browse to the *Windows/ Fonts* folder.
3. Now for a little trick: Select **Edit ▸ Select Items Matching**, type ***.ttf** in the box that appears, and click **OK** (Figure 18-3). This will select all the files in the folder with names ending in *.ttf*, which are all TrueType font files.
4. Copy the files to a convenient location (somewhere in your home folder should do it).

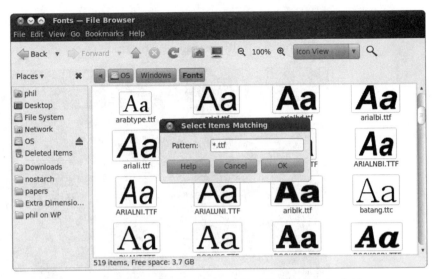

Figure 18-3: Selecting all the TrueType fonts in the Windows/Fonts *folder*

5. Now, go back to the *Windows/Fonts* folder, and select **Edit ▸ Select Items Matching** again. This time, however, type ***.TTF** in the box. This will select the rest of the font files—the item selection feature is case sensitive, and the filenames use different cases for some reason. Copy the selected files as you did previously.

6. With all the font files copied over into Ubuntu, you can now install them as you would any other font. At its simplest, this involves copying the files into the hidden *.fonts* folder in your home folder, but you should see "Project 8C: Installing TrueType Fonts" on page 143 for the full details.

Dual-Booting: Changing the Boot Order and Timeout

If you chose to install Ubuntu alongside Windows in a "dual-boot" setup, you'll be used to seeing the GRUB boot menu screen by now (Figure 18-4). This is the screen that appears every time you start up your computer and gives you the option of running either Windows or Ubuntu.

Ubuntu is started automatically if you don't select a different option after a few seconds. This is fine for people who want to use Ubuntu for almost everything but need to dip into Windows from time to time. If you spend more time in Windows, however, you might prefer to use that as the default operating system. To make the change, first use the Ubuntu Software Center to install StartUp-Manager, and then open it by selecting **System ▸ Administration ▸ StartUp-Manager**. You'll probably be asked to enter your password, so do that and then wait a little while as it loads. Click the **Boot options** tab in the StartUp-Manager window (Figure 18-5), and select Windows from the **Default operating system** drop-down list. The actual name of the Windows option will differ depending on which version you have installed—mine says *Windows 7 (loader)*, for example. From the next time you restart onward, Windows will boot automatically instead of Ubuntu.

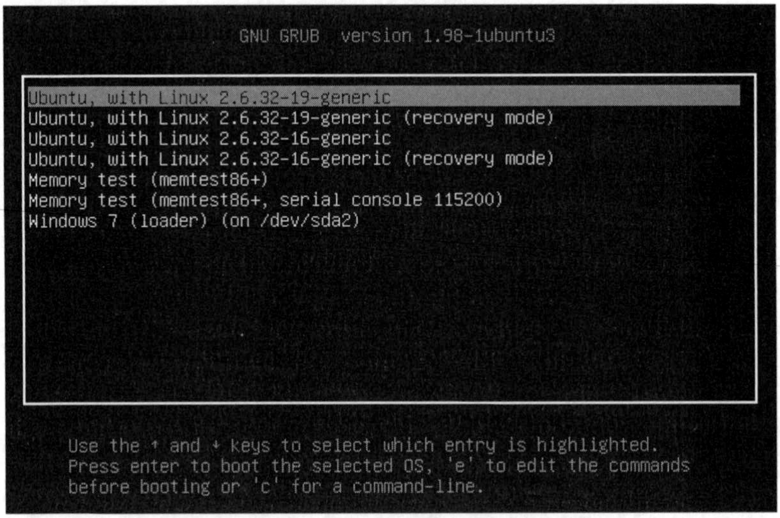

Figure 18-4: The GRUB boot menu screen

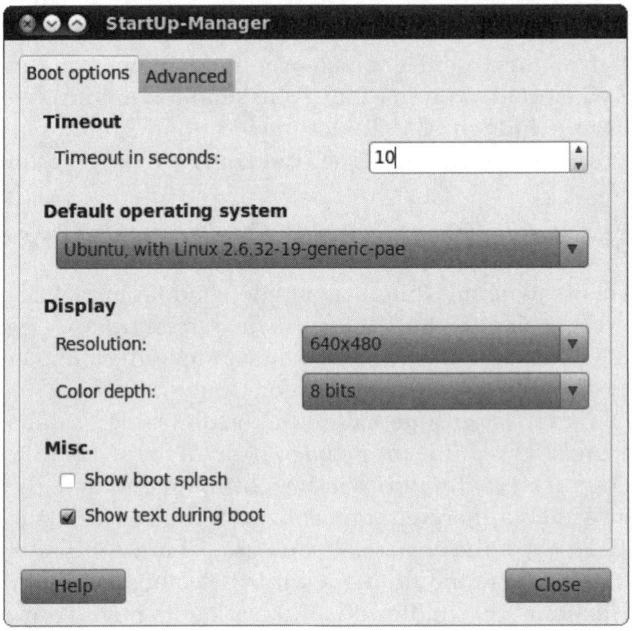

Figure 18-5: Changing boot options with StartUp-Manager

NOTE   *If you apply a major update to Ubuntu at some point, you may find that Windows is suddenly changed from being the default the next time you start the computer. This is because the update will have added a new entry to the boot list, causing the Windows* *item to slip down the list, where it won't be recognized as the default any more. To fix this problem, open the StartUp-Manager, and reselect Windows as the default operating system again.*

The StartUp-Manager lets you change the boot timeout too. By default, GRUB waits for 10 seconds before loading your default operating system, but I'm impatient and find this far too long to wait—so impatient, in fact, that I changed the Timeout in seconds option (also on the Boot options tab) to one so the menu is displayed only for a second. This might sound fast, but when I want to get into Windows, all I do is press the down arrow key a few times while my computer starts up. GRUB stops the timer when you press a key and just keeps the menu on the screen, so once that has happened, I'm free to choose the Windows option at my leisure.

Once you're happy with your revised boot timeout and/or default operating system, click **Close** to apply the settings. StartUp-Manager will spend a few seconds making the requested changes, after which it will close. Restart the computer to see the updated boot menu in action.

Linux Equivalents to Your Windows Applications

Before going through the trouble of running Windows programs in Ubuntu, it's a good idea to try some of the equivalent Linux applications. More often than not, there's a native Linux program that will do exactly what you need, without any of the headaches involved with running an application designed for another operating system.

First, however, you have to find those Linux equivalents. Luckily, plenty of websites list good alternatives to Windows software: *http://www.osalt.com/* and *http://www.linuxalt.com/* are quite comprehensive, for example. Or, you can simply root around the Ubuntu Software Center, installing applications that tickle your fancy. After all, the best way to see whether you like a program is to try it!

NOTE *Some Windows programs don't have direct equivalents in Ubuntu, so you might need to install a couple of programs to get similar functionality to your Windows software. In the rare cases where there aren't any suitable alternatives, you can try using Wine or installing Windows in a virtual machine, which I'll talk about next.*

Project 18C: Running Windows Programs

In Chapter 6 you learned a host of ways to add applications to your system, but you may not have considered one other method—installing Windows applications. Despite there being Linux equivalents for most of the Windows programs that you need, there may be one or two programs that you miss. Fortunately, it is possible to run some Windows applications from within Linux with the help of a program called *Wine*. The list of compatible software includes the likes of Microsoft Office, Internet Explorer, Adobe Photoshop, and a whole host of games, so if you're desperately missing a particular program, then it's definitely worth a look.

It is only fair to point out that Wine continues to be a work in progress. It works well with some programs and not at all with others. Things are improving, however, and Wine now seems to work better with more applications. If you are curious as to which apps are known to run under Wine and to what degree of success, check out the Wine home page at *http://www.winehq.org/*, and click the **AppDB** link. The AppDB entries for programs often contain helpful advice on getting them to run in Wine, so check there first if you run into problems.

18C-1: Installing and Testing Wine

You can get Wine via the Ubuntu Software Center by doing a search for *wine* and installing the Wine Microsoft Windows Compatibility Layer (it should be the first search result). Once the installation is complete, you can test it by selecting **Applications ▸ Wine ▸ Programs ▸ Accessories ▸ Notepad**. After a few seconds (longer the very first time you use Wine), the Windows Notepad will appear (Figure 18-6).

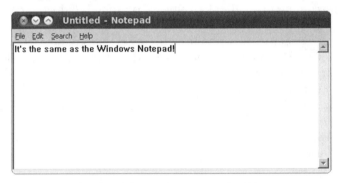

Figure 18-6: Windows Notepad running under Wine

18C-2: Installing a Windows Application in Wine

Now that you've seen one Windows application in action under Wine, you might as well learn how you can install more yourself. I will point you to one application that will definitely work—a pretty cool text editor called NoteTab Light (Figure 18-7).

To get NoteTab Light, go to *http://www.fookes.com/ftp/free/ NoteTab_Setup.exe*, select **Save File**, and click **OK** in the window that appears to save the file in your *Downloads* folder.

When the download is complete, go to the *Downloads* folder, right-click the *NoteTab_Setup.exe* file, and select **Properties** from the pop-up menu. Then, go to the Permissions tab and check **Allow executing file as program**. Close the Properties window, right-click the file again, and this time select **Open with Wine Windows Program Loader**. A few moments after that, the same sort of setup wizard that you would see if you were installing NoteTab in

Windows will appear (Figure 18-8). Go through the wizard, accept the license agreement, and then accept all the defaults along the way until the installation is complete.

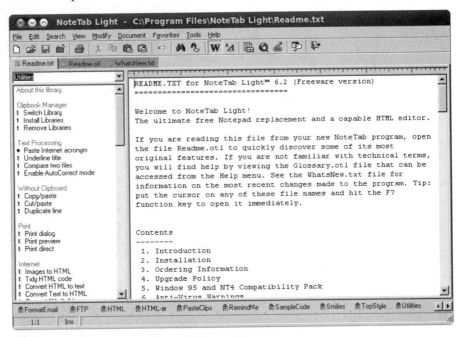

Figure 18-7: NoteTab Light running under Wine

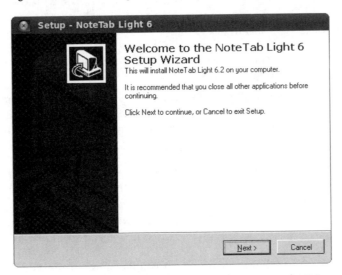

Figure 18-8: A Windows installation wizard running under Wine

Running NoteTab Light is quite easy because it provides you with a desktop launcher. You'll need to do a little more setting up first, though, because if you double-click the launcher now, you'll get a warning about an "Untrusted Application Launcher." To get rid of the warning, right-click the *NoteTab*

Light.desktop file on your desktop, and select **Properties**. Go to the Permissions tab, and check **Allow executing file as program** (as you did earlier).

With that done, just double-click that launcher, and NoteTab Light will soon appear, just like a regular Linux app would. You can also run NoteTab Light and other Windows applications installed under Wine by selecting **Applications ▸ Wine ▸ Programs** and then selecting the program you want to run. You might find, however, that some Wine-dependent applications will not appear in this menu until you log out and log back in after installing them.

18C-3: Getting Windows Apps to Work in Wine with PlayOnLinux

Some Windows software stubbornly refuses to work in Wine unless you have things set up in a specific way. The Wine website is full of tips on how to tweak settings until you hit on the magic formula that seems to work for a given program (settings that are practically guaranteed not to work for other programs you installed with Wine). Some instructions even ask you to install different versions of Wine for different programs! Fortunately, there's a neat way to side step these issues, called PlayOnLinux. It handles all the settings tweaks for you and supports many commonly used Windows programs (and an especially large number of games). You can install PlayOnLinux in the usual way from the Ubuntu Software Center.

Once it's installed, start PlayOnLinux by selecting **Applications ▸ Games ▸ PlayOnLinux**, and then click **Forward**. It'll spend a minute or two updating its database of supported programs and will leave you at the main PlayOnLinux window (Figure 18-9) when it's done. In that new window, click **Install**, and use the category pane or the search bar in the window that appears to look for a Windows program of your choice. In this example, I'll install the delightful Crayon Physics game:

1. Select the **Games** category, and find the Crayon Physics entry in the list (not the Deluxe version).

2. Select **Crayon Physics** (as in Figure 18-10), and click **Apply** to start the installation process. If the window freezes, click the window's close button, and then click **Force Quit** to convince the installer to start.

3. Click **Forward**, and wait as the game is downloaded.

4. If you like, check one or both of the boxes to put a shortcut to the game on the desktop and/or in your Applications menu. Then, click **Forward** and **Forward** again to finish the installation process.

5. To start playing, double-click the Crayon Physics entry in the list of programs in the main PlayOnLinux window, or select it from that list and click **Run**.

Assuming that the game was installed successfully, you'll be met with a Crayon Physics window. Click anywhere in that window, and you'll see a landscape scrawled onto your display in crayon, similar to the one in Figure 18-11. The aim of the game is to draw boxes on the screen with your mouse, which land in such a way as to roll the ball onto a star. Every time you get the star, you move to the next level, where you'll be forced to come up with a more ingenious ball-rolling strategy. It sounds simple, but I promise you it's addictive!

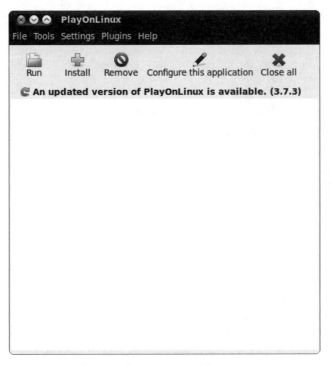

Figure 18-9: The main PlayOnLinux window

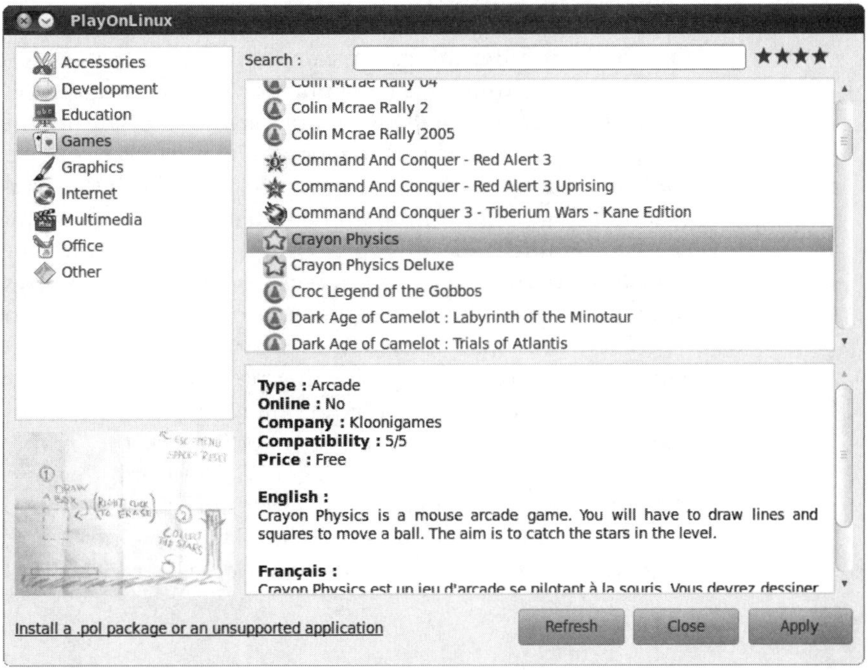

Figure 18-10: Selecting a Windows application to install in PlayOnLinux

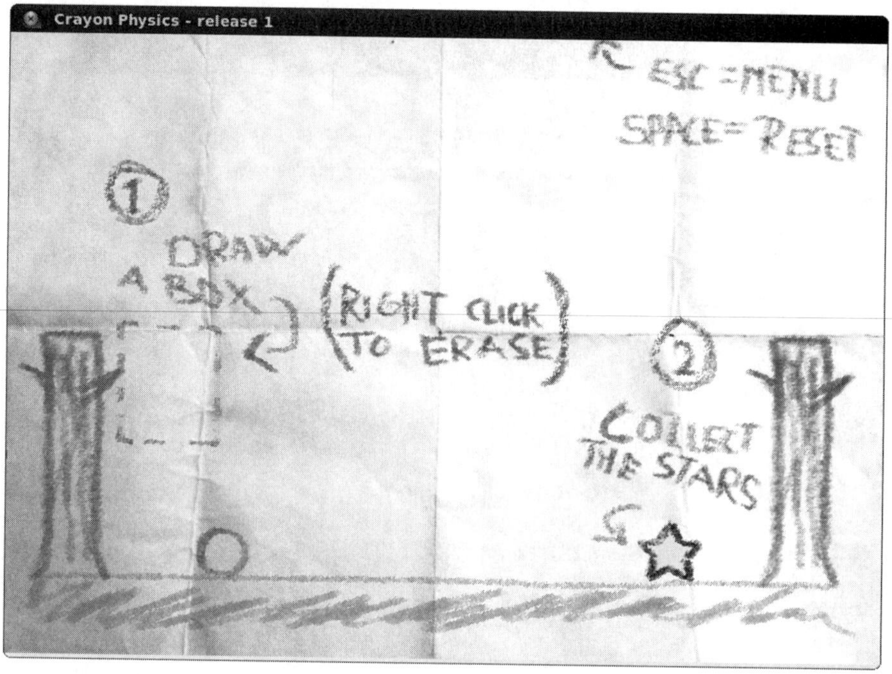

Figure 18-11: Playing the Crayon Physics game, courtesy of PlayOnLinux

Installing Windows Inside Ubuntu

One of the weirder things you can do with a computer is to run a simulation of a computer inside it. This simulation, known as *virtual machine (VM)* software, allows you to install one operating system inside another, so you can run both at once without having to reboot. This is handy if you need to run Windows for some reason, perhaps for some specialized software, but are too comfortable working in Ubuntu to even contemplate going through the somewhat time-consuming rebooting procedure that dual-booters must follow to get back into Microsoft territory. You can even get Windows to sit there in, well, a window, which can be opened and closed at will just like any other program.

There are some caveats. First, the virtual machine has to share your computer's resources with all your other programs, so it can slow things down if you're doing anything computationally strenuous. Second, it doesn't have the same access to your computer's hardware as the "real" operating system, so you probably won't be able to get Windows-only devices working through the virtual machine. Finally, and perhaps most awkwardly, you need a Windows installation CD to be able to put Windows into a VM, but most computers only come supplied with a recovery CD, which won't do the trick.

If you do have an installation CD, getting Windows into a VM doesn't take much more work than getting it onto a real computer:

1. Open the Ubuntu Software Center, and install VirtualBox. Other virtual machines are available, but I find this one the easiest to use.

2. Select **Applications ▸ System Tools ▸ Sun VirtualBox** to start it up, and click **New** followed by **Next**.

3. Choose a name and type for your VM. The name is up to you, but the operating system should be set to Microsoft Windows.

4. Click **Next**, and choose the amount of memory (system memory, not hard disk space) that you'd like the VM to have access to (Figure 18-12). This can be a tough decision; on one hand, you need enough memory for the "virtual" operating system to be able to run (Windows XP needs at least 128MB, for example), but you want to leave enough memory free for Ubuntu programs to be able to use it. VirtualBox normally suggests something sensible.

5. Click **Next** again, and choose **Create new hard disk** (Figure 18-13). Make sure that **Boot Hard Disk** is checked too, and click **Next** to open the Create New Virtual Disk window.

6. Run through the Virtual Disk Wizard, clicking **Finish** when you're done; the defaults should be fine for most of the options, but you might want to choose the size of the virtual disk yourself. This will be used as the hard disk of the virtual machine and is stored as a file in a hidden folder inside your home folder. Again, choose a size that's big enough to run the virtual OS but small enough that it doesn't engulf your entire hard disk.

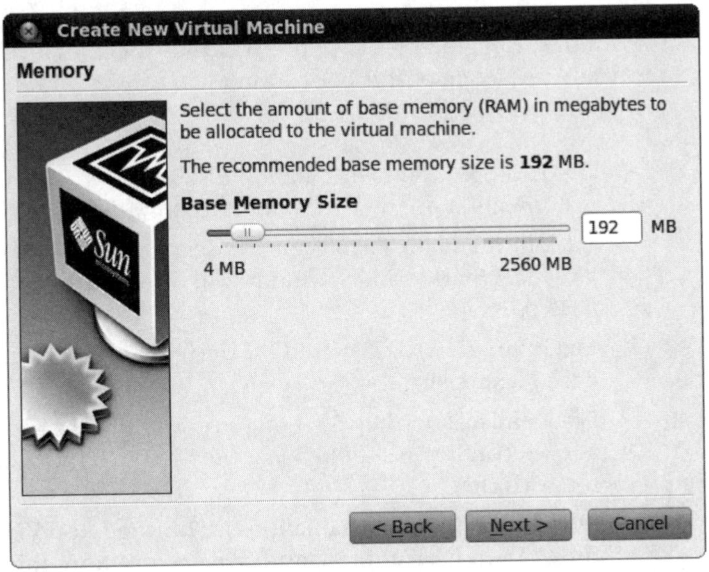

Figure 18-12: Choosing how much memory to allocate to the virtual machine

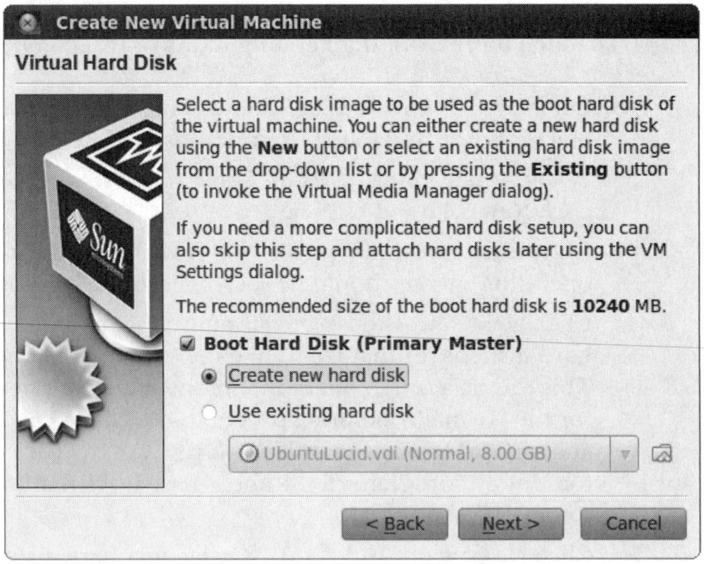

Figure 18-13: Creating a new virtual hard disk

NOTE   *If you choose Dynamically expanding storage as the storage type, the virtual disk will start off small and grow in size as you add more files in the virtual machine. This is a handy way of saving on disk space.*

7. With the virtual disk setup finished, you'll be taken to a summary page where you can click **Finish** to create the virtual machine.

So far, so good. With a VM ready and rarin' to go, it's now time to install Windows; I'm going to leave the Windows specifics up to you (they're a little outside the scope of this book, don't you think?), but here's what you need to do to get things started:

1. Insert the Windows installation disc into your CD drive, and close any windows that open and ask what to do with it.
2. Back in the main VirtualBox window, select your VM from the left pane, and click **Start**. A black window will open, along with a First Run Wizard; click **Next**.
3. Make sure that CD/DVD-ROM Device is selected under Media Type, and click **Next** again.
4. Click **Finish**, and the VM should try to boot from your Windows CD. After a few seconds you should be face to face with the Windows Installer. Have fun with that!
5. Once the Windows installation has finished, the VM will restart. Remove the CD when prompted, and, after a few more minutes of setup, you should be staring a Windows desktop in the eye. Phew, hard work over!

You can install Linux and other operating systems in virtual machines, as well as Windows. In fact, you could even install a VM within a VM, although you'd probably have to budget half a day to check your email if you had both of them running at once.

Sharing Files with Windows Users on Your Network

One of the main reasons for connecting to a network (apart from accessing the Internet) is to share files between computers. You might be familiar with this concept already; network shares are used in many workplaces, and you may have even set one up before on your home network. For the uninitiated, a network share is a folder on another computer that you can access as if it were on your own. Files are transferred around on the network, so there's no need to use a portable hard disk or flash drive to get them from one place to another.

Accessing Files Stored on a Windows Computer

Network shares are a two-way thing: You can either share your files with others by creating a *shared folder* or access existing shared folders created by other people. If you're connected to a network of Windows computers, then you probably have some network shares already. I talked about browsing network shares in some depth in "Using Nautilus as a Network Browser" on page 101, but to save you the anguish of flipping back so many pages, here's a quick outline of what you need to do to access a share from Ubuntu:

1. Select **Places ▸ Network**; Nautilus will open.
2. Double-click the *Windows Network* folder to see a list of all the Windows computers connected to the network.
3. Double-click one of the computers to see its shared folders.
4. Pick a shared folder, and double-click it to access the files inside it.

Making Your Files Accessible from a Windows Computer

Since your Windows computers have so gladly made their files available on the network, let's have Ubuntu reciprocate by sharing a folder of its own:

1. Open Nautilus and find the folder you want to share; then right-click it, and select **Sharing Options**.
2. Check **Share this folder** in the Folder Sharing window that appears.
3. You'll be told that the sharing service is not installed—click **Install service**, and wait for the installation process to finish.
4. Back in the Folder Sharing window (Figure 18-14), choose a name for the shared folder, and type a comment if you like.

Figure 18-14: Sharing a folder on the network

5. Check **Allow others to create or delete files in this folder** if you want other people on the network to be able to modify the files you have there. If you don't check this option, others will only be able to read and copy these files.

6. By default, only people with a user account on your computer can access your shared folders. To make it so anyone on the network can access your shared files, check the **Guest access** option.

7. Click **Create Share** to finish up.

Go to your Windows computer, and try to access the newly created share. Shared folders on Ubuntu computers can be accessed in the same way as any other share, so do whatever you would normally do to find it. (In Windows XP, for example, you'll find it in your *Network Shares* folder.) If you can open a file in the shared folder, you'll know that everything was set up correctly.

If you don't want to share a folder any more, right-click it in Nautilus, select **Sharing Options**, and uncheck **Share this folder**.

19

DEFENDING THE NEST

Security

Many a Windows user has entered the Linux fold after a host of bad experiences with *malware* in the Windows world—viruses, spyware, and all sorts of other malicious bits of software code, too numerous to imagine. Windows is also plagued by a seemingly endless array of security vulnerabilities, leaving the system easy prey to invaders with less than noble intentions. Every trip out into cyberspace thus becomes something like a run through the infectious diseases ward of a hospital. For a Windows user, it can sometimes seem that more time is spent ridding the system of viral pests and defending it from invaders than is actually spent getting things done.

Fortunately, Linux does not suffer greatly from such problems, leading to the much-touted claim that Linux is practically virus free and quite secure. Numerous lines of reasoning have been proffered to explain Linux's malware- and exploit-resistant nature. One reason is simply popularity—or lack thereof. Because Linux is not as widespread a system as Windows is, it is also a much less attractive target of digital evil-doers, who very often seem to be motivated by the challenge and headline-catching glory that comes with creating a truly global virus or finding a theretofore unknown back door.

Another reason is that Linux users, as a general rule, work on their computers in a nonprivilege mode, one in which the user does not have the right to install software without a password. This is not the case in some versions of Windows. A virus or other form of malware attached to an email or piggybacked upon another file or application cannot, therefore, install itself in your Linux system without that password . . . well, theoretically, at least. Of course, now that more recent versions of Windows use a privilege structure by default, this point is a bit less of an issue.

There is also the matter of structural design. Every system has security holes that can be exploited by digital and human foe alike. Windows might well be called the Swiss cheese of operating systems in this regard. Of course, Linux has its holes too, though far fewer of them than Windows does; and Linux plugs them through downloadable updates faster, once they are found.

Finally, Ubuntu's preconfigured security policy brings a defensive edge—there are no open incoming ports in Ubuntu desktop systems. This means your Ubuntu Linux system is even less susceptible to unwanted intrusions.

Does My System Need Protection?

So, with all this talk about Linux's great security, you may wonder whether you need to bother worrying about it at all. Well, if you take a look at the Ubuntu forums, you might find yourself a bit confused. When asked whether Linux users need to install antivirus software or firewalls, most users answer with an emphatic *no*. On the other hand, you'll find that an awful lot of people have installed or are trying to install that software. Hmmm.

So, what's a Linux user to do?

If you are on a network where you transfer a lot of files among a lot of Windows machines, you might want to think about installing some antivirus software, if for nothing more than the good of the Windows systems involved and the users of those systems—your unenlightened (i.e., Windows-using) email pals, for example. You might also want to give it a go if you are, by nature, on the cautious side of the spectrum. Basically, if it makes you feel safer to install some protection, go ahead. If it makes you feel safer to go whole-hog and install the full line of defense mechanisms I cover in this chapter, go ahead. After all, either way you go, it isn't going to cost you anything, and it certainly isn't going to hurt you any.

The First Line of Defense

Regardless of the system you happen to be using (though I am assuming that you have become a Linux devotee by now), the first line of defense for any computer permanently hooked up to the Internet is a *router*—an electronic device that allows a number of computers on a local network (such as in your home or at your office) to connect to and share a single connection from your

Internet service provider (ISP). While the router is connected to your modem via cable, the connection from the router to the computers on your local network can be wired, wireless, or both.

What does a router have to do with the defense of your computer? Well, most routers include a *firewall*, which essentially functions to keep all of the bad stuff on the Web away from your computer, much in the way that the firewall in your car keeps the heat, fumes, and noise from your engine out of the passenger compartment. This built-in firewall is one reason that even people with only one computer, who could just as easily connect their computer directly to their cable or DSL modem, use a router. Of course, just how much security the firewall in your router provides depends on which filters you select in the firewall setup software. For example, a very common and useful filter (particularly for those with a wireless network) limits Internet access to those machines specified on the firewall's access list. This prevents your next-door neighbors from hitching a wireless ride via your ISP connection. They aren't paying the bill, after all.

The setup software for a router is built into the router, so you don't have to worry about software installation and system compatibility. Using your router with Linux is no different from using it with Windows. You can access the software and modify your settings via a simple web browser, as you can see in Figure 19-1. Just type the IP address of the router (usually provided in the owner's manual) in the browser's location bar, press ENTER, and you'll be ready to go.

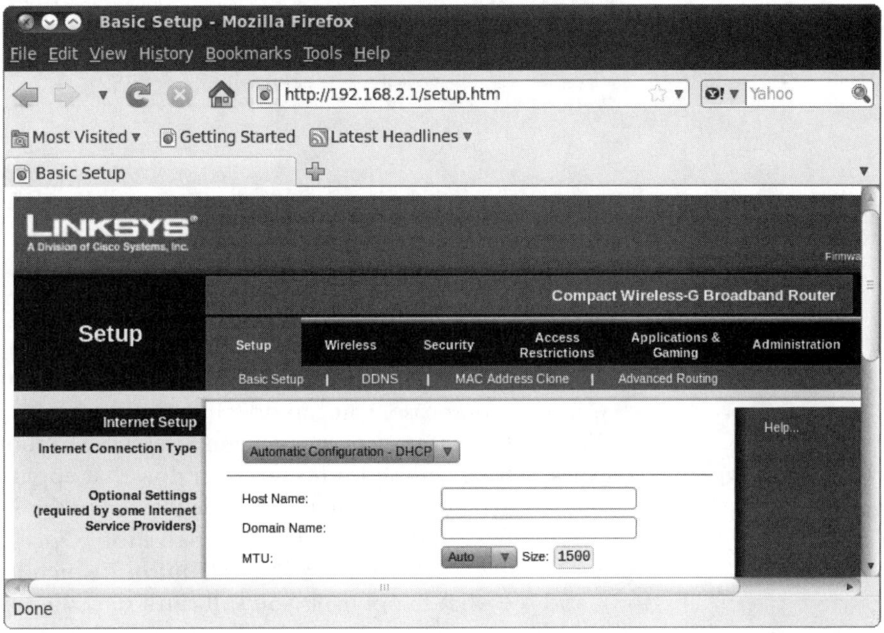

Figure 19-1: Setting up a router

Software Firewalls

If you don't have a router and don't plan on getting one or if you have one but are bordering on paranoia, you might want to consider using a software firewall, in particular one of the most popular software firewalls available for Linux, Firestarter.

You can get Firestarter via the Ubuntu Software Center by searching for *firestarter* and installing it. Once it is installed, run it by selecting **System ▸ Administration ▸ Firestarter** (you might be asked for your password). Firestarter will open with a self-explanatory setup wizard the first time. Just read each screen carefully; make whatever selection are suggested, if any; and click the **Forward** button in each of the wizard screens until you get to the last one (shown in Figure 19-2). On that screen, make sure that the box next to *Start firewall now* is checked, and then click the **Save** button. The wizard window will then close, and the main Firestarter window will appear. Assuming the correct network device was detected and selected and the correct wizard choice made, the firewall will be up and running.

Figure 19-2: The last screen of the Firestarter setup wizard

If the wrong network device was selected, a warning window will appear telling you so. In that case, you can do a bit of trial-and-error manipulation by selecting **Edit ▸ Preferences** in the main Firestarter window and then clicking **Network Settings** in the Preferences window that appears (Figure 19-3). In that window, select one of the other devices listed in the Detected device(s) drop-down menu, and then click the **Accept** button. Once back at the main Firestarter window, click the **Start Firewall** button (which looks like a Play button), and see what happens. If you still can't start the firewall, repeat the process I've just described, this time selecting a different network device.

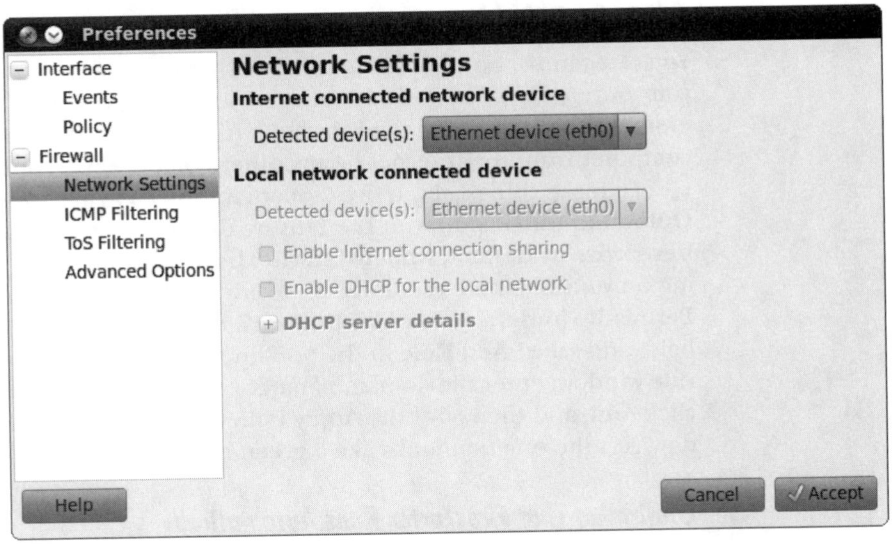

![Network Settings preferences window in Firestarter]

Figure 19-3: Selecting network devices in Firestarter

Once your firewall is up and running, there is nothing more that you really need to do. You can simply look at the Firestarter window (Figure 19-4) to see what is going on network-wise on your computer—which active connections you have, how much information has been coming and going, and whether there have been any events in which, for example, the firewall has blocked an intruder. If you click the **Events** tab, you can then see the details of those events, such as what connection attempts were blocked, where they came from, and when they happened.

Figure 19-4: Firestarter in action

Taking Control of Firestarter

You can control how Firestarter deals with various network events by creating your own *policies*. The default policy set in Firestarter allows you to do whatever you normally do via the Internet, while it blocks new connections to your computer from the Internet or any other computer on your network.

To make things a bit more draconian, you can click the **Policy** tab, select **Outbound traffic policy** in the Editing drop-down menu, and then select **Restrictive by default, whitelist traffic**. If you just want to deny anyone working on your computer access to a specific website, for instance, simply select **Permissive by default, blacklist traffic**, right-click the **Deny connections to host** field, and select **Add Rule** in the pop-up menu. In the Add new outbound rule window, enter the domain name for the targeted site (as in *example.com*), click **Add**, and then click the **Apply Policy** button in the main Firestarter window (it's the one that looks like a green check mark).

Confirming That Firestarter Runs Automatically

After you run Firestarter the first time, it will set itself to automatically start up whenever you start your system. Don't be concerned when you don't see the graphical interface you saw when you first started it; Firestarter will be running in the background, silently protecting your computer.

If you are the doubting type, you can check to see whether Firestarter actually is running in the background by opening a Terminal window, typing `sudo /etc/init.d/firestarter status`, and then pressing ENTER. If Firestarter is running, you will see the message `* Firestarter is running...` in the Terminal window. Worries over. If Firestarter isn't running, the response will read `* Firestarter is stopped`.

Finding Out More

If the world of firewalls is new to you, you can check out the Firestarter home page to learn a bit more. To check out the online manual, just to go to the Firestarter **Help** menu, and select **Online Users' Manual**, which will open the page in your web browser. If you prefer to check out the manual before installing Firestarter, point your browser to *http://www.fs-security.com/docs/*. You will also find a pretty good quick tutorial there.

ClamAV: Antivirus Software, Linux Style

Despite the lack of viruses that can wreak havoc upon your Linux system, your computer could still act as a transmitter of Windows viruses. As a result, a number of free antivirus scanners are available for Linux users interested in helping protect Windows users from viruses. These include Panda Desktop Secure (*http://www.pandasecurity.com/usa/homeusers/downloads/desktopsecure/*), f-Prot (*http://www.f-prot.com/*), and numerous others. For most Linux users, however, the virus scanner of choice is the open source contender: ClamAV.

Although it can be used on a number of operating systems, ClamAV is considered to be *the* Linux antivirus software package. It is open source and totally free, and you don't have to worry about licenses or suffer the bother of renewing them. Unfortunately, on its own, ClamAV is a command-driven application, which makes it a bit less user-friendly. Fortunately for all involved, a graphical interface, albeit a simple one, is available; it goes by the name of ClamTk. Both ClamAV and ClamTk are available via the Ubuntu Software Center—just search for *clamtk*, and install Virus Scanner. The Ubuntu Software Center will then automatically install ClamAV and all other packages it needs in order to run.

Once ClamAV is installed, you can perform a virus scan by selecting **Applications ▸ Accessories ▸ Virus Scanner**. This will open the ClamTk Virus Scanner window (Figure 19-5).

Once up and running, you can scan your system on demand from the Scan menu. To scan a single folder, select **A Directory**. To scan a directory and everything within it, choose **Recursive Scan**. In either case, the Select a Directory window will appear. Select the folder or disc you want to scan, and click **OK**. ClamAV will then start scanning your system. ClamTk will let you know what it is scanning at any given moment in the empty space just below the button bar. If it finds anything suspicious, it will list that item in the main pane of the window.

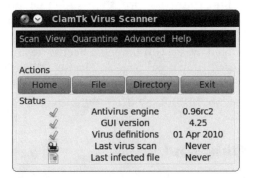

Figure 19-5: ClamTk—the graphical interface for ClamAV

ClamAV is set up by default to check for *signature updates* when it starts. These signature updates tell ClamAV what new viruses to be on the lookout for. If you leave your machine on for days and days at a time, it is probably also a good idea to set things up so that ClamAV will automatically check for signature updates daily rather than just on startup. To do this, go to the **Advanced** menu, and select **Scheduler**. In the Schedule window, select a time for ClamAV to do its update check in the bottom half of the window. Click the **Add** button when done. You can also use this window to set up a time to regularly scan the system—just select the time you'd like the scan to occur, and click **Add**. When you're finished, click **Close**.

As I mentioned, the only viruses you are likely to encounter during a virus scan are those designed for Windows systems, which cannot affect your Linux system. Although it won't hurt you any to scan your entire system for viruses, it is probably better to focus your virus-scanning activities on your Windows partition, if you have one, and on any files that you will be sending as email attachments, particularly to Windows users.

Project 19A: Virus Scanning with avast!

Although ClamAV may be the virus scanner of choice in the Linux world, my personal favorite is still avast!, which defended me during my Windows years. I think it is easier to use and, for what it's worth, nicer to look at. On the downside, it does require you to register every year so that you can get a license key, but that is hardly a monumental task, and it is still free.

19A-1: Downloading the avast! DEB Package and License Key

First you have to get the avast! file and license key. You can do this by opening your web browser and going to *http://www.avast.com/linux-home-edition/*. Once you're there, click the **Download** tab, and then download the DEB package of the avast! Linux Edition.

Once the download is complete, double-click the DEB package, and when the Package Installer window appears, click the **Install Package** button. You will then be prompted for your password, so provide that, and click **OK**. The download and installation will then begin. When these processes are complete, close the notification window and the Package Installer. Once you've downloaded and installed avast!, you'll need a license key in order to use it. Just go back to the avast! Download page in Firefox, click the **registration form** link, and then fill out and submit that form. You should receive your license key by email a few minutes later (though the page says it could take up to 24 hours).

19A-2: Running and Using avast!

Once avast! is installed, you can run it by selecting **Applications ▸ Accessories ▸ avast! Antivirus**. The first time you run avast!, a small window (Figure 19-6) will appear asking you to input your license code. Assuming you registered your free copy of avast! at the beginning of the project as I instructed you to do, your registration key should already be waiting for you in your email inbox. Copy the key, and paste it into the text field in the Registration window using CTRL-V or by right-clicking in the box and selecting **Paste**. Once the license key is in place, click the **OK** button.

The main avast! window (Figure 19-7) will now appear, but before you get started scanning away, it is a good idea to check for any updates to your virus database. New viruses are constantly appearing in cyberspace, so you should keep avast!'s virus database up-to-date so that it recognizes any viral newcomers. To perform the update, just click the **Update database** button, and let avast! do its thing.

Figure 19-6: Entering your avast! license key

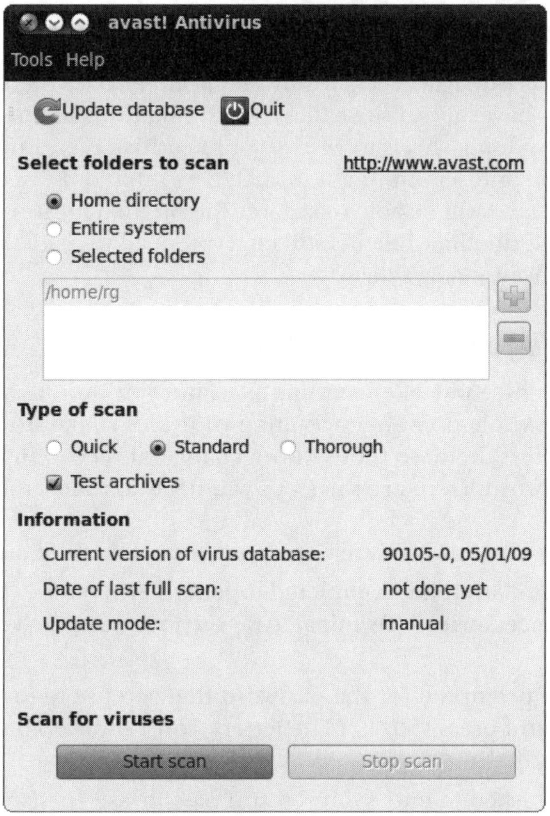

Figure 19-7: avast! virus scanner

When avast! is done updating the virus database, you can get on to the work of virus scanning by first deciding whether you want to scan just your home directory, the entire system, or selected folders. You can also decide how thorough a scan you want to perform via the three choices available in the middle of the window: Quick, Standard, or Thorough.

Which one of these sensitivity modes you choose depends on how thorough you want the scan to be. The Quick scan just scans files that end in certain extensions (*.exe*, *.scr*, *.com*, *.doc*, and so on), because these are the file types that are most often virus carriers. The Standard scan targets more files, ignoring extensions but still limiting the scan to those file types that are usually associated with viruses. Finally, the Thorough scan scans everything and searches for every type of virus.

Once you have made your selections, click the **Start scan** button, and avast! will start doing exactly that—showing its progress within the same window. When the scan is complete, a small window will pop up telling you, ideally, that no viruses were found. When was the last time you got a message like that on your Windows machine?

Project 19B: Encrypting Your Files

Protecting yourself against Internet nasties is all well and good, but what if someone gains physical access to your computer? Data theft is a serious business, so if you have any sensitive files, you should think about protecting them. A good way of doing this is to *encrypt* your sensitive files. Encryption is a way of taking a file and scrambling it in such a way that only a person with the right *decryption key* will be able to recover the original information. If someone tries to look at the file while it's still encrypted, all they will be able to see is a bunch of nonsense characters.

19B-1: Creating an Encrypted File Folder

Ubuntu has a nice way of encrypting files, but you should take care when using it! The whole point of encrypting your files is that no one but you will be able to access them, so there's little chance of recovering them if you forget your password. Here are the steps you need to follow to get encrypted:

1. Open the Ubuntu Software Center, and search for and install *ecryptfs-utils*.
2. Once installation has completed, open a Terminal by clicking **Applications ▸ Accessories ▸ Terminal**, type `ecryptfs-setup-private`, and press ENTER.
3. You'll be prompted for the password that you use to log in to Ubuntu. Type it, and press ENTER. (The letters won't show up on the screen, but that's normal.)
4. You'll be asked to enter your mount passphrase (password). Pick something *very* memorable—there's no recovering this password if you forget it! Press ENTER, retype the password (to make sure there were no typos), and press ENTER again.
5. Close the Terminal window, log out of your user account, and log back in again.
6. When you log in, an Update information window will appear (Figure 19-8). Click **Run this action now**, type your login password into the window that appears (it will look as if nothing is being typed again), and press ENTER.

7. Your mount password (also referred to as *encryption passphrase*) will be displayed on the screen. Make a careful note of it, press ENTER, and then click **Close** in the Update information window to continue logging in.

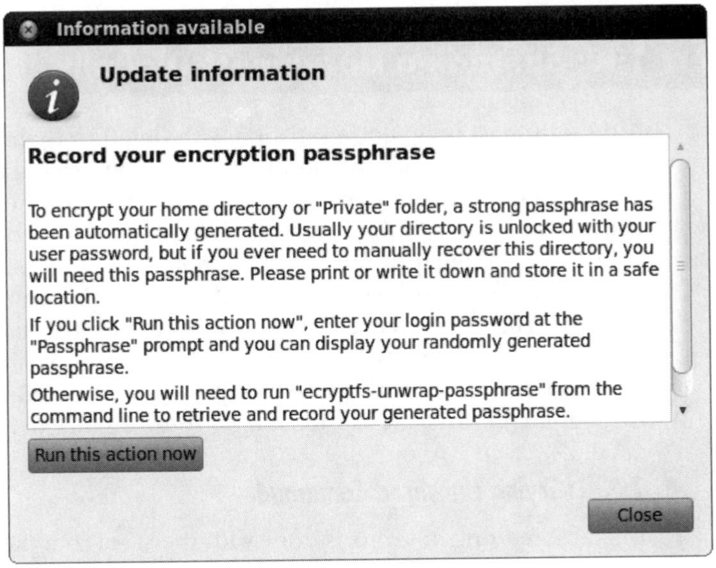

Figure 19-8: Checking your encryption passphrase

If you open your home folder, you'll now see a folder called *Private*. Anything you put in this folder will be encrypted and will be safe from prying eyes. This is especially useful if your computer gets stolen—only someone with your mount password will be able to look at the files, and ideally the only person who knows it is you!

19B-2: Recovering Encrypted Files If Something Goes Wrong

If you have problems with your computer and need to recover the files in the encrypted *Private* directory, use the following steps after you get Ubuntu up and running again. If you don't feel confident following these instructions, you should definitely ask for advice on the Ubuntu forums first.

1. Open a Terminal, type `sudo mount -t ecryptfs /home/`*username*`/.Private /home/`*username*`/Private`, and press ENTER. You should, of course, replace *username* with your own username.

2. You'll be asked for your passphrase. Type your mount passphrase (password), and press ENTER.

3. Now you'll be prompted a few times to make a section. Hit ENTER a few times until you're given a WARNING message.

4. Type **yes**, and press ENTER; then type **no**, and press ENTER.

5. If you entered the right mount password, the *Private* folder will be decrypted, and you'll be able to access your files. Copy them from that folder to somewhere safe!

If you have no luck recovering your files, take a look at *https://help .ubuntu.com/community/EncryptedPrivateDirectory/* to see whether there's anything further you can try.

Project 19C: Shredding Documents Digitally

Although most people are satisfied with deleting their files when they no longer need them, they may not realize that the deleted file data is still retrievable. This may pose little concern when it comes to photos of your summer trip to Maryland or reports you may have written for a class on Thai cooking, but it is a completely different situation if you've been storing bank details or other confidential information on your hard disk. Even if you reformat that disk, the data stays. That is great news if you want to retrieve any files you may have accidentally deleted (or formatted away), but it isn't such good news if your computer gets lost or stolen or if you just decide to give it away. In such cases, it might not be a bad idea to do some digital shredding.

19C-1: Trying the shred Command

Digital shredding in Linux is done with the shred command. Its usage is very similar to the rm command you learned to use in Chapter 9, though in terms of removal, shred is much more thorough. To give it a try, create a dummy file by going to the **File** menu of a Nautilus window, and selecting **Create Document ▶ Empty File**. Name the new document **myShredExp.txt**, and then double-click the file. This will open gedit. Type a couple of sentences in the document—anything will do—and then save it. Close gedit. The first couple of words you typed should now appear on the icon of the new dummy file you created (as shown in the example on the left side of Figure 19-9).

myShredExp.txt   myShredExp.txt

Figure 19-9: Files change their appearances after being shredded.

With your new file in hand and placed in your home folder to make it easier to follow along, you are ready to try shred. Open a Terminal window, type **shred myShredExp.txt**, and then press ENTER. If you now look in your home folder, you will notice the difference right away: Your original file is still there, but the text on the icon now looks like gibberish (as you can see in the example on the right side of Figure 19-8), which is what your file has become. If you double-click the file, gedit will open like it did before, but this time around, it won't be able to read your file, and it will tell you so (Figure 19-10).

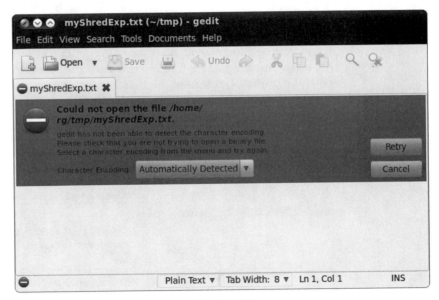

Figure 19-10: gedit can't open your shredded files.

So, now you've got yourself a shredded file sitting in your folder, but it sure would be handy to get rid of the file rather than just have it sitting there littering things up, wouldn't it? Of course, you can remove the file via the Terminal by using the rm command, but it would be easier to get future shredded files deleted immediately after being shredded. Fortunately, this is easy enough to do by using the shred command with the -u flag. You can try it on the file you've already shredded by opening a Terminal window, typing **shred -u myShredExp.txt**, and then pressing ENTER. Your file will then be further shredded and deleted.

19C-2: Taking the shred Command Graphical in Nautilus

Although using the shred command isn't all that difficult, most average users would prefer to do things graphically. After all, you don't *have* to type commands to delete or move a file, right? You can do all of that easily enough through Nautilus, and it's the same with shred. The only difference is that shred's functionality does not come bundled into Nautilus out of the box— you have to add it yourself. Here are the steps you need to follow:

1. From the Ubuntu Software Center, search for *nautilus-actions*, and install Nautilus Actions Configuration. This package allows you to add commands and other functionality to Nautilus.

2. Once the installation is complete, select **System ▸ Preferences ▸ Nautilus Actions Configuration**.

3. When the Nautilus Actions windows appears, click the **Add** button.

4. In the Add a New Action window that appears, type **Shred** in the Label box and **Erase files more securely** in the Tooltip box.

5. If you want to choose an icon for your Shred menu entry in Nautilus, click the arrow button to the left of the Browse button, and then select an icon of your choosing (I just used the delete icon). When you're finished, your window should look like that in Figure 19-11.

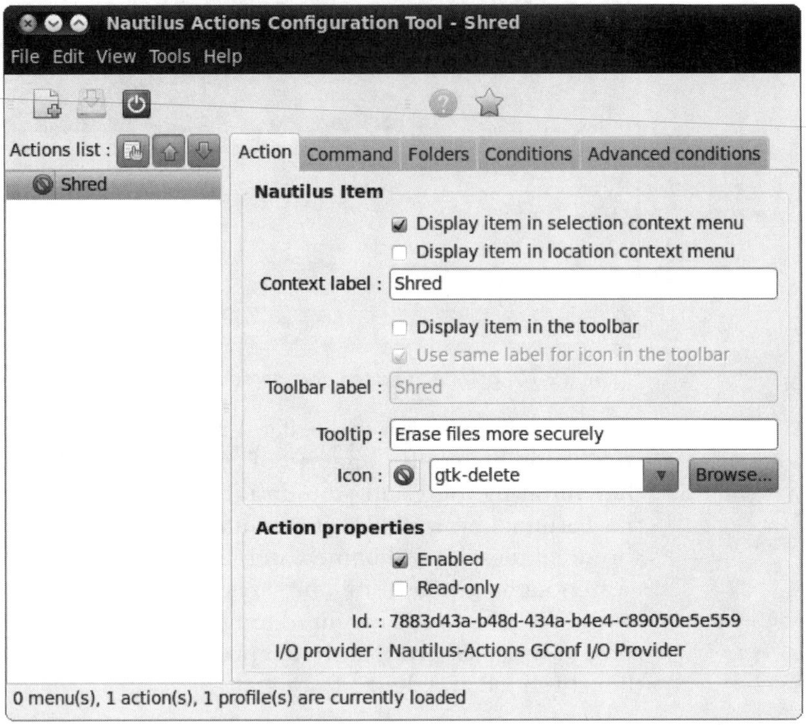

Figure 19-11: Making the shred command graphical via Nautilus

6. Next, click the **Command** tab, and type **shred** in the Path box, and **-f -u -v -z %M** in the Parameters box (making sure you use an uppercase *M*).

7. Now click the **Conditions** tab. In the Appears if selection contains section of that tab, choose whether you want the new Shred menu to appear only when you have selected a file, only when you've selected a folder, or both. To play it safe at first, you might want to stick with the default, Only files, so you don't inadvertently shred a whole folder full of important files. Once done, check the **Appears if selection has multiple files or folders** box, and then save your work by going to the **File** menu and selecting **Save**.

8. The label for the shred command in the left pane of the still-open Nautilus Actions window will now no longer be in italics. Click the **Close** button in that window.

To put shred to work in its new graphical manifestation, you must first log out and log back in to your account. After, that just right-click a file you want to shred, and then select **Shred** from the pop-up menu (Figure 19-12). The file will be securely, and permanently, deleted. Decidedly cool.

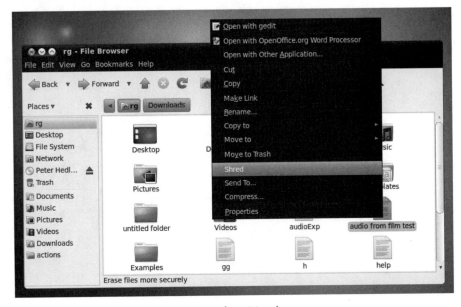

Figure 19-12: Invoking the shred command via Nautilus

20

A COLONY OF PENGUINS

The Ubuntu Community

One thing that really sets open source apart from the commercial software world is the importance placed on the *community*. This can include pretty much anyone who has anything to do with the software: The people who use it, the people who design it, the people who help others with problems . . . every last one of them is a valued community member.

Consider the commercial software world, where things tend to be quite top-down. When you have a problem, you go to some company that provides you with support. This company probably also designed and sold you the software, and you probably played no part in that process—you're the customer; they're the vendor. Open source is different: Rather than one business managing everything, everyone pitches in together and helps each other. People write software and fix faults because it helps other people and because they want to help. Everyone can play their part in offering feedback and suggestions and helping others with problems, and no one is in absolute control of the whole process. All in all, it's much more democratic and, in my opinion, much more fun!

The Ubuntu community in particular is large, vibrant, and notoriously friendly. In this chapter, you'll learn how to get the most out of it and how you can play your part by joining in and giving something back (if you like).

Take Me to Your SABDFL

Open source communities tend to have a well-defined structure, and Ubuntu is no exception. At the top of the pile is Ubuntu's founder, Mark Shuttleworth, whom you met in Chapter 1. He's the Self-Appointed Benevolent Dictator For Life (SABDFL), and according to *http://www.ubuntu.com/community/ ubuntustory/governance/*, his role is to "provide clear leadership on difficult issues and set the pace for the project." This doesn't mean that he makes all of the plans and decisions—that's more the job of the Technical Board, a group of senior Ubuntu contributors who figure out what shape the next Ubuntu release will take. Mark is just there to step in if no one can agree.

There's also the Community Council, which oversees the teams of contributors that make up the bulk of the project. There are lots of teams with all sorts of responsibilities: The Documentation Team writes the documentation for each release of Ubuntu, the Installer Team looks after the software used for installing Ubuntu, and so on. You can find a list of them at *https:// wiki.ubuntu.com/Teams/*. Teams consist of members from all over the world (Figure 20-1), and people on the team may have all sorts of responsibilities: Developers, for example, are the people who write and update the software. Last, but certainly not least, are the millions of Ubuntu users worldwide who form the biggest part of the community. This group includes you!

Figure 20-1: A world map showing the locations of the members of the Ubuntu Documentation Team

Everyone who participates is expected to abide by the Code of Conduct (*http://www.ubuntu.com/community/conduct/*), and people who make changes to the project (like developers) are asked to sign a copy of this document to show their commitment to the principles of Ubuntu. One final note: Ubuntu is a *meritocracy*, where the people who've contributed most to the project get the biggest say. The most prolific contributors are awarded with *Ubuntu membership* (if they apply for it) and benefit from such perks as an *ubuntu.com* email address.

Launchpad: Your Passport to the Ubuntu Community

Every open source software project needs a place to call home. In Ubuntu's case, this is Launchpad, a sort of project information website on steroids. Whether you want to report a problem, ask for help, design a cool new feature, or write your own program, Launchpad is where you go.

Fire up Firefox, and browse to *http://www.launchpad.net/*. Unless you've signed up before, you'll want to register for an account, so click **Log in / Register** at the top of the page, and answer the questions under the "Not registered yet?" heading. Hit **Register**, and go check your email for details on how to finish signing up. When the message arrives, click the first link, fill in your details, and click **Continue** on the page you get sent to so you can start using your account.

Once that's all done and dusted, click your name in the top right of the page to see your profile. It's probably looking pretty empty at the moment, apart from a bunch of three-letter acronyms and a mysterious invitation to change your "branding." Click one of the round, yellow pencil icons to start changing your details. You can put as much or as little information on your account as you want—for example, if you'd like people to be able to find you on IRC (see "Chatting on IRC" on page 367), make sure you enter your nickname on the page (Figure 20-2). Otherwise, you can leave most things blank.

If you've just created your account, you might notice a sad little zero hanging around in the "Karma" section. Fortunately, it's not karma of the metaphysical sort, and your eternal soul isn't in any danger. Rather, it's a points system for recognizing people who have helped make Ubuntu better. The more you contribute, the more karma points you get, and hence the greater your bragging rights over your Ubuntu-obsessed friends (that's all of them, right?). Check out *https://help.launchpad.net/YourAccount/Karma/* for details on how it all works.

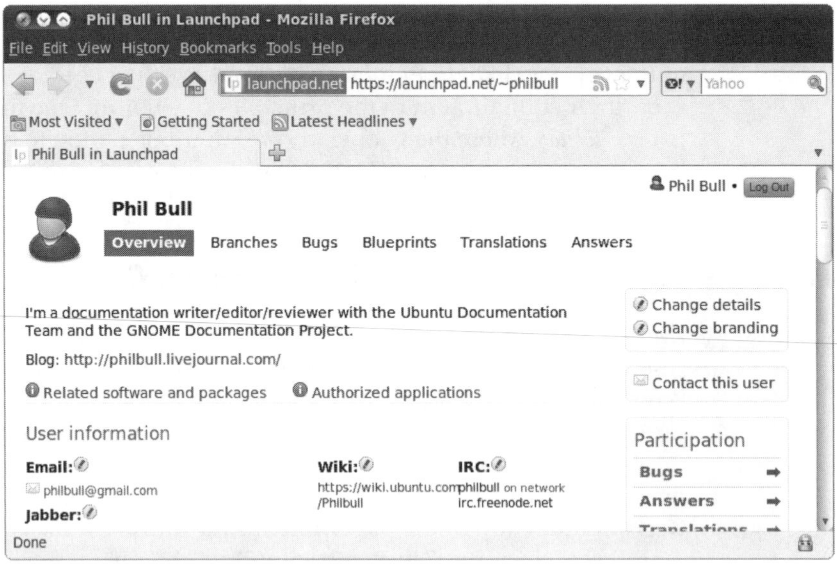

Figure 20-2: My Launchpad account page

Bugs, Bugs, Glorious Bugs

The computers of yesteryear were enormous, complicated beasts, filling entire rooms with delicate electronics and whirring tape drives. Renowned computer scientist Grace Hopper, on retrieving a moth from a relay in one such giant, taped the offending insect into her log book and remarked that she had found a "bug" in the computer. Well, computers may have changed a lot since the 1940s, but some of the terminology hasn't. Whether it's as major as a program crashing or freezing or as minor as a missing icon, any problem that you find with a piece of software is still referred to as a *bug*.

You've almost certainly come across a bug before—no software, whether commercial or open source, is ever perfect. The difference with open source is that you're strongly encouraged to report problems wherever you see them. Developers need feedback in the form of bug reports so they know what needs fixing, and problems get fixed more quickly if they're reported sooner. Filing a bug report is a relatively easy way of giving something back to the community; it doesn't take long, it helps to improve the software for everyone, and you get an annoying software problem fixed for free!

What Counts as a Bug?

There are lots of different types of bug, but you can usually fit them into one of the following categories:

- When a program crashes, freezes, or shows an error message for no good reason (for example, Figure 20-3)

- When something doesn't work (for example, when a button does nothing when you click it)

- When hardware (such as a printer or your sound card) misbehaves or doesn't work at all

- Typos, missing icons, and other cosmetic mistakes

If your problem fits any of these descriptions, then you likely have a bug on your hands! You should be aware of a few notable exceptions, though. First, if a program is missing a feature, that's not a bug. You can make a feature request using the Brainstorm website (see "Sharing Ideas on How to Improve Ubuntu" on page 364). Second, you shouldn't ask for help with software by reporting a bug, since you probably won't get a response. Use the forums or IRC instead; find out more on those in "The Ubuntu Forums" on page 365 and "Chatting on IRC" on page 367. Finally, it's important that the bug is *reproducible*. This means that you can provide a set of instructions for someone else to follow, and they will experience the same problem as you. Sometimes computers just do one-off weird things, so if it's not repeatable, there's little chance that the problem can be identified and fixed.

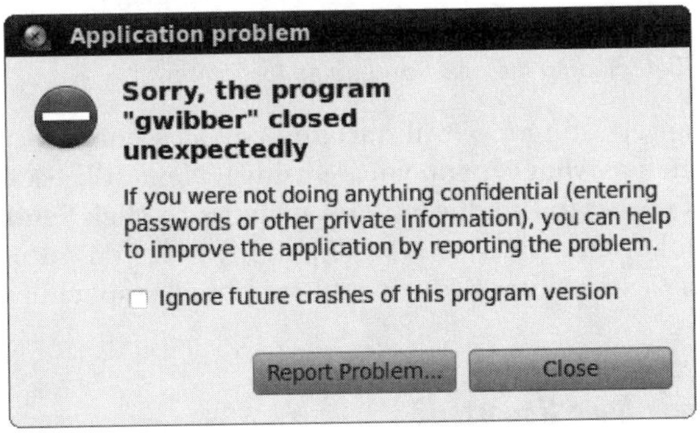

Application problem

Sorry, the program "gwibber" closed unexpectedly

If you were not doing anything confidential (entering passwords or other private information), you can help to improve the application by reporting the problem.

☐ Ignore future crashes of this program version

Report Problem...   Close

Figure 20-3: If a program crashes (like Gwibber here), it's probably a bug

Reporting a Bug

If you're confident you've found a bug, it's time to tell someone about it! If it happened in a specific program, select **Help ▸ Report a Problem** in that program's menu, if that option exists, and skip to the next paragraph. If that option isn't there, you'll have to get your hands a little dirty. First you need to find the command name for the offending program. This isn't always the same as the name that appears in the title of the window, so you'll have to do some digging to make sure you get it right:

1. Select **System ▸ Preferences ▸ Main Menu** to open the menu editor.

2. Use the Menus list to the left of the window to find your program. For example, if you want to report a bug about the Tomboy note-taking program, you'd click the **Accessories** item and find *Tomboy Notes* in the Items list in the middle of the screen.

3. Right-click the name of your program, and choose **Properties** from the menu that pops up.

4. When the Launcher Properties window appears, take a look at the contents of the Command box—for Tomboy it should say `tomboy --search` (Figure 20-4). You can ignore everything after the first space (only the first part matters)—so in this case, the program's command name is `tomboy`.

5. Press ALT-F2 to open the Run Application window, type **ubuntu-bug tomboy** (replacing **tomboy** with the command name for your program), and click **Run**.

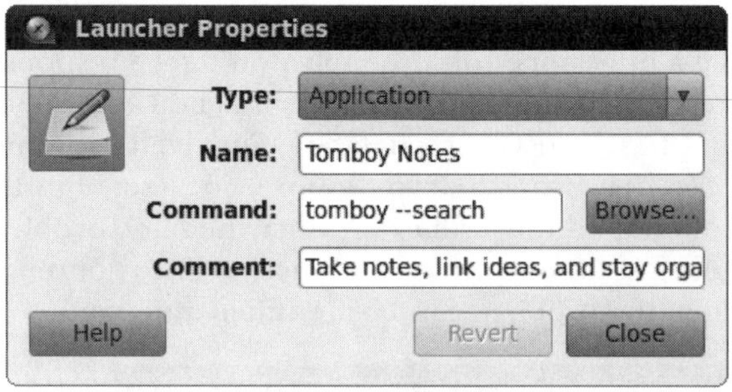

Figure 20-4: Finding the command name for Tomboy

The bug-reporting tool will start and collect some information about the program (such as what version you're using). Next, it'll ask whether you want to send this report to the developers—you do, so click **Send Report**, and a web page will open (log in to Launchpad if you haven't done so already). Type a brief description of your problem, being as specific as possible, and click **Next**.

Has It Already Been Reported?

Lots of people are using the same programs as you, so there's a good chance that someone has gone to the trouble of reporting your bug already. Launchpad will go off to look for existing bugs that it thinks match the description you gave, so take a look at the list that appears and see whether any of the results sound familiar (Figure 20-5). If you find one that does, click the arrow next to it, read the description to make sure, and click **Yes, this is the bug I'm trying to report**. This could be a good sign, because someone just might be working on a fix already!

Choose **Just mark the bug as affecting me**, and click the green check button to go straight to the bug page (the alternative option, Subscribe me as well, means that you will receive an email every time someone posts a comment about the bug). Take a look at the comments that others have made about the bug, and see whether there's anything useful that could help you work around the problem. Comments are sometimes technical in nature, so it might be necessary to ask around on the forums for help with some of the more cryptic instructions. If you can't see anything helpful, you can try to provide some more details on the problem to help a developer track it down. They often ask for you to provide a copy of the output of some command, which they can use to figure out what's going wrong. If you think you can help, scroll down to the bottom of the bug page, and put what you know in the comment box.

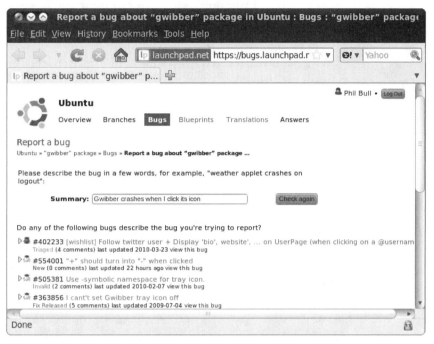

Figure 20-5: A list of bugs that Launchpad thinks are similar to the one you're reporting

A New Bug

If no one else seems to have the same problem, then you've got a live one! Click **No, I need to report a new bug** at the bottom of the page where the list of suggested bugs appeared, and write a description of the bug in the Further information box. Here are some tips on how to write a breathtakingly beautiful bug report:

Only report one problem per bug. If you report more than one problem at a time, it will be difficult for the developers to keep track of what they've fixed and what they haven't.

Describe what you were doing at the time the bug occurred. Context is important, so you should describe what you were doing when you experienced the problem. For example, if your music player crashed when you plugged in your iPod, then you should mention that.

Mention which version of the program you're using. The bug-reporting tool should have automatically provided information about software versions, but it's a good idea to make a note of them yourself too. Selecting **Help ▶ About** in the program's menu will usually give you the version number of the program, and you can find out which Ubuntu version you're running by selecting **System ▶ About Ubuntu**.

Describe how to reproduce the bug. Developers need to see how the bug happens in order to fix it. Provide a step-by-step list of instructions that describe how someone could make the same problem happen on their computer. If you don't know how to make the bug happen again, just describe in as much detail what you clicked or changed when the bug happened.

Once you've packed the report with information, click **Submit Bug Report** to finish the process.

What Happens Now?

You'll receive an email from Launchpad confirming that your bug was reported successfully, but this isn't the end of the story. Let's take a look at a typical bug to see how things pan out: Open Firefox, and head over to *https://bugs .launchpad.net/ubuntu/+bug/121853/* to see a bug I reported for the Rhythmbox music player in 2007. The first thing to note is the information at the top of the page (Figure 20-6): The *Affects* column lists which packages are affected by the bug, *Status* tells you how far the bug has made it on the road to being fixed, *Importance* tells you how serious the bug is, and *Assigned to* is the name of the developer or team responsible for fixing the bug. These details are changed by developers as progress is made on identifying and fixing the problem.

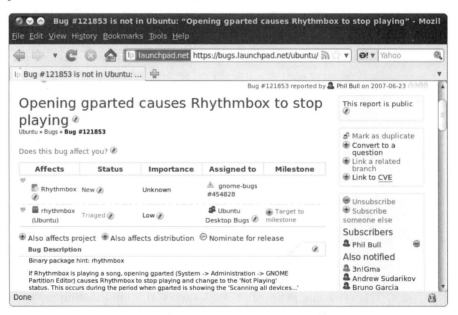

Figure 20-6: The Launchpad bug report page for my Rhythmbox bug

NOTE   *It's bad practice to change the status or importance of your own bug since people often overestimate the importance of their problem. Leave it up to an Ubuntu developer or another community member.*

Further down, you'll see my original bug report followed by a question from superstar Ubuntu developer Sebastien Bacher. There's a bit more to-and-fro until the bug gets sent *upstream*—that is, to a different open source project that handles the bugs for Rhythmbox. From there, I just had to wait for the Rhythmbox developers to fix the problem.

If you've reported a bug, keep an eye on your email. You'll be notified every time the bug is changed or a comment is made. If someone asks for more information on the problem (like Sebastien did with mine), all you need to do is reply to the email. Your reply will be automatically added to the bug report for everyone to see. The more information the developers have, the faster they will be able to fix the problem.

When Will My Bug Be Fixed?

Hundreds of new bugs are reported for Ubuntu every day, which isn't so surprising when you think that there are something like 30,000 packages available for you to install. The sheer volume of bugs isn't easy to cope with, and dealing with them has been likened to "drinking from a firehose." To calm the chaos, an army of volunteers called the Bug Squad pore over all the new bugs, categorizing them, identifying ones that have already been reported, asking for details on how the bug happens, and generally trying to get enough information together for a developer to be able to swoop in and fix the issue. In practical terms, this means it can take quite a while for a problem to be fixed, although the actual timescale will depend on how important the bug is judged to be. I normally reckon on waiting two to three months for an "average" bug. Having said that, my Rhythmbox bug hasn't been fixed yet, and it's several years later! (To be fair, it was a particularly minor problem that few people are ever likely to experience.)

Once a bug is fixed, its status is changed to Fix Released, and the Ubuntu developers will often provide an updated package that you can install to fix the problem on your computer. Fixes aren't made available straightaway, since they have to go through a series of stringent tests to make sure that they don't screw up anything else. This means that some bug fixes might not even be available until the next version of Ubuntu is released!

Faster Fixes

If you know that a problem has been fixed but an updated package hasn't been released yet, there may be a way around the delay—if you don't mind taking a small risk. When updates are being tested to get them ready for official release, they are made available online for anyone to try. There's a chance that the updated versions could cause problems (after all, they're being tested!), but they're usually fine. There are also *backported* packages, which are unofficially updated versions of programs. These will have been tested, just not very rigorously, so use these at your own risk too.

To gain access to these less-stable packages, select **System ▶ Administration ▶ Software Sources**, and click the **Updates** tab. Make sure that **Proposed updates** and **Unsupported updates** are checked (as in Figure 20-7), and click **Close**. You'll be greeted by a message saying that the information about available software is outdated, so hit **Reload**, and the new information will be downloaded. Once that's finished, select **System ▸ Administration ▸ Update Manager** to see which packages can be updated.

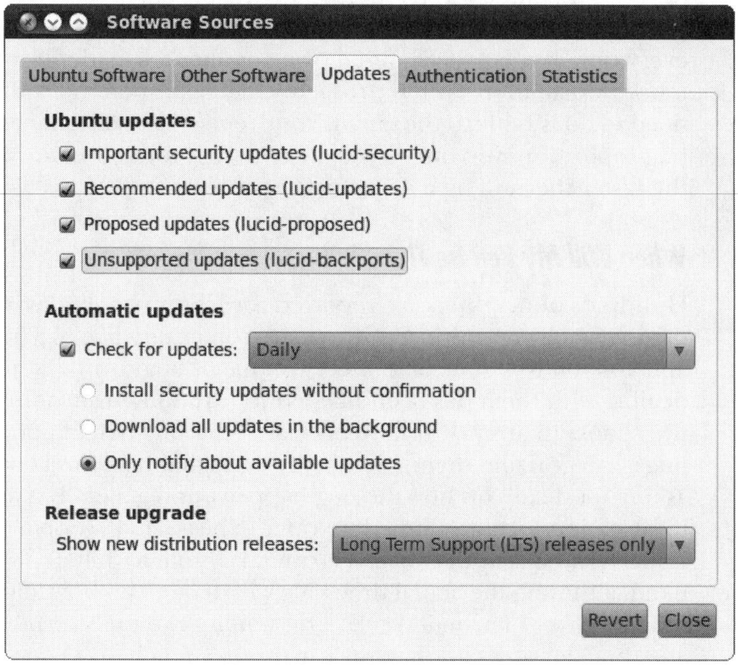

Figure 20-7: Using the Software Sources tool to enable proposed and unsupported updates

WARNING   *You really do need to be careful when using untested updates. One package that commonly causes problems is the Linux kernel itself—scroll down the list of packages in Update Manager, and look for the "Proposed updates" section, if there is one. If you find a package that has a name like* linux *or* linux-generic *in there, consider unchecking the box next to it to prevent it from being updated for the time being.*

Sharing Ideas on How to Improve Ubuntu

Have you ever sat in front of your computer and thought, "This would work better if . . ." but dismissed the idea because you had no one to tell? Bring forth your best brainwaves: Ubuntu has a place for visionaries like you. It's called Brainstorm, and it's where you can share your ideas about how you'd like to see things change in the next release of Ubuntu. Head over to *http://brainstorm.ubuntu.com/* to see what I'm talking about. The theory is that you write a description of your awesome idea, and other people vote on how important they think it is or whether they think some other plan would work better.

You have to log in to the site to be able to participate. Unfortunately, you can't sign in using your Launchpad username but must create a new account by clicking **Log in** at the top of the page and then filling in the Create new account tab.

There are thousands of submissions already on the site, and you can see a list of the most popular ones right there on the Brainstorm front page. If you find something compelling, just click the green arrow next to it to vote for it (or click the red arrow to register your disapproval). Of course, you can put your own ideas up there too: From the front page, click **Submit your idea**, and follow the instructions onscreen.

What happens to all of these ideas? A really good, popular idea might find its way to an Ubuntu developer who wants to turn it into reality, but there are no guarantees this will happen. Click the **Implemented ideas** link at the top of the Brainstorm page to see which submissions got picked up recently—chances are there won't be many. It's not the end of the world if an idea doesn't get adopted *officially*, though. The Ubuntu community is bursting with people who're willing to have a go at writing software, so somebody might see your idea and put it into practice.

THE HACKER CULTURE—A BRIEF ASIDE

If Linus Torvalds hadn't shared his hobby project with the world, we wouldn't be here talking about Ubuntu, or any form of Linux (see Chapter 1 if you have no idea what I'm talking about). The open source movement is founded on the hard work and ingenuity of people like Linus, who are affectionately known by the community as *hackers*. By this I vehemently *don't* mean the people who break into computers, write horrible computer viruses, or otherwise spoil the party for everyone. There's an alternative usage of the term *hacker* that goes much further back in computing history: Put simply, it means someone who writes computer programs as a pastime. The guys who founded Microsoft and Apple were hackers—enthusiasts playing around with early desktop computers in their respective garages.

The hacker culture extends beyond computers to all sorts of activities. It's about experimenting, coming up with cool ideas, and then sharing them amongst similar-minded people, and it's this philosophy that has made the open source movement possible.

The Ubuntu Forums

An online *forum* is a place where you can post messages about some topic that other forum users can read and respond to publicly. There are thousands of forums on the Web, bringing people from all over the world together to talk about all sorts of stuff. The Ubuntu forums are a great place to ask questions, get help, and converse with other people using Ubuntu. There are around 50,000 active users, and more than a million posts have been made to date. If you do have a question, there's a good chance that it's already been answered somewhere or that someone will be able answer it for you.

Dust off your explorer's hat, and let's go take a look around the forums. Head over to *http://www.ubuntuforums.org/*, and the first thing you'll notice is that there are lots of different categories on the front page. Choosing the right category is pretty straightforward—people seeking help with computer problems will post their questions in one of the Main Support categories, for example. For now, let's check out the part of the forum set aside for new

Ubuntu users. Click the **Absolute Beginner Talk** link, and scroll down to the bit that says *Sticky Threads* (Figure 20-8).

A *thread* is a collection of messages about the same topic. You can post replies to existing threads or start new threads yourself. A *sticky* thread is one that the forum moderators (the head honchos who make sure everything runs smoothly) deem important enough that they should stick around permanently, for everyone to read. Normal threads don't stick around and slowly make their way down the list as new threads are started and added to the top. To read a thread, just click its name.

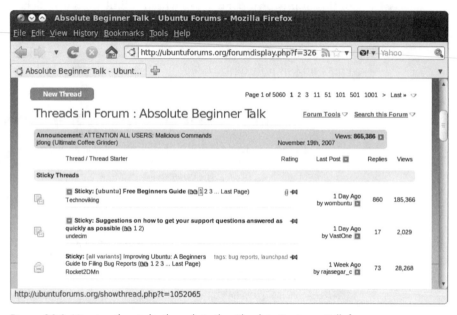

Figure 20-8: Viewing the sticky threads in the Absolute Beginner Talk forum

There are so many threads on the forums that sifting through them manually would take a lifetime. Luckily, there's a pretty good search feature. Just click the **Search** button at the top of the page, type some search terms in the box that appears, and click **Go** to see what turns up.

Replying to a Post

You can read any of the threads on the forums without a user account, but you do need to be logged in to reply to one of them. Click the **Register** link at the top of the page to create an account. You'll need to click through a couple of pages, entering your details as you go, but it should be quite straightforward. Click **Complete Registration** when you're finished, and go check your email. Once the confirmation email arrives, click the first link that it contains to finish setting up your account, and log in using the form at the top right of the page.

Now that you're logged in, find the thread you want to reply to, and click the **New Reply** button at the top (or bottom) of the page. Type your message, click **Submit Reply**, and your post will be added to the end of the thread. If you realize that you made a mistake in your reply, you can go back to the thread and click the small **EDIT** button in the bottom-right corner of your post.

Creating Your Own Thread

If you search through the forums but can't find anything relevant to your problem, why not create a new thread? The first step is to find the category that best fits the topic you want to discuss. Head back to the forum front page, and browse through the list until you find something that looks suitable. If you have a burning question about your wireless connection, for example, you'd click the **Networking & Wireless** category under the "Main Support Categories" heading.

Once you've found a category, click its name to view all of the threads it contains. Click the **New Thread** button at the top of the page to start writing. Make sure that you choose a descriptive title for your new thread, and include plenty of details if you're asking a question about a problem you're having. To finish off, click **Submit New Thread**, and wait for the replies to roll in!

What's All This Bean Business?

You might have noticed a lot of talk about coffee and beans on your travels through the forums. Don't worry, you haven't wandered into a caffeine addiction support group—beans are just a way of keeping track of how many posts a person has made. (It's supposedly an inside joke, referring to geeks' love of coffee, but personally I can't stand the stuff!) You're given a bean for every reply or thread you make, and as you collect more beans, you'll find that the description that appears under your name will change. As of this writing, I'm informed that my beans are green, with the chances of my ever becoming an "Ultimate Coffee Grinder" looking slimmer by the day.

Chatting on IRC

Internet Relay Chat (IRC) is the where Ubuntu users can go to talk to one another online. Chats happen in real time and are very similar to using an instant messaging service. They're particularly good if you can't wait for a reply on the forums and want to talk to someone ASAP about a question you have.

IRC can be daunting at first, so let's walk through a typical session. First, you'll need to make sure you have the right chat software. Open the Ubuntu Software Center, search for *XChat IRC* (not to be mistaken for XChat-GNOME), and install it. Once you've done that, limber up your clicking finger, and follow these steps:

1. Select **Applications ▸ Internet ▸ XChat IRC** to start XChat. A Network List window like the one in Figure 20-9 will appear.

2. Make a few choices for your nickname. Your nickname is how other users will be able to identify you, so choose something that befits your uniqueness (mine is *philbull*). You should try a few alternatives in case

someone has already used your first choice—adding random numbers to the end of your first choice seems to work well. Just make sure not to use spaces in your nickname.

3. Make sure that *Ubuntu Servers* is selected in the Networks list, and then click **Connect**.

4. A load of text will flash across the screen as you are connected to the IRC server. After a few seconds, you'll be switched over into the *#ubuntu* channel.

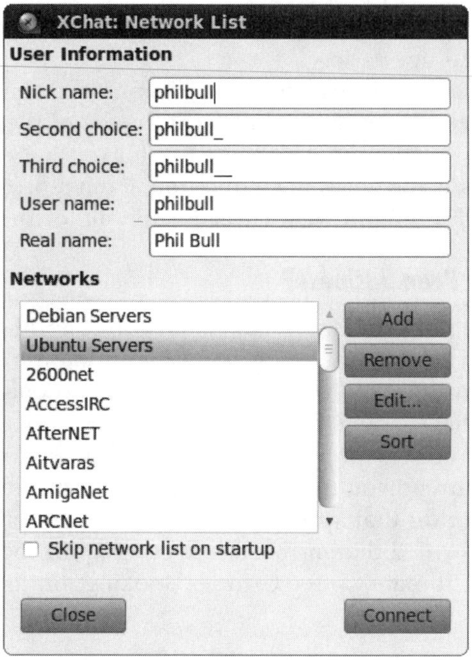

Figure 20-9: XChat's Network List window

Don't panic if things look confusing; you'll figure it all out now. Call it a crash course in IRC!

A *channel* is just a place where you can go to talk to other people. There are lots of them on IRC, each one dedicated to a different topic. In XChat there is a list of channels that you're connected to in the pane on the left side of the window, so you should be able to see that you're currently in *#ubuntu*, which is for general Ubuntu help and support. You could select **Server ▸ Join a Channel** to connect to a different one, but for now there's no need, since we're already in the right channel. In the right pane is a list of other users who are currently connected to the same channel; *#ubuntu* is very popular, so there are probably quite a few of them!

When you entered the channel, a bunch of messages will have passed by in the pane in the center of the screen. The first few are automated messages that describe what the channel is for, set some ground rules, and so forth, but by now you should see messages from other people scrolling up the screen too (Figure 20-10). The nickname of the person talking is to the left of the vertical dividing line, and their message is on the right. Everyone in the channel can see the same messages, and there are typically several conversations going on at once. You'll also see messages in different colors when someone joins or leaves the channel. People are coming and going all of the time, so you can just ignore these messages.

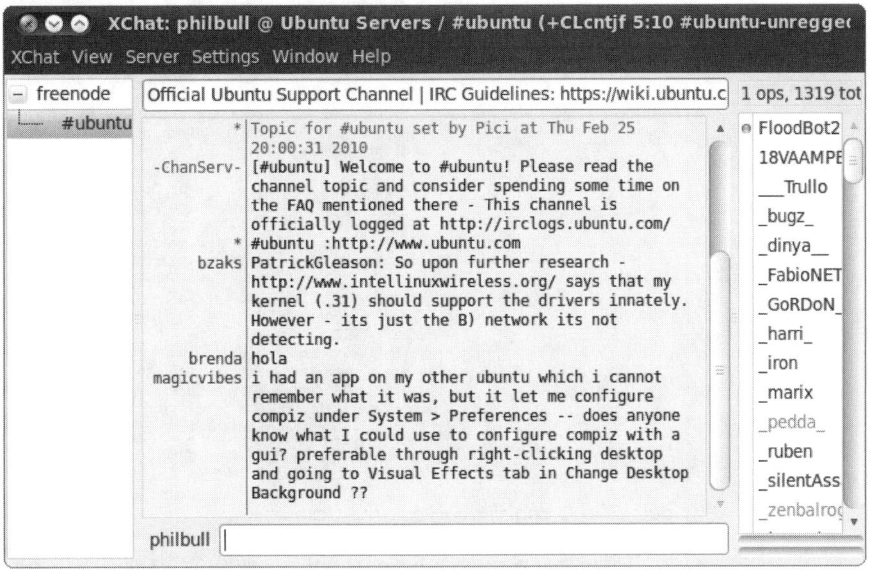

Figure 20-10: Other users chatting in the #ubuntu IRC channel

If you want to send a message, type it into the message box next to your nickname at the bottom of the screen, and press ENTER. You'll see your message appear in the center pane, and so will everyone else who's in the *#ubuntu* channel. All you have to do then is wait for a reply . . . .

Registering Your Nickname

It's a good idea to register your nickname so nobody else can steal it and so people will recognize you the next time you use IRC. In the pane on the left of the window, click the **freenode** item to switch to a welcome channel for Freenode, the IRC server used by Ubuntu (Figure 20-11). Now, type **/ns register** *password email* into the message box, replacing *email* with your email address and *password* with a good password. For example, typing **/ns register nopeeking joe@example.com** would do the trick if those were your details. Press ENTER to finish the registration.

If everything went according to plan, you'll see a message saying something like An email containing nickname activation instructions has been sent to joe@example.com. Check your email, and there should be an activation email containing instructions to type something like **/msg NickServ VERIFY REGISTER** *nickname* **jeaxzqxmgzqv** into the Freenode channel you were in earlier. Do this, and you should see a message along the lines of -NickServ- nickname has now been verified. That's it, you've registered! Click the *#ubuntu* channel in the left pane to return to where you were before.

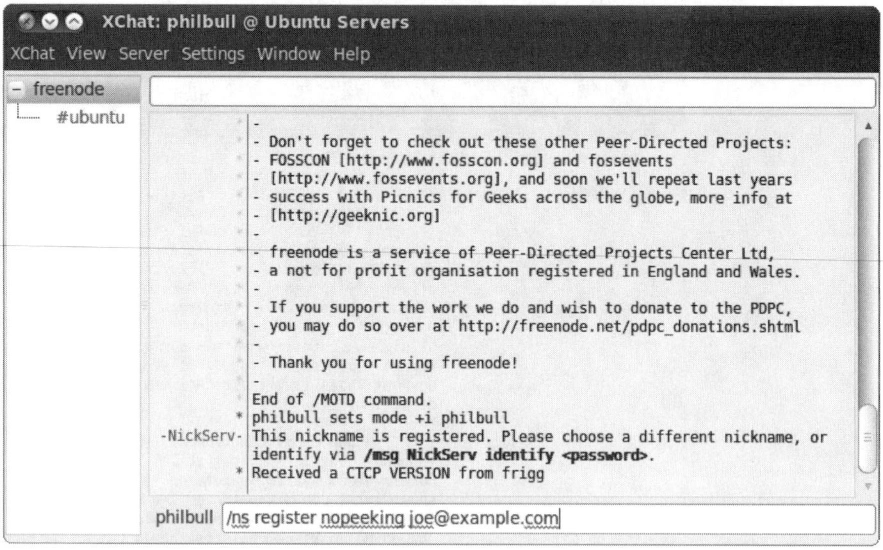

Figure 20-11: Registering your IRC nickname

If you got a message saying *nickname* is already registered instead of the one about an activation email, someone has already registered the nickname you're using. In this case, type **/nick *newname***, replacing *newname* with a new choice of nickname, and press ENTER. You'll see a message that says You are now known as *newname*. Ideally no one else has the same name this time, so try to register again.

The next time you go on IRC, you can retrieve your registered nickname by going to the *freenode* channel, typing **/nick *nickname***, and pressing ENTER. Then type **/msg NickServ identify *password***, and press ENTER again. Of course, replace *nickname* and *password* with your own nickname and password.

IRC Etiquette

There are rules and social norms to follow on IRC just like anywhere else. It goes without saying that you shouldn't go out of your way to offend or harass anyone, just as you wouldn't in the "real world." There are a few more subtle conventions that you should be aware of, though:

Don't shout. Writing in ALL CAPITALS is the IRC equivalent of shouting all the time. There's a special circle of hell for shouters; this is pretty much everyone's pet peeve, and you're bound to get censured for doing it.

Say things only once. Sometimes you won't get a reply for a while, so it can be tempting to keep repeating the same message until someone acknowledges it. Repeating yourself too many times is also considered annoying. Being patient is a necessary skill on IRC because people tend to dip in and out of chats sporadically rather than watching them all of the time. It's OK to repeat your message if you don't get a reply after 10 minutes or so, though.

Don't send loads of text. Sending more than a few lines of text at once is called *flooding*. It makes it difficult for other people to have a conversation, so you should avoid doing it. If you have lots of text that you want people to read, use a service like *http://pastebin.com/* to hold the text, and simply post a link to it on IRC.

Stay on-topic. There are different channels for different purposes, so you should try to stick to the topic for which a particular channel is intended. Advertising is considered to be off-topic in most channels and is particularly frowned upon.

Smile for the camera. Most of the conversations in the public Ubuntu chat rooms are logged and can be viewed at *http://irclogs.ubuntu.com/*. This is useful if you forgot a link that someone mentioned last week, but it can be awkward if you said something that you shouldn't. As a general rule, never post any sensitive or personal information on IRC (especially your password or credit card details), because it could come back to bite you in the posterior.

More Help with IRC

I hope this first expedition into IRC hasn't put you off for life. Lots of people find it confusing at first, but it's a really great way to talk to other Ubuntu users once you're comfortable with it. If you feel like you need to hone your IRC skills, the IRC Help website at *http://www.irchelp.org/* is a very useful resource.

An IRC Alternative: Mailing Lists

If you can't get the hang of IRC, there's another, more gentle, option available to you in the form of the support mailing lists. All you need to do is send an email to the appropriate list and hope for a reply. Visit *https://lists.ubuntu.com/* to see your options—the *ubuntu-users* list is probably the one you want.

Keeping Up with the News

If you want to find out what's going on in Ubuntu-land, there's no shortage of news outlets. Here are just a few of them (you'll also find additional resources in Appendix D):

Full Circle Magazine (*http://fullcirclemagazine.org/*): Full Circle is an independently produced Ubuntu magazine that is free to download in PDF. It contains everything you might expect to find in a traditional dead-tree magazine, such as reviews, interviews, stories from readers, and handy how-to guides.

Ubuntu Weekly Newsletter (*https://wiki.ubuntu.com/UbuntuWeeklyNewsletter/*): The UWN aims to provide an overview of the goings-on in the community each week and typically includes notable Ubuntu news stories, interviews with developers, and updates on recent changes to software. It's pitched at the geekier end of the spectrum.

The Fridge (*http://fridge.ubuntu.com/*): The Fridge is a place where people in the community can stick notes and updates on upcoming events. Interviews are sometimes posted here too.

Planet Ubuntu (*http://planet.ubuntu.com/*): This is where you can read the personal blogs of Ubuntu developers. Some of the posts are technical, but if you're interested in cutting-edge developments, this is where you need to go.

News and opinion get passed around on microblogging services too. Subscribe to the *#ubuntu* hashtag on Twitter, or join the Ubuntu group on Identi.ca (*http://identi.ca/group/ubuntu/*) to join in the tweeting, denting, or whatever you want to call it.

LoCos and LUGs

So far, the whole Ubuntu community thing might seem a bit, well, *virtual* to you. Why shouldn't it? Ubuntu is a very international venture, and communicating online is the most practical way of getting things done. Regardless, there are plenty of opportunities to contact and meet other Ubuntu users in your area through Local Community (LoCo) teams and Linux User Groups (LUGs). These groups often have a membership with diverse computing skills, so they can be a good place to go to get help with Linux, among other things.

LoCos tend to cover reasonably large geographic areas, normally on the scale of whole countries or states. As such, they tend to meet in person less regularly, although many LoCos arrange Ubuntu-related events throughout the year, including "launch parties" around the time of each Ubuntu release. You can find a list of LoCo teams at *https://wiki.ubuntu.com/LoCoTeamList/*.

LUGs are much more widespread than LoCos and tend to have a greater emphasis on meeting up. Typically, a LUG will hold regular meetings in a local community center (a pub, if you're lucky) and might organize talks or other Linux-related activities. You can find your nearest LUG at *http://www.linux.org/groups/*.

Stickers and Other Goodies

If you have a penchant for showing off your Ubuntu addiction, then you're in luck! Free stickers are available from Ubuntu-friendly computer manufacturer system76, and they're just great for replacing the unsightly Windows logo that you probably have hiding somewhere on your computer's case (see Figure 20-12). To order yours, browse to *http://www.system76.com/ article_info.php?articles_id=9*, and send a stamped, addressed envelope to the relevant address on that page. No club would be complete without a membership badge, would it?

If stickers leave you cold, other Ubuntu-branded goodies are available for purchase through the Canonical Store (*http://shop.canonical.com/*).

Figure 20-12: My laptop, complete with Ubuntu sticker (I couldn't remove the Windows one)

Getting Involved

Lots of people enjoy being part of the Ubuntu community and want to give something back by volunteering to help. Reporting bugs and using Brainstorm are great ways of making a contribution, but that's only the start of it!

If you talk to existing contributors, you'll soon see that everyone's story is different. I stumbled into contributing to Ubuntu in early 2006, when I started tidying up some bug reports that were missing information. It was something to pass the time and took up about half an hour per day. This was back when Launchpad was new and all the bugs were being transferred from the old system, so the work was pretty fun. The members of the Bug Squad were incredibly encouraging, and I soon found myself spending more and more time doing Ubuntu stuff. As time went on, I started editing help pages on the wiki (*https://help.ubuntu.com/community/*) and eventually found my way to the Documentation Team, where I coauthored a guide on switching from Windows to Ubuntu. Nowadays I'm one of the maintainers of the official help files, among other things. Being a contributor has been a great experience—I've met tons of interesting new people, indulged my interests in writing and computers, traveled to conferences around the world, and, most importantly, had tons of fun in the process.

Browse to *http://www.ubuntu.com/community/* to get some ideas on how you might be able to help. You don't need to be a geek to get involved: Artists, writers, multilinguists, marketers . . . the list of ways to participate just goes on. You can even attend a conference and have as much fun as the contributors in Figure 20-13! To get started, all you need to do is join the relevant team and introduce yourself on their mailing list. If you are interested, one thing in particular that you should look out for is Ubuntu OpenWeek, where all of the Ubuntu teams hold talks and tutorials on IRC. Check out *https://wiki.ubuntu.com/UbuntuOpenWeek/* to see when the next one will be.

Figure 20-13: Just a few of Ubuntu's many contributors at a conference (image created by Kenneth Wimer; used under Creative Commons license; original can be found at http://en.wikipedia.org/wiki/File:Uds_karmic.jpg)

21

WOUNDED WINGS

Fixing Common Problems

Like death and taxes, computer problems are an inescapable fact of life. Ubuntu suffers from its fair share of annoyances, and although I seem to spend far less time fixing things on Ubuntu than I ever used to on Windows, it's best not to ignore the possibility that you might some day experience a hardware hiccup or sticky software situation.

The purpose of this chapter is to arm you with some general-purpose tips, tricks, and troubleshooting hints. You'll find explicit instructions on how to fix several specific problems, but for the most part I've tried to keep the discussion general. This is because the way you resolve some issues will depend heavily on the peculiarities of your setup, and there just isn't a bookshelf big enough for a guide that covers every possible eventuality in suitable detail. Fortunately, the Internet harbors a sizable collection of Ubuntu-related guides, so even if you don't arrive at the exact answer you were looking for here, I hope you'll be able to use some of my tips to help you find the right information on the Web.

If you've run into a problem, flip through this chapter to see whether there's anything that might help. I've covered problems with installation, booting, sound and video, Internet and network connections, hard disks and storage, and displays and graphics cards, along with pesky software issues such as programs freezing or slowing down your computer. If you're not beset by any particular computer quandary, you might like to skim through this chapter to give you some idea of what to do if misfortune does befall you in the future. Or, you could take my preferred route: Make yourself a hot beverage and head back to the games chapter (Chapter 17) for some well-deserved R&R.

I Can't Get Ubuntu Installed

Not being able to install Ubuntu is a particularly unhappy problem because it means that you've probably been denied all the fun from the previous 20 chapters of this book! Never fear; there's plenty you can do to convince Ubuntu to install itself on your computer, and if you're still struggling, you can try alternative installation methods like booting from a USB stick, which I've covered in Appendix A.

My Computer Won't Boot from the CD

If you tried to start your computer from the Ubuntu installation CD but never even got to the purple boot screen (see "Going for a Dip" on page 12) or if the computer just boots into Windows every time, try one of the following options:

Check the boot order   When your computer starts up (*boots*), it goes through a list of devices in a set order, checking to see whether they have an operating system on them. As soon as it finds an operating system, the computer will boot from that device, and it won't check any of the other devices. This means that if the hard disk comes before the CD drive in the boot order, the computer will boot from the hard disk rather than the CD drive. To boot from the CD, you need to make sure that the CD drive comes first in the boot order. See "Going for a Dip" on page 12 for instructions on setting up the boot order correctly.

Check the integrity of the CD   You could have a faulty or damaged CD that your computer isn't able to boot from. It's possible to check whether a disc has faults on it by doing a *checksum* test. A checksum is sort of like a fingerprint; you take the checksum of your Ubuntu CD and compare it with the checksum of an Ubuntu CD that is known to be free of faults. If there is but one tiny difference between the two discs, the checksums will be different too—the fingerprints won't match. Ubuntu uses the MD5SUM program to do its checksums. Go to *https://help.ubuntu.com/community/ HowToMD5SUM/*, and scroll down to the "MD5SUM on Windows" section to see how you can find the checksum of your disc. If it turns out that the checksums don't match, you'll need to get another CD (for example, by downloading a CD image from *http://www.ubuntu.com/getubuntu/ download/* or by contacting No Starch Press to ask for a replacement).

Make sure you burned the disc correctly   If you downloaded a CD image (*.iso*) file instead of using the CD that came with this book, make sure that you burned the CD correctly. A common mistake that people make is to just copy the *.iso* file onto a CD, as if it were a normal file. This won't work; you need to use the Burn Disc Image option (or something similar) in your CD-burning software to do it properly. See *https://help.ubuntu.com/ community/BurningIsoHowto/* for instructions on how to do this.

I Can't Get the Installer to Run

If you can boot from the Ubuntu CD (so that the purple boot screen in Figure 21-1 is displayed) but when you choose to try or install Ubuntu, something goes wrong and you never get to the installer screen, the computer might be struggling to start some of the software required to run the live CD. You can try the following:

Try some kernel options   As soon as you get to the purple boot screen, press any key (my favorite is the spacebar), and choose your language from the list that appears by using the arrow keys and ENTER. Then, press F6 to open a little menu with a list of cryptic options (Figure 21-2). These are *kernel options* and can be used to turn off features that sometimes cause problems when you're trying to start the computer. Use the arrow keys to go up and down the list and the ENTER key to select an option (an x will appear next to it). In the first instance, I recommend selecting acpi=off, noapic, nodmraid, and nomodeset. Then, press ESC to hide the menu, and try to boot from the CD normally by selecting one of the options in the main list and pressing ENTER. If that didn't do anything, you might need to apply some good ol' trial and error to the kernel options to find a combination that works for you.

Try an alternate CD/memory stick   Some computers are simply unable to run the live CD. An alternative text-based installation CD is available from *http://www.ubuntu.com/getubuntu/downloadmirrors#alternate/*; you'll have to download the CD image (*.iso*) file yourself and burn it to a disc before you can use it (see *https://help.ubuntu.com/community/BurningIsoHowto/* for details). This installation method isn't as user-friendly as the graphical installation from the live CD, but it's much more likely to work if you're having problems. You could also try installing from a USB memory stick, as described in Appendix A.

Figure 21-1: The purple boot screen is displayed when you first boot from the Ubuntu CD.

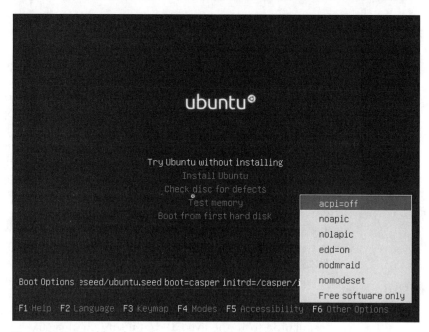

Figure 21-2: Disabling kernel options via the Ubuntu live CD boot menu

The Installer Stops Partway Through

This is probably one of the most annoying problems you can encounter. You boot from the Ubuntu CD, go through all the pages of options described in Chapter 2, and then click **Install** to start installing Ubuntu. But, after all that, the installer doesn't finish and gets stuck a few percent shy of 100.

There are lots of reasons why this might happen, most of which relate to misbehaving hardware. I've briefly described a few of the things you can try in this section, but because the underlying problem might be peculiar to the hardware in your computer, you will probably need to ask for help on the Ubuntu forums.

Wait for a while Installation takes longer on some computers than others. There are many reasons why this could happen (such as problems getting hardware to work), but if you give it an extra 20 or 30 minutes, it might finish.

Disconnect from the Internet If you are connected to the Internet, the installer might try to fetch extra settings or look for package updates while it is running. If something goes wrong when it tries to do this, it could stall, and the installation won't finish. Restart your computer and boot from the live CD again, but this time make sure you disconnect from the Internet before starting the installer.

Disconnect any unnecessary devices Some computer hardware can confuse the installer just by being plugged in. Turn off your computer, and disconnect or switch off any devices that you don't absolutely need to have attached. Printers, scanners, USB wireless cards, and external hard disks in particular should be disconnected. Then, start the computer, and attempt the installation again. Once installation is complete, you should be able to plug everything back in without any problems.

Check the integrity of the CD If the CD has a fault on it, the installer might not be able to access something that it needs from the disc. See "My Computer Won't Boot from the CD" on page 376 for advice on how to check the integrity of the CD.

Something Goes Wrong Before Ubuntu Finishes Booting

Boot problems are especially awkward—if Ubuntu won't start, how can you access the software you need to fix the problem? To get around this particular annoyance, you might need to start the computer from a live CD (like the one included with this book) or use some special options to help the process along.

This section covers the two most common classes of boot problems, GRUB errors and kernel problems. There's some general advice for other types of boot problem too, including tips for dual-booters struggling to get Windows to start.

I Get a GRUB Error

When you try to start your computer, you might be left with a black screen, which says that there was a GRUB error. This means there is a problem with the GRUB bootloader, which is responsible for telling your computer's hardware how to start Ubuntu. Fixing these errors tends to involve typing a few cryptic-looking commands or booting off a live CD, so be prepared for that. You can find a short guide to handling common GRUB errors at *https://help.ubuntu.com/community/Grub2#GRUB%20Errors/*.

I Get a Kernel Panic or the Computer Freezes

Kernel panics have a scary name for a reason. If you get an error message saying that there was a kernel panic, something pretty serious went wrong in Linux-land, and you'll probably find that you can't use the computer until you fix the problem. Fortunately, such errors are rare, and even if you do get one, you should be able to fix it without too much work. I should also note that kernel panics are only serious in that they make it difficult to run software on the computer—the physical hardware side of your computer won't be damaged at all, so once you get the software working again, everything will be back to normal. So really, there's no need to panic at all.

Freezes and kernel panics often go hand in hand, but they're not necessarily the same thing. You've probably seen a computer freeze up before—moving the mouse or pressing keys on the keyboard does nothing, and the display stays frozen. If the computer freezes, all you can do is give it a minute or two to see whether it wakes up and, if not, restart the computer or turn it off by holding down the power button for a few seconds.

You can try a few things if you keep getting kernel panics or freezes, detailed in the following sections. If nothing seems to be working, ask for advice in the Ubuntu forums, and, with a bit of luck, you'll soon be up and running again.

Unplug Unnecessary Hardware

A lot of freezes are caused by problems with hardware devices. If you recently bought some new hardware, try unplugging it and see whether you still get the freezes. If you recently installed some system updates, the driver for some hardware could be causing the problem too. It's worth unplugging any unnecessary hardware (such as scanners, printers, external hard drives, and the like) to check whether they're causing the problems.

Disable Restricted Drivers

Some freezes are caused by problems with accelerated graphics drivers (see "Games/Compiz Don't Work: Installing Accelerated Graphics Drivers" on page 394) or restricted drivers for other hardware (see "Installing Drivers for Your Network/Wireless Card," on page 390). If you suspect that this might be the case, disable the restricted drivers if you can. To do this, select **System ▸ Administration ▸ Hardware Drivers** to open the Hardware Drivers tool (Figure 21-3). Select a currently activated driver, and click **Remove**. Then, restart the computer to see whether you experience any more freezes.

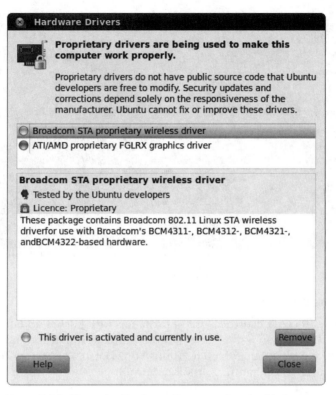

Figure 21-3: Using the Hardware Drivers tool to disable a restricted driver

Check Your System Memory for Defects

Your system memory (also known as RAM) is vital to the operation of your computer. It's where all your programs (and Linux itself) store information when they're running. If a fault develops in your system memory, freezes and crashes can start happening for seemingly no reason.

To check for problems with the system memory, boot from the Ubuntu CD included with this book (see Chapter 2 to remind yourself how to do this). As soon as the purple boot screen appears, press a key and select your language from the gray menu that pops up. Then, choose **Test memory** from the main menu, and press ENTER. The screen will turn blue, and the Memtest86 program will start running (Figure 21-4).

Memtest86 repeatedly writes things to your system memory and then accesses them a few moments later. It's sort of like a stress test for your RAM. Let it run until the Pass percentage at the top right of the screen has gone past 100 percent once or twice—this might take as long as an hour or two, depending on how much system memory you have. By that time, Memtest86 should have found any faults in the system memory and reported them on the screen. If it does find a problem, you might need to get some of your RAM replaced, because it could be damaged.

You can turn off your computer at any time while Memtest86 is running—you don't need to shut it down properly as you usually would.

```
   Memtest86+ v4.00       | Pass  2%
Intel Core 2 1489 MHz     | Test 12% ####
L1 Cache:   32K    539 MB/s | Test #3  [Moving inversions, 8 bit pattern]
L2 Cache: 3072K   1132 MB/s | Testing:  176K -   384M  384M
L3 Cache:         None    | Pattern:    40404040
Memory  :   384M    713 MB/s |-------------------------------------------
Chipset : Intel i440FX


  WallTime   Cached  RsvdMem   MemMap   Cache  ECC  Test  Pass  Errors ECC Errs
  --------   ------  -------   ------   -----  ---  ----  ----  ------ --------
   0:00:25    384M      0K     e820      on   off  Std    0       0



-----------------------------------------------------------------------------
(ESC)Reboot  (c)configuration  (SP)scroll_lock  (CR)scroll_unlock
```

Figure 21-4: Checking for memory faults with Memtest86

Use an Older Kernel

Some freezes occur because of problems with kernel updates or drivers. You can try using an older version of the Linux kernel if you have one installed. Take a look at "If an Update Ruins Your Day . . . or System" on page 84 for instructions on running an older kernel.

Use Rescue Mode

If you've asked for help online, chances are you'll be called upon to type some commands to try to fix your computer. There's no way of entering any commands if you can't get it to start up, though, so you'll need to use the rescue mode to get yourself to a command line.

Restart your computer, and, as quickly as you can, hold down the SHIFT key until a GRUB boot menu like the one in Figure 21-5 appears. If you have a dual-boot setup, you'll be used to seeing this boot menu anyway. Then, use the keyboard to select the topmost item with (*recovery mode*) in its name, and press ENTER. Text will flash across the screen for a while, and you'll be left at the Recovery Menu screen.

Use the arrow keys to highlight the netroot option, and press ENTER. After some more text passes by, you'll be dropped to a root command line, which says something like root@rg-laptop:~# and has a blinking cursor. From here, you can type commands that could help you fix the computer.

In particular, you might like to try updating your system to see whether a subsequent update fixes your problem. (This will work only if you're connected to the Internet.) Type apt-get update; then press ENTER, and wait for the list of packages to be updated. Then, type apt-get dist-upgrade to see whether any more updates are available for you to install.

NOTE   *Wireless Internet connections are unlikely to work in recovery mode. Plug your computer in with an Ethernet cable if you can.*

Figure 21-5: The GRUB boot menu

Reinstall Ubuntu

It pains me to say it, but if you just can't fix the problem no matter what you try, it might be worth reinstalling Ubuntu. To do this, follow the instructions in Chapter 2. You might need some of the advice on manual partitioning from Appendix C too.

Before you reinstall, remember to back up any files that you want to keep. You can do this by copying them to an external hard disk or USB memory stick while you're running the live CD—all you need to do to access the files is mount your hard disk as described in "Project 18A: Accessing Files on Your Windows Partition (for Dual-Booters)" on page 324 (but mount your Ubuntu partition rather than your Windows one).

Windows Won't Boot

If you installed Ubuntu in a dual-boot setup, you may find that the computer restarts or displays an error message when you try to boot Windows instead of Ubuntu. Dual-boot Windows setups sometimes have a problem with hibernation and disk checking, so try the following steps to see whether you can get it working again:

1. Boot into Ubuntu, and mount your Windows partition (see Chapter 18 for details on how to do this).

2. Find *hiberfil.sys* (it should be in the top-level folder of your Windows partition, as shown in Figure 21-6), and rename it something like *old_hiberfil.sys*. This will cause Windows to ignore all of the hibernation information it has stored.

3. Restart your computer, and boot into Windows by selecting it from the GRUB boot menu. Ideally, Windows will now boot.

4. If Windows does not boot and you get a blank screen or it restarts, reboot the computer into Windows again, but this time press the F8 key a few times immediately after choosing to boot Windows from the GRUB menu. A Windows boot menu should appear.

5. Select the **Safe Mode (with Networking)** option, and see whether that runs. If it does, perform a disk check in Windows. You can do this by going to (My) Computer, right-clicking your hard disk, and selecting **Properties**. You can find the Error-checking option you need on the Tools tab. Once the check is finished, restart the computer to see whether Windows will start normally.

You may need to repeat the rebooting-and-pressing-F8 procedure once or twice for it to stick—let it run a disk check whenever it ask to do so.

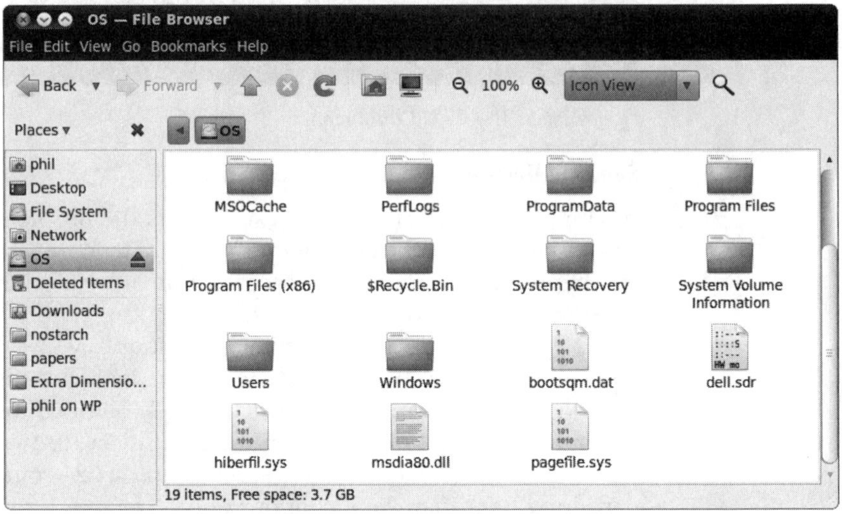

Figure 21-6: The top-level folder of a Windows partition, including the hiberfil.sys file

Sound and Video Problems

If you're met with silence when you try to watch a movie or play a song, either you've rented a Charlie Chaplin film or you're having issues with your sound card. Assuming it's the latter, you'll find that most sound-related problems in Ubuntu are caused by using incorrect sound card settings. Unfortunately, the number of these settings tends to be overwhelming, and it's rarely obvious which ones you should change to get things working. Trial and error is the order of the day when it comes to sound problems, I'm afraid, although I've tried to explain as many of the relevant options as possible in this section to help you out.

If the problem has more to do with what you're not seeing than what you're not hearing, then you're possibly in for an easier ride. Video problems tend to be easier to fix—most of the time, all you'll need to do is find the right piece of software to install and then, erm, install it. Skip to the end of the section for more on video issues.

Ubuntu Doesn't Play Any Sounds

There are many reasons why Ubuntu might not be playing any sounds. I'll concentrate on some of the more basic issues in this section, but if none of this helps, you can always try the Ubuntu forums or IRC; both are discussed in detail in Chapter 20.

To start troubleshooting, find a song on your computer and play it in Rhythmbox or the Totem Movie Player. (If you need it, there's a sample song available in the */usr/share/example-content/Ubuntu_Free_Culture_Showcase* folder, aptly called "Frustration Blues.") You need to have a sound file playing constantly in the background so that you can tell whether changing any of these settings has worked.

If you are unable to even start playing the file, Ubuntu may not have detected your sound card properly. Open a Terminal (**Applications ▸ Accessories ▸ Terminal**), type `aplay -l` into it, and press ENTER. If the list of playback hardware devices is empty, your sound card hasn't been detected. In this case, you'll definitely need to get some community support—see Chapter 20 for more information on using the Ubuntu forums and IRC.

Next, check that your speakers are turned on, turned up, and plugged into the correct socket on your computer (it's often a light green color). Many times in the past I've plugged my speakers into the microphone socket and sat there wondering why they were silent. When you're confident that your speakers are OK, try the following steps:

1. Click the speaker icon on the top panel, and select **Sound Preferences** from the menu that pops up. The Sound Preferences window will appear (Figure 21-7).

2. Make sure that the Mute option is not checked and that the Output volume slider at the top of the window is pulled all the way to the right.

3. Click the **Applications** tab, and make sure that none of the applications in the list is muted or set to a low volume.

4. Click the **Output** tab, and make sure that the right connector is chosen. If you're not sure, try choosing different connectors by trial and error until you get one that works. If none of them works, return this option to its original setting (usually Analog Speakers).

5. Click the **Hardware** tab, and choose a different device from the Profile option. Then, repeat the previous steps, checking that nothing is muted or at low volume and that the right output device is selected. Trial and error often works.

If none of this helped, check out *http://ubuntuforums.org/showthread .php?t=205449/.* It's a pretty comprehensive guide to identifying sound problems, though it requires quite a lot of work in the Terminal. (See Chapter 9 if you need to refresh your memory on how the Terminal works.)

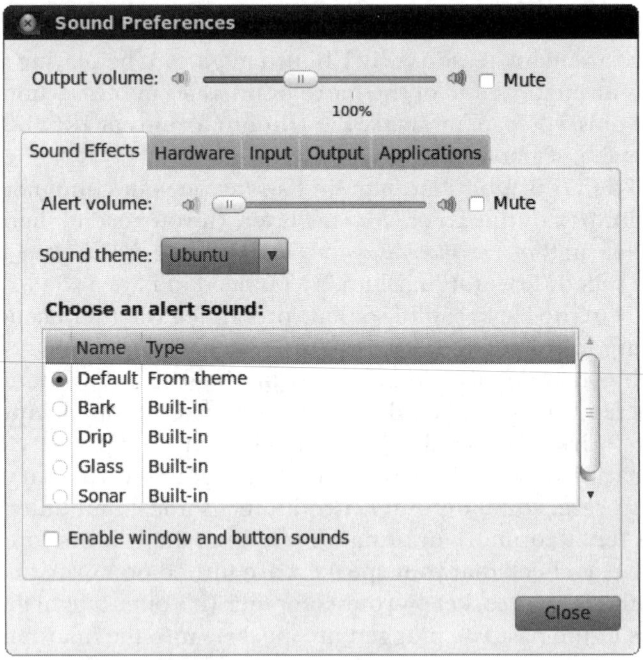

Figure 21-7: The Sound Preferences window

My Microphone Doesn't Work

As long as your sound card is detected correctly by Ubuntu, any microphone with a standard audio jack connection (similar to the connector on head-phones) should work.

To test your microphone, select **System ▸ Preferences ▸ Sound** to open the Sound Preferences window, and then go to the Input tab (Figure 21-8). There you'll see an Input level indicator, which should dance up and down when you make a sound. If nothing happens to the indicator when you make a noise, your microphone isn't being picked up, so try some of the following tips.

Plug it in   Check that the microphone is plugged into the correct socket (it should be marked by a small microphone symbol and is often pink). Also, be aware that some sound cards can switch inputs and outputs between different sockets, so what you think is the microphone socket might have actually been assigned to something else. In that case, try plugging the microphone into the other sockets.

Turn it up   Go back to the Input tab in the Sound Preferences window, and turn up the Input volume as high as it will go if necessary. If your sound card or microphone has a volume control, make sure that that is turned up too.

Check that it's not muted   Also on the Input tab, make sure that the Mute option next to the Input volume control is not checked.

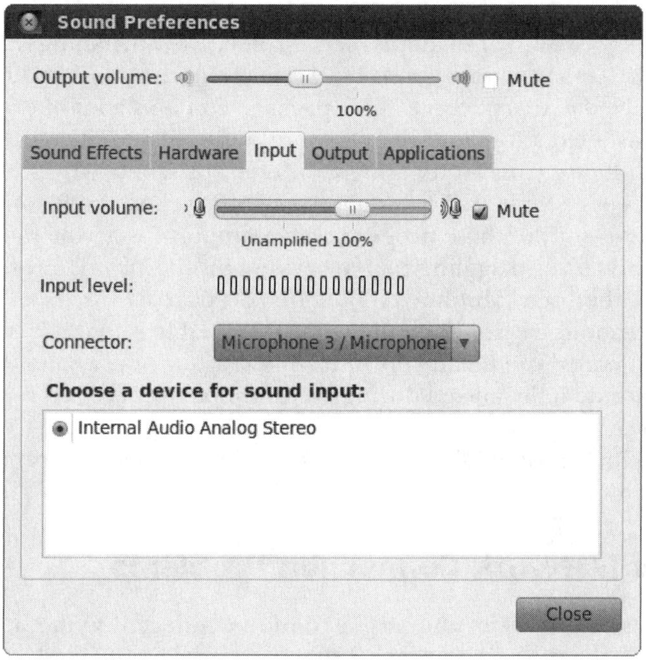

Figure 21-8: The Input tab of the Sound Preferences window

Choose the right device Ubuntu sometimes detects sound cards as being more than one device. Click the **Hardware** tab in the Sound Preferences window, and try choosing a different sound device from the list or a different profile for the device if you can. You could also try changing the device in the Choose a device for sound input list on the Input tab.

Choose the right input Some sound cards have more than one microphone input. This is often the case on laptops, which might have a microphone socket and a built-in microphone. Check whether you've enabled the correct input by changing the Connector option on the Input tab of the Sound Preferences window (Figure 21-8).

Test using a different program The lack of sound from your microphone could be a problem with the program you're using to record the sound rather than the way the microphone is set up. Try using a different program to test the microphone. The Sound Recorder (**Applications ▶ Sound & Video ▶ Sound Recorder**) is usually helpful.

NOTE   *One program that seems to suffer particularly heavily from microphone-related problems is Skype. See* https://help.ubuntu.com/community/Skype/ *for some Skype-specific sound troubleshooting tips.*

I Can't Play an Audio or Video File

The most common reason for not being able to play an audio or video file is that you don't have the necessary *codec* installed to play the file. A codec is a small piece of software that adds support for a given audio/video format into a program. Rhythmbox and the Totem Movie Player normally find the right codec for you (for example, see "Project 14A: Installing MP3 Support for Audio Apps" on page 262). However, if they fail, try installing the Ubuntu restricted extras package—this package contains a lot of extra codecs. Once it's installed, close and re-open your audio/video file and see whether it plays. If not, you can try using a different program, which might have the right codec built-in. Try installing the MPlayer Media Player or VLC media player—both of these programs have support for a wide range of formats.

If you're struggling to play a video on the Web (for example, one on YouTube), see "Multimedia Plug-Ins" on page 62.

Another reason for a file being unplayable is that it is damaged. If you downloaded the file, try downloading it again—occasionally, parts of the file are accidentally missed during the download process, so repeating the download should fix this.

Finally, you might have a problem with your sound card. See "Ubuntu Doesn't Play Any Sounds" on page 385 for advice.

Internet and Network Connection Problems

If you haven't been able to get Ubuntu connected to the Internet (or a network), the most likely cause is that your wireless/network card hasn't been detected correctly. Other people have probably had the same problem with the same network card before, so it's always a good idea to search online to see whether you can find specific instructions on setting up your card. You're not guaranteed to find something useful (or intelligible), however, so I've provided some general instructions on diagnosing connection problems and installing network and wireless card drivers in this section.

Finding the Cause of a Connection Problem

There are so many different causes of connection problems that it can be difficult to know where to start. In this section, I've provided a few tips on how you can get more information to help you figure out your connection problem. Unfortunately, some of the information is quite technical, so you might find some of the results of these tests confusing. If that is the case, just make a note of the results you get. The information might be useful to someone in the forums or elsewhere, who could help you fix the problem.

Do you have a connection to the Internet? Open Firefox, and try to visit a popular website, like *http://www.google.com/* or *http://www.bbc.co.uk/*. If neither of those pages loads and you get a "Server not found" message or similar, you may not have a link to the Internet, or you might just have a problem with Firefox. To check, open a Terminal (**Applications ▶ Accessories ▶ Terminal**), and then type ping 209.85.227.106 into it, followed by ENTER. This should ping Google's servers; *pinging* a server is a way of checking whether your computer can communicate with it. If you receive a message starting with the text 64 bytes from (as shown in Figure 21-9), you have a working Internet connection. Press CTRL-C to stop pinging

Google. In this case, the problem might be with your DNS settings or some other software, rather than your connection or your network/wireless card. If you get any other message, you probably aren't connected to the Internet, so it could be a hardware problem.

```
● ● ●   phil@panther: ~
File  Edit  View  Terminal  Help
phil@panther:~$ ping 209.85.227.106
PING 209.85.227.106 (209.85.227.106) 56(84) bytes of data.
64 bytes from 209.85.227.106: icmp_seq=1 ttl=241 time=135 ms
64 bytes from 209.85.227.106: icmp_seq=2 ttl=241 time=137 ms
64 bytes from 209.85.227.106: icmp_seq=3 ttl=241 time=140 ms
64 bytes from 209.85.227.106: icmp_seq=4 ttl=241 time=135 ms
^C
--- 209.85.227.106 ping statistics ---
4 packets transmitted, 4 received, 0% packet loss, time 3000ms
rtt min/avg/max/mdev = 135.118/137.032/140.027/2.084 ms
phil@panther:~$ []
```

Figure 21-9: The results of pinging one of Google's servers if you have a working Internet connection

Is your card recognized?   Open a Terminal, and type `lshw -c network -short`, and press ENTER. A list of the network and wireless cards that were recognized on your computer will be displayed, similar to the one shown in Figure 21-10; check whether any of them have a description matching the make or model of your card. If they do, the card has been recognized but may not necessarily have the right drivers.

```
● ● ●   phil@panther: ~
File  Edit  View  Terminal  Help
phil@panther:~$ lshw -c network -short
WARNING: you should run this program as super-user.
H/W path          Device   Class      Description
=================================================================
/0/100/1c.1/0     eth1     network    BCM4312 802.11b/g
/0/100/1c.2/0     eth0     network    88E8040 PCI-E Fast Ethernet Controller
phil@panther:~$ []
```

Figure 21-10: The list of recognized network and wireless cards on my computer

Is your card turned on?   If you have a wireless card, it may have been turned off. See the instructions in "No Wireless Networks Are Found" on page 392 for advice on how to check whether this is the case.

Are you using the right drivers?   Ubuntu sometimes uses the wrong driver for a network/wireless card. To check which driver is being used for your card, open a Terminal, and type `lshw -c network` followed by ENTER. Scroll down through all of the text, and find the card that has a product or vendor matching those of your card. Then, scroll down a few more lines until you get to the configuration line. This will tell you which driver is being used and the version number of the driver. You can compare this with the information for your card at *https://wiki.ubuntu.com/ HardwareSupportComponentsWiredNetworkCards/* (for wired network cards) or *https://help.ubuntu.com/community/WifiDocs/WirelessCardsSupported/* (for wireless cards).

Have you checked your settings? Select **System ▸ Preferences ▸ Network Connections**, and find the entry for your connection on the appropriate tab. Then, select the connection, and click **Edit**. Check through the settings in the Editing window to see whether any of them are wrong—the usual suspects are your default gateway and DNS servers (if you have a manually configured wired network) and the wireless security key (if you have a wireless connection).

For those of you struggling with a wireless connection, you can find a wireless troubleshooting guide at *https://help.ubuntu.com/community/WifiDocs/ WirelessTroubleShootingGuide/*. It's quite technical in places, though, so you might prefer to ask for help on the Ubuntu forums.

Installing Drivers for Your Network/Wireless Card

If your network card or wireless card hasn't been recognized or isn't working as expected, you might need to install some different drivers for it. You can try a few methods, and the one that works will very much depend on the make and model of your card. I've included two of the most general ones in the following sections, but some cards need you to follow very specific instructions to get them working. The lists at *https://wiki.ubuntu.com/ HardwareSupportComponentsWiredNetworkCards/* (wired cards) and *https:// help.ubuntu.com/community/WifiDocs/WirelessCardsSupported/* (wireless cards) should be able to help you figure out which method to use.

Check for Restricted Drivers

Some network/wireless cards have *restricted drivers* that you can download to get your card working. These drivers are normally provided by the manufacturer of the card and are "restricted" in the sense that they can't be fixed by Ubuntu developers if something goes wrong with them (in other words, they're not open source).

You need to be connected to the Internet to download restricted drivers. If you don't have a working connection (probably because you're currently in the process of trying to get your card working!), try using an Ethernet cable to plug the computer directly into your wireless router or cable modem (see Chapter 4 for more information). This will work only if you have a functioning wired network card. If your wired network card doesn't work, you won't be able to follow these instructions.

1. Select **System ▸ Administration ▸ Hardware Drivers**. Ubuntu will search for restricted drivers. If it finds any, they will be displayed in the list at the top of the window (as in Figure 21-3).

2. Check to see whether any of the restricted drivers have anything to do with networks or wireless (it should say in their descriptions). If you find one that does, select it, and click **Activate** to download and install it. Some cards require two drivers, so if you find two drivers that look relevant, install them both.

3. Once the installation has finished, you'll probably be told to restart the computer. It's a good idea to do this anyway, so restart.

4. Ideally, after restarting and logging in again, you'll now be able to use your network/wireless connection. See Chapter 4 for details on how to get connected.

Install Windows Drivers

Believe it or not, you can sometimes get the Windows drivers for your network/wireless card working in Ubuntu. To do this, you'll need the Windows driver for your card, plus a program called *ndiswrapper* that converts the driver into something more Ubuntu-friendly. Full instructions are available at *https://help.ubuntu.com/community/WifiDocs/Driver/Ndiswrapper/*, but here's an outline to help you get started:

1. Find the Windows drivers for your card. These normally come supplied on a CD with your computer, or you may be able to download them from the card manufacturer's website. A list of drivers is available at *http://sourceforge.net/apps/mediawiki/ndiswrapper/*.

2. Find the *.inf* file for the Windows XP version of your card's drivers. The drivers are normally provided as Zip files, which you can open and search inside for the INF file, or in folders on the driver CD. If you can't find the file, you might be able to get more information on the ndiswrapper website mentioned in the previous step.

3. Save the *.inf* file on your desktop or in some other convenient location.

4. Borrow a computer with Internet access, and download the *.deb* files from the following links (you'll need to click the link for a nearby location before the file can be downloaded):

   http://packages.ubuntu.com/lucid/all/ndiswrapper-common/download
   http://packages.ubuntu.com/lucid/i386/ndiswrapper-utils-1.9/download
   http://packages.ubuntu.com/lucid/i386/ndisgtk/download

5. Save the three *.deb* files to a memory stick or some other storage device, and use it to copy them onto your Ubuntu computer. Again, copying them onto the desktop would be convenient.

6. Now, double-click the *ndiswrapper-common* file, and install it (see "Project 6B: Installing Software from a PPA: OpenSonic" on page 88 to learn how to do this).

7. Once that's installed, install the *ndiswrapper-utils* file. The order that you install these files in is important.

8. Finally, install the *ndisgtk* file.

9. Now, select **System ▸ Administration ▸ Windows Wireless Drivers**, and enter your password if prompted. The Wireless Network Drivers window will open (Figure 21-11).

10. Click **Install New Driver**, and then click the **Location** button. Select the *.inf* file you found earlier, and click **Open**.

11. Click **Install**. If everything goes to plan, the Windows driver for your card will be installed.

12. Restart your computer, and try to get connected once you've logged in again (Chapter 4).

Don't worry if something goes wrong—there are several minor problems that might trip you up during this process. Visit the ndiswrapper website mentioned in Step 1, or ask on the Ubuntu forums for more specific advice.

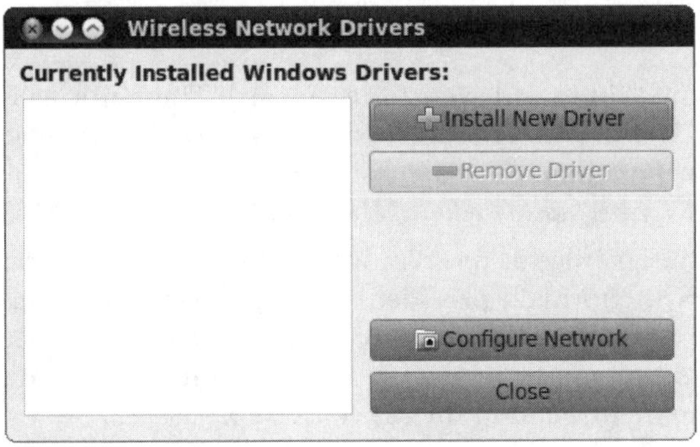

Figure 21-11: The Wireless Network Drivers window

No Wireless Networks Are Found

If you know that your wireless card is working in Ubuntu but you can't seem to find any networks, try the steps in this section:

1. Check to make sure that your wireless card is turned on. Many laptops have a keyboard shortcut that toggles the wireless card on and off (on mine it's FN-F2). Some cards have a physical switch that you need to flip instead. If your card has an antenna with a cable, make sure that it's firmly secured to the card too.

2. Now, right-click the Network Manager icon on the top panel, and make sure that **Enable Networking** and **Enable Wireless** are checked (Figure 21-12). If they aren't, check them, and wait a minute or two while the wireless card wakes up.

3. If the Enable Wireless option was already checked, try unchecking it, waiting for a minute or so, and then checking it again. Your wireless card might have needed turning off and on again to wake it up. You can also try doing this with the hardware switch/keyboard toggle I mentioned in Step 1.

4. If none of this has any effect, try restarting your computer. Some wireless cards work fine until you hibernate or suspend the computer, after which they fall into a deep sleep. Restarting should be enough to wake it up.

5. You should also check that the network you want to connect to doesn't have a hidden network name (also called an *SSID*). If it does, it won't appear in Network Manager's list, and you'll have to manually enter its name to be able to connect. To do this, click the Network Manager icon, choose **Connect to Hidden Wireless Network** from the menu, and fill out the details in the window that appears.

6. Finally, if you're still struggling, are you sure that you are sufficiently close to a wireless base station? If the signal is too weak, your card might not pick up the network at all.

Figure 21-12: Making sure that wireless and network connections are enabled in Network Manager

Other Users on My Computer Can't Connect

If you have more than one user account on your computer, you might find that you can connect to the Internet, but other users can't. To fix this problem, you need to make your network connection available to all users:

1. While working in your user account, select **System ▸ Preferences ▸ Network Connections**.

2. Find the network connection that you use on one of the tabs. For example, if you use a wireless network called "Marconi," you would click the **Wireless** tab and look for *Marconi* in the list there.

3. Select the network, and click **Edit**.

4. Check the **Available to all users** option at the bottom of the screen, and click **Apply**.

5. Type your password when prompted. The network will disconnect, and you may need to reconnect it by using the Network Manager icon on the top panel (see Chapter 4 for further details on connecting).

6. Log in to a different user account. You should now be able to connect to the network in that user account too.

Problems with the Display and Graphics Cards

Recently, Ubuntu has been doing an excellent job of detecting graphics cards, so it's unlikely that you'll ever be left staring at a blank screen. Things aren't guaranteed to turn out perfect, however. This section covers such problems as getting 3D acceleration support (if it's missing) and adjusting your screen resolution (if it's looking weird). Just in case, there's something to help you with a dreaded blank screen too.

Games/Compiz Don't Work: Installing Accelerated Graphics Drivers

If you can't get Compiz or a certain game to work, you might need to install some accelerated graphics drivers. This is because only basic drivers (which can't handle fancy effects and 3D games) are installed for some graphics cards by default, due to the lack of availability of suitable open source alternatives. If accelerated drivers exist for your card, you can install the more powerful (but possibly less open source) drivers by selecting **System ▸ Administration ▸ Hardware Drivers**, selecting the graphics driver from the list, and then clicking **Activate** to install it. Once it's installed, restart the computer, and the new driver should be enabled.

You can directly download Linux graphics drivers from some manufacturers. These tend to be updated more regularly than the ones that come with Ubuntu, and they may have some extra features too. The next couple of sections cover how to get these drivers for the two biggest manufacturers, ATI and nVidia.

ATI Cards

1. Go to *http://support.amd.com/us/gpudownload/Pages/index.aspx/*, and select *Linux x86* from the list on the left side of the page.

2. Choose the type of card you have from the next list, and choose the model/series of your card from the list next to that.

3. Click **GO!**, and you'll be taken to a download page for the driver. Scroll down to the bottom of the page, and click **Download**.

4. When prompted, click **Save File** to download the driver.

5. When the download finishes, find the driver file. It will probably be saved in your *Downloads* folder, and its name should end with *.run*.

6. Open a Terminal (**Applications ▸ Accessories ▸ Terminal**), and type `cd Downloads` (followed by ENTER) to change to your Downloads folder (if it's stored in there).

7. Now, type `chmod +x ati-driver*.run`, and press ENTER to make it so that you can run the file as a program.

8. To start the installer, type `sudo ./ati-driver`, and then press the TAB key. This should complete the name of the installer file for you, so you can press ENTER and run the installer.

9. Enter your password. Then, follow the instructions on the screen to install the driver.

nVidia Cards

1. Go to *http://www.nvidia.com/object/unix.html*, and click the link for the latest version under the "Linux IA32" heading (or the "Linux IA64" heading if you're running the 64-bit version of Ubuntu).

2. Click **Download** and then **Agree & Download**. When prompted, click **Save File** to download the driver.

3. Find the driver file; it will probably be in your *Downloads* folder, with a name ending with *.run*.

4. Open a Terminal (**Applications ▸ Accessories ▸ Terminal**), type `cd Down-loads`, and then press ENTER to change to your *Downloads* folder (if it's stored in there).

5. Now, type `chmod +x NVIDIA-Linux*.run`, and press ENTER to make it so that you can run the file as a program.

6. To start the installer, type `sudo ./NVIDIA-Linux`, and then press the TAB key. This should complete the name of the installer file for you, so you can press ENTER and run the installer.

7. Enter your password, and then follow the instructions on the screen to install the driver.

NOTE   *Because they're not open source, the quality of some of the graphics drivers can vary, and problems can't be fixed by the Ubuntu developers (as they can be with open source ones). As such, some accelerated graphics drivers can cause problems, most often when you try to hibernate or suspend your computer. If you do run into problems, consider uninstalling the driver so that you revert to the default open source one.*

The Screen Looks Stretched or the Wrong Size

If your screen doesn't look quite right, the screen resolution has probably been detected incorrectly. To fix this problem, select **System ▸ Preferences ▸ Monitors**, and change the Resolution setting to match the default resolution of your screen (trial and error will suffice if you don't know what the default is).

Click **Apply**; if everything looks OK, click **Keep This Configuration**. If your screen goes blank, don't worry—just wait for 30 seconds, and the resolution will be returned to its original setting.

If the correct resolution for your monitor isn't available from the list, you might have to use a different display driver. See "Games/Compiz Don't Work: Installing Accelerated Graphics Drivers" on page 394.

The Screen Is Blank

One possible cause of a blank screen is that something went wrong with your graphics card or its drivers. Thankfully, this is a reasonably rare occurrence, and it's much more likely that something minor (and easy to fix) happened. Peruse the following tips before you start worrying about some sort of graphics card apocalypse scenario:

Check that the display cable is connected   Most desktop computers have a separate monitor that plugs into the back of the computer. Look at the back of the monitor, and make sure both of the cables coming out of the back of it are firmly plugged in at both ends. You might also want to check that the display is switched on and that its power cable hasn't fused.

Try to wake up the computer   Your computer may have gone into a power-saving (sleep) mode, which you can wake it up from by moving your mouse or pressing keys on the keyboard. If that doesn't work, try pressing the power button on your computer once. This sometimes wakes computers up from their sleep too.

Switch to a command line   The part of the Ubuntu that's responsible for displaying things on the screen is called *X11*, or just *X*. Sometimes X fails to start. To see whether this is the case, press CTRL-ALT-F2. You should see a login: prompt if everything but X is working properly. You can type your username and password (pressing ENTER after typing each one) to access a command line, just like the Terminal you met in Chapter 9. While you're using the command line, try typing **sudo startx**, followed by ENTER, and type your password again if prompted. This will try to start X; it might work, or it might give you an error message telling you what the problem is. Alternatively, type **sudo reboot** to restart your computer. (If you're wondering what happened here, pressing CTRL-ALT-F2 switched you to a different *virtual terminal*. Ubuntu starts a few virtual terminals and uses them for different things; pressing CTRL-ALT-F7 will switch you back to the virtual terminal used by X to display everything.)

Restart the computer   Some computers occasionally start up without turning on the graphics card or the monitor. (This tends to be more of a problem on older computers.) As a last resort, try turning the computer off and then on again by pressing the power button. If the computer won't turn off, hold down the power button for a few seconds until it does.

Hard Disks and Storage Problems

I never really understood how you could completely fill up your hard disk until I bought a digital video camera. If you have a similarly expensive disk usage habit, this section is for you. There are a few tips on how to free up some disk space and, worst-case scenario, how to deal with a *completely* full disk.

My Disk Is Almost Full

If your hard disk is almost full, Ubuntu will pop up a warning message similar to the one in Figure 21-13. Click the **Examine** button to start the Disk Usage Analyzer—it will scan your disk and display a colored chart showing you what is using most of the disk space. You can use this information to hunt down the files and folders that are taking up most of your disk's capacity. If you're wondering exactly how much disk space you have left, select **System ▸ Administration ▸ System Monitor**, and look on the File Systems tab to see how much space is left on each disk.

Figure 21-13: A message warning you that your disk is almost full

Apart from rooting through your home folder and deleting unwanted files, you can try a few other things to free up some disk space:

Empty your Trash   When you delete files, they get moved to the *Trash* folder in case you change your mind about having removed them. To empty the *Trash* folder (thus permanently removing all the files in it), click the **Trash** icon on the bottom panel, and click the **Empty Trash** button in the Nautilus window that appears.

Clean up unwanted packages   When you remove a package using the Ubuntu Software Center, it sometimes leaves other packages that were installed at the same time on the system, even though they're not needed anymore. To remove them, open a Terminal, type `sudo apt-get autoremove`, and then press ENTER. Type your password when prompted, followed by ENTER, and see whether there are any leftover packages that can be removed. If there are, press Y and then press ENTER to remove them.

Empty the package cache When the Ubuntu Software Center installs a program, it keeps the package used to install it for a little while in case it's needed again. These cached files can take up quite a bit of disk space, but it's fine to delete them (the program won't be uninstalled or anything like that). Open a Terminal, and type **sudo apt-get clean**, followed by ENTER. Type your password if prompted, and then press ENTER to empty the cache.

My Disk Is Completely Full

If your hard disk is completely full, you may not be able to start Ubuntu at all, and all you'll get is a blank screen. If this happens, press CTRL-ALT-F2 to change to a Terminal login prompt. Type your username, followed by ENTER, followed by your password, followed by ENTER again, to access a command line. Once there, try clearing some disk space by typing some of the commands recommended in "My Disk Is Almost Full" on page 397. You can also use the rm command to remove some files in your home folder, but be careful: There's no undo when using rm.

Once you've cleared a little disk space, type **sudo reboot** to restart the computer. With any luck, there will be enough disk space for you to be able to log in now.

I Can't Delete a File

The usual reason for not being able to delete a file is because you don't have the right permissions to delete it (see Chapter 7 for an explanation of file permissions). Right-click a blank area of the folder that the file is stored in, choose **Properties**, and select the **Permissions** tab. If you are listed as the owner, make sure that your Folder Access permissions are set to Create and delete files. Click **Close**, and then try to delete the file again.

If you are not the owner of the folder, you'll have to gain ownership of it before you can delete the file. This is where you need to ask yourself, "Should I really be deleting someone else's file?" Sometimes file permissions get messed up and so the file might be yours—in that case, it's OK to delete it. If it's someone else's file, though, ask for their permission first. If you're convinced that deleting the file is a good idea, open a Terminal, and use the **chown** command to change the owner of the folder. Here's how it works: If I wanted to delete a file called *cats.jpg* from the *Pets* folder in my *Pictures* folder, I would type **sudo chown phil ~/Pictures/Pets**, followed by the ENTER key (remember, ~ means "my home folder"). After typing my password and pressing ENTER again, I would become the owner of the *Pets* folder and could delete *cats.jpg* as normal. Of course, you should substitute the name of the folder and your username in place of mine for this to work for you.

NOTE *Don't use this method to delete system files (in other words, files that aren't stored in the* /home *folder) unless you're sure you know what you're doing. You don't have permission to delete system files for a reason; you could really screw up your system if you remove something vital.*

Software Installation Problems

Ubuntu's software management tools tend to operate pretty smoothly these days. Nevertheless, I've included some troubleshooting tips for two or three problems that used to be common (but seem to be getting rarer with each release). If you're having a problem with installing, removing, or updating packages, this section is for you.

I Get an Error About Unauthenticated Packages

If you get an error message about unauthenticated packages when you try to install a program, try the following:

1. Select **System ▸ Administration ▸ Update Manager** to open the Update Manager.
2. Click the **Check** button, and enter your password if prompted. The package list will be updated, along with all the files that are used to check whether your packages are "authentic."
3. When it has finished updating the package list, close the Update Manager, and try to install your program again.

If you're still getting the error message, you may have added a software repository without adding its GPG key. The GPG key is required to do the authentication stuff that the error message is talking about. If this is the case, look at "Adding Extra Software Repositories" on page 86 for instructions on how to add the GPG key for a repository.

I Get a dpkg Error

There are a couple of common reasons why you might get an error message related to dpkg when you try to install, update, or remove a software package.

If you get an error saying E: Sub-process /usr/bin/dpkg returned an error code (1), you could have a broken package on your system. Here are some techniques you can try to fix a broken package:

1. Select **Application ▸ Accessories ▸ Terminal** to open a Terminal.
2. Type `sudo apt-get install --fix-broken`, and press ENTER. Type your password when prompted, and press ENTER again. This command looks for broken packages and tries to fix them.
3. With any luck, this will fix the problem; try installing a package via the Ubuntu Software Center to see whether you still get the dpkg error message.
4. If you do still get the error message, type `sudo dpkg --configure -a` into the Terminal, and press ENTER. This command tries to fix half-installed packages if there are any.
5. Try installing a package from the Ubuntu Software Center again. If you're still getting an error message, ask for help on the Ubuntu forums.

If you get an error message saying E: Could not get lock /var/lib/dpkg/ lock - open (11: Resource temporarily unavailable) or E: Unable to lock the administration directory (/var/lib/dpkg/), you are probably running more than one package manager (APT frontend) at the same time (see the note at the end of Chapter 6). For example, if you are installing a package using the apt-get command in a Terminal while simultaneously trying to install a program with the Ubuntu Software Center, you will get this error message.

Wait until one of the package managers finishes what it's doing, and then close it and try to use the other one again. If no other package managers are running, you won't get this error message. If you don't think you have any other package managers running, the Update Manager could be running in the background and causing the problem. Wait for a few minutes for the Update Manager to finish what it's doing and then try again.

I Have a Broken Update

If you update your computer using Update Manager but receive an error message saying that you have a broken update, try the instructions in "I Get a dpkg Error" on page 399 to try to fix the problem. If that doesn't work, try asking on the Ubuntu forums for help—there may be a bug in the package that was being updated when the error occurred.

Common Problems with Applications

So many applications are available for Ubuntu that it would be impossible to go through each one and point out what might possibly, some day, go wrong. Instead, in this section I've chosen to provide some general advice on how to deal with misbehaving programs, plus a sneaky little section on a particularly common Firefox problem. If it is something specific that you need to handle, it's never a bad idea to try looking at the help files for a given program. Selecting **Help ▸ Contents** should get you to a manual for most software. Failing that, a Google search often does the trick for me.

Firefox Says It's Already Running

When you exit Firefox, it sometimes takes a while to close itself down properly—the window will disappear, but Firefox could still be running somewhere in the murky depths of your computer. When you try to open Firefox again, you may receive a message that Firefox is running in the background, so you can't open a new window. This is no good, because you want a Firefox window that you can see! If this happens, open a Terminal (**Applications ▸ Accessories ▸ Terminal**), type killall firefox, and then press ENTER. (The command is case sensitive, so be sure you're typing in all lowercase.) This will force Firefox to shut down immediately. With that done, try to open Firefox again, and the window should pop up as normal. If it still isn't working, try repeating the previous command one or two more times.

A Program Always Crashes

If you have a program that keeps crashing, try running it in a Terminal to see what's going wrong. You'll have to get the name of the command needed to run the program first—see "Reporting a Bug" on page 359 for information on how you can find it. Once you have the command, type it into the Terminal, and press ENTER. The program should run as normal, so keep using it until it crashes. When it does, look at the Terminal to see whether it left any clues as to what's going wrong in there. Error messages in the Terminal can be quite cryptic, so you might like to ask someone on the forums or IRC (both of which are discussed in Chapter 20) if they know what it means.

If the messages in the Terminal are no help, you should report a bug. See "Bugs, Bugs, Glorious Bugs" on page 358 for details.

A Program Won't Start

If a program doesn't start when you click its shortcut in the Applications menu, try running it in the Terminal, as described in the previous section. It could be crashing soon after starting and might leave some information about the crash in the Terminal.

My Computer Is Running Slowly

Certain tasks take up lots of computing power and cause your computer to run slowly. Burning a CD, installing software, and converting music files to a different format all tend to strain your system, so you shouldn't be surprised if things feel a little sluggish when something like that is running. But what if your computer is running slowly even if you're not running anything intensive? You can investigate the cause of the slowdown by selecting **System ▸ Administration ▸ System Monitor** to open the System Monitor. Select the Resources tab, and check your CPU (processor) usage—if it's around 100 percent, then a program running in the background is probably responsible for the problem (for example, the one in Figure 21-14). Choose the Processes tab, and click the % CPU column heading a couple of times until it has an "up" arrow next to it. This will sort the list of programs in order of how much of the processor they are using. The one that's using all of the CPU should appear at the top of the list.

It's normally best to wait a few minutes and see whether the program reduces its CPU usage by itself. After all, it could be some system software running a scan or some other maintenance operation. If it doesn't go away, the program might have gotten stuck, so select it and click **End Process** to force it to close. Your system should return to its usual speed within a few seconds.

If you didn't notice high CPU usage on the Resources tab, then it's possible that something is overusing your hard disk instead. Programs that do this almost always finish what they're doing within five or ten minutes, so you should probably ride it out. If it persists, the easiest way of fixing the problem is by restarting the computer.

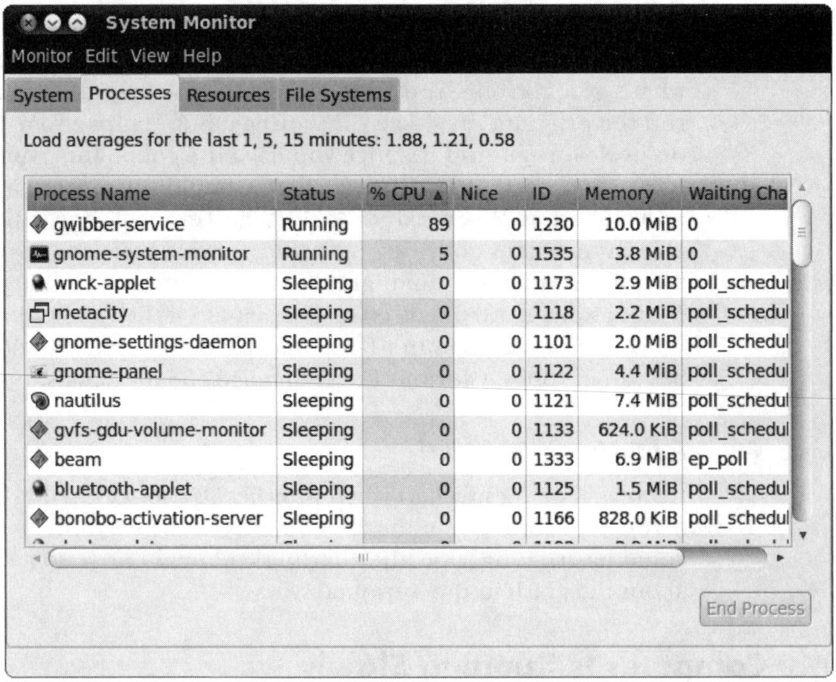

System Monitor

Monitor Edit View Help

System Processes Resources File Systems

Load averages for the last 1, 5, 15 minutes: 1.88, 1.21, 0.58

Process Name	Status	% CPU ▲	Nice	ID	Memory	Waiting Cha
gwibber-service	Running	89	0	1230	10.0 MiB	0
gnome-system-monitor	Running	5	0	1535	3.8 MiB	0
wnck-applet	Sleeping	0	0	1173	2.9 MiB	poll_schedul
metacity	Sleeping	0	0	1118	2.2 MiB	poll_schedul
gnome-settings-daemon	Sleeping	0	0	1101	2.0 MiB	poll_schedul
gnome-panel	Sleeping	0	0	1122	4.4 MiB	poll_schedul
nautilus	Sleeping	0	0	1121	7.4 MiB	poll_schedul
gvfs-gdu-volume-monitor	Sleeping	0	0	1133	624.0 KiB	poll_schedul
beam	Sleeping	0	0	1333	6.9 MiB	ep_poll
bluetooth-applet	Sleeping	0	0	1125	1.5 MiB	poll_schedul
bonobo-activation-server	Sleeping	0	0	1166	828.0 KiB	poll_schedul

End Process

Figure 21-14: The System Monitor, showing the gwibber-service program using an unhealthy 89 percent of the processor

Lost Files

Losing an important file is one of those uniquely frustrating experiences in life. If you've looked in all of the most likely locations (like your home folder), try one of the following:

Recent Documents Select **Places ▸ Recent Documents** to see whether the missing file is in the list of recently edited files. If it was an office document, try the **File ▸ Recent Documents** menu in OpenOffice.org too.

Basic search The basic Search for Files tool is useful only if you can remember part of the file's name. Select **Places ▸ Search**, type part of the file's name in the Name contains box, and click **Search**. It might turn up in the list of search results.

Heavy-duty search The more advanced Tracker search tool can look inside documents, which is handy if you don't remember the file's name but you do remember some of its contents. Install the Tracker Search Tool from the Ubuntu Software Center, and select **System ▸ Preferences ▸ Search and Indexing**. Check the **Enable indexing** option on the General tab, and click **Apply**. Click **Restart** in the warning window that appears, and wait for Tracker to build its search index (about 15 to 20 minutes should do it). When it has finished, select **Applications ▸ Accessories ▸ Tracker Search Tool**, and search for your lost file there.

Look in the Trash   It's possible that you accidentally deleted the file. Click the **Trash** icon on the bottom panel, and look for it in there.

Another explanation for the lost file might be that it was saved in a temporary folder. This happens when you open an email attachment, for example—the file is put in the temporary folder by your email client and then opened using the default application for that type of file. Unfortunately, some programs don't realize that it's a temporary file, and they let you save it in the temporary directory . . . which is periodically wiped clean. If you suspect that this may have happened and you have restarted your computer since you last saved the file, then it's probably gone forever.

If you haven't restarted, there may still be hope; try opening the (unmodified, original) file again to see which folder it gets stored in by selecting **File ▶ Save As** (or similar) in the program you're using. Then, check which folder the Save window opens up to. For example, the Evolution mail client temporarily stores attachments that you open in a randomly named folder within the */home/username/.evolution/cache/tmp* folder (see Figure 21-15 for an example). Note the name of the folder, and open your home folder. Then, select **Go ▶ Location**, type the name of the folder in the box that appears, and try to find your file in the folder that opens. It's hardly convenient, but it might just help you find your file.

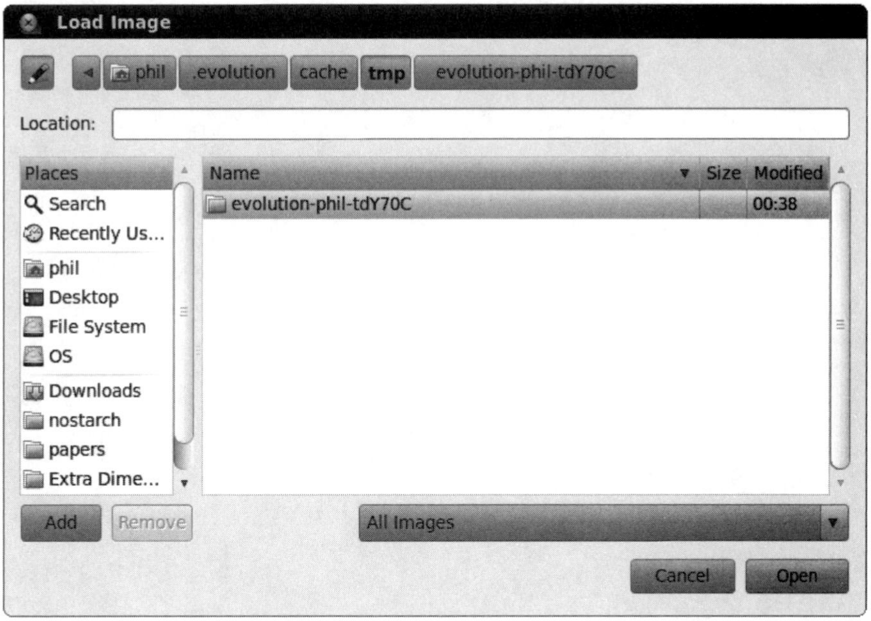

Figure 21-15: Looking for a file that was saved in a temporary folder by Evolution

Where Can I Go to Get More Help?

Many of the instructions in this chapter are quite general, so they might miss out on the specifics that you need to get your computer behaving properly. If you suspect that this is the case or if nothing in this chapter seemed to help with your problem, then it's a good idea to seek help elsewhere. Ubuntu has a large and thriving online support community that prides itself on being friendly and helpful. There are quite a few options for you to choose from:

- Visit *https://help.ubuntu.com/*, and use the search to find help guides and tutorials.
- Ask a question on the *#ubuntu* IRC channel (see "Chatting on IRC" on page 367).
- Ask a question on a mailing list (see "An IRC Alternative: Mailing Lists" on page 371).
- Post a question on the Ubuntu forums (see "The Ubuntu Forums" on page 365).

From here on out, it's up to you and the Ubuntu community to figure out what's going on. Good luck fixing your problem!

A

INSTALLING UBUNTU FROM A USB FLASH DRIVE

If you have a netbook or some other computer that doesn't come with a CD drive, don't worry: You can install Ubuntu using a USB flash drive. Booting from a USB drive can be a little more involved than simply booting from a CD or using Wubi, but once the installer is up and running, the installation process is identical. I'm going to assume that you're using Windows for the rest of this appendix, but it's possible to create a USB install disk with other operating systems too; see *https://help.ubuntu.com/ community/Installation/FromUSBStick/* for instructions.

NOTE   *Some older computers don't have the ability to boot from USB disks. If this is the case, you won't be able to use this method to install Ubuntu. Other alternative installation methods are available, such as downloading Wubi directly; see* https://help.ubuntu.com/ community/Installation/ *for a list of options.*

Preparing the Installer Files

First, you're going to need a flash drive with sufficient capacity to hold the Ubuntu installer: About 2GB should do it. Make sure that you don't have any files on the flash drive, either—you'll be formatting the drive shortly, so any files on there will be permanently deleted.

Next, you'll need to download an Ubuntu CD image. If you're feeling clever, you can use your CD-burning software to make an *.iso* image from the CD provided with the book, but otherwise head over to *http://www.ubuntu.com/ getubuntu/download/*, select your location from the drop-down list, and click **Begin Download** to download an Ubuntu CD image. The image is large at around 700MB, so it might take a while to squeeze its way down your Internet connection.

Sometimes, large downloads don't finish properly, and you could be left with an incomplete CD image. An easy (but not foolproof) way to check whether the image downloaded correctly is to open the folder where you saved it, right-click the image, and select **Properties**. Check that the size of the image file is *almost* 700MB (690MB, say).

The final thing you need is the software used to put the installer onto the USB drive. Use your web browser to download the Universal USB Installer from *http://www.pendrivelinux.com/downloads/Universal-USB-Installer/Universal-USB-Installer.exe*.

Creating a Bootable Installer Disk

With the installation files downloaded, you'll now be able to make a bootable Ubuntu flash disk. Plug your USB drive into the computer, and follow these instructions:

1. Double-click the **Universal-USB-Installer.exe** file you just downloaded to run it.

2. A License Agreement screen will appear. Click **I Agree**, and you'll be taken to the Setup Your Selections page.

3. Where it says *Step 1*, choose **Try Some Other Live Linux ISO** from the list.

4. Click the **Browse** button under Step 2, and find the Ubuntu CD *.iso* image that you downloaded earlier. Click once to select it, and then click **Open**.

5. Under Step 3, select your flash drive from the list (make sure it's the right one; otherwise, you could wipe a bunch of important files from some other disk!), and check the box next to it to say that you want to format the drive. Your screen should now look like the one in Figure A-1.

6. Click **Create**, and wait for a few minutes while the installer is put on the disk.

Once the process has finished, close the Universal USB Installer window, and safely eject your flash drive, as you normally would.

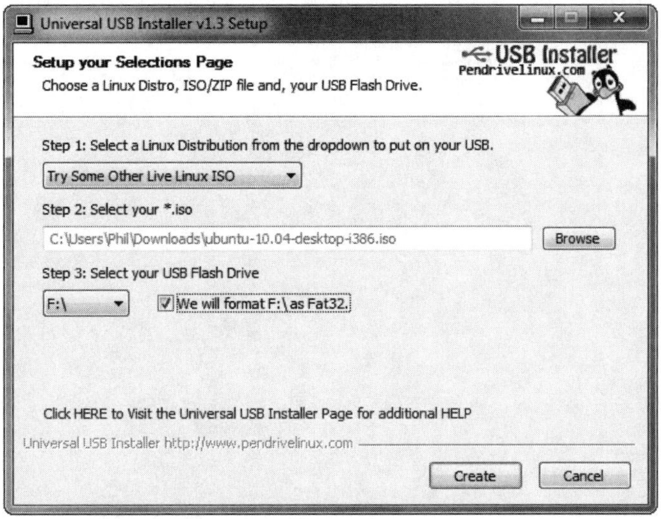

Figure A-1: Creating a bootable USB install disk

Booting from the USB Disk

Now, plug the flash drive back in, and restart the computer. This is where you find out whether you're set up to boot from USB drives—if you get a purple Ubuntu boot screen, you're all ready to go! The rest of the process will be the same as the usual installation from a CD, which you can read about in Chapter 2.

If the computer just boots back into Windows (or whatever operating system you're using), you'll need to change some settings to get it to boot from the flash drive. Restart the computer again, and look on the screen for text related to the boot order or BIOS settings for your computer. You'll normally have to press a key (such as DELETE, F2, or ESC) to access these settings, but this very much depends on the make and model of your computer. More information on accessing your BIOS is given in Chapter 2.

Once you've found the settings screen, find the option where you can choose to boot from a USB drive (that is, make the USB drive the first boot device), save your changes, and restart. Ideally, you'll now be taken to a purple Ubuntu boot screen. In that case, head over to Chapter 2, and continue the installation as normal.

If you run into any problems, take a look at *https://help.ubuntu.com/ community/Installation/FromUSBStickQuick/* for hints and tips, or head over to the forums (*http://www.ubuntuforums.org/*) for advice.

B

UBUNTU DESKTOP CDS FOR AMD64, OPTERON, OR INTEL CORE 2 USERS

 As I mentioned in Chapter 1, the version of the Ubuntu Desktop CD that comes with this book is designed to work with i386 processors, either in PCs or Intel-based Macs. It will also work with AMD64 or Intel Core 2 processors, albeit not in 64-bit mode. In order to use Ubuntu with these processors (or any other machine based on AMD64 or EM64T architecture) in 64-bit mode, you must get a different disc on your own. There are several ways of doing this: downloading an ISO (disc image) and then burning it to CD yourself, ordering the CD from Ubuntu (for free), or ordering it from an online Linux CD provider (for a nominal cost).

Downloading and Burning Ubuntu Desktop CD ISOs to CD

To download an ISO of the Ubuntu Desktop CD, go to the Ubuntu website at *http://www.ubuntu.com/*, find the link to the download page, and then select and download the appropriate version for your machine. Remember that the ISO file you will be downloading is a heavyweight, weighing in at just under

700MB, so the download will take a bit of time. Don't count on getting it all downloaded and done before dinner . . . or, if you happen to be using a dial-up Internet connection, before dinner tomorrow. Yikes!

Burning the ISO to CD in Windows

Once the Ubuntu Desktop CD ISO has been downloaded, you need to burn it to CD before you can use it. Although Windows has built-in CD-writing capabilities, not all versions have the built-in ability to burn ISOs. To burn an ISO to CD in Windows 7, just right-click the ISO file, select **Burn disc image**, and then click the **Burn** button in the window that appears. In all other versions of Windows, however, you must use a third-party commercial application, such as Nero. If you don't have a commercial disc-burning utility installed on your system, try the free and handy ISO Recorder.

To get ISO Recorder, visit *http://isorecorder.alexfeinman.com/isorecorder.htm*. Once the download is complete, double-click the *ISORecorderSetup.msi* file on your hard disk to install it. After the installation is complete, burn your ISO to CD by right-clicking the Ubuntu ISO file on your machine and selecting **Open with ▶ ISO Recorder** in the pop-up menu. A CD Recording Wizard window will appear.

It is generally best if you burn installation or live CDs at a lower speed than the maximum speed allowed by your drive in order to reduce the chance of error (with 2X to 4X speeds considered optimal). To do so, make your choice from the Recording speed drop-down menu. Next, pop a blank CD into the drive, and click the **Next** button. The CD-burning process should begin. Once it's done, the CD should pop out of the drive, and if all goes well, you'll have yourself an AMD64-compatible live CD. You can then use it by following the directions at the beginning of Chapter 2 for using the live CD that comes with this book.

NOTE   *If your CD does not seem to work, there could be a problem with the ISO file you downloaded. Find out by doing an integrity check as explained at* https://help.ubuntu.com/community/HowToMD5SUM/.

Burning the ISO to CD in OS X

Although Ubuntu no longer comes in PowerPC editions, the i386 editions can be installed and run on Intel-based Macs. You can also, of course, download ISOs for other architectures on your Mac and then burn them to CD for use on other machines.

To burn an ISO file to CD in OS X, first check to make sure the ISO image is not mounted by opening a Finder window and checking the disc in the area at the top portion of the left pane. If the disc is mounted, a drive icon will appear in that location. If the drive icon is there, click the arrow next to that entry to eject, or *unmount*, it.

After that, click **Applications** in the same Finder window, and then look for and open the **Utilities** folder. In that folder, find and then double-click **Disk Utility**. If the ISO is not listed in the left pane of the Disk Utility window when it opens, go back to the Finder window, locate the Ubuntu Live CD ISO you just downloaded, and then drag it to the left pane of the Disk Utility window, just below the listings for your current drives. Once the ISO file appears in that list, click it once to highlight it.

To complete the process, click the **Burn** icon in the Disk Utility window's toolbar, and then insert a blank CD in your drive when prompted to do so. Once the blank disc is inserted and recognized, you will be able to adjust the burn speed from the drop-down menu next to the word *Speed*. Select as low a speed as your hardware will allow, which, depending on the age of your Mac, will probably be 4X to 8X. Finally, click the **Burn** button in that same window, and the burning process will begin.

Ordering an Install Disc from Ubuntu

The easiest and most foolproof way to get an Ubuntu Desktop CD is to simply order one (or more) for free from Ubuntu; you don't even have to pay shipping or handling. Of course, the only downside to this approach is time. It can take up to ten weeks for you to get the CDs in this manner, so if you're impatient, you might want to opt for one of the other methods. To order your install CDs from Ubuntu, go to *https://shipit.ubuntu.com/*, and follow the directions there. It's easy.

If you need faster service or larger numbers of Ubuntu CDs and don't mind paying a small amount for the service, then you can order your discs through the Canonical store instead (*https://shop.canonical.com/*).

Ordering an Install Disc from Other Online Sources

If you are in a hurry to get your install CD, you can also order a copy from an online source, such as CheapBytes (*http://www.cheapbytes.com/*) and OSDisc.com (*http://www.osdisc.com/*).

C

MANUALLY PARTITIONING YOUR HARD DISK

When you're partitioning your hard disk with the Ubuntu installer, the first two options (use the whole disk and resize an existing partition) should cover most eventualities. They're both discussed in Chapter 2. But if you're in a geekier mood, there are a few fancy ways to carve up your disk space. For example, you can create a shared data partition so your files can be shared between Windows and Ubuntu, or you can make a separate partition for your */home* directory so you can reinstall Ubuntu (or install a different Linux distro) without having to fully back up all of your files.

When you get to the Prepare disk space screen of the installer, choose **Specify partitions manually**, and click **Forward**. You'll be presented with a colored-bar view of your current partition setup (Figure C-1) and a list of your partitions below that. None of the changes that you make in this window will be applied until you click **Forward** again, and you can click the **Back** button if you want to forget about making the manual changes altogether. (There is one exception: Changes are made immediately and irreversibly when you resize a partition. See "Editing Existing Partitions" on page 416 for more on this.)

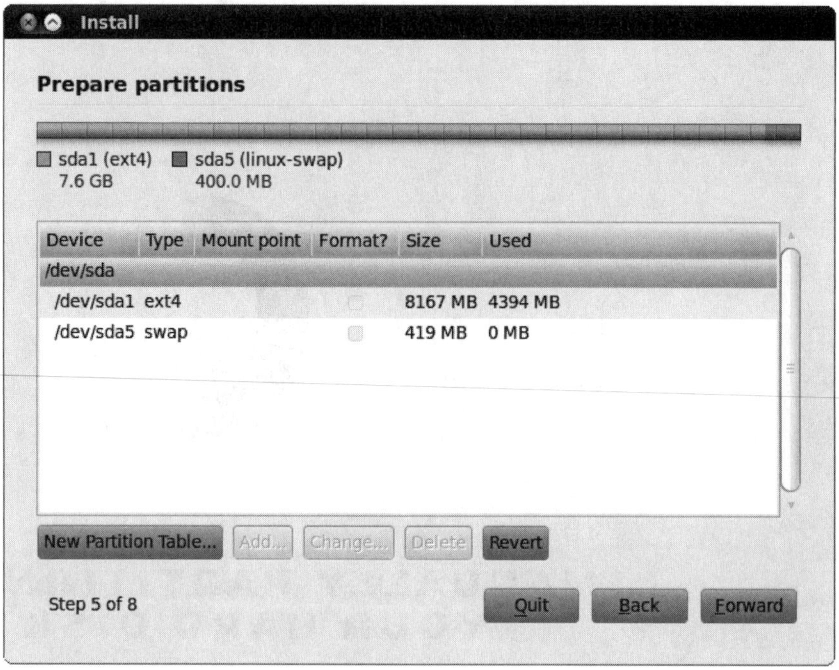

Figure C-1: Using the manual partitioning tool

Creating and Deleting Partitions

You can create new partitions only if you have some "free space" to put them in. This is free space in the sense that there's not already a partition on that part of the disk, not that there are no files there. One way of creating free space is to delete an existing partition; to do this, click the list item for the partition, and click **Delete**. After a few seconds it'll change into free space in the list (Figure C-2). Alternatively, if you're planning to completely change your partition setup, select the hard disk you want to modify, and click **New Partition Table**. You'll be left with a completely blank slate, where all you need to do is add new partitions.

Select any free space, and click **Add** to put a new partition in it. You'll be presented with a Create new partition window (Figure C-3), which will ask how big you want to make the partition in megabytes. (1GB is roughly 1,000MB.) See "Varieties of Partitions" on page 416 for advice on how big to make your partitions.

The Use as option lets you specify the filesystem you want to use. A *filesystem* tells your operating system how to store files on the partition. There are a number of different filesystems that you can choose, but not all of them can be understood by Windows and Mac OS. Ext4 is the best choice for a partition that will be solely used by Linux, but FAT32 is the one you need if you want to share files with Windows or Mac OS.

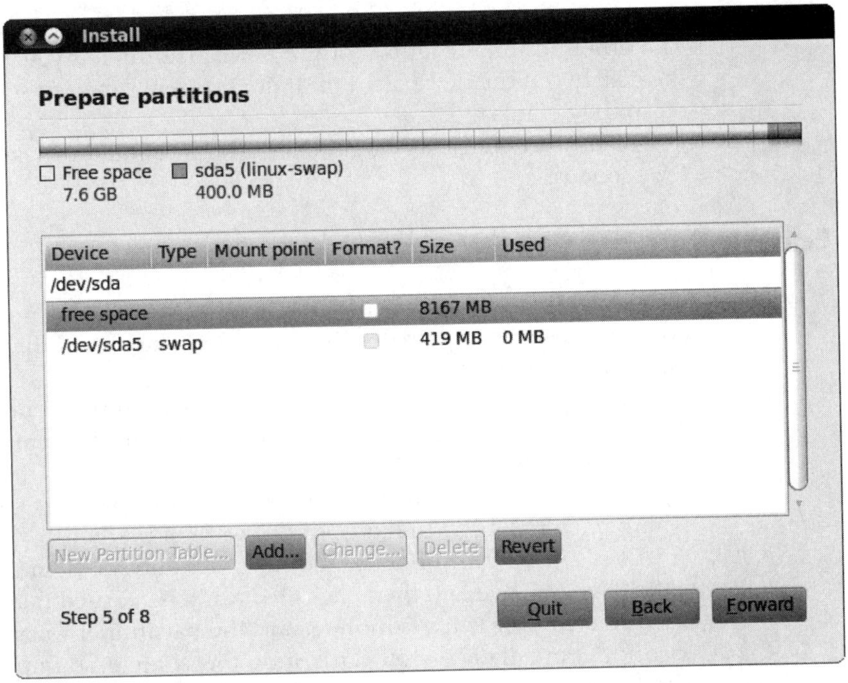

Figure C-2: Creating some free space

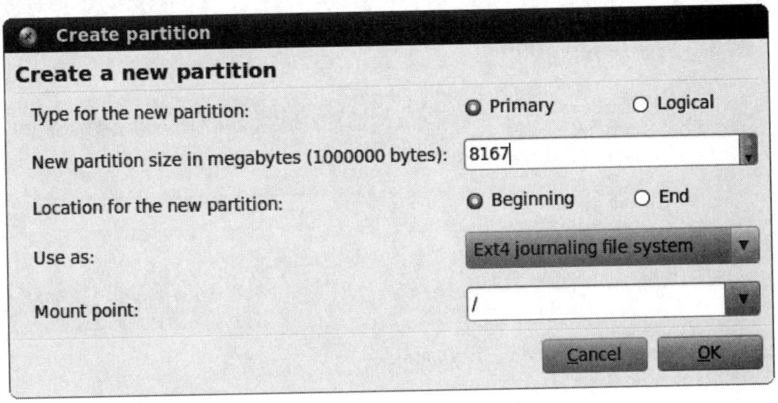

Figure C-3: Creating a new partition

You can also select the *mount point*, which is where Ubuntu will put the folder that corresponds to this partition (see Chapter 7 if you're not familiar with how Linux organizes folders). For example, you would mount the home partition as the */home* folder. More detail on mount points is given in "Varieties of Partitions" on page 416.

There are two more options in the Create new partition window, both of them rather technical and boring. The Type for the new partition option gives you a choice between creating a *primary* or *logical* partition. You can have a maximum of four primary partitions on a disk but lots of logical partitions—the disk partitioner will choose the right option for you, so there's no need to alter this setting (it doesn't affect how you use the partition in any way). The other option, Location for the new partition, lets you choose where on the disk to put the new partition. It doesn't really matter, so leave this option set to the default too.

Click **OK** to finish adding the partition; it should appear in the list after a few seconds.

Editing Existing Partitions

If you have an existing partition that you'd like to resize or change its mount point or filesystem type, select it and click **Change**. An Edit partition window will appear (Figure C-4).

The Use as and Mount point options work in the same way as those in the Create new partition window. You can also check **Format the partition** if you'd like all the data on it to be erased so you can start fresh. You have no choice but to format if you're changing the filesystem of a partition (for example, from FAT32 to Ext4), so be aware of that too.

To resize the partition, use the New partition size in megabytes option. If you change the size and then click **OK**, you'll be warned that the changes will be written to disk. Click **Continue**, and the partitioner will start to resize the partition immediately—you can't undo this change, so think carefully about whether you've chosen the right options before hitting Continue.

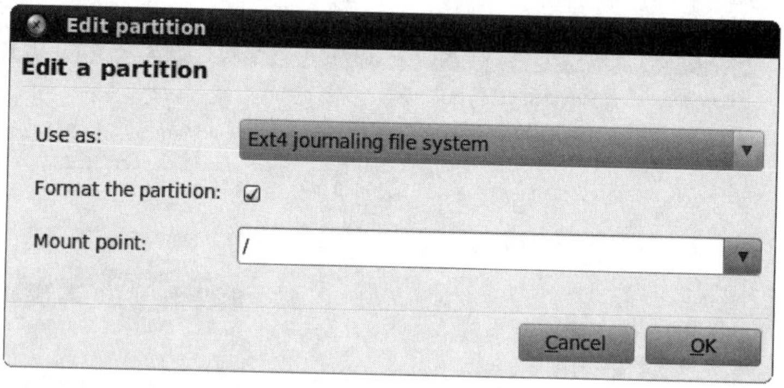

Figure C-4: Editing a partition

Varieties of Partitions

You'll need to be familiar with a few varieties of partitions when you manually partition your disk. I've summarized these in the following sections and provided some tips on choosing their size, mount points, and filesystems.

Root Partition

You must have a root partition; it's where important system files are stored and software is installed. I recommend making it at least 8GB in size, but aim for 10GB to 15GB if you can to leave room for installing new programs. If you're not going to have a separate home partition (described in a moment), all of your files will be stored in the root partition too, so you should make it as big as possible to accommodate all your stuff in that case. The mount point should be set to / and the filesystem to *ext4*.

Swap Partition

You must have a swap partition. The swap partition is like an extra area of system memory (RAM); if your computer's system memory gets full, it will start using this partition to handle the overspill. It's also used to store the contents of your system memory (like all of your open files and programs) when you hibernate the computer. See *https://help.ubuntu.com/community/SwapFaq/* for more details on swap.

As a rough guide, it should be a little larger than the amount of RAM that your computer has. For example, if you have 2GB of RAM, make a 2.2GB swap partition. The filesystem should be set to *swap area*, and there's no need to set a mount point.

NOTE   *It's possible to get away without a swap partition by creating a* swap file *after you've installed Ubuntu. The method for doing this is beyond the scope of this book.*

Home Partition

The */home* folder can be put in a separate partition. You don't need to do this, but it's useful if anything ever goes wrong and you need to reinstall Ubuntu—all your personal files and configuration settings will be left intact on the home partition while Ubuntu is reinstalled on the root partition. This can save a lot of work when restoring your system. If you don't have a separate home partition, the */home* folder will be put in your root partition with everything else. The way you access your home folder (for example, through the Places menu) will be exactly the same whether you put it on a separate partition or not.

The home partition is where all your files and settings are stored, so you'll want to make it as big as possible. The filesystem should be *ext4*, and the mount point should be set to */home*.

Windows Partition

If you have Windows installed, you will need to resize the Windows partition to make room for Ubuntu. When you do this, be sure to leave at least enough disk space for Windows to function properly. Windows XP needs a partition at least 2GB in size, and for Vista and Windows 7 you should leave at least 16GB. You will probably want to leave more space than this so that you can install programs and save files when using Windows, and remember to leave space for your existing Windows files too. The Used column in the main partitioning window will tell you how much space your Windows files are currently taking up.

Windows partitions will be of type NTFS or FAT32. Remember not to format the Windows partition, or your current installation of Windows will be erased.

Shared Partition

If you want an easy way to share files between Windows and Ubuntu, create a shared partition. In both operating systems, it will appear as a separate hard disk, which you can use to store whatever you like.

Make the partition as big as you think you'll need: If you only ever copy small files between Ubuntu and Windows, then 1GB to 2GB should be plenty; if you want to permanently store all your Windows and Ubuntu files in there (sort of like a shared home folder), make it as big as possible. You should choose FAT32 as the filesystem, but you can use almost anything for the mount point—/*windows* will be one of the default suggestions, but you could type something like /*shared* or /*blackhole* into the Mount point box if you liked. Just make sure you use a name without any spaces in it.

Example Partition Layouts

Partitioning can be confusing if you've never done it before, so I've provided a few example partition layouts that should make things clearer. In all of these examples I've used a 100GB hard disk, but you can scale all the partition sizes up or down for your disk according to the advice in "Varieties of Partitions" on page 416.

Standard Ubuntu-Only Installation

Only Ubuntu will be installed on the disk, so only the root and swap partitions are needed (Figure C-5). Since I have 4GB of RAM, I made the swap partition 4.2GB. The root partition filled up the rest of the disk space to give me as much room for files and programs as possible. (There was no need to partition the disk manually in this case; the Ubuntu installer's Erase and use the entire disk option would have achieved the same result.)

Ubuntu-Only with a Separate Home Partition

Only Ubuntu will be installed, but there will be a separate home partition to keep my data safe in case I ever need to reinstall (Figure C-6). I'm planning to store home movies on this one, which means lots of very large files, so I went for a smallish 10GB root partition and a slightly undersized 4GB swap partition. This leaves lots more space for the home partition (and my videos), which takes up the remaining 86GB of the disk.

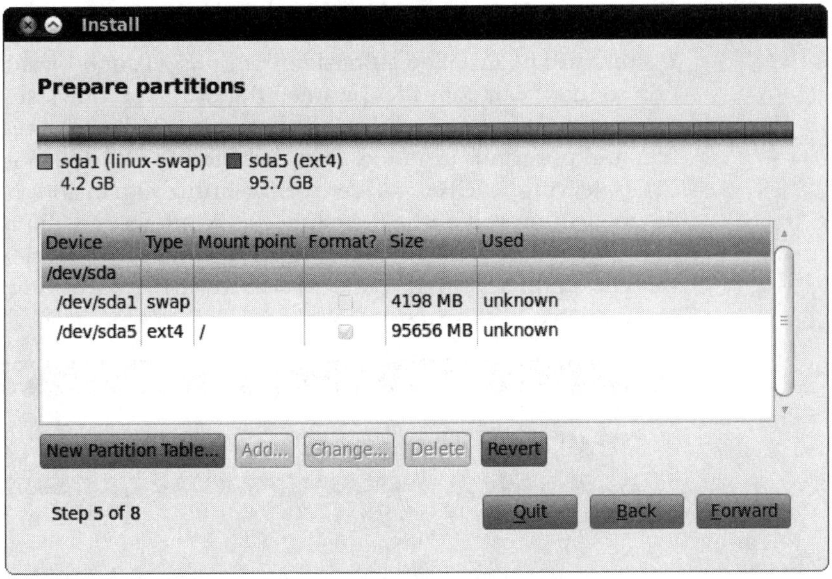

Figure C-5: A simple Ubuntu-only partition layout

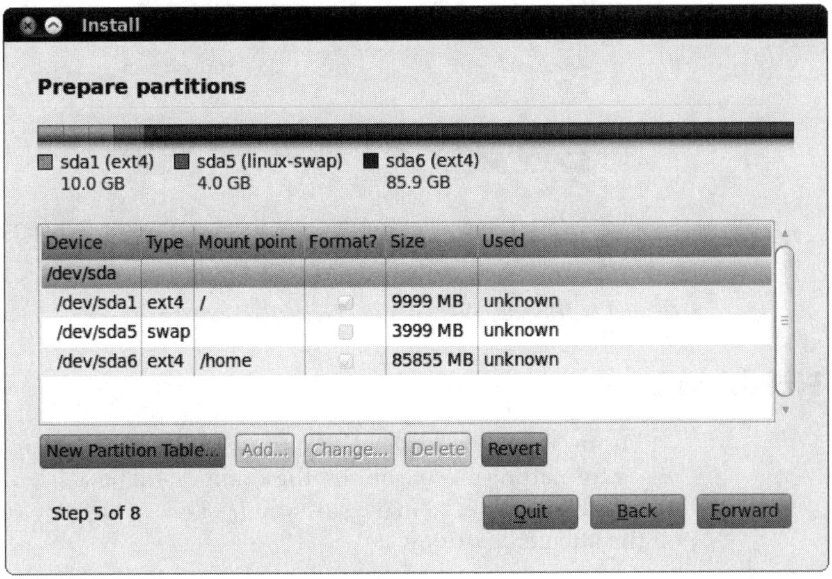

Figure C-6: The partition layout for Ubuntu with a separate home partition

Ubuntu and Windows with a Shared Partition

Ubuntu will be installed alongside Windows XP, and I want a shared partition so that I can copy files between the two operating systems (Figure C-7). My existing Windows installation was using 7.3GB of the disk because I had files and programs installed on it. I resized the Windows installation to 15GB, leaving 7.7GB of space free for future expansion. Note that the Windows partition will *not* be formatted, so Windows and all my files on that partition remain intact. I created a 40GB Ubuntu root partition and a 4.2GB swap partition and then created a shared FAT32 partition in the remaining 40GB or so of disk space.

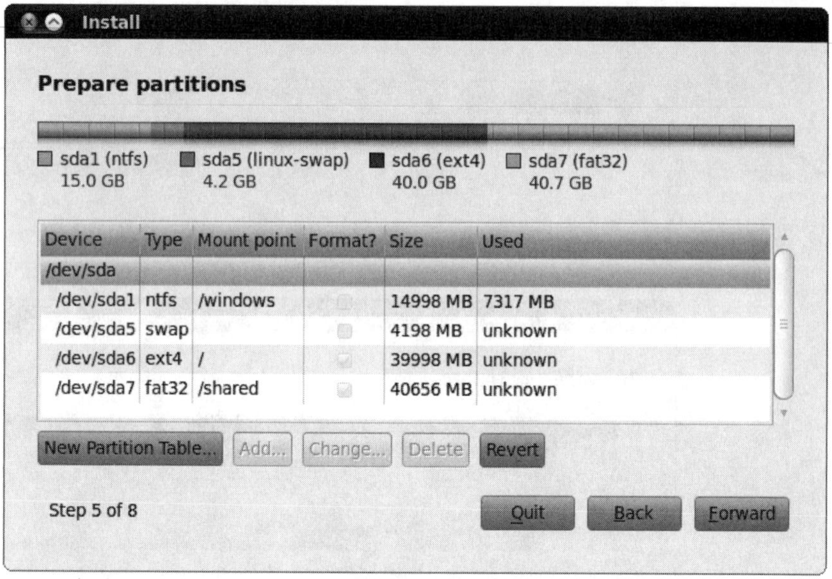

Figure C-7: Ubuntu, Windows, and a shared partition

Finishing Up

When you've finished, click **Forward** to finalize your changes. If you're deleting or formatting any partitions, the changes will be written to disk. This is an irreversible change, so make sure you backed up any valuable data that was on the affected partitions!

D

RESOURCES

Because Linux owes much of its growth and development to the Internet, it should come as no surprise that there is a wealth of information about the various flavors of Linux, including Ubuntu, available to you online. In addition to the usual news, how-to, and download sites, you will also find a variety of tutorials, forums, blogs, and other sources of useful information—all of which you can turn to as you use and learn more about your system.

Forums

When you are looking for advice, trying to solve a particular problem, or just looking for some general tips, online forums are the way to go. Fortunately, Ubuntu has a forum all its own, and since Ubuntu is primarily a desktop-oriented Linux distro, you are likely to find many fellow newbies and newbie-friendly posters there, rather than the hard-core geekiness you might find on some other sites. There are, of course, other newbie-friendly forums, which, although not Ubuntu-specific, should also be able to provide you with lots of helpful information.

Regardless of which forum you are posting in, just be sure to mention that you are using Ubuntu, which version you have (Lucid Lynx, in case you forgot), and that you are new to Linux. And remember to always seek clarification when you get an answer you don't understand. The same poster will usually come back and clarify things for you. You should feel right at home at most of these sites, though you will probably come to like one or two more than the others.

http://ubuntuforums.org/   This is the official Ubuntu community forum, which was covered in detail in Chapter 20. This is always a good place to start when you're in a fix, have a question, or just want to find out what's going on.

http://www.ubuntux.org/forum/   This is another, slightly smaller Ubuntu-specific forum. This is a good place to turn if you find UbuntuForums.org a bit too much to wade through.

http://www.kubuntuforums.net/   This is a forum dedicated to Kubuntu, an official Ubuntu edition based on the KDE desktop environment.

http://www.justlinux.com/ and *http://www.linuxquestions.org/*   If you can't find what you want in the previously mentioned forums, you can try these forums dealing with general Linux issues. You are sure to find many Ubuntu users on them.

Linux Reference

These are sites, many of which are geared toward newbies, where you can learn more about using Ubuntu or Linux in general:

http://www.ubuntu.com/products/whatisubuntu/   An overview of Ubuntu and its features

http://ubuntuguide.org/wiki/ubuntu:lucid   An unofficial Ubuntu startup guide

https://help.ubuntu.com/   Official documentation for the current release of Ubuntu

http://www.tuxfiles.org/   Lots of tutorials and information for Linux newbies

http://www.linuxcommand.org/   Where you can learn to use commands in Linux

http://www.linux.org/   News, book reviews, downloads, and all sorts of other stuff—all about Linux

http://openoffice.blogs.com/openoffice/   Tips for users of Ubuntu's OpenOffice.org office suite

Blogs

You can also find a lot of great information in blogs. In these blogs, you can discover the findings of fellow users as they try new things, share tips, and offer solutions to problems:

http://www.ubuntux.org/blog/   This is mostly an Ubuntu-oriented news blog.

http://www.ubuntugeek.com/   Despite having the word *geek* in the name, this is a pretty accessible set of mostly useful Ubuntu system and software tweaks.

http://embraceubuntu.com/   This is an archive of Ubuntu tips (although it hasn't been updated in a while).

Hardware Compatibility Issues

If you want to find out whether or not your hardware is compatible with Linux or if you want to read up on other matters related to hardware support, take a look at the following sites:

https://wiki.ubuntu.com/HardwareSupport/   This contains Ubuntu-specific hardware compatibility information.

http://www.linuxcompatible.org/compatibility.html   This has numerous compatibility lists, arranged by distribution.

http://www.linuxfoundation.org/   This is a great spot for reading up on printer compatibility issues.

http://www.linmodems.org/   Find out if your modem is supported.

http://www.sane-project.org/   Check to see if your scanner is Linux compatible, and look for fixes if it isn't.

http://www.linux-laptop.net/   Have laptop, want Linux? Check it out here.

http://www.tuxmobil.org/   This site has information for using Linux with anything that isn't stuck to your desk (laptops, PDAs, phones, and so on).

Wireless Connections

If you use a wireless card to connect to the Internet and have trouble getting your card to work or if you just want to know where all the free wireless hotspots happen to be, the following sites should help:

https://help.ubuntu.com/community/WifiDocs/

http://www.linuxwireless.org/

http://www.hpl.hp.com/personal/Jean_Tourrilhes/Linux/

http://www.ezgoal.com/hotspots/wireless/

Free Downloads

If you find yourself looking for more goodies to play around with, you should be able to find plenty of free stuff to download at one of these sites.

Applications and Other Packages

http://www.getdeb.net/

http://sourceforge.net/

http://www.freshmeat.net/

http://www.gnomefiles.org/

Free Fonts

http://www.fontfreak.com/

http://www.fontparadise.com/

http://fonts.tom7.com/

News and Information

These sites are mainly informational, keeping you abreast of what's going on in the Linux world as a whole (I covered some Ubuntu-specific ones in Chapter 20). DistroWatch focuses on the various distributions available out there, whereas Linux Today and LinuxPlanet fit better in the online magazine/ newspaper genre.

http://www.distrowatch.com/

http://www.linuxtoday.com/

http://www.linuxplanet.com/

Magazines

If you are more of a tactile type who enjoys the feel of paper pressed between your fingers, then you might want to turn to some of the Linux magazines available at most major newsstands. All have a good deal of online content, so even if you're not interested in the pleasures of holding a magazine in your hand, their sites are worth checking out.

http://www.tuxmagazine.com/   (now out of publication but still has back issues)

http://www.linux-magazine.com/   (European)

http://www.linuxmagazine.com/   (U.S.)

http://www.linuxjournal.com/

There are two (unrelated) magazines sharing almost the same name: One of these is from the United States; the other is from Europe. Newbies who want some pizzazz in their reading materials, plus some useful tips and some things to play around with, should go for the European version. The U.S. version is targeted toward business users and power geeks, not newbies.

Books

Once you've finished working through this book, you should be able to do just about whatever you want in Ubuntu. Still, your interest may have been piqued enough that you want to find out a bit more about Linux. Here are some books that might help in that quest:

How Linux Works by Brian Ward (No Starch Press, 2004)

The Debian System by Martin Krafft (No Starch Press, 2005)

The Linux Cookbook 2nd Ed. by Michael Stutz (No Starch Press, 2004)

Running Linux by Matthias Dalheimer and Matt Welsh (O'Reilly Media, 2005)

Linux Multimedia Hacks: Tips & Tools for Taming Images, Audio, and Video by Kyle Rankin (O'Reilly Media, 2005)

Linux Pocket Guide by Daniel J. Barrett (O'Reilly Media, 2004)

Ubuntu CDs

To order an AMD64 version of the Ubuntu Desktop CD, get a replacement for the i386 version that comes with this book, or get the next version of Ubuntu when it comes out (if you don't want to or can't download it), just place an order with any of the following sites. (CDs from most suppliers will cost $5 to $10 or so.)

http://shipit.ubuntu.com/

http://shop.canonical.com/

http://www.cheapbytes.com/

http://www.linuxcd.org/

INDEX

C

cable
  for providers without DHCP, 47
  Internet connection,
    connecting, 46
CAD (computer-aided design),
    QCad for, 258
Calc (OpenOffice.org), 228
  Easter egg in, 230
  uses for, 230
calendar command, 162
canceling print job, 202–203
Canonical store, 372
capturing and editing digital video,
    Kino for, 300–301
case sensitivity of commands, 158
cd command, 163–164
CD Creator window,
    switching to, 109
CD drive, changing boot
    sequence, 12
CD/DVD, ejecting, 106
CD-RW discs, 108, 109
CDs
  burning, 106–107, 109
    ISO images, 109
    multisession, 110
  duplicating, 111
  for AMD64 users, 409
  for Intel Core 2 users, 409
  in book, 1
    compatibiliy with 64-bit
      systems, 9
  reading, 106
cellphones, working with, 282
Centrino IPW-2100 and IPW-2200
    cards, 49
channel, IRC, 368
character encoding, for web
    pages, 212
Character Map utility, 213, 216
characters, typing nonstandard,
    213, 216
chat. See IM (instant messaging)
CheapBytes, 411
checksum, 376
children, Tux Paint for, 260

Chinese
  input with IBus, 219–222
  recommended input
    methods, 220
chmod command, 165, 167
ClamAV, 344, 346
clipart, adding to OpenOffice
    gallery, 234
Code of Conduct, 357
codec, 387
coffee, 367
color, Nautilus side pane, 129
command line, user reaction to,
    155–156. *See also* Terminal
command-line driven operating
    system, 2
commands
  apt-get, 168
  aptitude, 169
  calendar, 162
  case sensitivity of, 158
  cd, 163, 164
  chmod, 165, 167
  cp, 164
  df, 161
  exit, 162
  finding for applications, 359
  fine tuning with flags, 161
  finger, 159
  gunzip, 173
  gzip, 173
  ln, 171
  locate, 167
  ls, 162
  mkdir, 163
  mv, 163
  pwd, 161
  rm, 164
  rmdir, 165
  sudo, 167
  tar, 171, 173
  touch, 163
  updatedb, 168
  use of flags with, 161
  whoami, 158
commercial software, 355
compiler, 184

hardware
    bugs, 359
    checking that your wireless card
        is recognized, 389
    compatibility issues, 7–8, 423
    drivers, installing, 391
    graphics cards, 394
    minimum requirements, 9
    modems, cable or ADSL, 52
    modems, dial-up, 53
    software for checking, 82
    wireless Internet connection,
        49–50
hardware acceleration, checking
        for, 310
Hardy Heron, 10
help. *See also* troubleshooting
    community help website, 373
    from mailing lists, 371
    from Ubuntu Forums, 365
    on IRC, 367
    top panel launcher for, 27
hiberfil.sys, 383
hibernation
    role of the swap partition in, 417
    Windows, problems with, 383
hidden files
    displaying, 162, 174
    .plan file as, 174
hiding Nautilus side pane, 95
high-level programming languages,
        184–185
high-speed Internet connection,
        setup, 46
hiragana, 217
History view of filesystem, 95
Hoary Hedgehog, 10
Hobbyist, role in open source, 365
/home directory, creating separate
        partition for, 413
Home folder, 94, 100
    encrypting, 22
    keeping private, 105
home partition, 417–418
Hopper, Grace, 358
HWiNFO, 8
Hyperlink window, 233

I

IBus (Intelligent Input Bus), 219
    Chinese, recommended input
        methods, 220
    Japanese, recommended input
        methods, 220
    Korean, recommended input
        methods, 220
    Selecting input method
        modules, 219
    setting up to automatically start
        at log in, 223
IcedTea. *See* Java
icons
    changing in desktop menus, 38
    changing sets, 134, 136
    installing additional, 136–137
    on GNOME desktop top panel, 27
    stretching, 140
    top desktop panel, 27
ideas on improving Ubuntu, 364
Identi.ca, 372
IM (instant messaging), 71
    client, 71
    explanation, 71
    instant status, 73
    IRC, 367
    sending files, 73
IME, defined, 217
import process, for digital
        photos, 247
Impress (OpenOffice.org)
        presentation application, 231
indicator applet, 69
inkjet printer, scanned image
        resolution and, 208
INSTALL files, in source code
        packages, 186
Installer Team, 356
installing applications. *See also*
        applications; Software
        Installation window
    Art Manager, 133
    Briscola, 180
    by downloading a DEB
        package, 90
    Firefox extensions, 62, 68–69

The Electronic Frontier Foundation (EFF) is the leading organization defending civil liberties in the digital world. We defend free speech on the Internet, fight illegal surveillance, promote the rights of innovators to develop new digital technologies, and work to ensure that the rights and freedoms we enjoy are enhanced — rather than eroded — as our use of technology grows.

PRIVACY EFF has sued telecom giant AT&T for giving the NSA unfettered access to the private communications of millions of their customers. eff.org/nsa

FREE SPEECH EFF's Coders' Rights Project is defending the rights of programmers and security researchers to publish their findings without fear of legal challenges. eff.org/freespeech

INNOVATION EFF's Patent Busting Project challenges overbroad patents that threaten technological innovation. eff.org/patent

FAIR USE EFF is fighting prohibitive standards that would take away your right to receive and use over-the-air television broadcasts any way you choose. eff.org/IP/fairuse

TRANSPARENCY EFF has developed the Switzerland Network Testing Tool to give individuals the tools to test for covert traffic filtering. eff.org/transparency

INTERNATIONAL EFF is working to ensure that international treaties do not restrict our free speech, privacy or digital consumer rights. eff.org/global

EFF.ORG
ELECTRONIC FRONTIER FOUNDATION
Protecting Rights and Promoting Freedom on the Electronic Frontier

EFF is a member-supported organization. Join Now! www.eff.org/support

More no-nonsense books from **no starch press**

MY NEW™ iPAD
A User's Guide

by WALLACE WANG

Apple's iPad has revolutionized the way consumers experience the Web, email, photos, and video. As with all Apple gadgets, the basic features are easy to access and understand. But there's a world of possibility beyond the basics, and many users need guidance to make the most of their iPads. *My New iPad* takes readers step by step through the iPad's many useful features—like surfing the Internet, sending email, listening to music, taking notes, reading ebooks, using iWork, and playing with digital photos. And since no one wants to read a long, dry textbook to learn how to use their new toy, author Wallace Wang takes a practical, easy-to-follow approach and keeps the tone light.

JUNE 2010, 368 PP., $24.95
ISBN 978-1-59327-275-3

THE ESSENTIAL BLENDER
Guide to 3D Creation with the Open Source Suite Blender

edited by ROLAND HESS

Blender is the only free, fully integrated 3D graphics creation suite to allow modeling, animation, rendering, post-production, and real-time interactive 3D with cross-platform compatibility. *The Essential Blender* covers modeling, materials and textures, lighting, particle systems, several kinds of animation, and rendering. It also contains chapters on the compositor and new mesh sculpting tools. For users familiar with other 3D packages, separate indexes reference topics using the terminology in those applications. The book includes a CD with Blender for all platforms as well as the files and demos from the book.

SEPTEMBER 2007, 376 PP. W/CD, $44.95
ISBN 978-1-59327-166-4

FORBIDDEN LEGO
Build the Models Your Parents Warned You Against!

by ULRIK PILEGAARD *and* MIKE DOOLEY

Written by a former master LEGO designer and a former LEGO project manager, this full-color book showcases projects that break the LEGO Group's rules for building with LEGO bricks—rules against building projects that fire projectiles, require cutting or gluing bricks, or use nonstandard parts. Many of these are back-room projects that LEGO's master designers build under the LEGO radar, just to have fun. Learn how to build a catapult that shoots M&Ms, a gun that fires LEGO beams, a continuous-fire ping-pong ball launcher, and more!

AUGUST 2007, 192 PP., $24.95
ISBN 978-1-59327-137-4

THE MANGA GUIDE™ TO PHYSICS

System and Network Monitoring

by HIDEO NITTA, KEITA TAKATSU, *and* TREND-PRO CO, LTD.

The Manga Guide to Physics teaches readers the fundamentals of physics through authentic Japanese manga. Megumi, an all-star tennis player, is struggling to pass her physics class. Luckily for her, she befriends Ryota, a patient physics geek who uses real-world examples to help her understand classical mechanics. Readers follow along with Megumi as she learns about the physics of everyday objects like roller skates, slingshots, braking cars, and tennis rackets. As the book progresses, Megumi begins to master even the toughest concepts of physics, like momentum and impulse, parabolic motion, and the relationship between force, mass, and acceleration. Using a lively and quirky approach, *The Manga Guide to Physics* combines a whimsical story with real educational content so that readers will quickly master the core concepts of physics with a minimum of frustration.

MAY 2009, 248 PP., $19.95
ISBN 978-1-59327-196-1

THE LEGO MINDSTORMS NXT 2.0 DISCOVERY BOOK

A Beginner's Guide to Building and Programming Robots

by LAURENS VALK

The LEGO MINDSTORMS NXT 2.0 Discovery Book teaches readers how to harness the capabilities of the NXT 2.0 set. With building and programming instructions for eight different robots, readers become master builders and reach an advanced level of programming skill as they learn to build robots that move, use advanced programming techniques like data wires and variables, and monitor sensors. Additionally, numerous building and programming challenges throughout the book encourage readers to think creatively and to apply what they've learned as they develop the skills essential to creating their own robots. Readers learn how to build Strider, a six-legged walking creature; the CCC, a climbing vehicle; the Hybrid Brick Sorter, a robot that sorts by color and size; the Snatcher, an autonomous robotic arm; and more!

APRIL 2010, 336 PP., $29.95
ISBN 978-1-59327-211-1

PHONE:
800.420.7240 OR
415.863.9900
MONDAY THROUGH FRIDAY,
9 A.M. TO 5 P.M. (PST)

FAX:
415.863.9950
24 HOURS A DAY,
7 DAYS A WEEK

EMAIL:
SALES@NOSTARCH.COM

WEB:
WWW.NOSTARCH.COM

MAIL:
NO STARCH PRESS
38 RINGOLD STREET
SAN FRANCISCO, CA 94103
USA

COLOPHON

Ubuntu for Non-Geeks, 4th Edition is set in New Baskerville, Futura, and Dogma. The book was printed and bound by Transcontinental, Inc., at Transcontinental Gagné in Louiseville, Quebec, Canada. The paper is Domtar Husky 50# Smooth, which is certified by the Forest Stewardship Council (FSC). The book has an Otabind binding, which allows it to lie flat when open.

UPDATES

Visit *http://www.nostarch.com/ubuntu4.htm* for updates, errata, and other information.

ABOUT THE CD

This software is released for free public use under several open source licenses. It is provided without any warranty, without even the implied warranty of merchantability or fitness for a particular purpose. See the license text included with each program for details. Source code for Ubuntu can be downloaded from *http://archive.ubuntu.com/ubuntu/dists/lucid/main/source/* or can be ordered from Canonical at the cost of the media and shipping. Ubuntu and Canonical are trademarks of Canonical Ltd. All other trademarks are the property of their respective owners.

Ubuntu's official documentation is online (*https://help.ubuntu.com/*), and free technical support is available through web forums (*http://www.ubuntuforums.org/*), mailing lists (*http://www.ubuntu.com/support/community/mailinglists*), and IRC (*#ubuntu*). Commercial support is also available from Canonical (*http://www.canonical.com/consumer-services/support*).

Ubuntu is sponsored by Canonical Ltd. For more information, visit *http://www.ubuntu.com/* and *http://www.canonical.com/*. To request free Ubuntu CDs, visit *https://shipit.ubuntu.com/*.

The Intel x86 Edition packaged with this book will run on Intel x86–based systems (including Intel Pentium and AMD Athlon). See "Version Compatibility" on page xxxi for more information. This and all other versions of Ubuntu are available for download at *http://www.ubuntu.com/desktop/get-ubuntu/download*.

No Starch Press does not provide support for Ubuntu. However, if the Ubuntu CD packaged with this book is defective, broken, or missing, you may email *info@nostarch.com* for a replacement.

You are legally entitled and encouraged to copy, share, and redistribute this CD. Share the spirit of Ubuntu!